Hiking
Southern New England

Second Edition

Rhonda and George Ostertag

FALCONGUIDES ®

GUILFORD, CONNECTICUT
HELENA, MONTANA

AN IMPRINT OF THE GLOBE PEQUOT PRESS

Contents

Acknowledgments

We would like to acknowledge the work of the trail associations and individual volunteers who help blaze and maintain southern New England's trails, the efforts of the preservationists who work to save the area's landscape and history, and the generosity of landowners who have allowed the tristate trail system to grow and endure.

We also would like to thank the individuals who helped with our research and volunteered their ideas or faces to this book, and our East and West Coast base camps for freeing us to work.

Legend

Interstate	95	Wetland	
U.S. Highway	101	Campground	▲
State or County Road	○	Picnic Area	
Paved Road		Trail Shelter	△
Gravel Road		Bridge	)(
Unimproved Road		Building	
Trailhead/Parking	Ⓟ	Cemetery	
Starting Point	Ⓟ	Mine/Quarry	✕
Described Trail		Viewpoint	⊙
Alternate Trail		Point of Interest	★
Brook		Power line	
River		Lookout Tower	
Body of Water		Railroad	
Summit	2,477ft.	Scale	0 0.5 1 Miles
Waterfall		Spring	
Dam			

Overview

A. Western Massachusetts
B. Central Massachusetts
C. Eastern Massachusetts
D. Western Connecticut
E. Eastern Connecticut
F. Rhode Island

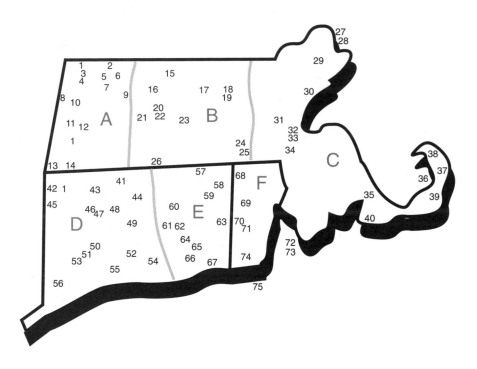

Introduction

The trails of Massachusetts, Connecticut, and Rhode Island weave an intriguing tapestry that invites exploration. Hundreds of trail miles entice hikers to lace on their boots to experience tours ranging from short nature walks to rugged skyline hikes to wilderness beach strolls. Trails wandering through natural areas and extensive forested reaches offer a winning diversity, rich in geological and cultural history.

The trails in this book explore many of southern New England's premier parks, forests, peaks, coastal flatlands, swamps, beaches, and private reserves and sanctuaries. Travel past charming waterfalls and daunting cliffs, revel in summit views and wilderness solitude, shuffle across the leafy carpet of autumn-blazed woods, and dig your toes into clean white sand. Turtle, fish, salamander, deer, raccoon, porcupine, eagle, hawk, warbler, and gull share these byways with human visitors.

While traveling the trails, flip through the pages of history. Discover dinosaur tracks and Native American graves, see where the Pilgrims first tasted the sweet water of the New World, make a pilgrimage of your own to a sacred Shaker society hilltop, and unravel the story of colonial settlement and the Industrial Revolution. When your boots are worn and your soul is primed, you can better appreciate nature and perhaps touch the spirit of Henry David Thoreau.

This guidebook features a regionwide sampling of nature walks, a full range of day-length hikes, and, where available, backpacking trips. The collection serves as a launching pad to both the sport of hiking and to the foot-travel possibilities of this tristate area.

WEATHER

Southern New England offers fairly reliable three-season hiking, with days of no or minimal snow extending the season into winter. Several trails also serve as winter cross-country ski or snowshoe routes. Spring and fall offer the preferred mix of mild temperatures and low humidity levels, while summer can bring extremes in both categories. Spring and summer hikers should come prepared for biting insects.

TERRAIN

Glaciers sculpted the face of southern New England, grinding down ridges, broadening valleys, and depositing rocky glacial debris. The tristate area offers hikers a landscape of outcrop vistas and traprock ridges, tranquil waterfalls, broad rivers and clear-coursing streams, reservoirs, beaver ponds, swamps, rolling hardwood forests, and exquisite coastal sands.

Junction sign, Norman Bird Sanctuary, RI.

LANDOWNERSHIP

While this book concentrates primarily on public land offerings, trails also cross private, utility, trustee, Audubon sanctuary, and conservancy lands. Hikers assume full responsibility for their own well-being when traveling on private lands, and implicitly consent to abide by posted rules. Stay on designated trails, leave gates as you found them, and pick up and pack out litter left by other trail users as well as your own trash. "Pack it in, pack it out."

We make every effort to indicate if and where a trail traverses or abuts private land. Occasionally, landownership changes or a landowner may withdraw the privilege of thru-travel; respect such closures.

Publicly held lands. Trails traveling lands managed by state, local, and federal agencies are the core of this book.

State parks typically show greater grooming and development and possess more facilities. At most state parks, expect to pay a seasonal entrance fee.

State forests, reservations, and *management areas* account for much of the region's open space. These minimally developed woodland sites typically offer a wilder experience, with few or no facilities. Some may charge a seasonal or campground fee.

Public wildlife management areas and *national wildlife refuges* primarily promote and sustain waterfowl and wildlife populations, with hunting and fishing, bird-watching, and hiking allowed as compatible recreations.

Privately held lands. The privately held lands of the *Trustees of Reservations* in Massachusetts offer outstanding hiking opportunities. The Trustees, a nonprofit entity and the world's oldest land trust (founded in 1891), purchase and preserve properties of exceptional scenic, historical, and ecological value throughout Massachusetts for public use and enjoyment. Their mission is supported by membership dues, contributions, admission fees, and endowments. When visiting Trustees sites, obey the posted rules that protect the unique qualities of each property, confine your visits to daylight hours, and keep vehicles on designated roads.

The Nature Conservancy (TNC), an international nonprofit organization devoted to the protection of biodiversity, opens its trails to the public for hiking, nature study, and photography. Please note that straying from the trails, hiking with pets, collecting, smoking, picnicking, camping, building fires, swimming, and bicycling are forbidden activities.

TNC extends hiking privileges only where and when compatible with their primary mission of conserving and preserving the land, its habitats, and inhabitants. Donations defray the cost of maintaining existing preserves and acquiring new ones.

National and state *Audubon Society* lands welcome travelers, but visitors must hold Audubon membership or pay a visitor fee. Respect the posted rules and any closures designed to protect the wildlife and natural habitat. Picnic only at established sites, leave pets at home, travel by foot only—no mountain bikes—and no collecting.

Eastern forest, Chatfield Hollow State Park, CT.

White Memorial Foundation, in Litchfield, Connecticut, maintains a remarkable 4,000-acre gift from a farsighted brother and sister committed to preserving nature and its tranquility, and to providing future generations the opportunity to enjoy and explore the land. The site promotes conservation, research, education, and compatible forms of recreation in a natural arena. Heed trail-use restrictions. No collecting.

TRAIL MARKINGS

Decades or centuries of use, rather than planned cutting, have created most trailbeds in the tristate area. The predominance of leafy woods (which often obscure trails) makes necessary some manner of trail blazing (paint, diamond, or disk markers) to guide hikers. A double blaze typically warns of a change in direction, with the top blaze offset in the direction of the turn.

While the intervals between blazes can vary greatly from trail to trail, the spacing on a particular trail often has a consistent rhythm. If you note the frequency of blazes along a trail, an uncommonly long lapse between blazes can warn that you have strayed from course. In autumn, be especially alert, because fallen leaves can conceal the tracked path.

The Connecticut Forest and Park Association marks its 600-odd miles of forest, park, and private land trails with a blue paint blaze; side trails typically bear a colored dot within the blaze.

The Appalachian National Scenic Trail brands its route with white blazes as it slices across the northwest corner of Connecticut and through western Massachusetts.

On Massachusetts Audubon lands, find letter- and number-coded junction and site markers with orientation arrows keyed to the area map. You may also find a directional blazing scheme that uses blue blazes to indicate travel away from the trailhead or nature center and yellow blazes for travel toward the trailhead or nature center.

On private lands, consult a mapboard or flyer before plotting your course; some trails are marked for one-way travel only. Following these trails in reverse, without the aid of markers, could result in hikers becoming lost.

THE VOLUNTEER COMPONENT

Devoted, energetic volunteers and established hiking organizations, such as the Appalachian Mountain Club, help maintain, promote, and expand the regional trail system. Hikers can encourage and support this work by becoming members of these groups and by purchasing their maps and materials. The maps produced and sold by the volunteer organizations are often the best and most current available, containing up-to-date information on the lay of the trail, landownership, shelters, facilities, and obstacles.

Hikers are likewise indebted to the private landowners who allow trails to cross their lands. Many trails would not exist without their cooperation.

Within this recreation dynamic, trail users have an obligation to use the land responsibly and to protect and preserve trails and the landscape they traverse. Respect switchbacks, contours, and other design features intended to retain the integrity of the land. Remember, your adventure should not come at the cost of the land or the enjoyment of the trails by future generations.

How to Use This Guide

To help you decide which trails you would like to hike, we have grouped the trails into six geographical regions and provided a trail-at-a-glance summary at the head of each write-up.

Summary entries provide a character sketch of the trail, its general location, special attractions, length, elevation change, difficulty, available maps, special requirements or concerns, season, and an information resource. (Find contact information for each listed resource in appendix D.) The key points and elevation profiles further help you visualize a trail. Although the handful of key points allows a quick check on progress, the listing cannot replace the hike text for guiding you along the trail. At the end of each summary, you will find detailed directions to the trailhead.

"The hike" component of the write-up describes the progress of the trail, drawing attention to special features and alerting you to obstacles and potentially confusing junctions. Habitat changes, seasonal surprises, sidelights, and unusual discoveries flesh out the tour description. Where appropriate, we mention flaws and disappointments for a balanced view.

Mountain laurel.

The maps in this book are not intended to replace the more detailed agency maps, road maps, state atlases, and/or topographic maps, but they do indicate the lay of the trail and the site's attractions, helping you visualize the tour.

AN EXPLANATION OF SUMMARY TERMS

Listed distances represent pedometer readings. Backpacking excursions—sometimes dictated by distance, sometimes by attraction—are left to the hiker's judgment and the rules of the appropriate agency.

The assignment of a subjective classification of "easy," "moderate," or "strenuous" considers overall distance, elevation change (the difference between the trail's elevation extremes), cumulative elevation (how rolling a trail is), trail surface, obstacles, ease of following, and its relative difficulty to other hikes in the book.

We do not estimate hiking times, because personal health, party size, the interest of the trail, the weather, and the trail's condition can all influence the time needed to complete a hike. Instead, gain a sense of your personal capabilities and hiking style and judge the time for yourself based on the distance, the elevation change, the difficulty rating, and what you glean from the text. Customize the hike to fit your needs; you need not continue just because a description does, nor must you stop where the description stops. Interlocking loops, side trails, and alternative destinations may await.

GLOSSARY

Car-shuttle hikes. Typically, these are linear routes that require a drop-off and pickup arrangement, spotting a second vehicle at trail's end, or hiking back to the trailhead you started from.

Corduroy. This side-by-side alignment of logs, boards, or branches provides dry passage over soggy trail segments or delicate meadow sites.

Forest lanes, carriageways, cart paths. These routes typically are narrower than a woods road, yet wider than a trail, serving foot and horse travelers.

Jeep trails. These doubletrack routes typically serve foot and horse travelers. Most are no longer drivable.

Service roads. These routes carry minimal traffic, allowing official vehicles only.

Woods roads. These dirt, grass, or rocky routes are abandoned logging, farm, and town roads that have been reclaimed as trails. Most are closed to vehicle travel, although some may allow snowmobile or mountain bike use. We alert you if we are aware of vehicle use (legal or illegal).

Outdoor Primer

Whether wilderness trekking is a revitalizing experience or an ordeal depends largely on preparation. Nature is not without inherent risks and discomforts, but learning to anticipate and mitigate them clears the way to great outdoor fun.

PREPARATION

Ten Essentials. Outdoor experts recommend "Ten Essentials" for safe backcountry travel. They are:

1. Extra food
2. Extra clothing
3. Sunglasses
4. Knife
5. Candle or chemical fuel to ignite wet wood
6. Dry matches
7. First-aid kit and manual
8. Flashlight with bulb and batteries
9. Maps for the trip
10. Compass

Dress. The amount and types of clothing worn and carried on a hike depend on the length of the outing, the weather, and personal comfort. Layering is the key to comfort and well-being; select items that can serve more than one purpose. A long-sleeve shirt may be layered for warmth, lends sun protection, hinders mosquitoes, and protects against ticks. A lightweight raincoat may double as a windbreaker.

Choose wool or good-quality synthetic fleece for cold, wet, or changeable weather conditions; these fabrics retain heat even when wet. Choose cotton for dry summer days. For their weight, hats play an invaluable role, shielding eyes, face, and top of head, and preserving body heat.

Footwear. While sneakers may be passable for nature walks, for long hikes and uneven terrain, wear boots for both comfort and protection. Sock layering, with a light undersock worn next to the foot and a second wool sock worn atop, helps prevent rubbing, cushions the sole, and allows absorption of perspiration. Avoid socks with a large cotton content; they are cold when wet and slow to dry.

Food. Pack plenty: Hiking demands a lot of energy. Pack foods that will not spoil, bruise, or break apart in the pack. Maximize the energy value for

Lily pads, Miles Standish State Forest, MA.

the weight, particularly when backpacking. Food fends off fatigue, a major contributor to accidents on the trail.

Equipment. The quantity and variety depend on the length and nature of the hike and on the season (appendix A offers a checklist of commonly carried items), but a good pack for transporting the gear is essential. A day pack with padded straps, a reinforced bottom, and side pockets for water bottles works for most short outings. For overnight trips, select a backpack that has a good frame and balance and supports the weight without taxing hips, neck, or shoulders.

Because backpacks represent a major investment, newcomers should first try renting one. You cannot evaluate a pack in the store with only a few sandbags for weight. A trail test delivers a better comfort reading; it also demonstrates how well the unit packs with your personal gear. Many back-packing stores with a rental program will allow the rental fee to be applied to the purchase of a new pack; ask the manager.

Map and compass. All hikers should learn to read maps in conjunction with a compass. Maps provide orientation to an area, suggest alternative routes, and aid in planning and preparation for the journey.

Become familiar with the United States Geological Survey (USGS) topographic maps. While most of these quads for southern New England are too dated to show the current lay of the trail, they provide information about the steepness of the terrain, the vegetation (or lack of it), the course of waterways, and the location of man-made structures. The USGS offers topo maps at two scales: 7.5-minute and 15-minute series.

Remember when using a compass that true north does not equal magnetic north. For the region, the mean declination is about 14 degrees west. Search the map border for the specific declination.

TAKING TO THE TRAILS

Pacing yourself. Adopt a steady, comfortable hiking rhythm, take in the surroundings, and schedule short rests at regular intervals to guard against exhaustion.

Wading streams. Cross at the widest part of a watercourse, where the current is slower and the water shallower. Sandy bottoms suggest a bare-foot crossing; fast, cold waters and rocky bottoms require the surer footing of boots. For frequent stream crossings or for hiking streambeds, lightweight sneakers earn their passage.

Hiking cross-country. For safe cross-country travel, you must have good map and compass skills, good survival skills, and good common sense. Steep terrain, heavy brush, and downed timber physically and mentally tax hikers, increasing the potential for injury. This, of all hiking, should not be attempted alone. Even know-how and preparation cannot fully compensate for nature's unpredictability and human fallibility.

Hiking with children. For young children, choose simple destinations and do not insist on reaching any particular site. Allow for differences in attention span and energy level. Enjoy the scenery, and share and encourage children's natural curiosity. Come prepared for sun, mosquitoes, and poi-

Trailhead information board, Bald Hill Reservation, MA.

son ivy, and discuss what to do should you become separated. Even small ones should carry a pack with some essential items: a sweater, water bottle, and food.

A WILDERNESS ETHIC

Trails. Keep to the path. Shortcutting, skirting puddles, and walking two abreast all contribute to erosion and the degradation of trails. Report any damage.

Permits and registration. In sensitive areas, land agencies may require trail or camp permits to help monitor and manage the sites and minimize overuse. To protect the integrity of the wild, keep party size small.

At trail registers, take the time to sign both in and out and to comment on the condition of the trail and its markings. The collected information affects the allotment of funds and labor for trail improvement and expansion.

For designated backpacking trails in Connecticut, hikers must request camping permits in writing two weeks before an overnight stay. The permit request letter should list the camp area(s), the date(s), the name and address of the leader, and the number and ages of the group's members. Limit camping to a one-night stay per location, and leave pets at home. For a list of backpacking trails, or to submit a permit request, contact the Connecticut Department of Environmental Protection, Bureau of Outdoor Recreation; the address is in appendix D.

Pets. Owners should strictly adhere to posted rules for pets. Controlling your animal on a leash is not just a courtesy reserved for times when other hikers are present; it is a responsibility to protect the wildlife and ground cover at all times.

Camping. Low-impact camping should be everyone's goal. Camp only where it is allowed. Select an established campsite and do not alter the ground cover, bring in logs for benches, bang nails into trees, or dig drainage channels around tents. Leave no (or few) clues that a hiker has passed this way.

Where no established campsite exists, select a site at least 200 feet from the water and well removed from any trail. Avoid delicate meadow and alpine environments, and do not camp at lakeshores, waterfalls, overlooks, or other prized sites.

Reduce comforts (as opposed to necessities). Carry a backpacker's stove for cooking; when a campfire is unavoidable, keep it small. Snags and live trees should never be cut.

Sanitation. For human waste disposal, select a site well away from the trail and at least 300 feet from any water body. Dig a hole 8 inches deep in which to bury the waste. This biologically active layer of soil holds organisms that can quickly decompose organic matter. If the ground prohibits digging a hole of the specified size, dig as deep a hole as possible and cover well with gravel, bark, and leaves.

Use tissue sparingly, and for day excursions, carry a zipper-seal plastic bag for packing out soiled tissue. Burying often results in the tissue becoming nest-building material for rodents or unsightly garbage scattered by salt-seeking deer.

Litter. "Pack it in, pack it out." This includes aluminum foil, cans, orange peels, peanut shells, cigarette butts, and disposable diapers. It takes nature six months to reclaim an orange peel. A filter-tip cigarette butt takes ten to twelve years to decompose, and disposable diapers have become an incredible nuisance and contaminant in the wild. Burying is not a solution.

Garter snake, Macedonia Brook State Park, CT.

Outcrop passage, Westwoods Preserve, CT.

Washing. Washing of self or dishes should be done well away from the lake or stream. Carry wash water to a rocky site and use biodegradable suds sparingly, remembering that even these soaps can degrade water quality.

SAFETY

Water. Water is the preferred refreshment; carry a reserve of safe water at all times, as wilderness sources often dry up or become fouled. Know that caffeine and alcohol are diuretics that dehydrate and weaken.

All wilderness water (even from the most pristine-appearing streams) used for drinking, food preparation, and washing dishes should be treated to remove or destroy *Giardia lamblia* (a waterborne organism causing stomach and intestinal discomfort) and other disease-causing organisms.

Water purification systems that remove both debris and harmful organisms offer the most common and satisfactory treatment for natural water sources. The alternative is to bring the water to a full boil for at least five minutes. Iodine tablets do not protect against *Giardia*, do not fully protect against other waterborne diseases, and are not considered safe for pregnant women.

Getting lost. Prior to departure, notify a responsible party of your intended destination, route, and time of return. Then keep to your plan and notify the party upon your return.

If lost, sit down and try to think calmly. No immediate danger exists, as long as you have packed properly and followed the notification procedure. If hiking with a group, stay together. Short outward searches for the trail, returning to an agreed-upon, marked location if unsuccessful, are generally considered safe. If near a watercourse, following it downstream typically delivers a place of habitation or a roadway, where help may be sought. Aimless wandering is a mistake.

Blowing a whistle or making loud noises in sets of three may summon help. If late in the day, prepare for night and try to conserve energy. Unless you have good cross-country navigational skills, efforts are best spent conserving energy and aiding rescuers by staying put and hanging out bright-colored clothing.

Modern aids—global positioning system (GPS) receivers, cell phones, walkie-talkies, and the like—can reduce the risk of becoming lost or speed rescue.

Hypothermia. This dramatic cooling of the body occurs when heat loss surpasses body-heat generation. Cold, wet, and windy weather commands respect. Attending to the Ten Essentials, eating properly, avoiding fatigue, and being alert for hypothermia's symptoms—sluggishness, clumsiness, and incoherence—among party members remain the best protection. Should a party member display such symptoms, stop and get that member dry and warm. Dry clothing, shared body heat, and hot fluids all help.

Heat exhaustion. Strenuous exercise combined with summer sun can lead to heat exhaustion, an overtaxation of the body's heat regulatory system. Wearing a hat, drinking plenty of water, eating properly (including salty snacks), and avoiding fatigue are safeguards.

Poison ivy and poison sumac. The best way to avoid contact with these and other skin-irritating plants is to learn what they look like and in what environments they grow. Consult a good plant identification book. Vaccines and creams are beginning to come on the market, but science has yet to conquer these irritating plant oils. If you suspect you have come in contact with one of these plants, rinse off as soon as possible and avoid scratching, which spreads the oils.

Ticks, stings, and bites. Again, the best defense is knowledge. Learn about the habits and habitats of snakes, bees, wasps, ticks, and other "menaces" of the wild and how to deal with the injuries they may cause. Also, become aware of any personal allergies and sensitivities that you or a party member might have.

Lyme disease, transmitted by the tiny deer tick, has become a serious concern in the East, but it need not deter you from the outdoors. Hikers come into contact with ticks amid grasses and shrubs; the ticks do not drop from trees. Wear light-colored long pants and long-sleeve shirts, and keep your layers tucked into one another. This will help you identify any ticks and keep them on the outside of your garments. While hiking, make frequent checks for the unwanted hitchhiker. When at home, shower and search skin surfaces thoroughly, and launder hiking clothes directly.

Should a tick bite and become anchored in the skin, remove the tick by drawing evenly on its body, disinfect the site with alcohol, and monitor over the next few weeks. Look for a red bull's-eye swelling at the site of the bite; also be alert to inexplicable muscle pain, tiredness, or flu-like symptoms. Consult a physician immediately should any kind of symptom occur.

Bears. The black bears in the East represent more nuisance than threat. Use common sense; do not store food near camp, and especially not in the tent. If clothes pick up cooking smells, suspend them along with the food from an isolated overhanging branch well away from camp. Sweet-smelling creams or lotions should be avoided.

Hunting. Although most public lands open to hunters do not prohibit hiking during hunting season and few have any record of conflict, we would still advise fall hikers to point their boots toward lands and trails where hunting is not allowed. If you hike where hunting occurs, wear bright orange clothing and keep to the trail. Rhode Island law demands each hiker wear a fluorescent orange hat or vest from October 1 through February 28.

Trailhead precautions. Unattended hiker vehicles are vulnerable to break-ins, but the following steps can minimize the risk:

- Whenever possible, park away from the trailhead at a nearby campground or other facility.

- Do not leave valuables in the car. Place keys and wallet in a button-secured pocket or remote, secure compartment in the pack where they will not be disturbed until your return.

- Do not leave any visible temptations; stash everything in the trunk, and be sure any exposed item advertises it has no value.

Poison ivy, Vin Gormley Trail, Burlingame State Park, RI.

• Be suspicious of loiterers and do not volunteer the details of your outing.

• Be cautious about the information you supply at the trailhead register. Withhold information such as license plate number and duration of stay until you are safely back at the trailhead. Instead, convey that information to a responsible party back home.

Backcountry travel includes unavoidable risks that every traveler assumes and must be aware of and respect. The fact that a trail or an area is described in this book is not a representation that it will be safe for you. While the book attempts to alert users to safe methods and warn of potential dangers, it is limited. Time, nature, use, and abuse can quickly alter the face of a trail. Let independent judgment and common sense guide you.

For more detailed information about outdoor preparedness, consult a good instructional book or enroll in a class on outdoor etiquette, procedure, and safety. Even an outdoor veteran can benefit from a refresher.

Western Massachusetts Trails

Western Massachusetts encompasses the attractions of the Berkshires and Taconics, boasting the highest peaks in the three-state region of southern New England. Hike through northern hardwood forest and enjoy rare pockets of boreal evergreens and mountain ash at the highest elevations. Southern hardwoods in the lower foothill and valley realms produce a salute to autumn that is among the nation's finest. Trails explore skyline ridges, tag vista points, and journey along brooks and picturesque mountain ponds. Delicate waterfalls, an attractive skyline war memorial, a rare cobble, and blueberry patches contribute to the discovery. Scenic river valleys and pockets of population part the steep-sided ridges of the region.

1 Appalachian National Scenic Trail

General description:	This 2,155-mile national scenic trail, journeying from Springer Mountain, Georgia, to Mount Katahdin, Maine, traverses the northwest corner of Connecticut and western Massachusetts, touring forest, field, and mountaintop. It offers various tour options for round-trip, shuttle, and thru-trail hikes.
General location:	Northwest corner of Connecticut through the Berkshires of western Massachusetts.
Special attractions:	Vistas, ponds, waterfalls, the Housatonic River, hardwood and boreal forests, spring blooms, fall foliage.
Length:	141.4 miles one-way (53 miles in Connecticut; 88.4 in Massachusetts).
Elevation:	Travel between a low point of 250 feet along the Housatonic River and a high point of 3,491 feet at Mount Greylock in Massachusetts. The high point for the trail in Connecticut is 2,330 feet at Bear Mountain.
Difficulty:	Strenuous.
Maps:	Appalachian Trail Conference map, Appalachian Trail Guide to Massachusetts–Connecticut.
Special concerns:	Thru-hikers must plan how to pick up supplies along the route and what to do in case of emergency. They also need to arrange for transportation at the end of the trail. The trail is rocky and difficult in spots, and hikers should have strong map and compass skills.

Season and hours: Spring through fall.
For information: Appalachian Trail Conference (ATC).

Key points:

0.0	New York–Connecticut border; follow AT northbound.
11.5	Connecticut Highway 341.
15.8	St. Johns Ledges.
17.3	West bank Housatonic River.
32.0	Sharon Mountain.
38.3	Falls Village, Connecticut.
40.6	Prospect Mountain.
51.5	Bear Mountain.
53.0	Connecticut–Massachusetts state line; proceed north.
57.8	Mount Everett.
66.6	U.S. Highway 7.
74.3	Massachusetts Highway 23.
95.0	US 20.
114.0	Dalton.
119.1	Gore Pond.
131.4	Top Mount Greylock, near Bascom Lodge.
137.3	Cross MA 2 in North Adams.
141.4	Massachusetts–Vermont state line.

Finding the trailhead: The Appalachian Trail crosses many Connecticut and Massachusetts state routes and traverses several state parks and state forest lands. Find the southernmost highway access to the Connecticut–Massachusetts segment along CT 55 at the New York–Connecticut border. The northernmost road access lies along MA 2 in North Adams.

The hike: The first trail in the nation to win national scenic trail designation, the **Appalachian Trail (AT)** passes through the mountain wilds of fourteen eastern states. Conceived in the early 1920s, the ribbon of the AT rolls atop the ancient Appalachian Mountains, dipping to cross important eastern river valleys. Most of the AT greenway has received permanent public protection; some 4,000 volunteers along with 200 public agencies maintain and oversee the trail.

In Connecticut and Massachusetts, the AT rolls along the Housatonic River Valley, up and down the peaks of northwestern Connecticut, and through the forests of the southern Berkshires. The tour concludes with rigorous climbs and descents, traversing the high peaks of northwestern Massachusetts.

Although a boreal complex crowns Mount Greylock, hardwood forests are the norm on this hike. Swamps, fields, streams, lakes and ponds, the Housatonic River, and picturesque southern New England villages complement the tour. Ledges and clearings regularly reward with views.

Open to hiking only, the white-blazed AT advances primarily via foot trail, with some sections of abandoned woods road. In rare places, it travels developed roads, including a 2-mile stretch between CT 4 and Falls Village. The terrain can be rocky and steep, so expect to use your hands occasionally for steadying, climbing, and easing yourself over rocks. Stay on the trail

Appalachian National Scenic Trail

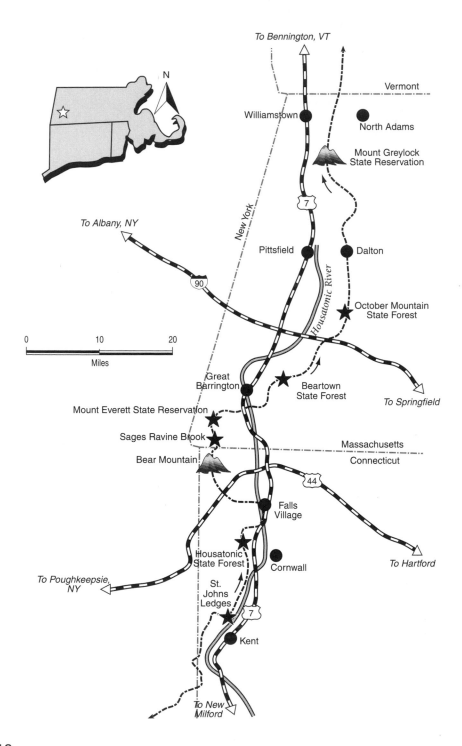

to avoid straying onto private land; the protected AT greenway is often quite narrow.

Some fifteen lean-tos and shelters lie along or just off the AT, providing convenient, dry overnight waysides, but, since they cannot be reserved, a tent should be standard equipment. Gambling that you will arrive early enough to claim a lean-to for the night is an unwise and unnecessary wilderness risk. Camp in established sites to minimize environmental harm.

From south to north, the Connecticut–Massachusetts leg of the AT sashays back and forth between New York and Connecticut for the first 7 miles, then settles in Connecticut for the next 46 miles. From the Housatonic River Valley, the trail mounts a ridge, where ledges provide a raven's-eye view of the river.

The tour crosses Caleb's Peak and passes the renowned St. Johns Ledges, popular for rock climbing. Red pines add to the oak–deciduous tour. Where the trail drops from the ridge, it follows the west bank of the Housatonic River for a 5-mile stretch—one of the longest river segments on the entire Appalachian Trail.

The trail returns to the ridge, overlooking the river, crossing Sharon Mountain, and passing through Housatonic State Forest. A 2-mile road stretch interrupts the reverie of the trail, where the AT twice crosses the river, the second crossing occurring in Falls Village.

The tour then passes from the Housatonic Valley floor over Prospect Mountain to tag the southern end of the Taconic Range. Some brook crossings mark off distance. Atop Bear Mountain (the highest peak in Connecticut), a tower, now half its original size, provides an exciting three-state panorama. Side trails branch off to visit waterfalls as the trail resumes its rolling rhythm.

Appalachian Trail sign, MA.

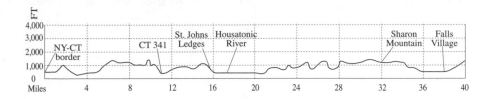

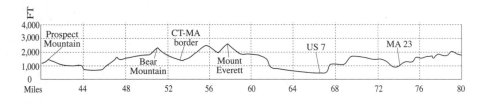

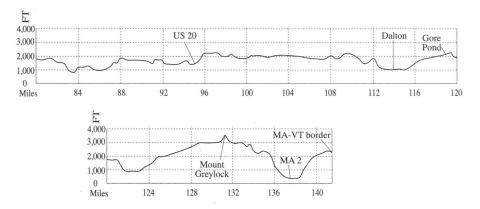

Sages Ravine Brook, just across the Connecticut–Massachusetts line, delights with cascades, waterfalls, and towering trees. Where the trail again rolls skyward, Race Mountain and Mount Everett reward with vistas.

From the mountains, the AT dips once more to the Housatonic Valley, touring a flat stretch, sometimes on road, passing through pasture, field, and swamp. Stone walls hark to the early settlers of the valley.

The tour now stays mainly in forest, touring ridge and summit for frequent vistas. Where the AT crosses MA 23, an area of snapped trees commemorates the spring 1995 tornado that swept through Great Barrington. The storm cut a broad path of destruction. To the north, the AT traverses Beartown State Forest, passing again through tranquil hardwood–conifer forests and skirting Benedict Pond. Beaver ponds likewise mark the tour.

The trail passes briefly through the valley of Hop Brook, encountering further areas impacted by beaver. At Lower and Upper Goose Ponds, hikers may want to adjust the day's planned mileage to allow for a long stop. A rolling tour through October State Forest follows. Where a long forested ridge then advances the trail, the views are few. The occasional stone wall or swampy passage provides visual interest.

Near Gore Pond, the AT passes from the Housatonic to the Hoosic River drainage. This more demanding section journeys to the top of Mount Greylock. At the summit, find rustic stone-and-wood Bascom Lodge and the site's inspiring war memorial. Greylock's chiseled drainages and steep plunging flanks add to its commanding presence in northern Massachusetts. Seldom reaching this far south, a boreal forest of fir and spruce engages hikers.

The trail continues north along Mount Greylock's summit ridge, eventually dropping to cross MA 2 in North Adams. For the final miles, the trail parallels a brook north to ascend East Mountain. Soon after tagging the quartzite outcrop of Eph's Lookout, the AT leaves Massachusetts to enter Vermont.

Thru-trail travelers and hikers planning short excursions along the AT should contact the ATC for its official maps and guides. Entire books have been devoted to this premier hiking trail and to the Massachusetts–Connecticut component alone. They are likely available at your local library, bookstore, or backpacker/outfitters supply store.

2 Monroe State Forest

OVERVIEW

This 4,321-acre Massachusetts state forest in the northern portion of the Hoosac Range features the beautiful mixed woods along Dunbar Brook and the enfolding rounded hills. Remote, sparkling, and pristine, Dunbar Brook hosts the best brook hike in the entire three-state area. Elsewhere, trails travel hill, ridge, and hollow.

General description:	Two short hikes explore brook and summit and may be combined for a single long tour. Brookside campsites and a trail shelter provide overnight accommodations.
General location:	In Monroe and Florida, Massachusetts.
Special attractions:	Beautiful energetic brook, rich mixed woods, scenic big boulders, woods flora, fall foliage.
Length:	Dunbar Brook Trail, 5.6 miles round trip; Spruce Mountain Trail, 3.2 miles round trip.
Elevation:	Dunbar Brook Trail, 700-foot elevation change; Spruce Mountain Trail, 1,000-foot elevation change.
Difficulty:	Both moderate.
Maps:	State forest map.
Special concerns:	Heed posted trailhead hours for the lower trailhead: 6:00 A.M. to 9:30 P.M. Backpackers should park at the Raycroft Trailhead. With a recent decline in maintenance, trail and junction markings have become unreliable.

Season and hours: Spring through fall.
For information: Monroe State Forest.

Key points:
Dunbar Brook Trail:
- 0.0 Lower (River Road) trailhead; ascend service road.
- 0.7 Dunbar Brook bridge.
- 1.2 Overnight shelter.
- 2.8 Upper (Raycroft Road) trailhead; backtrack or add Spruce Mountain Trail.

Spruce Mountain Trail:
- 0.0 Raycroft Road trailhead.
- 1.6 Spruce Mountain; backtrack.

Finding the trailhead: From Massachusetts Highway 2 in Florida, turn north onto Florida–Monroe Road/Main Road and go 3.9 miles. Find the upper Dunbar Brook and Spruce Mountain Trailhead by turning right (south) onto Raycroft Road, an unmarked dirt road opposite North Road. Locate trail parking for a handful of vehicles on either side of the Dunbar Brook bridge. Although Raycroft Road continues south through forest, drive no farther than the bridge without a four-wheel-drive vehicle.

For the lower Dunbar Brook Trailhead, remain on Florida–Monroe Road another 2 miles and turn right onto Kingsley Hill Road. In 1.2 miles, meet and bear right onto River Road. Find the trailhead parking lot on the right in another 1.7 miles; New England Power maintains the site. The power company's Bear Swamp Visitor Center is another 0.7 mile south on River Road.

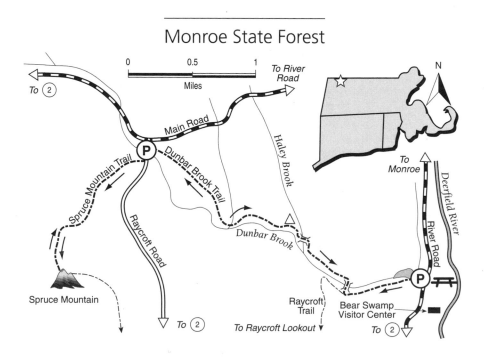

Monroe State Forest

For an alternative approach to the lower trailhead, turn north off MA 2 onto Zoar Road at the east end of the Mohawk Indian Bridge (2 miles west of Charlemont). Go 2.4 miles and turn left at the T-junction, following the Deerfield River north via River Road. Reach Bear Swamp Visitor Center in another 7.4 miles and the lower trailhead 0.7 mile past the center.

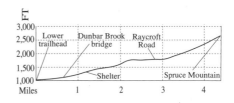

The hikes: From the River Road trailhead, ascend the service road near the utility line to begin **Dunbar Brook Trail.** Hike the south shore upstream, paralleling a boardwalk that leads to a small dam. Dunbar Brook feeds into the Deerfield River, a critical water in this power company corridor. Initially, overlook a deep, narrow reservoir shaped by the dam; the wild brook awaits upstream.

By 0.25 mile, travel a steep bank 15 feet above the natural brook; hardwoods and evergreens cloak the slope. In autumn, eddies along the brook lasso the colored leaves into scenic pools. The trail rolls, journeying upstream. Descend to a small camp flat at 0.5 mile; there, enjoy overlooks of the sterling brook, its cascades and pools. Ahead, moss- and fern-decorated boulders claim the slope.

At 0.7 mile, the Raycroft Trail charges uphill to the left to reach the Smith Hollow Trail and Raycroft (Hunt Hill) Lookout. Bear right to cross the footbridge, continuing on the Dunbar Brook Trail; beware of broken planks.

Continue upstream along the north bank, passing three desirable brook campsites to ascend amid a woods showing large spruce and pine. Find more birch and a tilted footbridge over Haley Brook as the trail approaches the overnight shelter (1.2 miles). The lean-to sleeps five and has a wooden floor, fire ring, grill, and privy in disrepair.

At the left side of the lean-to, veer right, hiking past the privy, to resume the tour; avoid a tracked path that follows Haley Brook downstream. Find a steady ascent through mostly deciduous woods, passing under a utility line at 1.5 miles. While markers are rare, the trail remains followable.

Dip and rise at a deep drainage lined by birch. Farther upstream, travel a scenic hemlock stand where the forest floor seemingly erupts with mossy boulders. Cross a large side brook via stone, log, or wading at 1.8 miles and traverse a woods flat within feet of Dunbar Brook.

Enjoy a series of picture-pretty cascades, riffles, boulders, and window-clear pools. Hobblebush, striped maple, and fern contribute to the understory. Proceed along or just above the brook, touring a brief swampy area with remnant corduroy. The trail slowly climbs; where it plateaus at 2.1 miles, watch for red, yellow, or blue blazes indicating a sharp right turn. Ascend away from the brook, angling northwest uphill, zigzagging among some gargantuan boulders.

At the upper slope, bear left, continuing northwest well removed from the brook. The path broadens to a woods road; the rushing sound of the brook still carries upslope. Descend, again gaining filtered looks at the prized waterway. Cross a side brook atop slippery rocks, pass a pair of 6-foot-high mossy rock walls, and watch for blue blazes as the hike follows a faint, rolling trail to Raycroft Road at 2.8 miles.

Backtrack, or bear left, cross the bridge, and follow Raycroft Road uphill, reaching Spruce Mountain Trail on the right (3 miles). From the bridge, admire the energetic wild, clear water coursing over gneiss–schist outcrop and boulders.

Find the blue-blazed **Spruce Mountain Trail** heading right off Raycroft Road, 0.1 mile south of the Dunbar Brook bridge. Be alert for its start. Look for a large roadside boulder and downed trail post.

Ascend steeply via a charming foot trail framed by fern, aster, and club moss. Seasonally, a vibrant tapestry of fall color and shape may regale the eye. The ascent briefly levels at 0.25 mile and then resumes amid fern-dressed rocks and ledges. Black cherry, birch, maple, beech, striped maple, and hobblebush contribute to the mix. At 0.7 mile, meander through a scenic log-strewn woods.

With a sudden climb, contour the slope, finding spruce. At times, eyes must strain for the next marker. Quartzite appears in some of the rock; a grouse sounds in the distance. Ascend steadily as the midstory vegetation frisks passersby.

At 1.6 miles, find a trail fork atop Spruce Mountain (elevation 2,730 feet). The right fork (straight ahead) leads to an outcrop in 150 feet for limited seasonal looks and an ending point to the tour. While the destination no longer affords open views, it still offers a tranquil retreat. Return as you came.

Alternatively, the left fork continues across Spruce Mountain ridge and descends southeast to Raycroft Road, the Raycroft (Hunt Hill) Lookout, Smith Hollow, and ultimately the Raycroft Trail and Dunbar Brook. This 9- to 10-mile loop travels trail and drivable dirt road. Before attempting it, inquire about trail conditions and the reliability of trail markings.

3 Mount Greylock State Reservation: North

OVERVIEW

In the northern Berkshires of Massachusetts, this 12,500-acre reservation protects the state's highest peak, Mount Greylock (elevation 3,491 feet) and its mostly wild flank. The mountain, topped by an inspirational 100-foot-tall stone war memorial, commands the setting for miles in any direction. The Appalachian Trail travels the spine, serving as a critical link for loop hikes. Centuries-old spruce, five-state panoramas, and wilderness challenges and reverie appeal to hikers. Fifty miles of interlocking trail trace wooded flank, razorback side ridges, and wind-tortured summit.

General description: Two summit treks and a short hike to a waterfall represent the hiking in the northern reservation.

General location: Midway between Lanesborough and North Adams, Massachusetts.

Special attractions: Historic war memorial and Bascom Lodge; a 100-mile, 360-degree tower vista; waterfalls; boreal and northern hardwood forests; spring and summer wildflowers; fall foliage.

Length: Appalachian Trail (AT) to Mount Williams, 5.2 miles round trip; AT–Overlook Loop, 2.4-mile loop; Money Brook Falls Hike, 1 mile round trip.

Elevation: AT to Mount Williams, 790-foot elevation change; AT–Overlook Loop, 600-foot elevation change; Money Brook Falls Hike, 300-foot elevation change.

Difficulty: All moderate.

Maps: State reservation map.

Special concerns: White blazes indicate the AT; blue blazes, all other trails.

Season and hours: Spring through fall for hiking. Day use: 7:00 A.M. to 8:00 P.M.; visitor center, 9:00 A.M. to 5:00 P.M. daily; war memorial, 10:00 A.M. to 5:00 P.M. summer weekends.

For information: Mount Greylock State Reservation.

Key points:
AT to Mount Williams:
    0.0   AT Trailhead, Mount Greylock summit; hike AT northbound.
    1.3   Mount Fitch.
    2.6   Mount Williams; backtrack to trailhead.

AT–Overlook Loop:
    0.0   AT Trailhead, Mount Greylock summit; hike AT southbound.
    0.1   Loop junction; head right.
    0.5   Cross Notch Road.
    1.9   AT junction; go left.
    2.4   End at summit trailhead.

Money Brook Falls Hike:
    0.0   Notch Road trailhead.
    0.2   Meet Money Brook Trail; turn left.
    0.5   Money Brook Falls vista; backtrack to trailhead.

Finding the trailhead: Find the southern approach through Lanesborough, Massachusetts. From the center of town, go 1.2 miles north on U.S. Highway 7 and turn right onto North Main Street, following signs. In another 0.7 mile, bear right onto Rockwell Road. Find the visitor center on the right in 1 mile; reach the summit in another 8 miles.

For the northern approach, from the Massachusetts Highway 2–MA 8 junction in North Adams, go 1.1 miles west on MA 2 and turn south onto Notch Road at the sign. In 1.2 miles, turn left, staying on Notch Road. Reach the summit in another 7 miles.

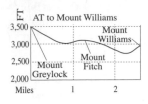

AT to Mount Williams

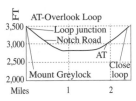

AT-Overlook Loop

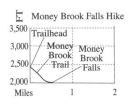

Money Brook Falls Hike

The hikes: Start the **AT to Mount Williams** at the summit; look for the painted AT crosswalk on the park road near Bascom Lodge. Follow the AT northbound as it heads east on a gravel walk to the war memorial. A moving tribute to Massachusetts's war dead, this 100-foot-tall stone tower lifts skyward an attractive spire-topped sphere of metal and glass. When open, the tower's steps ascend to a grand 360-degree view.

The AT then rounds the memorial and veers left, touring the summit. At 0.1 mile, find a sign for the AT at the north end of the parking lot. Descend sharply via shrub-clad outcrop and loose rock, crossing Summit Road.

Views pan east, overlooking the community of Adams. Small aspen, birch, fir, bramble, and hobblebush frame the tour. The path remains steep and eroded, with broad fern shoulders. Look for the occasional white blaze. At 0.4 mile, a blue-blazed cutoff trail heads left to Notch Road, and 20 feet farther north the breakneck Thunderbolt Trail plunges right. Watch for the AT to bear left, entering a high-elevation woodland, where the blue-blazed Bellows Pipe Trail descends east 1 mile to a lean-to.

At 0.5 mile, bear right, crossing seasonal wet spots atop hewn logs, and pass from a boreal fir–spruce forest to northern hardwoods. As the AT rolls along a thin ridge, pass a ledge outcrop with an eastern perspective before descending to a moist saddle or col.

With the trail's return to the ridge, tour the east shoulder of Mount Fitch (elevation 3,110 feet). Where the AT next descends, reach a trail intersection at 2.4 miles. Here, a steep 0.2-mile descent to the right leads to an unreliable spring; the path to the left descends 0.3 mile to Notch Road, passing the chimney from what was the Williams College Outing Club Cabin. The AT proceeds forward.

Ascend steadily, topping Mount Williams (elevation 2,951 feet) at 2.6 miles. To end at a register and vista outcrop, continue briefly for a mild descent and bear right, skirting a vernal pond. The vantage overlooks the Hoosic River Valley, the ridges rolling east, and the peaks of New England. Backtrack to the Mount Greylock summit (5.2 miles), or continue north on the AT as it descends amid forests of hardwood and spruce, reaching Notch Road in another 0.7 mile.

For the **AT–Overlook Loop,** again start at the summit crosswalk near Bascom Lodge and the war memorial, but follow the AT south. Pass a flagpole, snaring nice over-the-shoulder looks at the memorial, dazzling when framed by blue sky or storm-blackened cloud. Follow a wide, trimmed track across the summit meadow and descend the paved driveway toward the radio tower building. Below the building, locate the marked Overlook Trail and follow it right.

Mount Greylock State Reservation: North

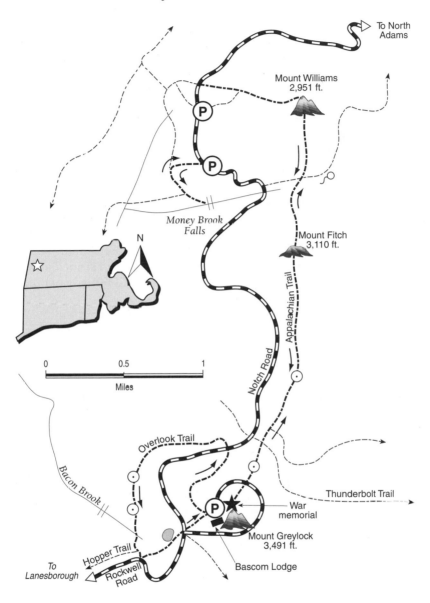

Skirt below the building and the fenced radio tower, descending a tight fir–spruce corridor, absent of views. The firs show the protective skirts of a high-elevation forest. In places, the thin rocky soil has worn down to the bedrock.

Cross Notch Road (0.5 mile) and settle into a contouring course, with gentle rolls. At 1.2 miles, a spur to the right reaches a clearing at the edge of the slope, where hikers gain a U-shaped view of "the Hopper," a glacier-carved ravine secluding old-growth spruce. The Hopper carries "unique natural area" distinction. To the west stretch valley farms, the Taconics with Petersburg Pass, and the distant Adirondacks—a view that applauds Massachusetts, New York, and Vermont.

Resume the Overlook Trail, encircling the upper reaches of Mount Greylock. Hewn logs ease passage over soggy reaches. At 1.6 miles, cross the headwaters of Bacon Brook, which spills to the March Cataract. Now ascend relatively steeply to meet the Hopper Trail. To the right lies the campground; go left to complete the summit loop.

Bear left as the trail nears Rockwell Road and continue bearing left, touring boreal forest en route to the summit. At 1.9 miles, go left on the AT, following its white blazes past a small pond. Cross over the park road at the juncture of Summit, Notch, and Rockwell Roads, closing the loop near the memorial at 2.4 miles.

The **Money Brook Falls Hike** starts at the parking turnout on the west side of Notch Road, 3 miles north of the Rockwell–Notch Road junction, 5 miles south of MA 2; parking accommodates four vehicles.

Follow the blue-blazed trail leaving the north side of the turnout, passing among birch, large-diameter ash, black cherry, both sugar and striped maple, beech, and hobblebush. The rootbound, rock-studded trail initially parallels Notch Road before descending steeply away.

At 0.2 mile, meet the actual Money Brook Trail and follow it left toward the falls. Contour the slope, entering the Money Brook drainage. There, descend steeply, watching your footing. A few azalea dot the area.

At 0.4 mile, reach Money Brook; the main trail continues right. Go left, ascending stone steps for a square-on view of the falls, located 100 feet upstream from the spur's end. The highest falls in the reservation, 40-foot Money Brook Falls dances over sheer black rock before racing downstream through a rock jumble. Return as you came.

4 Mount Greylock State Reservation: South

OVERVIEW

In the northern Berkshires, stretching some 11 miles north to south, Mount Greylock (elevation 3,491 feet) reigns over the neighboring landscape, inspiring hiker, poet, author, and one of the earliest conservation movements in the state of Massachusetts. Beginning in 1898, the state set aside great portions of this mountain to be kept wild. Today, the reservation encompasses more than 12,500 acres and 50 miles of trail, with 1,600 acres recognized as a national natural landmark. At the summit, find a war memorial tower and rustic stone lodge, both dating to the 1930s. Old-growth spruce, stirring vistas, and wilderness escape recommend the mountain.

General description: A blueberry patch and vista outcrop tour, a ridge circuit, and a pair of waterfall hikes encapsulate the offering found in the southern extent of the reservation.

General location: Midway between Lanesborough and North Adams, Massachusetts.

Special attractions: Historic war memorial and Bascom Lodge, vistas, waterfalls, boreal and northern hardwood forests, blueberry patch, a 1945 airplane crash site, fall foliage.

Length: Rounds Rock Trail, 1 mile round trip; Ridge Circuit (linking the CCC Dynamite Trail, Jones Nose Trail, Appalachian Trail or AT, and Old Adams Road), 6.4 miles round trip; Deer Hill Falls Hike, 0.8 mile round trip; March Cataract Trail, 1 mile round trip.

Elevation: Rounds Rock Trail, Deer Hill Falls Hike, and March Cataract Trail each show between 180 and 200 feet in elevation change; the Ridge Circuit shows an 800-foot elevation change.

Difficulty: Rounds Rock Trail, easy; Ridge Circuit, strenuous; the Deer Hill Falls Hike and March Cataract Trail are both moderate.

Maps: State reservation map.

Special concerns: Challenging terrain. Note that white blazes indicate the AT; blue blazes, all other trails.

Season and hours: Spring through fall for hiking. Day use: 7:00 A.M. to 8:00 P.M.; visitor center, 9:00 A.M. to 5:00 P.M. daily; war memorial, 10:00 A.M. to 5:00 P.M. summer weekends.

For information: Mount Greylock State Reservation.

Key points:
Rounds Rock Trail:
  0.0   Southern terminus; ascend west on foot trail.
  0.2   Rounds Rock spur.
  0.7   Plane crash site.
  1.0   End loop; returning to parking.

Ridge Circuit:
  0.0   CCC Dynamite Trailhead.
  1.2   Jones Nose Trail; turn left.
  1.7   Saddle Ball Mountain; follow AT right.
  2.6   Mark Noepel Shelter.
  4.1   Cross Kitchen Brook bridge.
  5.2   Close loop at 1.2-mile junction; backtrack to trailhead.

Deer Hill Falls Hike:
   0.0   Start in Sperry Campground near site 5.
   0.4   Falls; backtrack to trailhead.

March Cataract Trail:
   0.0   Start near Sperry Campground fee station.
   0.5   March Cataract; return as you came.

Finding the trailhead: Find the southern approach through Lanesborough, Massachusetts. From the center of town, go 1.2 miles north on U.S. Highway 7 and turn right onto North Main Street, following signs. In another 0.7 mile, bear right onto Rockwell Road. Find the visitor center on the right in 1 mile; reach the summit in another 8 miles.

For the northern approach, from the Massachusetts Highway 2–MA 8 junction in North Adams, go 1.1 miles west on MA 2 and turn south onto Notch Road at the sign. In 1.2 miles, turn left, staying on Notch Road. Reach the summit in another 7 miles. Descend south from the summit on Rockwell Road for the visitor center.

Locate all trails off Rockwell Road between the visitor center and summit.

The hikes: Locate the parking for the **Rounds Rock Trail** 3 miles north of the visitor center on the right (east) side of Rockwell Road. The trail is on the left. Find its southern terminus 200 feet farther north, and its northern terminus 0.1 mile north of the parking turnout.

Start at the southern terminus, following a moderate-grade foot trail uphill through northern hardwood forest, followed by a shrub–meadow complex and an open blueberry patch mazed by side trails. The first spur to the left as the trail returns to woods leads to Rounds Rock, which is indicated by a survey marker. This bare outcrop overlooks the leafy tree crowns of the immediate setting.

The hike resumes traversing the broad hilltop, passing a 1912 pillar that marks the New Ashford–Cheshire town line. Descend into a spruce stand. At 0.4 mile and again at 0.5 mile, spurs lead left to scenic overlooks featuring the Taconics, Catskills, and Berkshires, with reservoirs to the south. Cairns and blazes point the way over outcrop and through berry patch.

The hike concludes passing amid maple, black cherry, beech, ash, and birch. At 0.7 mile, pass a rusty steel frame and small wooden cross hinting at a 1945 plane crash site. Beautiful 4-foot-tall interrupted ferns adorn the woods. Meet Rockwell Road and turn right for the parking lot at 1 mile.

For the **Ridge Circuit,** start at the CCC Dynamite Trailhead for a 6.4-mile hike, beginning and ending with a scenic woods amble. Locate the trailhead on the east side of Rockwell Road, opposite Sperry Road (the campground access). For a 4-mile loop alone, start at the Old Adams Road/Jones Nose Trailhead, east off Rockwell Road, 3.7 miles north of the visitor center, 3.3 miles south of Notch Road.

The 1.2-mile CCC Dynamite Trail offers one of the easiest tours in this landscape of distinct ups and downs. Enjoy a scenic rolling meander through northern hardwoods, with hobblebush, fern, bramble, sarsaparilla, and whorled aster adorning the deck. At 0.1 mile, pass an old storage box that

Mount Greylock State Reservation: South

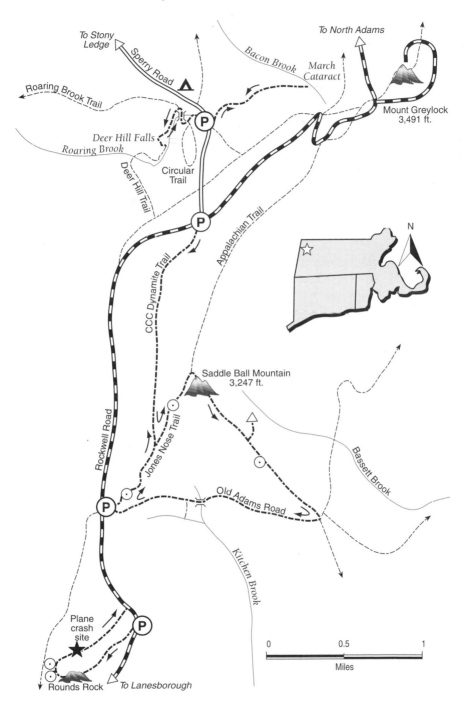

To Stony Ledge

Roaring Brook Trail

Sperry Road

Bacon Brook

March Cataract

To North Adams

Mount Greylock 3,491 ft.

Deer Hill Falls

Roaring Brook

Circular Trail

Deer Hill Trail

CCC Dynamite Trail

Appalachian Trail

N

Saddle Ball Mountain 3,247 ft.

Jones Nose Trail

Rockwell Road

Old Adams Road

Bassett Brook

Kitchen Brook

Plane crash site

Rounds Rock

To Lanesborough

0   0.5   1

Miles

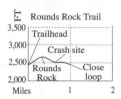

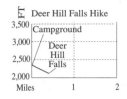

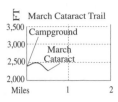

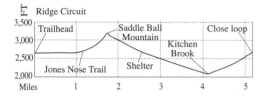

contained the dynamite for road building in the 1930s. Hewn logs cross sodden stretches; large sugar maples enrich the tour.

At 1 mile, stone-step over a brook, and at 1.2 miles meet the Jones Nose Trail. Follow it left for a clockwise tour of the Ridge Circuit.

Find a fairly steep ascent amid black cherry, maple, and beech trees. Soon after, traverse an area of rock outcrops clad with low, dense spruce and mountain ash. A 30-foot spur to the left offers a 90-degree southwestern view, featuring the Taconics and Catskills. Stair-step up the schist outcrop to meet and follow the AT south (right) at Saddle Ball Mountain (1.75 miles). Northbound, the AT reaches the summit, Bascom Lodge, and the war memorial in another 2.6 miles.

Keep to the Ridge Circuit, following the AT south, passing a blue-blazed spur to a former vista stolen by enfolding conifer. Enjoy a rich tour often through boreal forest, a rarity this far south. The steady descent shows less gradient than the Jones Nose Trail; schist continues to make up the trailbed. At 2.5 miles, a 0.1-mile spur leads left to the Mark Noepel Shelter at Bassett Brook. A luxury lean-to that can sleep a dozen hikers, this site offers a table, fire ring, usable privy, and nearby water source (purify all natural sources).

Resume the AT south, still descending. A spur to the right at 2.9 miles offers a grand look out the Kitchen Brook drainage, especially appealing when splashed with autumn red and orange. Where the descent eases, the trail rounds a large boulder with an overhang shelter before weaving among fractured boulders.

Pass among tall spruce and travel logs over muddy areas, reaching the Old Adams Road Trail. Turn right toward Jones Nose Parking on this single-lane dirt road, now a mountain biking trail; leafy branches lace over the route. Keep descending along the main woods road.

After crossing a small drainage, find beech trees replacing the spruce. At 4.1 miles, cross the bridge over upper Kitchen Brook; jewelweed and bramble dress the drainage. At the 4.25-mile junction, turn right to avoid private land. The route now ascends, with aspen and black cherry filling out the ranks. In 200 feet, bear right, passing amid shrubs. At 4.7 miles, round a gate and reach the Old Adams Road/Jones Nose Parking Area.

Resume the circuit tour, following the Jones Nose Trail, heading right. Ascend the ridge, passing through woods and a broad mountain meadow, reaching the junction with the CCC Dynamite Trail at 5.2 miles. Retrace the dynamite trail left, ending at 6.4 miles.

Both the **Deer Hill Falls Hike** and **March Cataract Trail** start in Sperry Campground. Day-use parking is on the left, 200 feet past the fee station. For Deer Hill Falls, hike into the campground, taking the first left to begin near site 5. For March Cataract, hike back toward the fee station and turn left per the sign. The trailhead is where the road curves toward the group sites.

On the **Deer Hill Falls Hike,** leave the campground, immediately cross a footbridge over a headwater fork of Roaring Brook, and turn right, descending within a setting of hardwoods. At 0.1 mile, bear right, recrossing the brook; the Circular Trail heads left just prior to the bridge. In another 50 feet, follow the Deer Hill Trail downhill to the left. The Roaring Brook Trail continues forward. All junctions are well marked.

The Deer Hill Trail descends, briefly pulling away from the brook only to switchback toward it. At 0.4 mile, arrive at the falls spur; the Deer Hill Trail proceeds downhill. The 30-foot spur leads to the base of this weeping-garden-like falls with ledges of moss, fern, wildflower, and grass. From the serene falls, the water threads through schist slabs and drops steeply away. Return as you came.

For the **March Cataract Trail,** hike a narrow, rocky footpath angling uphill to the east. In 50 feet, a little-tracked 0.2-mile Nature Trail journeys left through woods and fern pockets to campsite 16 (an alternative start/return for campers).

A full, rich forest enfolds the cataract trail. Ascend, crossing a rocky drainage to tour a narrow wooded terrace. At 0.25 mile, earthen steps quicken the descent. At the base of the first set of stairs, find a mammoth yellow birch. At the base of the second set, switchback right to cross a pair of hewn logs over a steep, pinched gulch. By weaving among rocks and boulders and passing beneath large maples, reach the base of March Cataract on Bacon Brook at 0.5 mile. The water streaks and skips over a sheer dark outcrop that broadens at the base; small ledges redirect the flow. After plummeting 30 feet, the water tumbles through a steep rocky cataract. Return as you came.

5   Savoy Mountain State Forest

OVERVIEW

This northern Berkshire Mountains retreat unites quiet waters, thriving swamps, and relaxing forest settings. Although removed from the core flyway for the fall hawk migration, the count station atop Spruce Mountain still documents up to 500 birds, mostly seen in pairs or solitary flight. Vistas and the companionship of chickadees help pass the wait for sightings. A network of interlocking trails explores this 10,500-acre state forest. Because most hikers manage to find their way to Bog Pond and Tannery Falls, this description introduces three other possible hikes.

General description: Three hikes introduce the heights, ponds, and swamps of this state forest.
General location: 5 miles east of North Adams, Massachusetts.
Special attractions: Summit vistas, evergreen–hardwood forests, ponds and brooks, mountain laurel, autumn hawk-watch, and colorful fall foliage.
Length: Busby Trail, 2.5 miles round trip; North Pond Loop, 2.4-mile loop; South Pond–Tyler Swamp Loop, 3.7 miles round trip.
Elevation: Busby Trail, 700-foot elevation change; North Pond Loop, 250-foot elevation change; South Pond–Tyler Swamp Loop, 100-foot elevation change.
Difficulty: Busby Trail, moderate to strenuous; the North Pond Loop and South Pond–Tyler Swamp Loop are both moderate.
Maps: State forest map (available at the forest headquarters).
Special concerns: Keep dogs leashed at all times. Blue markers indicate hike and ski routes.
Season and hours: Year-round; spring through fall for hiking. Day use ends at 8:00 P.M.
For information: Savoy Mountain State Forest.

Key points:
Busby Trail:
  0.0   Central Shaft Road trailhead.
  1.0   Spruce Hill summit loop.
  1.2   Summit.
  1.5   Complete summit loop; backtrack to trailhead.

North Pond Loop:
  0.0   Start at North Pond Picnic Area.
  0.4   Junction; proceed forward.
  2.4   End at North Pond Picnic Area parking lot.

South Pond–Tyler Swamp Loop:
  0.0   Start at campground entrance.
  0.4   Spur to South Pond.
  0.7   Swamp loop junction; bear left onto Tyler Swamp Trail.
  1.5   Cross swamp outlet.
  2.9   Complete swamp loop; retrace South Pond Trail (left).

Finding the trailhead: From the junction of Massachusetts Highway 2 and MA 8 in North Adams, go east on MA 2 for 5 miles and turn right (south) onto Central Shaft Road for Savoy Mountain State Forest. Go 2 miles and turn right (still on Central Shaft Road) to enter the state forest, reaching the

Savoy Mountain State Forest

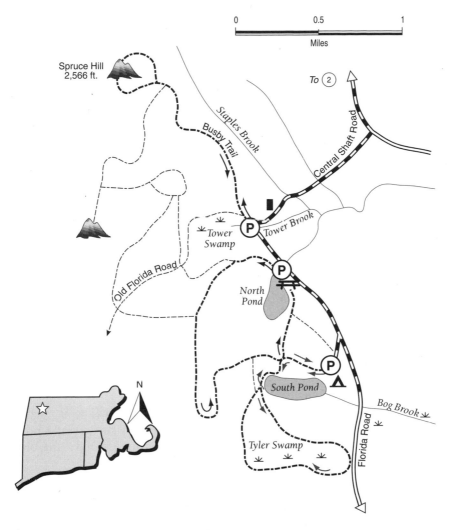

headquarters in another 0.9 mile. Locate the trails off Central Shaft Road past the headquarters.

The hikes: Locate the start for the **Busby Trail** 0.1 mile west of the forest headquarters at the turn for North Pond; there is head-in parking along the road shoulder at the turn.

Follow the dirt road heading west off Central Shaft Road for 100 feet and turn right at the sign for Busby Trail/Spruce Hill Hawk Lookout. The hike remains on an old road grade. After crossing a shrubby utility corridor, take the bypass route left to avoid an often muddy stretch of road. Hemlock and spruce contribute to the woods; aster, fern, and hobblebush color the roadsides. At the second utility-line clearing, spy the fall color mosaic of a neighboring ridge.

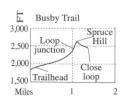

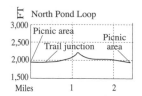

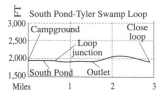

A narrower, rockier roadbed passing through stands of planted spruce and draping deciduous forest continues the hike. Where the trail parallels a drainage, find a steady, even ascent. The route crosses side drainages before passing a stone cellar (0.9 mile) with a birch growing from it. Abandoned fruit trees are also seen. The climb grows more serious with switchbacks and a fairly steep gradient.

Cross the stone wall at 1 mile, coming to a junction. A left leads to the 2,416-foot bump shown on the forest map, but it offers no view. Straight continues to Spruce Hill (elevation 2,566 feet), reaching the summit loop. The left (or south) fork offers a steep assault; the right (north) fork holds the more gradual approach.

The impatient should take the left fork, coming to a rocky climb in 0.1 mile. Nooks and ledges shape toe- and hand-holds. Top Spruce Hill at two survey markers, gaining a 270-degree panoramic view of Mount Greylock, Hoosic Valley, the town of Adams, distant peaks to the north, and the Taconics to the west. A couple of large reservoirs break the treed expanse. A stroll of the summit pieces together the remaining 90 degrees. The summit's hawk-watch monitoring equipment occupies the northern set of rocks; do not disturb. Complete the summit loop (1.5 miles) and return to the trailhead (2.5 miles).

For the **North Pond Loop,** start at the North Pond Picnic Area parking lot (0.5 mile southwest of the forest headquarters). Hike 0.1 mile north along Central Shaft Road and turn west at the gated road. Follow the blue-marked trail angling to the right before the first gate.

The hike enters a beautiful woodland of maple, beech, black cherry, birch, and ash. Fern, striped maple, and hobblebush add texture. An autumn spangling of colored leaves makes the path particularly eye-pleasing. Boots shuffle up mini collages. After paralleling the park road, the trail curves away and bears left at 0.25 mile, avoiding a stone-blocked trail to the right. The route widens to cart path width and has a moderate incline. At 0.4 mile is a junction. The Old Florida Road Trail heads right; proceed forward for the North Pond Loop. At 0.75 mile, the pond loop heads left, now on foot trail. Conifers briefly punctuate the leafy forest.

At 1.1 miles, the grade steepens as the trail weaves uphill and tops out. A slow descent follows. Pass attractive beech stands and an unusual rock arrangement, with small rock bracing a much larger boulder. Pass through sag at 1.5 miles for a faster, slope-wrapping descent. In 0.3 mile, the South Pond Loop heads right; continue forward, passing an ancient red maple and an assembly of boulders. At the three-prong junction at 2 miles, head left to continue the North Pond Loop.

The descent resumes. Corduroys, hewn logs, and stones span muddy spots in the hemlock–maple woods. Find patches of laurel and bowls of fern. At the next junction, the foot trail to the left advances the loop. A low slope isolates the trail from the park road. At 2.25 miles, emerge at a gated road and turn left to reach North Pond Recreation Area. Return to the North Pond Picnic Area (2.4 miles), ending the hike with views of the tree-rimmed pond at the foot of the ridge.

Begin the **South Pond-Tyler Swamp Loop** near the campground entrance. Follow the campground road, taking the right toward the cabins and nature center at 0.1 mile. Go past the group site and take the woods road (trail) that heads right as the road curves toward the cabins. From it, bear left per the trail user sign; a campsite is to the right. Travel a hemlock–maple–birch woods and descend a rocky slope, coming to a three-way junction at a big split boulder (0.25 mile). Go left for a clockwise loop.

This scenic footpath shows a modest grade. Where the trail bears right uphill (0.4 mile), a 100-foot spur through a hemlock stand leads to the South Pond shore. South Pond is a big, open-water pond rimmed by overhanging red maple and mountain laurel with a hemlock background. In spring, the pond reflects the laurel bloom; in autumn, the red foliage.

The trail continues with an easy rolling tour of the slope, passing some 200 to 300 feet away from shore. Although the hike affords pond glimpses, there are no other access spurs. At 0.75 mile, the trail drifts from the pond to a junction. Bear left on the Tyler Swamp Trail to add the second part of this hike.

Tyler Swamp Loop, Savoy Mountain State Forest, MA.

The swamp trail offers a basically level stroll through similar woods, with a few soggy spots and boulder accents. As the trail rounds the swamp on an old road grade, discover lighting changes but no swamp views. The trail turns right before reaching a forest road and crosses Tyler Swamp outlet, a stone crossing. This next stretch of trail, although traceable, receives little use and can be overgrown. Hobblebush and striped maple abound in the swamp periphery, and black cherry appear in the mix. As the trail ascends, it crosses a couple of small drainages. Forest changes are subtle. After the trail tops out and again descends, first glimpse snag-riddled Tyler Swamp (2.5 miles). Swamp views build to include the snarl of logs, snags, and twisted branches. The swamp's red maples offer a colorful contrast to the gray wood.

The trail rolls along the slope to the junction at 2.9 miles. Head right to complete the swamp loop in a matter of strides, and then angle sharply left to retrace South Pond Trail to the campground.

6 Mohawk Trail State Forest

OVERVIEW

In the northern Berkshires of Massachusetts, this 6,457-acre state forest encompasses steep-sided mountains, rich hardwood forest, abundant mountain laurel, deep ravines, and a historical Indian trail. Cold River bisects the property, the Deerfield River flows along the northeast boundary, and Trout and Wheeler Brooks drain the hillsides. Despite the significant role of water in this terrain, the hikes focus travel on mountain flank and crest, with only limited overlooks of the drainages.

General description:	Three short hikes of varying difficulty attain vantages and present the forest offering.
General location:	4 miles west of Charlemont, Massachusetts.
Special attractions:	Outcrop vistas, mountain laurel, relaxing hardwood forest, fall foliage, wildlife.
Length:	Indian Trail, 4.5 miles round trip (visiting both Todd and Clark Mountains); Thumper Mountain Trail, 0.5 mile round trip; Totem Trail, 2.2 miles round trip.
Elevation:	Indian Trail, 600- to 800-foot elevation change (depending on selected turnaround points); Thumper Mountain Trail, 100-foot elevation change; Totem Trail, 700-foot elevation change.
Difficulty:	Indian Trail, strenuous; Thumper Mountain Trail, easy; Totem Trail, moderate.
Maps:	State forest map (generally available at site).
Special concerns:	Admission fee. Portions of the first 0.5 mile of the Indian Trail are exceedingly steep and may require the use of hands for balance. Boots are recommended.

Season and hours: Spring through fall.
For information: Mohawk Trail State Forest.

Key points:
Indian Trail:

- 0.0 Indian Trailhead.
- 0.5 Saddle junction; head right.
- 1.2 Top Todd Mountain; backtrack to saddle.
- 2.0 Saddle junction; follow Mahican–Mohawk Trail west.
- 3.0 Halt in field below Clark Mountain; return to trailhead (4.5 miles).

Thumper Mountain Trail:

- 0.0 Thumper Mountain Trailhead; head southeast.
- 0.2 Top outcrop vantage; return as you came.

Totem Trail:

- 0.0 Totem Trailhead; ascend south at monument.
- 1.1 Totem Viewpoint; return to trailhead.

Finding the trailhead: From the junction of Massachusetts Highway 2 and MA 8A South (0.4 mile west of Charlemont), go west on MA 2 for 3.5 miles, and turn north for the state forest campground and Indian and Thumper Mountain Trails. Find day-use parking near the headquarters.

Continue west on MA 2 for 0.7 mile to find the Totem Trail as it heads south off MA 2 at a monument. The picnic area turnoff is 0.1 mile farther west on the north side of the highway. Park there and carefully cross the road for the Totem Trail.

The hikes: For the **Indian Trail,** from the day-use parking at the headquarters, hike the state forest road northwest for 0.6 mile, finding the marked trailhead on the north side of the road where it hooks left to campsites 36 through 56.

From the trailhead, log-reinforced steps ascend the hillside, which has a varied cloak of hemlock, ash, birch, oak, maple, striped maple, witch hazel, and mountain laurel. After contouring, the trail bears right in 250 feet. It then charges steeply uphill, crossing over rock outcrops, advanced by a marked switchback partway to the saddle. Lichens encrust the rock and nearby oak trunks, and the Cold River rushes in the basin below. Although markers are few, the trail is well worn.

At 0.5 mile, top the saddle, arriving at a junction. To the right (east) lies Todd Mountain with its tree-framed vistas in 0.75 mile. The Mahican–Mohawk Trail heads left, quickly splitting into forks (be alert—the split is

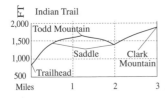

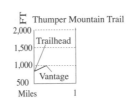

easily missed). The left fork leads west to Clark Mountain; the right fork crosses over the saddle and descends the back side of the ridge before emerging at the start of the Nature Trail near the group sites (consult a map and remain alert for markers and other trail clues if you choose this option). The gentle tour to Clark Mountain rounds but does not top the peak before halting in 1 mile at an open field.

For this area sampling, first hike east along the ridge toward Todd Mountain. The trail rolls along the crest and then ascends, passing between and over rocks; be careful when it is wet or overlain with leaves and pine needles. Pass a scenic congregation of rocks that allows stolen looks south. Later, gain better outward looks before claiming the summit (elevation 1,711 feet). Here, views extend south and east and overlook the Cold River drainage, the opposite steep-sided ridge, and rural valley of MA 2. Quartzite veins riddle some rocks, while reindeer lichens accent others.

Return to the saddle junction and descend to camp for a 2.5-mile round trip, or add the westbound tour to Clark Mountain.

An aisle of mountain laurel ushers hikers west along the rolling ridge toward Clark Mountain. In 0.2 mile, a gap offers a look across the Cold River drainage. Within a hemlock flat, the trail widens to carriage width. Where the ridge sags, reach another flat just below the summit. Here a pair of stone foundations, semimasked by ferns, signals a potential ending at 0.75 mile. The shady stroll, however, continues. It rounds the north flank of Clark Mountain, ending at an open field edged by picturesque birch in another 0.25 mile.

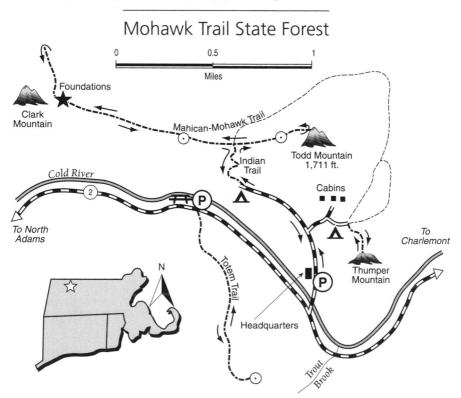

Mohawk Trail State Forest

0   0.5   1

Miles

Foundations

Clark
Mountain

Mahican-Mohawk Trail

Cold River

Indian
Trail

Todd Mountain
1,711 ft.

Cabins

2

P

To North
Adams

To
Charlemont

Totem Trail

Thumper
Mountain

N

Headquarters

P

Trout Brook

This time, upon returning to the saddle junction, descend to camp for a total 4.5-mile round trip. Exercise caution on the descent, particularly if conditions are wet.

The **Thumper Mountain Trail** is reached by going 0.4 mile northwest from the headquarters and turning north for the cabins and group campsites. The trail starts at the end of the road in another 0.2 mile. Hikers may only park in this area during low-use times. Generally, use the day-use parking near the headquarters and walk to the trailhead.

Look for this trail's signpost east past the group campsites; the Nature Trail heads north at the gate. Periodic markers, sometimes ambiguous, point the way on the Thumper Mountain Trail. Hemlock, white pine, hardwood, and laurel shape the setting. In 250 feet, bear right, ascending and traversing a ledge. In another 0.1 mile, climb steeply left. As the outcrop destination comes into view, bear right, rounding to the top. Find a framed view south-southwest looking across the Cold River drainage at a wooded skyline knoll. Noise from MA 2 carries to the site. Return as you came.

The **Totem Trail** leads to Totem Viewpoint, elevation 1,500 feet; a few blue and orange markers assist hikers. Ascend south at a roadside monument noting the establishment of the forest in 1921. In 100 feet, turn left, crossing a broad rocky drainage. A foot trail now contours east uphill. Birch, small beech, maple, and a bounty of fern contribute to an eye-pleasing journey.

Ascend steadily; a few rocks and roots foul footing. At 0.25 mile, meet a former woods road and follow it east, still enwrapping the slope. Cross a rocky drainage at 0.6 mile, regaining both rocks and incline. For the next 0.4 mile, the hike remains along a drainage cut.

At 1 mile, follow a faint foot trail, contouring and descending east. Where it rolls uphill, reach the vista site (1.1 miles), a scooped and canted outcrop overlooking Trout Brook to the east and the Cold River drainage to the north. The neighboring wooded ridges especially enchant when awash with fall color. Return as you came.

7 Notchview Reservation— Windsor State Forest

OVERVIEW

In the northwest corner of Massachusetts, the adjoining lands of Notchview Reservation (a property of the Trustees of Reservations) and Windsor State Forest introduce the tranquility of the Hoosac Range. Rich hardwood forests and pine and spruce plantations enfold the area. Sparkling Steep Bank Brook ties together the reservation and state forest lands, ushering hikers between the two sites. Within the state forest, Windsor Jambs Scenic Area spotlights a small gorge and energetic rush of water.

General description:	This day hike travels between the two properties. Visit mixed woods, plantations, and wet meadow bottoms, crisscrossing Steep Bank Brook to admire the rocky gorge of Windsor Jambs.
General location:	20 miles northeast of Pittsfield, Massachusetts.
Special attractions:	Tranquil woods; rocky brooks; cascades; gorge (The Jambs); wildlife sightings of turkey, porcupine, and deer.
Length:	10.1 miles round trip; car-shuttle or shorter trips are possible.
Elevation:	Find a 1,000-foot elevation change, with the low point located on the Jambs Trail, the high point at Judges Hill (elevation 2,297 feet).
Difficulty:	Moderate; strenuous and treacherous when streambed rocks and mosses are wet.
Maps:	Reservation and state forest trail maps (generally available at the respective sites).
Special concerns:	Privately owned Notchview Reservation suggests a per-hiker donation, while the state forest charges a parking fee. Reservation travel is at your own risk; obey posted rules.
Season and hours:	Spring through fall for hiking. Reservation, 8:00 A.M. to dusk; Windsor Jambs Scenic Area, 8:00 A.M. to 8:00 P.M.
For information:	The Trustees of Reservations, Western Regional Office; Windsor State Forest.

Key points:

0.0   Budd Visitor Center trailhead; hike Circuit Trail clockwise.
1.4   Top Judges Hill.
2.1   Steep Bank Brook; first crossing.
3.2   Bathhouse at Windsor State Forest Headquarters.
4.4   Mouth of The Jambs.
4.7   The Jambs Scenic Area (car-shuttle hike ending); backtrack to Circuit Trail.
8.8   Circuit Trail; resume clockwise tour.
10.1 End at Budd Visitor Center.

Finding the trailhead: To reach the reservation, from Massachusetts Highway 9, 2 miles east of Windsor, turn north at the sign for Notchview Reservation. Go 0.2 mile to reach the Colonel Arthur Budd Visitor Center and trailhead parking area.

For the state forest, from MA 9, 6 miles east of Windsor, turn north onto West Main for West Cummington and Windsor State Forest. In 0.7 mile, turn

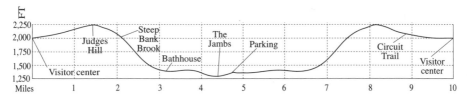

Notchview Reservation—Windsor State Forest

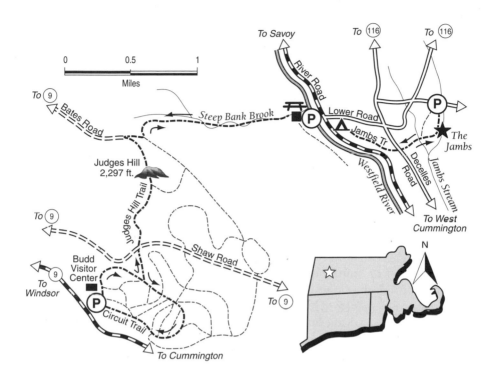

right onto River Road; reach the campground, picnic area, and headquarters in another 2.9 miles. From the headquarters area, follow graveled Lower Road southeast to reach the turn for Windsor Jambs Scenic Area.

The hike: On a west–east hike, travel the reservation's Circuit and Judges Hill Trails, the jointly held Steep Bank Trail, and the state forest's Jambs Trail. Look for yellow markers and signed junctions along the reservation trails; blue markers indicate the state forest trails.

From the Budd Visitor Center at Notchview Reservation, hike the mowed track beginning to the left of the trail information board. Pass north between a set of fences and bypass Kinder Loop, coming to the junction of the Circuit and Spruce Hill Trails in 250 feet. Go left for a clockwise tour of the Circuit Trail, traveling a time-healed woods roads of cushiony grass and needles. The Circuit Trail serves as a hub for the reservation trail system and doubles as a winter cross-country ski trail.

On the left at 0.3 mile, view an unusual beech tree displaying long, low, outward-spreading branches. Beyond the Anthill Trail, turn left onto the Judges Hill Trail to head toward Windsor Jambs; the Circuit Trail turns right.

Follow a grassy woods corridor, soon crossing dirt Shaw Road. Pass from ash swale to planted spruce, again on an old woods road; footboards and logs ease passage at wet areas. By 1 mile, find a steady ascent among mixed hardwoods. The grade steepens, drawing away from the marked Windsor Trail junction; stay on the Judges Hill Trail.

At 1.4 miles, top Judges Hill; the rockwork from an old picnic shelter and a stand of beautiful small- to midsize beech trees claim the summit. A quick descent to Bates Road (1.7 miles) follows. Turn right onto this former stage-coach route to find the Steep Bank Trail, descending left in 0.1 mile.

This trail escapes much of the area boot traffic for a pleasing woods and brook meander, but stay alert for the faint trail markers; a few red Trustees' disks help point the way. Descend through a maple woodland with a lush green understory, crossing over and pursuing the thin side drainages downstream.

Along a rock wall, curve right, cross a side brook, and follow the south (right) bank of Steep Bank Brook downstream. Big birch, smaller beech, and hemlock frame this tannin-colored water punctuated by mossy boulders and 1-foot-high cascades. Various ferns lend accent. Find the first stone-hopping crossing at 2.1 miles. Thirteen more follow, so be alert.

At times, the brook's trademark steep banks or downfalls push hikers higher up the slope. Spruce trees fill out the shady complex, and a few skewed state forest triangles can either mark or confuse the way. With the fourteenth crossing, return to the south bank and continue downstream, following a woods road contouring the slope above the brook. Turn right to reach the bathhouse at Windsor State Forest Headquarters at 3.2 miles.

Traverse the parking lot, cross River Road, and pass south through the campground, finding the Jambs Trail near the rest room building. A simple sign says TRAIL.

Blue markers and blazes now guide hikers through a dark hemlock–birch complex and plantations of spiny spruce. Where the soft earthen bed grows soggy, jewelweed, clintonia, and mayflower make a spotty appearance. After a slow ascent, head left on a woods road to cross dirt Decelles Road (3.8 miles) and angle left through another plantation.

Where footboards cross a wet site, find a marked junction. Left leads to upper Jambs, but for the best gorge viewing, go right as indicated for lower Jambs. Tour a hemlock–hardwood forest, following and crossing a side drainage to arrive at the mouth of The Jambs (the gorge on Jambs Stream) at 4.4 miles.

Follow the left shore upstream, separated from the gorge by a mesh fence. Massive green-stained rock slabs riddle the 15-foot-wide tannin-steeped watercourse pinched between 50-foot cliffs. The racing water cascades, riffles, and sheets over and around the rock, with the largest cascades plunging 12 feet. An early-morning chill often hangs in the gorge. At 4.7 miles, reach the Jambs Scenic Area Parking Lot, the ending for shuttle-tour hikers.

Round-trip hikers backtrack, returning to the Circuit Trail at Notchview Reservation (8.8 miles). Continue straight on the woods road to complete the clockwise tour, passing through spruce plantation and hardwood settings. Avoid the outward-radiating side trails to skirt a weathered-board garage, orchard, and field. A stately staircase to nowhere hints at an earlier time when these woods supported family farms. Proceed back to the visitor center, now within sight, ending at 10.1 miles.

Windsor Jams, Windsor State Forest, MA.

8 Hancock Shaker Village Trail

General description:	Constructed and maintained by the Boy Scouts of America, this circuit travels wooded, stream, and hilltop sites key to a nineteenth-century Shaker society. The hike visits an area that held a Shaker family residence, farm and pasture, mills, waterworks, and two holy summits; plaques identify the points of archaeological and historical note.
General location:	5 miles west of Pittsfield, Massachusetts.
Special attractions:	National historic trail with religious and historical sites, rock walls, mixed woods, fall foliage.
Length:	6.5 miles round trip.
Elevation:	From a trailhead elevation of 1,170 feet, top Mount Sinai (now Shaker Mountain) at 1,845 feet, Holy Mount at 1,927 feet.
Difficulty:	Moderate.
Maps:	Pittsfield State Forest brochure.
Special concerns:	Because this trail passes through the private Hancock Shaker Village (a not-for-profit museum village), hikers must first check in at the visitor center to secure a free hiker pass. Pass directly through the village property to the trail, avoiding all fee attractions: buildings, lectures, and demonstrations. Hikers interested in these attractions may instead purchase admission. No smoking and no pets within the village.
Season and hours:	Spring through fall; visitor center, 9:30 A.M. to 5:00 P.M. April through November.
For information:	Hancock Shaker Village; Pittsfield State Forest.

Key points:

0.0 Hancock Shaker Village; take crosswalk north.
0.5 Loop junction (above Lower Dam); cross bridge and head downstream.
0.7 North Family residence site; detour to cornfield.
2.1 Mount Sinai Summit Holy Ground.
2.9 "Great gulf" between summits.
4.0 Sacred Lot, Holy Mount.
6.0 Complete loop; backtrack to village.

Finding the trailhead: From the junction of U.S. Highways 20 and 7 in Pittsfield, go west on US 20 for 4.5 miles. Find visitor parking for Hancock Shaker Village on the south side of the highway. Park, check in, and cross US 20 at the crosswalk.

The hike: White circles within green triangles guide hikers into the world of an 1845 Shaker community. Although woods now conceal much of the story, some of the remaining stonework, fruit trees, and cellar holes help you visualize the area. The trail tags two holy summits: Mount Sinai,

Hancock Shaker Village Trail

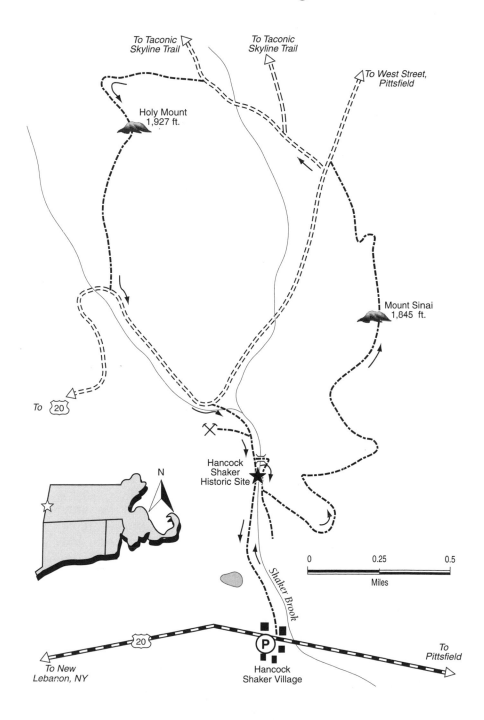

To Taconic Skyline Trail

To Taconic Skyline Trail

To West Street, Pittsfield

Holy Mount 1,927 ft.

Mount Sinai 1,845 ft.

To 20

N

Hancock Shaker Historic Site

Shaker Brook

0   0.25   0.5

Miles

20

To New Lebanon, NY

P

Hancock Shaker Village

To Pittsfield

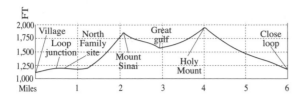

chosen by the Hancock Shakers; and Holy Mount, chosen by the Shakers of Mount Lebanon, New York.

A commitment to a common religion, culture, and lifestyle united the Shaker members into a cohesive community, isolated from the outside world. Hancock represents one of the earliest Shaker communes formed in the United States. The trail holds the distinction of being the first national historic trail in Massachusetts; pass gently and respectfully.

From the crosswalk, follow the grassy track north past a small garden plot and through a field. Looks west find an elevated reservoir first used in 1790. At 0.25 mile, bear right, passing the rusty remains of a steam boiler left over from a Shaker textile mill. At 0.3 mile, again bear right, entering woods on the historic road to the North Family residence; six such families made up Hancock.

The road travels upstream along the west shore of Shaker Brook, reaching the remnants of Lower Dam at 0.5 mile. This straight-built dam supplied power to the community. Built of rock slabs, it stands between 5 and 10 feet tall. While some of the cap rock has collapsed into the stream, it remains in remarkably fine shape. Just upstream lies the footbridge marking the start of the loop; cross, delaying a visit to High Dam until the end of the tour.

Proceed downstream along the east shore, again overlooking Lower Dam. A spur to the right reveals the stone foundation of the carding-, grist-, and saw-mills. At 0.75 mile, signs to the right indicate where the North Family residence stood, now an overgrown flat and cellar depression. Although the loop now turns left to ascend Mount Sinai, a 0.5-mile round-trip detour straight ahead adds looks at a scenic rock wall, cornfield, and ancient maple and ash for a sense of the land's historical use.

Resume the tour to Mount Sinai at 1.25 miles, hiking a trail of cart path width that mirrors and, in places, utilizes segments of the historical route. Find a steady, moderate grade winding skyward to the hallowed ground. Passage is through a mixed forest of white pine, maple, birch, ash, oak, hickory, and beech. Sarsaparilla, striped maple, and fern contribute to an understory profusion.

Twice pass under a power line. Blackened earth hints at the former charcoal pits; look for more along the hike's ending. At 2.1 miles, reach and cross the summit Holy Ground, abandoned to nature. Ferns and young trees hint at the open flats of ceremony and worship. At the high point (2.25 miles), find a wooden bench.

A woods descent follows, reaching what Shaker diaries refer to as the "great gulf" between the holy summits (2.9 miles). Here, off-road-vehicle tracks scar the trail as it meets a multiuse forest road. Turn left for the loop and bear right at the immediate road fork, keeping an eye out for the familiar green-and-white markers.

48

Stone wall on Holy Mount, Pittsfield State Forest, MA.

Beautifully constructed rock walls now line the trail as the loop arcs west to ascend Holy Mount. These walls formerly marked the north boundary of the Hancock Shaker property. Moss and lichen accent the flat rock slabs.

At 3.3 miles, bear left onto a narrower, less trafficked multiuse route, journeying through a mixed-age deciduous woods. The trail rolls and dips, crossing a side brook. At 3.8 miles, go left for a hiker-only segment snaking to the summit. Black cherry and white pine contribute to the woods, as do a few fruit trees.

A breach in the summit rock wall (4 miles) provides access to Sacred Lot; stone walls and foundations hint at the lay of the site. Curve right, following the signs south off Holy Mount. Low, multitrunked pines initially frame the descent, grading into a forest of oak and beech. Find a few steep pitches and canted trail segments before ascending among maple and birch. At 4.75 miles, turn left again, following a multiuse road that now parallels a side brook downstream.

At the fork at 5.2 miles, go right to continue the loop on a hiker-only road. After a couple of side-brook crossings, vehicle use again mars travel. At 5.5 miles, a 0.3-mile round-trip detour right finds a limestone quarry first used in 1785. Dense ferns mask the quarry depressions. Maidenhair ferns first cued the brethren to the likelihood of limestone beneath the surface.

At 5.8 miles, resume the loop, soon turning right to travel the road downstream alongside Shaker Brook. In 100 feet on the left, find the remains of convex-shaped High Dam, circa 1810. Close the loop at 6 miles, reaching the village at 6.5 miles.

9 D.A.R. State Forest

OVERVIEW

The Daughters of the American Revolution (D.A.R.) State Forest occupies 1,635 acres in the east-central Berkshires, serving up tranquil woods, two large lakes, and a fire tower delivering a five-state vista. The featured 5-mile hike ties together nearly all of the site's designated foot trails; another 10 miles of bridle trail extend the exploration.

General description:	This relaxing hike travels the northwest quadrant of the forest, visiting lakeshore, marshy drainage, mixed woods, and Goshen Fire Tower.
General location:	4 miles northwest of Williamsburg, Massachusetts.
Special attractions:	Quiet lakeshore, summit vistas, hemlock–hardwood forest, stone walls and ruins, mountain laurel and spring wildflowers, fall foliage.
Length:	Lake–Tower Hike, 5 miles round trip.
Elevation:	The trail shows a 250-foot elevation change.
Difficulty:	Moderate.
Maps:	State forest map.
Special concerns:	Fee admission site. Assistive listening devices and tapes for the Nature Trail are available at the ranger station.
Season and hours:	Year-round, spring through fall for hiking.
For information:	D.A.R. State Forest.

Key points:
- 0.0 Start at beach/day-use parking; cross dam.
- 0.2 Nature Trail.
- 0.5 Long Trail.
- 1.0 Loop junction; bear left.
- 3.0 Moore Hill; descend via Darling Trail.
- 3.6 Campground.
- 4.0 Close loop; backtrack to trailhead.

Finding the trailhead: From the junction of Massachusetts Highways 9 and 112 north of Goshen Center, follow MA 112 north for the state forest. Go 0.6 mile and turn right (east), reaching the beach/day-use parking (trailhead) in 0.3 mile.

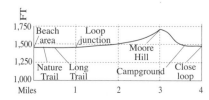

The hikes: This tour travels a portion of the self-guided **Nature Trail,** the **Long Trail,** and the **Darling Trail.**

From the day-use parking on the south shore of Upper Highland Lake, hike the footpath heading east along the shore and across the earthen dam to ar-

D.A.R. State Forest

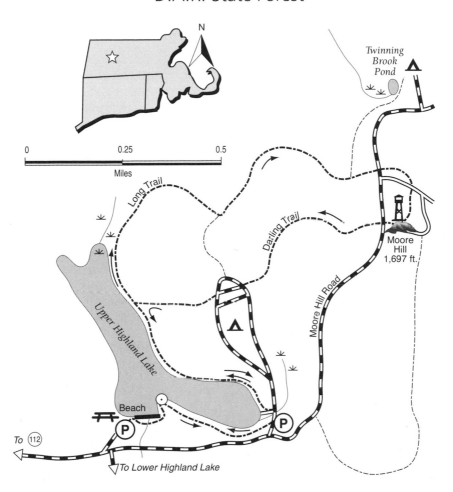

rive at the handicapped-accessible boat launch. From there, enter the woods of hemlock, white pine, and birch via the Nature Trail; maps are generally available at its start. This groomed, handicapped-accessible trail passes between the two launches on Upper Highland Lake; along it, rustic folk-art log and limb benches invite sitting. Where the trail rounds a small point (0.25 mile), find a log gazebo and rock-rimmed fishing access overlooking boot-shaped Upper Highland Lake; the still waters reflect the rimming trees and low terrain.

Continue the pleasant lake–woods stroll, gathering views and seasonal impressions. At 0.5 mile, the Nature Trail ends at the parking lot for the second boat launch. Emerge at a landscaped island and flagpole and turn left to continue the hike at the launch; a sign indicates the Long Trail.

With gas-powered boats prohibited, the peace is unchallenged. A few spruce, black cherry, and towering oak complete the woods. Pass above a small beachfront and through a gap in a stone wall, gaining an impressive mountain laurel midstory. Some beautiful big trees punctuate the dark woods. Where the slope steepens and the trail rolls, find a superb corridor of the 10-foot-tall laurel. At 1 mile, reach the loop junction and bear left; to the right sits the campground (0.2 mile).

A few azalea accent shore where the Long Trail curves away from the open lake at a marshy inlet cove. Follow the inlet brook upstream; paired logs, corduroys, and stones cross the wet reaches. At 1.9 miles, another spur branches right to the campground; continue forward. The woods remain lush, green, and marshy.

Slowly ascend through a hardwood forest with dispersed pine and spruce; blue markers aid travelers. From 2.3 to 2.5 miles, hike atop a low, bumpy ridge with a few outcrop ledges and boulders. A tumbled sign reads GREAT ANT HILLS.

Where the trail curves away left, take either trail fork; they soon merge again. Pass through a stone wall opening and over a drainage, finding the junction for Twinning Brook Group Camp (2.75 miles). A 0.25-mile spur heads left for the camp, descending along a thin drainage, with remnant stone walls and bountiful ferns. The camp sits above a tiny dammed pond.

For the Lake–Tower Hike, continue forward, crossing over paved Moore Hill Road and dirt Oak Hill Road, ascending through low-stature forest to reach the tower atop Moore Hill (elevation 1,697 feet) at 3 miles. Locate the return trail to your right as you reach the tower.

The public may ascend this nine-story tower, but the lookout loft remains closed. Views sweep the Berkshires, Taconics, and Holyoke Range, with the farthest bumps on the horizon representing New York, Vermont, New Hamp-

Upper Highland Lake, D.A.R. State Forest, MA.

shire, and Connecticut. The 360-degree view applauds a broad sweep of the wooded Massachusetts terrain, resplendent in fall.

Now follow the unmarked Darling Trail as it descends steeply away, passing beneath a utility line to the fire tower. Cross Moore Hill Road and descend amid shoulder-high shrubs, laurel, goldenrod, and small oaks and maples. Cross a boardwalk and pass an old stone cellar, returning to forest. The width of the trail fluctuates, but it remains easy to follow.

Stone walls parallel the trail as it approaches the campground at 3.6 miles. Hike the paved campground road ahead, passing a utility shed, site 47, and a rest room facility to resume on the foot trail (3.7 miles). It leaves the campground at a road juncture; look for the blue markers. Close the loop at 4 miles, and retrace the trail left to the trailhead at 5 miles.

10   Canoe Meadows Sanctuary

OVERVIEW

At this tranquil 262-acre retreat along the Housatonic River, hardwood forest, meadow, riparian corridor, pond, field, and swamp woodlands contribute to varied travel and fine wildlife-watching. Two short hikes introduce the area.

General description:	Sacred Way (a pond–river circuit) and Wolf Pine Trail (a woodland tour) explore the sanctuary.
General location:	In Pittsfield, Massachusetts, 1 mile from the town center.
Special attractions:	Bird-watching, canoeing, enclosed blind, a unique pine, wildflowers, fall foliage.
Length:	Sacred Way, 1.2 miles round trip; Wolf Pine Trail, 1.5 miles round trip (1.9 miles round trip adding the Owl Trail spur).
Elevation:	Sacred Way, flat; Wolf Pine Trail has less than a 40-foot elevation change.
Difficulty:	Both easy.
Maps:	Sanctuary trail map.
Special concerns:	A per-person admission fee or Massachusetts Audubon membership is required. No dogs or bikes. Find privies near the trailhead and wildlife observation building.
Season and hours:	Year-round; spring through fall for hiking; 7:00 A.M. to dusk, daily except Tuesday.
For information:	Massachusetts Audubon Society, Berkshire Sanctuaries.

Key points:
Sacred Way:
- 0.0   Sanctuary trailhead; head east.
- 0.1   Loop junction; go right.
- 0.6   Sackett Brook overlook.
- 1.1   Close loop; return to trailhead.

Wolf Pine Trail:
- 0.0   Sanctuary trailhead; head east–southeast on service road.
- 0.2   Wildlife observation building/loop junction; stay on service road.
- 0.7   View Sackett Brook at small dam; return to loop.
- 0.9   Wolf pine.
- 1.3   Close loop; backtrack right.

Finding the trailhead: From Interstate 90, take exit 2 for Lee. Then, from the town green in Lee, go 6.9 miles north on U.S. Highway 20 West, which merges with US 7 North. Turn right onto Holmes Road, go 2.5 miles, and turn right for Canoe Meadows.

The hikes: These relaxing strolls invite leisurely touring with binoculars and identification guidebooks in hand.

For **Sacred Way,** hike east on either the service road or the mowed track that enters a pocket of shrubs to the right of the kiosk and bear right to round West Pond, a small wildlife pond. Bramble and goldenrod claim its immediate bank, with a dense row of pine along the opposite shore.

Across the small concrete bridge, find the loop junction. Go right for a counterclockwise tour, paralleling the thickety shore of West Pond outlet downstream to the Housatonic River. An untamed field of tall grasses and milkweed sweeps away to the left. The wide mowed track offers easy walking.

At 0.25 mile, a cut-across path heads left; continue forward along the river amid a bottomland of dogwood, bramble, and woody shrubs. Oak, mixed maple, black cherry, elm, and cottonwood claim the skyline. River glimpses (best in fall) admire the 50-foot-wide smooth-flowing ribbon. Soon, the open pools and interlocking marsh of Oxbow Pond replace the flowing river. Look for duck, goose, northern waterthrush, alder flycatcher, muskrat, and beaver. Mature oaks and maples preside trailside, as does a grove of sinewy-trunked hornbeams.

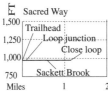

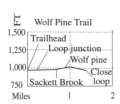

At 0.6 mile, overlook Sackett Brook before drifting away from the waterways, touring woodland. Beyond the trees to the right stretches the floodplain of Sackett Brook. At 0.8 mile, the cut-across arrives on the left; follow the boardwalk ahead through swamp woodland and floodplain forest. Alder, willow, and dogwood dominate. From the end of the boardwalk (1 mile), swing left along the shore of West Pond. Close the loop and return to the trailhead at 1.2 miles.

For the **Wolf Pine Trail,** hike the service road as it passes through a field, skirts West Pond, and trends

Canoe Meadows Sanctuary

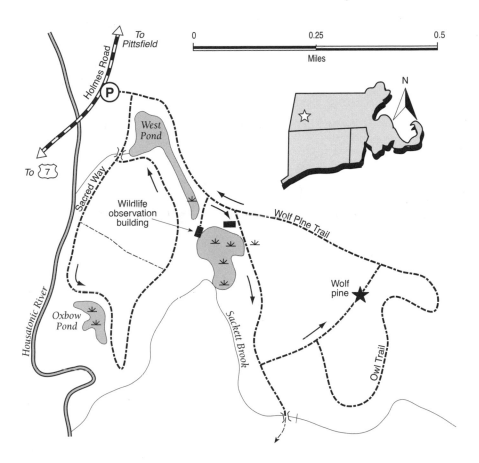

southeast along the watery link between West Pond and the wildlife observation pond. Maple, elm, and wild grape interweave the roadway's pine corridor. Stay southeast on the main service road, coming to a fork. To the right, find the wildlife observation building and a dugout canoe.

A boardwalk leads to the doorway of the enclosed wildlife viewing facility. Sliding Plexiglas windows on two sides present the area, keeping the elements out while allowing photographers a clean "shot" at their subject. Clumps of bog grass, drilled snags, and a long barn to the left contribute to views.

Resume southeast on the service road. Near the barn, find the first marked junction for the Wolf Pine Trail. Forgo taking it, staying on the service road for a counterclockwise tour. Pine stands, bog ponds coated in duckweed and rimmed by cattail, marshy woods, and hemlock vary viewing. Blue herons commonly draw attention.

At 0.6 mile, reach the second Wolf Pine Trail junction. A left continues the loop, although a brief detour southeast along the service road offers a look at Sackett Brook and its small dam washed by a 3-foot cascade. Signs

Wolf pine, Canoe Meadows Sanctuary, MA.

caution that PCBs pollute this stream; avoid contact with water, fish, frog, and turtle.

Resume the loop at 0.75 mile, traveling a scenic lane framed by hemlock, birch, beech, maple, oak, pine, and aspen. At 0.9 mile, the blazed Owl Trail heads right, offering an opportunity to lengthen the tour. It travels similar woods with a few smaller examples of this hike's signature "wolf pine"; continue forward to admire the featured pine.

In 100 yards near post 6, a crescent-shaped spur veers right for an audience with the starring wolf pine—a huge candelabra-shaped multitrunked pine within an entourage of maple. It requires no introduction. Upon resuming the loop, find the other end of the Owl Trail (on the right), offering a second chance to view its woods. Bear left, descending to the main service road (1.3 miles). Turn right to return to the parking area at 1.5 miles.

11 Monument Mountain Reservation

OVERVIEW

At this 500-acre mountain preserve owned by the Trustees of Reservations, visit a peak that not only inspired Nathaniel Hawthorne, Herman Melville, and William Cullen Bryant, but is also rich in Indian lore. A stone cairn marks the eastern precipice, the legendary site where a love-forsaken Indian maiden hurled herself from the cliff. From the cairn comes the name *Monument Mountain;* from the maiden, the name *Squaw Peak.*

General description:	A circuitous tour uniting the Hickey and Indian Monument Trails passes through mixed forest and tops Squaw Peak via a side-trip spur for stirring looks at the site's sheer quartzite cliffs and southern Berkshire neighborhood.
General location:	4 miles north of Great Barrington or 3 miles south of Stockbridge, Massachusetts.
Special attractions:	Vistas, white cliffs, historic literary landmark, Inscription Rock, seasonal waterfall, mountain laurel, fall foliage.
Length:	3.1 miles round trip, adding the Devils Pulpit spur. The hike may be shortened by following the Squaw Peak Trail, which bisects the loop.
Elevation:	Travel from a trailhead elevation of 900 feet to a summit elevation of 1,640 feet.
Difficulty:	Moderate, with a difficult summit stretch.
Maps:	Reservation map.
Special concerns:	Donation appreciated. Obey posted rules, and stay on trails to protect endangered species. No mountain bikes, and no climbing.
Season and hours:	Spring through fall, dawn to dusk.
For information:	The Trustees of Reservations, Western Regional Office.

Key points:

  0.0   Trailhead; hike north on Hickey Trail.
  0.7   Junction; detour on Squaw Peak Trail.
  1.0   Squaw Peak summit vantage.
  1.2   Devils Pulpit vantage; backtrack to 0.7-mile junction.
  1.8   0.7-mile junction; descend Indian Monument Trail.
  3.1   End at trailhead.

Finding the trailhead: From the junction of U.S. Highway 7 and Massachusetts Highway 41 in Great Barrington, go north on US 7 for 3.5 miles. Find a half-moon dirt parking lot, picnic tables, and a trailhead on the left. Look for the green Trustees sign.

The hike: From the kiosk, hike north following the white-blazed footpath of the Hickey Trail as it disappears into the red pine–deciduous woods at the foot of the slope; the return is via the Indian Monument Trail. The needle-strewn footpath broadens into a pleasant hiking lane, touring a varied woods of white pine, oak, striped maple, beech, birch, viburnum, sarsaparilla, and fern. Small boardwalks span the seasonally muddy segments before the more serious climb begins.

Despite the fairly steep incline, diagonal

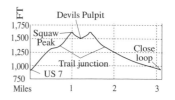

Monument Mountain Reservation

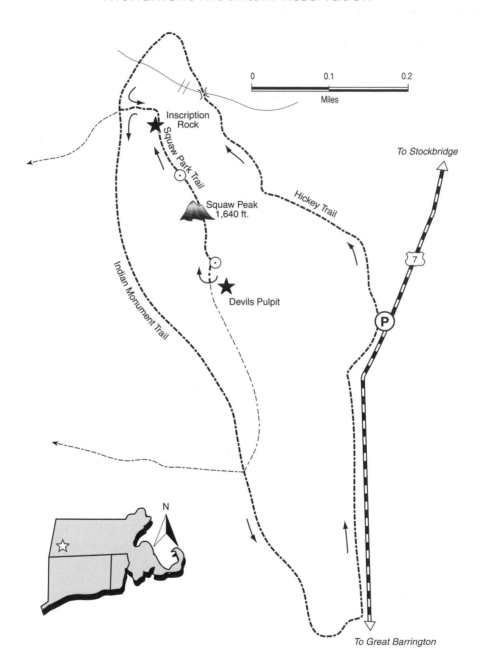

0   0.1   0.2

Miles

Inscription Rock

Squaw Park Trail

To Stockbridge

Hickey Trail

Squaw Peak
1,640 ft.

7

Indian Monument Trail

Devils Pulpit

P

N

To Great Barrington

drainages maintain the integrity of the trail. Pockets of big hemlocks and 3-foot-tall mountain laurel decorate the hillside. Round a bouldery slope and follow a steep drainage channel upstream, hiking past an abandoned side trail on the left. Cross a footbridge over the drainage and ascend the opposite bank.

A seasonal 12-foot waterfall marks the drainage, pretty when flowing; at other times, the cliff overhang and a 5-foot-deep hollow intrigue travelers. Round to the top of the falls, again crossing the drainage to follow the path curving east to the rocky summit crest. At 0.7 mile, the loop arcs right, following the Indian Monument Trail off the mountain.

For this hike, though, postpone taking the loop to visit the summit and overlook the eastern precipice. Proceed forward on the Squaw Peak Trail, finding Inscription Rock soon after the junction. Beautifully etched and brushed with fine sand, the inscription relates how Rosalie Butler gifted the mountain to the people in 1899, through the agency of the Trustees. Maple, birch, oak, chestnut, laurel, and witch hazel interweave the natural outcrops.

Ahead, the trail grows steep and eroded. Early views pan east-northeast, overlooking Monument Mountain Regional High School, a marsh, and valley farmland. Pitch pine, huckleberry, and small oak continue to intersperse the rocks. The rough quartzite supports lichen, while the smooth breaks, slick like soapstone, steal footing. Exercise care when scrambling south over the rocks, gathering views.

At 1 mile, come to a spectacular summit view overlooking the stunning eastern cliffs. The skyline pines and enfolding wooded terrain amplify the

Squaw Peak, Monument Mountain Reservation, MA.

whiteness and precipitous drop of the cliffs. Vultures and ravens ride thermals; peregrines once nested on the site's remote crags. Stretching south, the Housatonic River Valley completes the view.

For hikers wanting to extend the vista offering, pursue the trail as it continues south, descending and bearing right, coming to a signed junction in 0.2 mile. A left leads to the SCENIC VIEW; the Squaw Peak Trail continues its descent for an alternative loop return.

Head left, reaching the superb view of the dramatic broken pinnacle of Devils Pulpit with its complement of vultures, and gain new perspectives on the area. Afterward, backtrack to the Squaw Peak Trail, retracing your steps north past Inscription Rock to the 0.7-mile junction at 1.8 miles. Follow the Indian Monument Trail, turning left to complete the chosen loop.

The Indian Monument Trail follows a sharply pitching wide woods lane off the mountaintop. Bear left at the upcoming junction, continuing the descent. Hardwoods shade the trek, joined by a few hemlocks and pines. Before long, the grade eases into a relaxing stroll.

At the 2.2-mile trail fork, take either path, because they soon merge again; to the right, the trail follows an old ditch. In a hemlock grove at 2.5 miles, come to a four-way junction. The unmarked trail to the right is the Taggart Trail, back to the left is the Squaw Peak Trail, and ahead lies the return. The hike skirts a low rock wall, eventually paralleling US 7 northward, weaving among the quartzite boulders of the lower slope. Although US 7 proves a loud neighbor, the woods remain scenic. End the hike at 3.1 miles.

12   Beartown State Forest

OVERVIEW

Snuggled in the southern Berkshires, Beartown represents the third largest Massachusetts state forest, encompassing more than 10,500 acres. The site features rolling hills, mixed woods, a scenic pond, beaver-flooded bottomlands, and miles of foot, bridle, and all-terrain-vehicle trails. The Appalachian Trail slices south to north through the forest, passing two lean-tos during its Beartown sojourn.

> **General description:** A comfortable pond loop and challenging, often tricky-to-follow bridle trail loop explore the scenic woodland of this state forest. A self-guided walking brochure is available for the trail around Benedict Pond.
> **General location:** 8 miles east of Great Barrington, Massachusetts.
> **Special attractions:** Benedict Pond, beaver ponds and swamps, rich deciduous forest, limited vistas, flowering shrubs and wildflowers, wildlife discovery, fall foliage.

Length:	Benedict Pond Loop, 3.2-mile loop, including Appalachian Trail spur; Bridle Trail, 11.5 miles round trip.
Elevation:	Benedict Pond Loop, 300-foot elevation change; Bridle Trail, 500-foot elevation change.
Difficulty:	Benedict Pond Loop, easy; the Bridle Trail is moderate.
Maps:	State forest map.
Special concerns:	Day-use fee.
Season and hours:	Spring through fall for hiking; day use, 8:00 A.M. to sunset.
For information:	Beartown State Forest.

Key points:

Benedict Pond Loop:

  0.0 Start at pond bathhouse; head right along shore.

  1.2 Vista outcrop on AT; return to pond loop.

  3.2 Complete loop at pond bathhouse.

Bridle Trail:

  0.0 Start at Benedict Pond bathhouse; head left.

  0.5 Loop junction; head left.

  5.4 Beartown Road.

  7.3 First crossing of Wilcox Road.

  9.9 Second crossing of Wilcox Road.

  11.0 Complete loop; backtrack left.

Finding the trailhead: From the Massachusetts Highway 23–U.S. Highway 7 junction in Great Barrington, go east on MA 23 for 5.1 miles and turn north onto Blue Hill Road. Follow it 2.1 miles, and turn right onto Benedict Pond Road. Reach the day-use parking/trailhead at the pond in 0.5 mile.

  The hikes: Start the **Benedict Pond Loop** at the bathhouse/rest room. Head right (counterclockwise) around the ladle-shaped pond, first touring its lightly developed shore. Because several impostor paths thread this area, keep toward the pond; the true path reveals itself at the boat launch. Hemlock, maple,

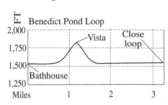

oak, mountain laurel, azalea, and highbush blueberry dress the shore. A vulture may soar through the dip in the opposite ridge, while a raven speaks in hysterics. Some roots and rocks erupt in the path. Outcrops invite anglers and dreamers aside.

  At 0.5 mile, the Appalachian Trail (AT) merges on the right, just as the pond trail crosses a boggy inlet via planks and hewn logs. A small rocky point next engages with a length-of-the-pond vista. Striped minnows and bluegills can be spied in the clearwater. After crossing the main inlet bridge (0.7 mile), the AT departs to the right; the loop continues forward.

  Briefly follow the AT to see a beaver swamp and take in a southern view. With a moderate climb, passing among big birch, outcrops, and mountain

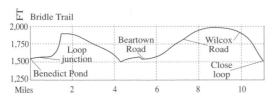

laurel, top a ridge (1 mile); after a few steps forward, find the beaver dam, pond, and swamp. Cross the footbridge to the right and negotiate some stepping-stones through a sulfurous reddish brown ooze to obtain the vantage in another 0.2 mile. This tiered outcrop looks out at Livermore Peak and Mounts Everett and Darby, as well as a reclaimed beaver pond.

Return to Benedict Pond (1.7 miles) and turn right, traveling an old woods road above shore. Wild geraniums spangle the woods floor. At 2 miles, descend left on footpath, passing below a canted outcrop and hemlocks. At the wide end of the pond, drift away from shore, touring corduroys through soggy reaches. Next, round a beaver extension, returning to the pond. Cross a footbridge, turn uphill, and pass the Ski and Bridle Trail on the right to cross the campground road. Soon afterward, cross the pond outlet to end the hike at 3.2 miles.

For the **Bridle Trail,** hikers should have a sense of adventure, possess good map and trail skills, and be willing to do some sleuthing; otherwise the hike will only frustrate. The forest supervisor has slated this trail for clearing and marking, which should ease travel.

Start by hiking clockwise on the pond loop, touring along the outlet and crossing over the campground road to take the Ski and Bridle Trail left at 0.3 mile. At the loop junction at 0.5 mile, again bear left for a clockwise tour. Red efts may animate the trail; a few orange markers point the way; and an explosion of green characterizes the multistory forest. At 1 mile, angle left on a paved road to pick up the bridle trail on the opposite side.

An overgrown two-track that can weight boots with mud next leads the

Benedict Pond, Beartown State Forest, MA.

Beartown State Forest

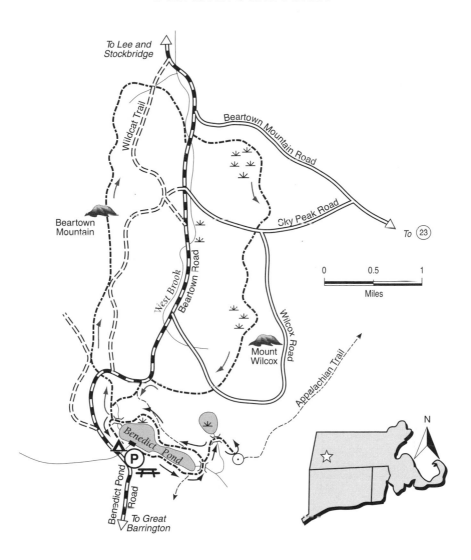

way. Reach a dirt jeep road and follow it right. Then at 1.2 miles, hike the overgrown foot trail uphill to the right; a left leads back to Benedict Pond. Generally, you can discern the underlying trail beneath the mesh of vegetation; waist-high ferns at times claim the ascending trail.

At 1.6 miles, reach the Wildcat Snowmobile Trail, turn left on it, and quickly turn left again to reenter woods. By 2 miles, travel a low wooded bench above a drainage, again finding laurel and hemlock. Woodpeckers, songbirds, and deer may add to the trek. Lady's slipper and azalea decorate the woods. A couple of drainage crossings mark off distance.

At 4.5 miles, turn right onto the Wildcat Snowmobile Trail, cross its bridge, and turn left following a grassy lane framed by big maples. Where the trail passes through a white pine grove, enjoy a cushiony needle-mat trailbed. At 5.4 miles, go left on a dirt road, reaching Beartown/Benedict Pond Road. Turn left onto this lightly trafficked road, cross its bridge, and resume the overgrown bridle trail on the right. A few more faint markers aid travelers.

At 5.8 miles, reach a beaver-influenced area and its associated reroute through forest that climbs from a boggy drainage to return to the original trail at 6.1 miles. Stay left to resume the loop. Not long after the route changes to a time-healed woods road, look for the path of the bridle trail to bear right. The path then curves left, crosses a drainage, and charges straight up a rocky slope; midway up, the path becomes more apparent. Continue contouring and climbing right.

At 7.3 miles, cross gravel Wilcox Road. After a couple of drainage crossings, the bridle trail ascends to contour the slope above the road. While somewhat overgrown, the trail is better worn. At 8.4 miles, descend amid a lush bed of ferns before finding another beaver-marsh passage/bypass. Bear left through woods, cross a drainage, and turn right to view the beaver dam and lodge. Now follow the original trail left through stands of pine and spruce.

Cross Wilcox Road a second time (9.9 miles) for a straightforward woods descent to Beartown/Benedict Pond Road at 10.3 miles. Turn left toward Benedict Pond, hike downhill 0.2 mile, and bear left onto a gated, overgrown road. In 100 feet, the bridle trail resumes on the right. Although now well defined, it still shows soggy reaches. Close the loop at 11 miles, and retrace the first 0.5 mile, returning to the bathhouse area at Benedict Pond (11.5 miles).

13   Alander Mountain Loop

General description:	In Mount Washington State Forest, this demanding all-day or overnight loop with side spurs travels the South Taconics, passing between Massachusetts and New York, gathering grand views.
General location:	The southwest corner of Massachusetts on the tristate border of Massachusetts, Connecticut, and New York.
Special attractions:	A springtime showcase for mountain laurel and azalea; fountains of fern; multistate views; fall foliage; sightings of beaver, frog, red eft, and wild turkey.
Length:	15 miles round trip (12.8-mile loop, plus 2.2 miles of round-trip side spurs).
Elevation:	Find an elevation change of 1,000 feet, with the low point at Lee Pond Brook and the high at Mount Frissell (elevation 2,453 feet).

Difficulty: Strenuous.

Maps: Mount Washington State Forest trail map (generally available at trailhead information board); New York–New Jersey Trail Conference map, South Taconic Trail.

Special concerns: Permit and fee required for overnight camping in the backcountry campsites of Mount Washington State Forest; preregister at headquarters (located at the trailhead).

Season and hours: Year-round; parts of the tour double as winter cross-country ski routes.

For information: Mount Washington State Forest.

Key points:

0.0   Headquarters trailhead; follow Alander Mountain Trail.
0.8   Loop junction; turn left onto Ashley Hill Trail.
5.2   Top Mount Frissell; return to loop.
6.2   South Taconic Trail; detour south.
6.6   Brace Mountain; return north.
11.4   Alander saddle, cabin, and junction.
11.6   Alander Mountain summit; backtrack to loop.
14.2   Close loop; backtrack to trailhead.

Finding the trailhead: From the junction of Massachusetts Highways 23 and 41 in South Egremont, take MA 41 south for 0.1 mile and turn right onto East Street. At its junction with Jug End Road in 1.7 miles, a sign indicates that drivers should stay on East Street for Mount Washington State Forest. In another 6.8 miles (having passed the turns for Mount Everett State Reservation and Bash Bish Falls), turn right for the headquarters and trail.

The hike: From the information board, follow the sign for the Alander Mountain Trail, passing through field and conifer–hardwood forest for the first 0.5 mile. After the footbridge crossing of Lee Pond Brook, pass the Charcoal Pit Trail to reach the loop junction at 0.8 mile. For a clockwise tour, follow the Ashley Hill Trail left, closing the loop via the Alander Mountain Trail (straight ahead). Either trail has access to the numbered backcountry campsites.

The woods road shows a modest ascent, contouring the slope above rushing Ashley Hill Brook; blue triangles and paint blazes point the way. Hemlock, maple, birch, and beech throw a pleasing shade. At 1.5 miles, a side trail descends right, reaching the campsites and Alander Mountain Trail; stay left for the loop.

Black oaks join the mix as a fern sea holds the eyes transfixed. After the overgrown Charcoal Pit Trail arrives on the left, find a precarious crossing of a side drainage. By 2.4 miles, enjoy an almost imperceptible incline, paralleling upstream along

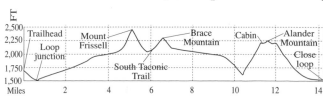

65

Ashley Hill Brook. Half a dozen beaver dams punctuate the 10-foot-wide brook.

A stone-hopping crossing offers an alternative to the decrepit footbridge at 3 miles. At the upcoming junction, stay left on the Ashley Hill Trail as it becomes more trail-like, climbing in pulses. At a clear-spilling headwater (3.5 miles), fill water bottles for the dry tour ahead; purify natural sources.

Tall, full mountain laurels wrap the trail in bloom mid-June through early July. Azaleas add their signature bloom a few weeks earlier. Past a Massachusetts–New York state line marker, reach a red-blazed trail junction (4.5 miles). Turn left for the Mount Frissell Trail and Tri-State Point; turn right to reach the South Taconic Trail and continue the loop.

A detour left follows foot trail through a low-stature woods, ascending over bedrock. Past another Massachusetts–New York state line marker, dated 1898, the climb steepens. Over-the-shoulder glimpses find Brace Mountain and Riga Lake. At 5 miles, a simple cairn marks Tri-State Point, the highest point in Connecticut.

Soon after, views expand, sweeping from South Brace Mountain in New York to Mount Plantain in Massachusetts, with Connecticut's Round, Gridley, and Bear Mountains. The top of Mount Frissell lies 0.2 mile farther, but the rimming 15-foot-high oaks steal any views.

Back at the 4.5-mile junction (5.9 miles), ascend the rock-studded red-blazed trail to a ridge junction with the white-blazed South Taconic Trail at 6.2 miles. From the intersection, a detour south adds an 0.8-mile round-trip visit to the summit of Brace Mountain; the loop follows the white blazes north.

For the Brace Mountain detour, follow the woods road south, bearing right at the fork. An open, shrubby complex enfolds the moderate-grade trail. At 6.6 miles, a spur left tops Brace Mountain (2,311 feet), where a 5-foot cairn puts an exclamation mark on the tour. Views sweep the tristate area.

Back on the loop at 7 miles, hike north along the rolling open ridge, traversing lichen-etched outcrops and overlooking rural New York toward Fox Hill. In 0.2 mile, a woods road, decorated with azalea and lady's slipper, continues the tour.

Past a blue trail, the South Taconic Trail briefly veers left from the woods road, passing among low shrubs and traversing outcrops for limited western views. The laurel again explodes. Elsewhere, rock walls or waist-high ferns decorate the going.

After the woods road bottoms out at a rocky drainage, the white-blazed South Taconic Trail turns right onto a steeply charging foot trail. Mixed deciduous trees dress the slope. Views build, climaxing in a 270-degree view encompassing Mount Frissell as well as Alander, Brace, and Round Mountains.

Atop Alander Ridge, go past the concrete platform of a former lookout tower, keeping an eye out for the faint blue paint blaze on an open rock at 11.3 miles. This signals where the loop leaves the South Taconic Trail to again follow the Alander Mountain Trail.

Descend right, following the blue blazes to a saddle (0.1 mile) where a quaint, tight-roofed cabin offers a dry overnight wayside on a first-come, first-served basis. Early-summer azalea and mountain laurel fancy it up. The loop

Alander Mountain Loop

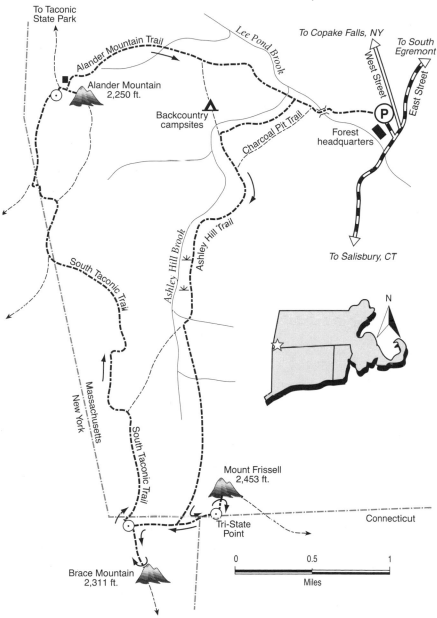

descends past the cabin, but to add another summit conquest, follow the blue trail ascending east. It tops Alander Mountain (2,250 feet) in 0.2 mile for an open view from New York's Brace Mountain to Massachusetts's Mount Darby.

From the summit, backtrack to the saddle (11.8 miles) and descend through Mount Washington State Forest on the Alander Mountain Trail. Some-

Fern meadow, Mount Washington State Forest, MA.

times rocky, sometimes muddy, the trail parallels a small drainage, crossing feeder streams. Glorious waist-high fern attract the eye, while oak, maple, birch, and beech weave a rustling canopy. Despite the few and faint markers, the trail remains well trampled.

At 12.5 miles, bear right. Before long, darker blazes, a milder gradient, and a defined woods road all ease travel. At the 13.3-mile junction, continue straight ahead to close the loop; to the right are the campsites.

The loop now contours and mildly descends, reaching a rock-hopping crossing of Ashley Hill Brook just upstream from its confluence with Lee Pond Brook. Ascend from the crossing (14.1 miles) to return to the loop junction at 14.2 miles. Retrace the first 0.8 mile to your vehicle.

14   Bartholomew's Cobble

OVERVIEW

Cobble knolls of limestone and marble formed 500 million years ago, one of the greatest concentrations of fern diversity in North America, diverse conifer–deciduous forests, grassland, pasture, and the sidewinding Housatonic River make this Berkshire reservation an exciting place to visit. Such natural attributes also won the Cobble (a property of the Trustees of Reservations) recognition from the National Park Service as a national natural landmark.

Spring and summer wildflowers and the fall hawk migration prove seasonal draws. The site's Bailey Natural History Museum displays letters of praise from distinguished naturalists, while the reservation's Colonel Ashley House, built 1735, holds the honor of being the oldest dwelling in Berkshire County. Weatogue Road partitions the 277-acre reservation into east and west halves.

General description: Three hikes present this outstanding property. Explore cobble, river, meadow, and woods.

General location: 10 miles south of Great Barrington, Massachusetts.

Special attractions: Cobble outcrops; bird- and wildlife-watching; nature study; flowering trees, shrubs, and annuals; fall foliage; museums.

Length: Eaton Trail, 0.2-mile loop; Ledges–River Hike, 2 miles round trip; Hurlburt's Hill Hike, 2 miles round trip.

Elevation: Eaton Trail, 50-foot elevation change; Ledges–River Hike, less than a 100-foot elevation change; Hurlburt's Hill Hike, 400-foot elevation change.

Difficulty: All easy to moderate.

Maps: Reservation map; The Ledges Trail brochure.

Special concerns: Admission fee, with a separate admission charged at the Colonel Ashley House. Find signs at the key junctions and white blazes through the wooded stretches, but carry a map to sort out trails.

Season and hours: Reservation, mid-April through mid-October, 9:00 A.M. to 5:00 P.M.; Bailey Natural History Museum, 9:00 A.M. to 5:00 P.M. Wednesday through Sunday. Colonel Ashley House, summer 1:00 P.M. to 5:00 P.M. Wednesday through Sunday and holidays.

For information: The Trustees of Reservations, Western Regional Office.

Key points:
Eaton Trail:
0.0   Trailhead kiosk; bear left, topping northern cobble.

0.1   Bailey Museum.
0.2   End at trailhead.

Ledges–River Hike:
0.0   Trailhead kiosk; hike east to The Ledges Trail.
0.7   Colossal cottonwood/Spero loop junction; head left.
1.8   Complete Spero loop; return to The Ledges Trail.
2.0   End at trailhead.

Hurlburt's Hill Hike:
0.0   Trailhead kiosk; hike right to cross Weatogue Road.
0.7   Hurlburt's Hill.
0.9   Tulip Tree Trail; head east.
2.0   End at trailhead.

Finding the trailhead: From the center of Sheffield, Massachusetts, go south on U.S. Highway 7 for 1.5 miles, then continue south on US 7A for another 0.5 mile. Turn right onto Rannapo Road. At its junction with Cooper Hill Road in 1 mile, a right leads to the Colonel Ashley House in 0.2 mile. To access the trails, continue straight, taking a quick right onto dirt Weatogue Road. Find parking on the left in 0.1 mile; signs aid travelers in finding the reservation.

The hikes: Start all hikes from the Cobble Parking Lot, east off Weatogue Road. Find the trailhead kiosk and fee station to the left of the Natural History Center.

For the sun-drenched **Eaton Trail,** bear left (north), ascending a dirt trail framed by cedar and goldenrod to encircle and top the northern cobble. A lofty wooden bench overlooks a horseshoe bend on the Housatonic River and the grassy peninsula of Corbin's Neck. The folded, pitted, and ledged outcrop supports fern niches and caps, lichen and moss, and alkaline-loving plants and wildflowers.

Where the trail descends, pass Bailey Museum, a rustic wooden building ringed by sweet pepperbush, wild grape, and mountain laurel, and bear right to return to the trailhead. Rest rooms can be found below the museum.

To the left of the kiosk, follow the hiker path heading east (straight) for the **Ledges–River Hike.** Pass the spur to Bailey Museum, quickly reaching a three-way junction; go left for The Ledges Trail (a 0.5-mile interpretive loop). The prongs for Craggy Knoll and Cedar Hill Trails welcome alternative looks at the limestone–marble outcrop.

The Ledges Trail rounds a scenic cobble knoll, passing amid hemlocks and overlooking the Housatonic River. Admire the weathered and polished

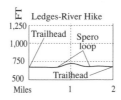

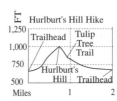

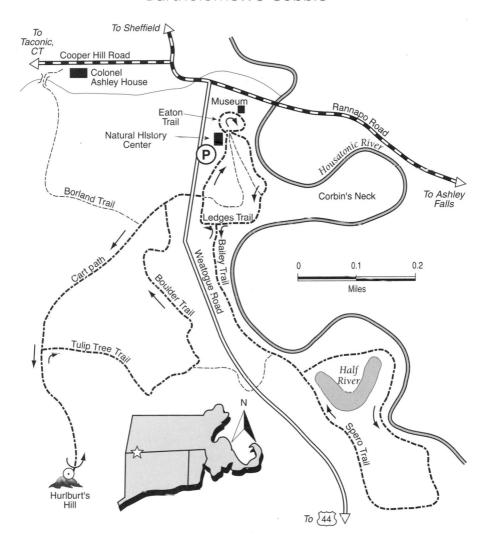

rock, worn niches, hollows, overhangs, and cavities. Even the untrained eye can detect an uncommon variety of ferns (best seen in June and July). At times, crickets enliven the air.

The trail rolls between the outcrop's waistline and the river level. Where it dips, expect rough footing. Oak, basswood, hop hornbeam, maple, and ash contribute to a varied canopy; the silk nests of the webworm ensnare a few leafy branches. Keep to The Ledges Trail.

At 0.2 mile, walk past the open pasture of Corbin's Neck and ascend the reinforced steps. Ahead, a wide travel lane replaces the footpath, and red cedars find suitable habitat in the more exposed rock. At 0.3 mile, depart

Tulip tree, Bartholomew's Cobble Reservation, MA.

The Ledges Trail, bearing left to follow the Bailey and Spero Trails for a rolling tour south along the Housatonic River.

Here, enjoy a rare opportunity to explore the grassland and riparian woodland of the river floodplain—habitats often privately held and closed to the hiking public. Although river views are few and filtered, chance bird and wildlife sightings exist. The diversity of the riparian environment includes elm, ash, willow, box elder, cottonwood, and silver maple, along with the richness of thick grass meadows interlaced with nettle, jewelweed, milkweed, joe-pye weed, and goldenrod.

At 0.7 mile, beside a colossal cottonwood measuring 6 feet in diameter, the Spero Trail swings a generous lasso around Half River, a shallow oxbow pond. Clockwise, travel floodplain, a deciduous rise with jumbles of gneiss, and a dark hemlock woods. The loop concludes by traveling a boardwalk, skirting a north-shore wetland of Half River.

Retrace the Spero and Bailey Trails to rejoin The Ledges tour at 1.8 miles; turn left. Round the cobble knoll, viewing overhangs, a glacial erratic atop the rim, and quartzite seams. At 1.9 miles, pass the hiker stile leading to Weatogue Road and the western half of the reservation. Continue along the knoll, finding the last interpretive post below a cavelike opening, and end the hike (2 miles).

For **Hurlburt's Hill Hike,** follow the trail heading south (right) from the kiosk, retracing the end of The Ledges Trail. Pass behind the Natural History Center and parking area and turn right. Exit a hiker stile and cross Weatogue Road to enter the western portion of the reservation.

Bear right, following a mowed cart path across the small field, passing under an elm to ascend amid woodland. At the 0.3-mile junction, the Borland Trail heads right to Colonel Ashley House; keep to the cart path for Hurlburt's Hill.

Pass through field and mixed woods of maple, hickory, ash, birch, black cherry, witch hazel, aspen, and hop hornbeam. Squirrels leap through the rustling canopy. At 0.5 mile, the Tulip Tree Trail heads left for a loop; remain on the cart path, ascending the high pasture for a hilltop vantage.

At 0.7 mile, reach the reservation high point on Hurlburt's Hill (elevation 1,050 feet) and a north-facing bench for a grand 180-degree view of the Berkshire–Housatonic neighborhood. Mid-September into October, the fall hawk migration draws enthusiasts for a sky-watch. The site also applauds the autumn fanfare.

Now backtrack, descending the pasture slope, to hike east on the Tulip Tree Trail. Pass mainly through leafy woods with small field breaks; a tree identification book earns its way. Beyond the hiker stile, hemlocks dominate. At 1.2 miles, pass beneath a 3-foot-diameter tulip tree, one of a few lending the trail its name. Deer sometimes startle, darting to safety.

A big boulder marks the junction where the loop turns left onto the Boulder Trail. More boulders punctuate the hemlock woods. Mixed fern, doll's-eye baneberry, and hog peanut spot the forest floor. Pass beneath another tulip tree and through a hiker stile, touring amid mixed deciduous woods to emerge at the small field along Weatogue Road. Turn right for the hiker stile, cross the road, and bear left to return to the trailhead at 2 miles.

Central Massachusetts Trails

This region boasts ancient mountain features, including monadnocks (erosion-resistant isolated peaks) and the northern traprock ridges (the elongated cliff-sided mountains rising from the Connecticut River Valley). In many ways, the abrupt ridges and lone-standing peaks afford some of the state's finest panoramas. In spring and especially in fall, watch for the hawk migration, with impressive groupings or "kettles" of broadwings. Bald eagles find habitat at Quabbin Reservoir. Mountain woodland, meadow, swamp, pond, and an intriguing rock chasm further characterize the region. In this central Massachusetts landscape, find historic industrial river towns and the rural charm of silos and church steeples.

15 Northfield Mountain Recreation Area

OVERVIEW

At this 1,500-acre playground, 25 miles of interlocking foot and carriage-width trails offer a variety of hiking and cross-country ski tours. Power lines and a reservoir overlook hint at the site's host, Northeast Utilities; the generating facility sits 700 feet underground. May through October, a bus tour runs to the summit, offering hikers the option of downhill travel only.

General description:	Two loops travel the west flank of Northfield Mountain, topping the peak and exploring its ledges. The web of trails offers numerous other hike options.
General location:	2 miles north of Millers Falls, Massachusetts.
Special attractions:	Conifer–deciduous forest, granite–gneiss ledges, mountain and sheep laurel, vistas, fall foliage.
Length:	Summit Loop, 5.8 miles round trip; Rose Ledge Loop, 3.1 miles round trip.
Elevation:	The Summit Loop shows an 800-foot elevation change; it advances via long, steep ups and downs, topping Northfield Mountain at 1,100 feet. Rose Ledge Loop shows about a 400-foot elevation change, with some sharp pitches.
Difficulty:	Summit Loop, strenuous; the Rose Ledge Loop is moderate.
Maps:	Northfield Mountain trail map (available on site).
Special concerns:	Colored diamond markers, trail signs, and numbered intersections help hikers negotiate the web of

avenues; carry a map to sort out options. For hikers interested in taking the bus to the summit, phone in advance to confirm that it is running. Because hunting is allowed on the mountain, keep to the trails within the no-hunting zone (check map) during the hunting season (times are posted in the Massachusetts Fish and Wildlife Abstracts).

Season and hours: Year-round, spring through fall for hiking. Visitor center, 9:00 A.M. to 5:00 P.M. Wednesday through Sunday, during the spring, summer, and much of the fall.

For information: Northeast Utilities, Northfield Mountain Recreation and Environmental Center.

Key points:

Summit Loop:

    0.0   Visitor center trailhead; follow 10th Mountain Trail.
    0.6   Chocolate Pot warming hut/loop junction.
    3.6   Summit/reservoir overlook.
    5.2   Close loop near Chocolate Pot; backtrack downhill to trailhead.

Rose Ledge Loop:

    0.0   Visitor center trailhead; hike to Rose Ledge.
    0.6   Loop junction; continue straight.
    0.9   Top first ledge.
    1.5   Base of cliffs.
    2.5   Close loop; retrace first 0.6 mile to trailhead.

Finding the trailhead: From the junction of Massachusetts Highways 2 and 63 in the village of Millers Falls, go north on MA 63 for 1.9 miles and turn right (east) for Northfield Mountain Recreation and Environmental Center. Start trails at the mapboard behind the visitor center.

The hikes: A 1-mile, fifteen-station **nature trail** marked by blue diamonds and interpretive plaques travels the foot of the mountain behind the visitor center. Because the two selected hikes each overlaps the nature trail, hikers also explore it.

The **Summit Loop** pursues several of the named carriage-width trails through the recreation area's core to claim the Northfield Mountain summit. Start by following the 10th Mountain Trail south (right) along the foot of the mountain, pass a wildlife pond, and continue on the 10th Mountain Trail as it curves left upslope. The trail's broad swath parts a mature pine plantation with dispersed birch and maple.

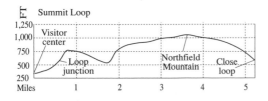

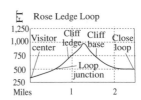

Northfield Mountain Recreation Area

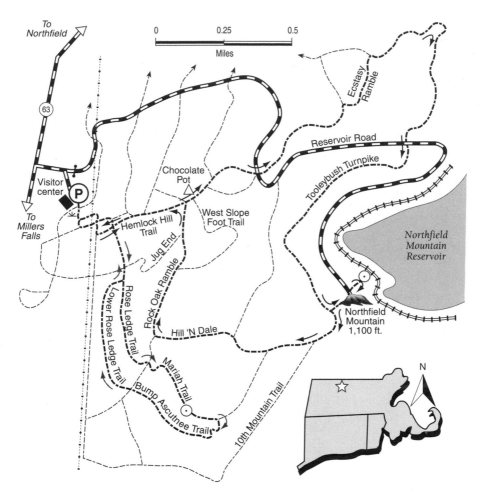

Curve past the switching station, cross the Rose Ledge Trail, and, at 0.25 mile, turn left onto the Hemlock Hill Trail, briefly passing under utility lines. Sumac, wildflowers, and bramble crowd the corridor. In hemlock–deciduous woods, again cross the Rose Ledge Trail for a moderate ascent.

Keep to the Hemlock Hill Trail. Platy outcrops and fractured boulders, fern, sarsaparilla, and club moss accent the forest floor. At junction 8 (0.6 mile), continue forward for a clockwise loop, soon finding a picnic site and the Chocolate Pot (a warming hut open during ski season). Rock Oak Ramble on the right marks the return. At 0.85 mile, a spur to the left leads to a chemical toilet.

The ascent adds oaks and chestnuts to the mix. The Hemlock Hill Trail then tops out and dips to cross Reservoir Road at a crosswalk. A hemlock-framed descent follows. At the 1.5-mile fork, turn right onto Ecstasy Ramble, continuing the descent to Tooleybush Turnpike at 1.7 miles.

Again turn right, finding a steep incline, including a tight bend dubbed the Chute by cross-country skiers. With the climb, transition back to woods of birch, beech, oak, and aspen; overhanging branches afford partial shade.

At 2.5 miles, again cross Reservoir Road; sweet fern and mountain laurel decorate the trail's shoulders as more maple appear in the mix. Find junction 32 at 3.4 miles. Turn left for the summit and reservoir overlook, reaching the spur to the viewing platform on the opposite side of the paved summit turnaround. Views feature sterile Northfield Mountain Reservoir, its dam and intake, and sentinel mountains Hermit and Crag. To the north rise Haystack and Stratton Mountains and Mount Snow.

Resume the loop at 3.8 miles, turning left at junction 32, once again on the 10th Mountain Trail. Sheep laurel abounds here and along the summit spur. At 4 miles, follow Hill 'N Dale, a grassy lane snaking downhill to the right, for a scenic stroll; keep to this trail for the loop. At 4.3 miles, it bears right for a roller-coaster descent.

Reach junction 16 at 4.7 miles, turn right, and follow Rock Oak Ramble for a meandering downhill hike in mixed woods. The descent sharpens past the West Slope Foot Trail. Hike past Jug End, bearing right to close the loop just beyond the Chocolate Pot (5.2 miles). Retrace the Hemlock Hill and 10th Mountain Trails, returning to the visitor center at 5.8 miles.

For the **Rose Ledge Loop** (a foot trail), again follow the 10th Mountain Trail south along the base of the mountain, but continue straight where it curves left up the hill. Find the marked turn for Rose Ledge on the left and ascend through a dark pine woods, with birch, maple, and oak. Roots riddle the bed; in places, the path becomes ill defined.

At 0.25 mile, cross the 10th Mountain Trail to travel an attractive woods, avoiding the open utility corridor. Before long, the ledge trail turns right; the nature trail continues straight.

Cross the Hemlock Hill and Jug End Trails for a rolling trek, contouring the slope. Mountain laurel, chestnut, and witch hazel contribute to the midstory. Reinforced steps and footbridges ease travel. At 0.6 mile, reach the loop junction; continue straight for a clockwise tour, still ascending. Dogwoods make a rare appearance in the low-stature woods. Top the first outcrop ledge at 0.9 mile. Trees at the foot of the slope steal or filter views; keep back from the edge. Rock tripe lichen adorns the rock, and mountain laurel crowns the ledge, making an early-summer visit worthwhile.

At 0.95 mile, hikers may shorten the loop, descending to the right. For the full 3.1-mile tour, follow the Rose Ledge/Mariah Trail for a steady, moderate ascent; spurs regularly top the ledge. Most views applaud the immediate area rims, cliffs, and forest; at 1.25 miles, claim a southwestern perspective spanning the Connecticut River Valley to the Berkshires.

At junction 33 (1.4 miles), the Bump Ascutnee Trail sharply descends to the right; follow it for the loop. This portion of the hike offers both side views and a neck-craning appreciation of the 50- to 80-foot vertical cliffs. Admire their subtle streaking and picturesque fracturing. At 1.5 miles, a ledge composed of tilted slabs precedes the base of a cliff favored by rock climbers. Descend and round to the right.

Rose Ledges, Northfield Mountain Recreation Area, MA.

At 1.8 miles, a 100-foot spur to the right presents a bold look at the main cliff, a feature of stark beauty. Broken rock at its base hints at how the cliff has changed over time. Cliffs continue to edge the tour, now more boxy in feature.

Cross Rock Oak Ramble at 2 miles to follow the Lower Rose Ledge Trail. After a steep pitch, skirt below low cliffs to travel the wooded edge of a utility-corridor meadow. Birch, maple, and white pine shape the passage. At 2.3 miles, tag a lower-tiered ledge for a western perspective overlooking the corridor. Return to woods, close the loop at 2.5 miles, and retrace the first 0.6 mile to the trailhead.

16 Mount Toby State Reservation

OVERVIEW

This reservation enfolds an ancient peak (elevation 1,269 feet) rising above the Connecticut River Valley. Outcrops of a coarse conglomerate called puddingstone, steep ravines, rich forested hollows, marshy bottoms, and dry ridges make the mountain a botanical treasure trove. Naturalists can discover forty-two varieties of fern, as well as prized orchids. The described loop travels to the top of Mount Toby, reaching an observation tower—a trek that has inspired area visitors since the 1800s.

General description:	Traveling part of the Robert Frost Trail and Summit Road (a restricted road closed to vehicles), this loop explores rich woods and obtains a summit panorama sweeping a 50-mile radius. Spurs visit a cabin ruin, side mountain, and Cranberry Pond.
General location:	10 miles north of Amherst, Massachusetts.
Special attractions:	Summit panoramas, rich forest, cool brook drainage, pond view, opportunity for solitude, fall foliage.
Length:	5.5-mile loop, including spurs.
Elevation:	Find a 750-foot elevation change.
Difficulty:	Moderate.
Maps:	Mt. Toby Trail Map by New England Cartographics, P.O. Box 9369, North Amherst, MA 01059 (available for purchase in area outdoor stores or by writing to the company directly).
Special concerns:	The reservation is a learning laboratory. Tread lightly, and do not disturb vegetation. Note that several trails branching from the loop lead to or pass through private property; carry a map and heed posted notices.
Season and hours:	Spring through fall; daylight hours.
For information:	University of Massachusetts—Amherst, Department of Forestry and Wildlife Management.

Key points:

0.0 Reservation Road trailhead; follow Robert Frost Trail (RF).
1.5 Summit lookout tower.
2.8 Metawamp Cabin ruins.
2.9 Top Roaring Mountain; return to Summit Road.
4.9 Cranberry Pond.
5.5 End at trailhead gate.

Finding the trailhead: From the junction of Massachusetts Highways 63 and 47 (4.5 miles south of Millers Falls), go south on MA 47 for 1 mile and turn left (east) onto Reservation Road. Find the gated trailhead on the right in 0.5 mile, with parking in another 50 feet next to a small headquarters building.

From the MA 47–MA 116 junction in Sunderland, go north on MA 47 for 3.8 miles and turn right onto Reservation Road.

The hike: For a counterclockwise tour, round the gate and take an immediate right onto the orange-blazed Robert Frost Trail (RF). This ascending woods lane alternately tours conifer–hardwood forest and pine plantation. Poison ivy, bramble, sarsaparilla, striped maple, and mountain laurel lend visual interest. Daring squirrels leap through the canopy, while deer flee to safety.

At 0.4 mile, the RF (now a footpath) heads left as a blue-blazed trail continues forward. In another 0.25 mile, the RF turns right, passing through a mature hemlock stand and below a lichen-painted outcrop rise.

Upon meeting a woods road at 1 mile, turn right to travel a steep shrub corridor, following telephone lines skyward to Mount Toby. Despite the congestion of fern, bramble, laurel, goldenrod, aster, small maple, and birch, the path remains clear. Summer heat though can create a sauna effect.

At the trail fork at 1.2 miles, keep to the right for the RF; the red-blazed Upper Link Trail continues forward. Be alert at this junction, because the red and orange markers can easily be confused. With a steep charge, the RF claims the tree-rimmed, grassy summit (1.5 miles) to find a fence-enclosed nine-story lookout tower. The public may ascend the tower when gates are open; mount at your own risk. Enjoy a 360-degree view, including Mount Monadnock in New Hampshire, Mount Ascutney in Vermont, and the Massachusetts landscape with Mount Greylock, the Berkshires, and the Connecticut River Valley and peaks.

Remain on the RF, now pursuing dirt Summit Road east from the lookout tower, slowly descending along the ridge of oak, maple, hickory, birch, and hemlock. Where the descent quickens, encounter cobbles. At 2.25 miles, go left for RF/Summit Road; to the right is the yellow-blazed Robert Frost Bypass.

Along a headwater fork of Roaring Brook, enjoy a serene dark hemlock woods. Within this reservation, hikers will find some of the finest eastern hemlock in all of southern New England.

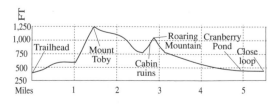

On the left at 2.5 miles, the Upper Link Trail offers an alternative return, looping back to the 1.2-mile junction with the RF. For the full 5.5-mile

Mount Toby State Reservation

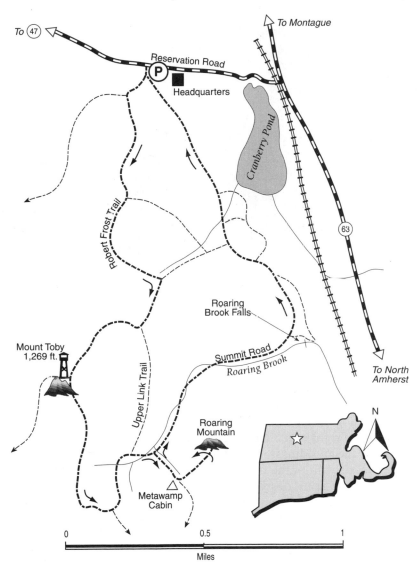

To (47)

To Montague

Reservation Road

P

Headquarters

Cranberry Pond

Robert Frost Trail

63

Roaring
Brook Falls

Mount Toby
1,269 ft.

Summit Road

Roaring Brook

To North
Amherst

Upper Link Trail

Roaring
Mountain

N

Metawamp
Cabin

0   0.5   1

Miles

tour, continue descending the woods road, reaching the first detour in 0.1 mile. Here, the Summit Road and RF part company. Head right on the RF to add a visit to Metawamp Cabin and Roaring Mountain. For the loop alone, continue forward.

The RF, now a footpath, parallels Roaring Brook upstream, coming to the cabin ruin and the white-blazed side trail to Roaring Mountain at 2.8 miles. Be careful near the ruins, because glass, nails, and splintered wood all contribute to the cabin character; a rock fireplace and sturdy door still remain in place.

Deciduous forest, Mount Toby State Reservation, MA.

From Metawamp Cabin, cross the brook and charge steeply uphill for 0.1 mile, reaching the broad summit plateau of Roaring Mountain. Although lacking vistas, this summit cloaked in oak, maple, mountain laurel, and huckleberry succeeds in delivering a reflective retreat. A cairn marks the high point.

Return to Summit Road (3.2 miles) and resume the descent, paralleling and crisscrossing Roaring Brook. Hemlocks shade one side of the drainage; deciduous trees the other. An occasional white blaze marks the tour. At 4 miles, the canyon opens up, cobbles disappear, and an easy-to-miss spur plunges to the right reaching a view of Roaring Brook Falls.

Some of the puddingstone outcrop borders Summit Road, while telephone poles rise out of the framing woods. At 4.8 miles, find the second detour, a 0.1-mile spur descending right to Cranberry Pond, a good-size, tree-rimmed pond with vegetated and open glassy waters. MA 63 travels along one side. Return to Summit Road and follow it right, returning to the trailhead gate at 5.5 miles.

17   Brooks Woodland Preserve

OVERVIEW

At this remote 464-acre woodland preserve of the Trustees of Reservations, the Swift River Tract offers hikers peaceful strolling through mixed woods; along river, brook, and pond; and past cultural sites. Ample opportunity exists for nature study, wildlife-watching, and solitude. Interlocking woods roads and trails pass freely among the adjoining lands of the Trustees, Harvard Forest, and Massachusetts Audubon.

General description: Three short hikes explore this preserve, traveling along pond, river, and brook, with the brook hike ending at the Indian grinding stones.

General location: 2 miles southeast of Petersham Center, Massachusetts.

Special attractions: Swift River, Moccasin Brook, and Connor's Pond; Indian grinding stones; stone walls and foundations dating back to the early 1800s; fall foliage; deer, fox, beaver, porcupine, and a host of birds.

Length: Connor's Pond Hike, 1.75 miles round trip; Swift River Hike, 3 miles round trip; Grinding Stones Hike, 2 miles round trip.

Elevation: Connor's Pond Hike, 50-foot elevation change; Swift River Hike, 250-foot elevation change; Grinding Stones Hike, 100-foot elevation change.

Difficulty: All easy to moderate.

Maps: Brooks Woodland Preserve, North Common Meadow, Swift River Reservation map. Purchase a copy from the Trustees of Reservations, Central Regional Office, prior to touring.

Special concerns: Obey the posted rules of the respective landowners; no facilities. Find numbered junctions keyed to the preserve map. The Brooks Woodland foot trails have colored trail markings; the woods roads do not.

Season and hours: Spring through fall, dawn to dusk.

For information: The Trustees of Reservations, Central Regional Office.

Key points:
Connor's Pond Hike:

0.0	Trailhead; cross bridge, turning right at junction 65.
0.6	Connor's Pond.
1.0	Audubon sanctuary; return to loop at junction 67.
1.7	End at trailhead.

Swift River Hike:

0.0	Trailhead; round gate into Harvard Research Forest.
0.2	Loop junction; keep to road.
2.0	Cross Swift River bridge.
2.7	Ford Swift River (avoid when water is high).
2.8	Close loop; turn left to return to trailhead.

Grinding Stones Hike:

0.0	Trailhead; cross bridge, turning left in 100 feet.
0.3	Moccasin Brook bridge.
1.0	Grinding stones; backtrack to trailhead.

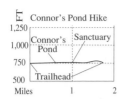

Connor's Pond Hike

FT
1,250
1,000 — Connor's Pond | Sanctuary
750
500 — Trailhead
Miles   1   2

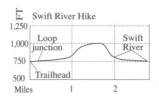

Swift River Hike

FT
1,250
1,000 — Loop junction | Swift River
750
500 — Trailhead
Miles   1   2

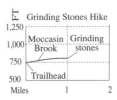

Grinding Stones Hike

FT
1,250
1,000 — Moccasin Brook | Grinding stones
750
500 — Trailhead
Miles   1   2

Finding the trailhead: From Petersham Center, go 1.8 miles south on Massachusetts Highway 32 and turn left (northeast) onto Quaker Drive. From Barre, go 5.6 miles north on MA 32/MA 122 and turn right for Quaker Drive. Go 0.2 mile, finding unsigned parking for a handful of vehicles on either side of Quaker Drive west of the Swift River bridge.

The hikes: The **Connor's Pond Hike** combines a counterclockwise woodland loop with a side trip along the east shore of Connor's Pond. Cross the Swift River bridge, turn right at junction 65, and skirt the cable to follow a scenic woods road downstream. From the bridge, admire small fish wriggling in the clear water of the brook-size river. Pines shade the corridor.

At 0.15 mile (junction 70), a yellow-marked foot trail veers right for a crescent-shaped detour. It stays along the Swift River, following it downstream to the marshy inlet of Connor's Pond. The main trail traverses a low ridge of pines and overlooks a wet meadow bottom on the left. The paths reunite at junction 71. Continue the counterclockwise tour in a pine–hemlock woods before dipping to the snag-riddled meadow bottom and rolling away. Beautiful ferns dress the floor.

At junction 67 (0.4 mile), turn right to visit the east shore of Connor's Pond; bear left for the loop alone. For the pond detour, again bear right at junction 68, descending among beech, birch, maple, hornbeam, hop hornbeam, black cherry, and witch hazel. Cross a scenic bridge over Rutland Brook and round a gate, entering a Massachusetts Audubon property.

Continue south on the wide grassy lane, cross a drainage, and bear right at the fork to skirt the pond's edge. Initial views find a vegetated cove with lily pads and arrowhead. In fall, goldenrod and aster claim the meadow bank. By 0.7 mile, overlook the dark open water, low rounded western hills, and stunning reflections. Abandoned beaver lodges and an island contribute to the view.

Where the trail meets the entrance road to the Audubon sanctuary (0.95 mile), turn back, retracing the tour to junction 67 (1.5 miles). Complete the loop, passing through similar woods. Turn left at junction 64 to return to Quaker Drive and the river (1.75 miles).

From the parking turnout at the northwest corner of Swift River bridge, round a metal gate, entering Harvard Research Forest for the **Swift River Hike.** Where the road curves right to parallel the Swift River upstream, it becomes more of a rustic country lane, softened by grass, littered with pine needles, and shaded by conifer–deciduous woods. Keep to the road (0.2 mile), avoiding the fording that completes the loop. Although the woods road and river at times drift apart, enjoy frequent looks at this sparkling brook-size

Brooks Woodland Preserve

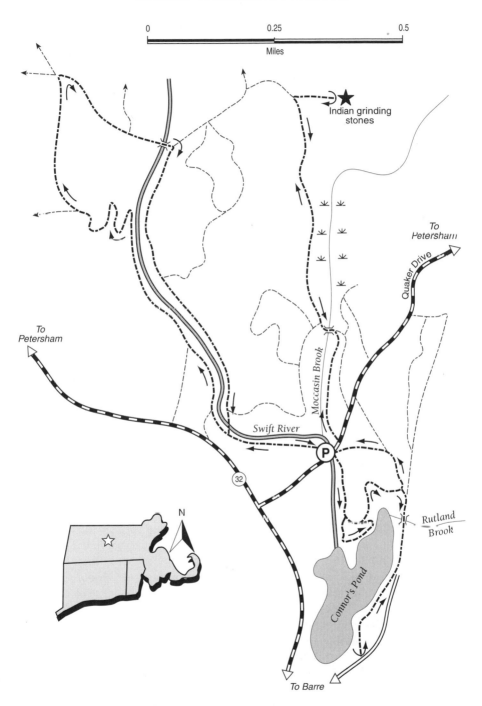

0   0.25   0.5

Miles

Indian grinding stones

To Petersham

To Petersham

Quaker Drive

Moccasin Brook

Swift River

P

32

To Barre

N

Connor's Pond

Rutland Brook

tannin-colored waterway. Fountains of fern, hobblebush, club moss, and sar-saparilla contribute to travel.

As secondary trails branch away, keep to the main woods road. At 0.8 mile, the river broadens, forming a scenic pool that reflects its treed shore. In an-other 0.1 mile, remain on the road as it arcs left and switchbacks away from the Swift River, touring a mostly deciduous woods interrupted by small groves of spruce, tamarack, hemlock, and pine. At the 1.25-mile fork, turn right, hiking on a long grassy straightaway sandwiched by rich ferns, a dark stone wall, and high-canopy woods.

At the 1.6-mile intersection, wooden gates bar the routes straight ahead and to the right, while an open woods road journeys left. For the loop, round the gate to the right, descending back toward the Swift River and Brooks Woodland Preserve. Again find stone walls and a rich woodsy charm. Be on the lookout for a good-size American chestnut tree—a rarity these days; chip-munks scold from nooks in the wall.

With a drainage crossing, travel a sunken grade between two low ridges resplendent in summer green. At junction 35, continue straight ahead to cross a wooden bridge over the Swift River. At the immediate T-junction (junction 45), turn right for the downstream return. Find a strollable woods road, hem-lock and towering pine, and soothing river views.

At 2.15 miles, the spur from the 0.9-mile river ford arrives on the right; continue downstream, drawing away from the river's edge. At junction 46, bear right, remaining along the river plain for a tranquil woodland journey. Where the woods road forks at 2.75 miles, veer right for a rock-hopping cross-ing or fording of the Swift River. Close the loop at 2.8 miles, turn left, and retrace the first 0.2 mile to the trailhead.

When waters are high, either backtrack the tour or head left on the woods road at 2.75 miles, bearing right at all subsequent junctions to return to Quaker Drive east of the bridge at junction 53.

For the **Grinding Stones Hike,** cross the Swift River bridge and continue northeast on Quaker Drive for 100 feet. There, look for a foot trail entering the dark hemlock woods on the left side of the road; an orange trail marker and a posted notice of the Trustees of Reservations signal the start.

Hike upstream along Moccasin Brook, a stream the size of Swift River. Pine, maple, oak, black cherry, and birch fill out the forest; beautiful ferns spread at their feet. Roots and an occasional mossy rock ripple the trailbed.

Cross over a couple of stone walls, reaching a woods road. Turn left, pass the plaque tribute to John Fiske, and cross the footbridge over Moccasin Brook. The hike now continues forward past junction 49 to skirt the large open marsh of upper Moccasin Brook; glimpse the marsh beyond the pines. At 0.4 mile, a blue trail heads left; proceed forward on the woods road for a rolling tour.

Step through a passage in a rock wall, reaching the 0.65-mile junction (junc-tion 48 on the map, but it may be missing its marker); bear right. A mild to moderate ascent follows, with more deciduous trees interweaving the for-est.

At the next rock wall (0.95 mile), find the signed junction for Indian grind-ing stones and turn right. In 100 yards, before the next stone wall, discover some large frost-fractured boulders and stones holding mortar depressions and trenches. Here the Nipmuck Indians, using stone pestles, ground acorns and maize and pushed the finished meal out the troughs into their baskets. Although subtle, the worn stone clues provide an interesting peek into the cultural past. Return as you came.

18 Wachusett Mountain State Reservation

OVERVIEW

This 2,100-acre state reservation protects Massachusetts's tallest mountain east of the Berkshires. The site features hardwood–conifer forest, rock ledges and outcrops, summit panoramas stretching from Boston to Mount Greylock, winter downhill skiing, and some 20 miles of hiking trail, including 4 miles of the long-distance Midstate Trail, which cuts south to north through the middle of the state.

General description: Two day hikes present the mountain offering: one rounds the eastern base of Wachusett Mountain to Echo Lake; the other scales the north flank and descends via the west flank, visiting Balance Rock and the summit.

General location: 4 miles north of Princeton, Massachusetts.

Special attractions: Summit panorama; mixed woods; spring and summer wildflower, azalea, and mountain laurel blooms; fall hawk migration; autumn foliage.

Length: Bicentennial–Echo Lake Hike, 2.5 miles round trip; Balance Rock–Summit Hike, 4 miles round trip.

Elevation: Bicentennial–Echo Lake Hike, 150-foot elevation change; Balance Rock–Summit Hike, 1,000-foot elevation change.

Difficulty: Bicentennial–Echo Lake Hike, moderate; the Balance Rock–Summit Hike is strenuous.

Maps: State forest map.

Special concerns: No overnight camping or fires. Keep dogs leashed. Visitor center parking can fill in September and October when fall hawk migrations and colorful autumn foliage swell visitorship.

Season and hours: Spring through fall for hiking, daylight hours. Visitor center, 9:00 A.M. to 4:00 P.M.

For information: Wachusett Mountain State Reservation.

Key points:
Bicentennial–Echo Lake Hike:
- 0.0 Headquarters trailhead; hike Bicentennial Trail south.
- 1.0 High Meadow Trail junction; turn left.
- 1.2 Echo Lake; backtrack to trailhead.

Balance Rock–Summit Hike:
- 0.0 Ski area trailhead; follow Midstate Trail.
- 0.4 Balance Rock.
- 0.7 Loop junction; continue forward.
- 1.8 Wachusett Mountain summit.
- 3.3 Close loop; go left, backtracking to trailhead.

Finding the trailhead: From Massachusetts Highway 2 west of Fitchburg, take exit 25 and go south on MA 140 for 2.1 miles. There, turn right per the sign, following Mile Hill Road. In 0.5 mile, bear right onto Bolton Road, and take an immediate left to enter the ski area parking lot and reach the trailhead for the Balance Rock–Summit Hike. For the Bicentennial–Echo Lake Hike, continue south on Mile Hill Road/Mountain Road for another 1.2 miles and turn right for headquarters/visitor center parking and the trailhead.

The hikes: For the **Bicentennial–Echo Lake Hike,** start on the west side of the headquarters parking lot at a sign for the Bicentennial Trail; blue blazes mark the way. Cross the footbridge and turn south, contouring the rocky eastern base of Wachusett Mountain above Mountain Road. On this rocky course, expect to do some high stepping. Enjoy wildflowers and a diverse canopy.

At 0.1 mile, the Pine Hill Trail arrives on the left to briefly share the trailbed before striking uphill to the right. At 0.25 mile, descend left; the Loop Trail claims the center and right forks. Oak, maple, birch, ash, hornbeam, hop hornbeam, hickory, and hemlock variously render shade. Mountain laurel lends a showy early-summer accent. Pass through a gap in a rock wall (0.5 mile) and descend away from the rockiness.

Next, cross the Mountain House Trail at 0.75 mile and continue contouring south. Old stone foundations punctuate the slope below the Bicentennial Trail, and a few old-growth oaks and maples frame the path. Owl, woodpecker, and songbirds may animate the treetops. Beyond the next stone wall, ascend.

At 1 mile, the Bicentennial Trail ends at its junction with the High Meadow Trail. To visit Echo Lake, go left on the High Meadow Trail, finding views of Little Wachusett Mountain as the trail travels a sumac–scrub clearing and a grove of spindly birch. Reenter woods, cross another rock wall, and descend

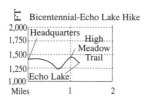

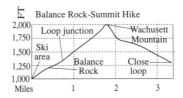

Wachusett Mountain State Reservation

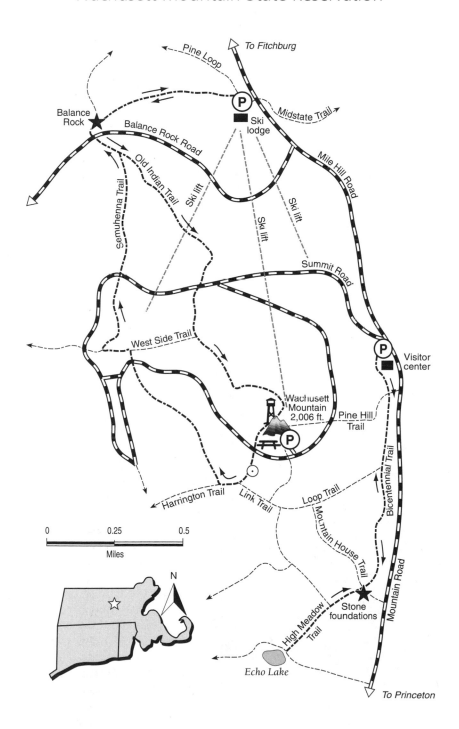

To Fitchburg

Pine Loop

Balance Rock

Balance Rock Road

Ski lodge

Midstate Trail

Mile Hill Road

Semuhenna Trail

Old Indian Trail

Ski lift

Ski lift

Ski lift

Summit Road

West Side Trail

Visitor center

Wachusett Mountain 2,006 ft.

Pine Hill Trail

Bicentennial Trail

Harrington Trail

Link Trail

Loop Trail

Mountain House Trail

Mountain Road

0   0.25   0.5
Miles

N

Stone foundations

High Meadow Trail

Echo Lake

To Princeton

to Echo Lake, with its shoreline picnic tables and a rock fireplace (1.25 miles). Ash, birch, oak, and maple rim this shallow pond dammed at its east end. Return as you came to the trailhead (2.5 miles) or devise a loop to the summit, utilizing cross trails.

The **Balance Rock–Summit Hike** starts at the ski area parking lot; find the trail at the base of the mountain opposite aisle post 5. Look for the yellow triangle of the Midstate Trail on a light post next to the path.

Angle into the woods to the right of the light post, meeting a wood-chip road in 50 feet. To the right is Pine Loop; go left toward Balance Rock Road. Ascend slowly in conifer–hardwood forest, reaching an unsigned fork at 0.3 mile. Bear right, staying on the Midstate Trail, passing through a breach in a rock wall to win an audience with Balance Rock (0.4 mile). Prominently located in the woods opening, this boxy rock pedestal balances an oversize round boulder.

Resume the hike heading uphill, still following the yellow triangles; a few species tags identify trees. At 0.5 mile, cross dirt Balance Rock Road, now ascending via the Old Indian Trail. Historically, Wachusett Mountain was a key gathering site for the Nipmuck Indians. The name *Wachusett* means "by the great hill." A deer or porcupine may precede you on the trail.

Ascend and contour fairly steeply, touring a pine–oak habitat, crossing a rock wall, and reaching the loop junction at 0.7 mile. The Semuhenna Trail heads right; continue forward on the Old Indian Trail for a clockwise summit loop. Contour the slope, crossing the meadowy ski runs, where downhill views find Wachusett Lake. Then follow the painted footprints across Summit Road at 1 mile and begin a steep rocky ascent, switchbacking amid platy outcrop ledges, and hike past the West Side Trail on the right.

At 1.5 miles, traverse the summit ridge, touring a low-stature forest. Pass behind the chairlift terminal and beside a war memorial, coming out at the broad

Balance Rock, Wachusett Mountain State Reservation, MA.

open summit (1.8 miles), attainable by road, with outward-radiating trails and vistas. Strolling the summit (elevation 2,006 feet), piece together a full 360-degree view, with Mount Monadnock and the Wapack Range, the Berkshires, the Taconics, Worcester, and Boston.

On a corner of the fence enclosing the summit lookout tower, find a sign for the Harrington Trail. Follow it west off the summit to complete the loop. Cross over a road linking picnic sites and angle left across an open outcrop, finding a rugged, rocky descent, sometimes requiring the use of hands. Watch for blazes; oaks clad the upper mountain reaches.

Cross Summit Road and find a difficult step over the 6-foot-tall stone wall. When wet or blanketed by leaves, the hillside rocks require even greater attention. At 1.9 miles, a spur left offers a limited view south toward the towers of Worcester Highland. As the woods grow more mixed, stay on the Harrington Trail, bypassing the Link Trail on the left. Just ahead, find the Semuhenna Trail; for the loop, go right.

The Semuhenna Trail offers a more relaxing stroll, enwrapping the slope. The woods feature hemlock, maple, birch, and beech. At 2.6 miles, cross Summit Road; find picnic sites on either side. Now stay left, following the West Side/Semuhenna Trails. At a drainage, veer right with the Semuhenna Trail; the West Side Trail continues forward. Once again pursue the yellow markers of the Midstate Trail.

Cross Summit Road, angling right. Descend through hemlock deciduous woods and pine plantation, crossing rock walls to close the loop at 3.3 miles. Go left, backtracking the Old Indian and Midstate Trails to the ski area at 4 miles.

19 Wachusett Meadow Wildlife Sanctuary

OVERVIEW

This sanctuary of the Massachusetts Audubon Society presents hikers a varied canvas to explore, with upland meadows, field, mixed woods, pasture, a beaver wetland, and a 1,300-foot monadnock (an erosion-resistant hill). Trails lead to an ancient maple, summit vistas, wildlife ponds, glacial erratics, and tranquil retreats. The fall hawk migration (September and October) and the turning of the red maple leaves are seasonal draws, but the variety of flora and fauna engages year-round.

General description: Two short loops (one to a summit, the other through pastures) explore the area, with sight-seeing options along the way. A third hike visits a pond and can be used to link the sanctuary and its neighbor to the north, Wachusett Mountain.

General location: 15 miles northwest of Worcester, Massachusetts.
Special attractions: Bird- and wildlife-watching, mature forest, fall foliage, spring and summer wildflowers, access to the Midstate Trail and Wachusett Mountain.
Length: Brown Hill Loop, 2.8 miles round trip; Chapman Trail, 2.8 miles round trip to Black Pond; Pasture Trail–Fern Forest Trail Loop, 2.5 miles round trip.
Elevation: Brown Hill Loop, 300-foot elevation change; Chapman Trail, 100-foot elevation change; Pasture Trail–Fern Forest Trail Loop, 50-foot elevation change.
Difficulty: Brown Hill Loop, moderate; the Chapman Trail and Pasture Trail–Fern Forest Trail Loop are easy.
Maps: Sanctuary brochure.
Special concerns: Per-person access fee or Massachusetts Audubon membership; obey posted rules. Trails are for foot travel only—no bikes or skis. Leave pets at home. Find the characteristic Audubon blazing, with blue heading away from the trailhead, yellow returning.
Season and hours: Year-round, Tuesday through Sunday and most holidays that fall on Monday. Closed Thanksgiving, Christmas, and New Year's Days. Trails, dawn to dusk; office, 10:00 A.M. to 2:00 P.M. Tuesday through Saturday.
For information: Wachusett Meadow Wildlife Sanctuary.

Key points:
Brown Hill Loop:
   0.0   North Meadow Trailhead; hike counterclockwise.
   0.1   Farm Pond.
   0.4   Loop junction.
   1.1   Otter Pond.
   1.8   Brown Hill summit.
   2.4   Complete loop; return to trailhead.

Chapman Trail:
   0.0   North Meadow Trailhead; hike north.
   0.1   Crocker maple.
   0.2   Chapman Trail.
   1.4   Black Pond; return as you came.

Pasture Trail–Fern Forest Trail Loop:
   0.0   Parking area; hike Goodnow Road west.
   0.2   Pasture Loop.
   0.6   Rock Fire Pond.
   0.8   Fern Forest Trail.
   2.5   Parking area.

Finding the trailhead: From the town common in Princeton, go west on Massachusetts Highway 62 for 0.6 mile and turn right onto Goodnow Road, a rough paved road. Go 1 mile, turning left for trail parking.

The hikes: For both the **Brown Hill Loop** and the **Chapman Trail,** start via the North Meadow Trail. From the parking area, cross Goodnow Road, passing through a breach in the stone wall to the right of the large white colonial house. Ascend north on mowed track to the loop junction. For the Brown Hill Loop, go right (counterclockwise); for the Chapman Trail, head left (clockwise).

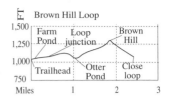

The sanctuary's **Brown Hill Loop** encircles the site's prominent monadnock feature, topping it via one of the Summit Trail spurs.

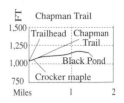

Counterclockwise travel on the North Meadow Trail takes the hiker briefly north through a hay field before turning right to visit Farm Pond, a small wildlife pond with cattails and tadpoles. Gray catbirds and red-winged blackbirds further add to its charm. Proceed east along the pond's southern shore, remaining on the North Meadow Trail. Bypass the Birch Trail and parallel stone walls, coming to a breach in the wall on the right at 0.3 mile.

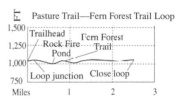

Pass through the breach and keep right on the Summit Trail to reach the Brown Hill Loop in 0.1 mile; turn right for a counterclockwise stroll, contouring the foot of Brown Hill. Pine, oak, hickory, maple, and birch dress the slope, with clearings of blueberry and juniper. At 0.9 mile, bear left past the Birch Trail, quickly coming to the next junction, where a side trip right leads to Otter Pond.

This side trip passes through young deciduous woods and transition meadow, reaching a research study area for the rare fringed gentian, a wildflower. After edging a hay field, overlook Otter Pond from its small dam. Bayberry, juniper, dogwood, oak, and maple rim the vegetated water, while Little Wachusett Mountain rises in the distance. Backtrack and resume the loop (1.2 miles), ascending steadily, advancing via a walkway of stones.

At 1.7 miles, reach the first of three possible summit ascents and turn left. Follow a stone wall, passing a scenic multitrunked pine, coming out on the shrub-clad hilltop. Continue 100 feet to the right to claim the topmost point, elevation 1,312 feet. Views sweep 360 degrees, with Wachusett and Little Wachusett Mountains, New Hampshire's Mount Monadnock, the Worcester Highlands, and the sanctuary's own Beaver Wetland. In fall, the hawk migration funnels south between Wachusett and Little Wachusett Mountains, making Brown Hill an ideal spot at which to stage a sky-watch.

Descend as you came, resuming the counterclockwise loop at 1.9 miles, rounding amid picturesque pines and a fern understory. Keep to the Brown Hill Loop, bypassing the Summit Trail on the left and Glacier Boulder Trail on the right. Upon passing the third summit spur mounting Brown Hill, complete the loop at 2.4 miles. From here, bear right, backtracking the initial

Wachusett Meadow Wildlife Sanctuary

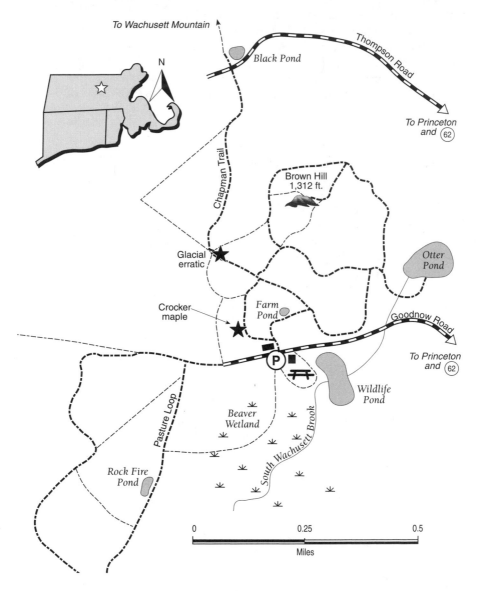

To Wachusett Mountain

Black Pond

Thompson Road

To Princeton and (62)

N

Chapman Trail

Brown Hill
1,312 ft.

Otter Pond

Glacial erratic

Crocker maple

Farm Pond

Goodnow Road

To Princeton and (62)

P

Wildlife Pond

Pasture Loop

Beaver Wetland

South Wachusett Brook

Rock Fire Pond

0   0.25   0.5

Miles

0.4 mile to the trailhead, passing back through the fence opening and taking North Meadow Trail to return to parking.

Alternatively, hikers can add to the loop by following the 0.5-mile Glacial Boulder Trail at 2.3 miles. This trail visits a room-size erratic surfed to this site on a retreating glacier some 12,000 years ago. Frost has since fractured the boulder into big chunks. From the boulder, follow the stone wall southeast back toward the breach in the stone wall first seen at 0.3 mile (2.8 miles). Pass through the breach and backtrack to the trailhead (3.1 miles).

For the **Chapman Trail/Midstate Trail North,** follow the North Meadow Trail as it ascends northwest, skirting a hay field, coming to the junction for the Crocker maple (0.1 mile).

A short detour left through the egress in the stone wall adds a visit to the Crocker maple, a 250-year-old monarch believed to be one of the largest sugar maples in the United States. It presides at the western edge of the pasture above a moist drainage; the area's natural springs contributed to the tree's enormity. Stout, with a lopped top and missing a major arm, this relic captivates and humbles onlookers. Conchs cling to the gnarled 6-foot-diameter trunk. Beware of poison ivy near the maple; a bench seat allows a comfortable view.

The North Meadow Trail then continues north at the outskirts of the hay field, paralleling the same stone wall to the next egress, the start of the Chapman Trail (0.2 mile). This sanctuary trail also advances the Midstate Trail, carrying it north through the property.

Pass through the sanctuary's remote western woods, a rich mixed-deciduous habitat, twice meeting the West Border Trail to exit at Thompson Road (a minimally used, rutted dirt road). Across the road sits tree-enclosed Black Pond (1.4 miles), a dark mirror of water with a soothing aqua hue. Aquatic vegetation or autumn leaves at times can claim the pool.

Northbound, the tour continues out of the sanctuary and across public lands to top Wachusett Mountain at about 4 miles; be alert for the Midstate Trail blazings as the route utilizes sections of woods roads weaving its way to the peak. Ask for a Wachusett Mountain State Reservation map at the sanctuary office. For this hike, though, the return is as you came.

For the **Pasture Trail–Fern Forest Trail Loop,** hike west from the parking area on Goodnow Road, now a scenic lane defined by stone walls and 200-year-old oak, beech, and ash trees. Round the gate and continue west past the northbound Midstate Trail, a long-distance trail stretched across Massachusetts from Rhode Island to New Hampshire. Soon after, at 0.2 mile, turn left for the Pasture Loop and southbound Midstate Trail. (A longer, alternative approach to the Pasture Loop is to follow the South Meadow Trail counterclockwise to the Beaver Bend Trail, joining the described loop at the south end of Second Pasture.)

The selected clockwise tour offers an exploration of the external loop traversing five pastures isolated by stone walls and forest buffers. In different stages of succession, each pasture boasts a signature flora and fauna. Travel mowed track, woods lane, and foot trail.

From Goodnow Road, hike south, proceeding forward at each of the first two junctions. The Beaver Bend Trail arrives on the left at the second junction (0.4 mile). Find both groomed and unruly meadow pastures. Those left wild show stands of waist-high grasses, bramble, milkweed, and goldenrod, with seedpods adding interest in the fall.

At 0.6 mile, between the Third and Fourth Pastures, find Rock Fire Pond, a charming dark-water pool with lily pads and a reflecting rock. Aspen, birch, and maple frame the pool, gentian dot its banks, and whirligig beetles enliven the surface. Warblers lend a cheerful note. Past Fourth Pasture, keep left to add the Fern Forest Trail extension; a right shortens the tour following the Pasture Trail alone.

Areas of pine, black cherry, and tall fern add to travel. After leaving the upland meadow of the Fifth Pasture, bear right, keeping to the selected external loop; the Midstate Trail continues south to the left. The loop travels a richly wooded slope, passing a large quartz boulder on the right at 1.1 miles. The white rock offers a stunning contrast to the dark pine trunks and vibrant ferns.

Now keep left to bring the loop to a close, enjoying a relaxing woods hike amid hemlock, oak, and beech, with areas of low-growing mountain laurel. A few disturbed openings record the injury and healing from the tornado of 1989. Later, a high-canopy deciduous woods escorts hikers onto the grassy retired lane of Goodnow Road at 2.1 miles. Turn right to end the hike at 2.5 miles.

20 Norwottuck Rail Trail

General description: This paved, abandoned stretch of the Boston & Maine (B&M) Railroad serves up a scenic travel corridor to hikers, cyclists, skaters, joggers, wheelchair users, and cross-country skiers. The route traverses rural, residential, and light industry/commercial areas.

General location: In Northampton, Hadley, and Amherst, Massachusetts.

Special attractions: Wildlife-watching, nature study, mixed deciduous woods, swamps, fields, wildflowers, fall foliage.

Length: 10 miles one-way.

Elevation: The rail-trail is virtually flat.

Difficulty: Easy.

Maps: *Guide to the Norwottuck Rail Trail* (free copies available at area bicycling and outdoor stores).

Special concerns: Keep to the right, keep dogs restrained on a short leash, and keep to the rail corridor, respecting the neighboring private properties. Rangers patrol regularly.

Season and hours: Year-round, generally spring through fall for hiking, 5:00 A.M. to 10:00 P.M.

For information: Norwottuck Rail Trail.

Key points:
    0.0 Western terminus (Elwell State Park); cross trestle bridge.
    1.5 Hadley Commons.
    3.0 Massachusetts Highway 9 tunnel.

3.7   Mountain Farms Mall.
6.2   Skirt Amherst College grounds.
7.0   Fort River bridge.
8.5   Station Road trailhead.
8.9   Lawrence Swamp.
10.0 End at eastern terminus (Warren Wright Road trailhead).

Finding the trailhead: Find the western terminus at Elwell State Park on Damon Road west of MA 9 in Northampton. Central accesses are found along the south side of Mountain Farms Mall in Hadley and on Station Road in South Amherst. Find the trail's eastern terminus on Warren Wright Road 0.6 mile south of its intersection with Station Road.

The hike: Start a west–east tour at Elwell State Park. Cross the scenic 0.25-mile-long trestle bridge spanning a side arm of the Connecticut River, sixty-acre Elwell Island, and the main flow of the river. Silver maple, elm, sumac, cottonwood, walnut, locust, and wild grape add to river views.

The bridge enchants with its diagonal-plank walk, rusting steel trestles, and overlacing greenery. Downstream views reveal the Calvin Coolidge Bridge. Coolidge was a native son and regular passenger on the B&M Railroad. Upstream views hold rural appeal.

The 7-foot-wide rail-trail offers comfortable travel. The recycled glass used in its pavement glints in the sun. This rail-trail parallels MA 9, drifting farther from the highway as it journeys east. Mileposts help hikers track progress, while road crossings mark off distance. Find crossings well marked for both motorists and rail-trail users.

Fields, nurseries, cropland, and even a pumpkin patch sweep away left. Autumn tours prove especially enjoyable with the rural backdrop, a dusting of colored leaves, and the noisy chaos of flocking blackbirds. At just under 1.5 miles, pass through historic Hadley Commons, a grassy wayside with tables, wastebaskets, and a seasonal drinking fountain; in the past, town citizens grazed their animals here.

Look for stone pillars bearing the letter *W;* these cued engineers to sound the whistle. On the eastern half of the tour (in Amherst), the path crosses over two granite tunnels dating back to the 1880s. These rail underpasses allowed cows to move between pastures without crossing tracks.

Intermittent breaks in the overlacing canopy and bordering trees open up the corridor. The long straightaways prove aesthetically pleasing. A beautiful maple swamp graces the tour approaching the Spruce Hill Road tunnel (2.75 miles). Ahead, travel a sunken grade with a junkyard on the rise to the right. An abundance of fern and overlacing trees quickly dismiss the intrusion.

At 3 miles, pass through the MA 9 tunnel, putting the highway and settlement to the left, the rural terrain to the right. Beware of poison ivy along

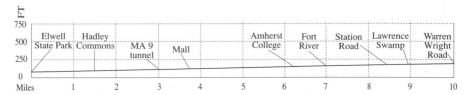

Norwottuck Rail Trail

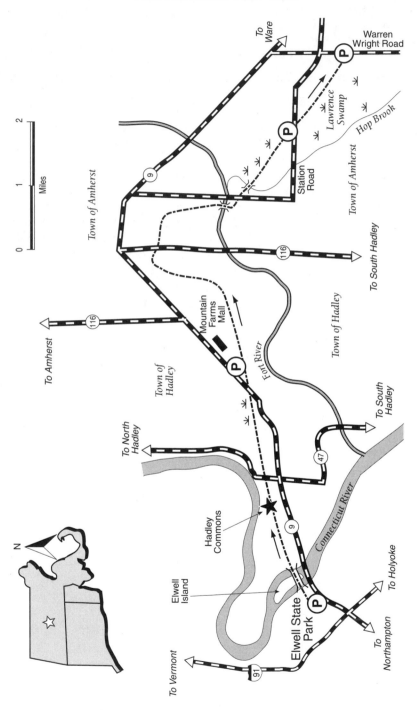

the shoulders. In another 0.2 mile, hike past a drive-in eatery that makes the most of having the rail-trail for a neighbor by welcoming and serving travelers and posting trail distances. Find benches and tables at the southwest and southeast corners of Mountain Farms Mall (3.75 miles). A dairy farm sprawls to the right. Dairy farming was once a major enterprise in the area.

After 4.25 miles, enjoy an isolated passage along undeveloped fields and woods. Cross-field views find Mounts Toby and Sugarloaf rising to the north. Southern vantages present the Holyoke Range. Maple, oak, and elm are familiar shade sources. Chances for wildlife sightings increase, with skunk, deer, woodpecker, and squirrel. A ranger mentioned a lone moose as a past visitor.

At 5 miles, pass between a golf course and deep woods. The trail alternately travels levee and sunken grades. By 6.25 miles, begin skirting the grounds of Amherst College, with its sporting fields, tennis courts, and posted spruce plantations. Wetlands and conservation lands next border the trail, holding new discovery, including beaver, heron, painted turtle, and frog. Turkey vultures assemble on a popular roosting snag.

At 7 miles, cross the bridge over Fort River, and at 7.25 miles pass Fort River Loop, a hiker-only path descending to the left. Cattail bogs and riparian woodland next host the rail-trail. Gaps in the border afford looks north and south.

Cross the bridge over Hop Brook (7.5 miles) and, soon after, pass segments of the K.C. Trail, another foot trail. Hornbeam commonly grows along the swamps. At 8.5 miles, reach Station Road, with parking for about twenty vehicles.

Connecticut River Bridge, Norwottuck Rail Trail, MA.

Across the road, the paved rail-trail continues east, rounding the barrier. To its right is the Caroline Arnold Trail, a footpath open to hikers only that travels the woodland bottom. The woods are richly varied with drapes of wild grape and poison ivy. An industrious woodpecker might betray its location on a snag. Where gaps open the woods to the left, glimpse a nearby existing railroad.

Later, shrub-filled Lawrence Swamp borders the grade, bringing a nice change of aspect. Croaking frogs, the lilting of songbirds, the wetland mosaic, the smell of methane, and the penetrating sun all contribute to the marsh offering. Skirt an off-limits water supply site and pass through a gate to emerge at the Warren Wright Road trailhead (10 miles).

21 Mount Tom State Reservation–Dinosaur Footprints Reservation

OVERVIEW

At these neighboring central Massachusetts sites, find perhaps the finest vista–ridge tour for the three-state area and walk where dinosaurs roamed. The long-distance Metacomet–Monadnock Trail slices south to north through Mount Tom State Reservation, offering two short skyline hikes with heart-quickening cliffs and restful Connecticut Valley views.

Dinosaur Footprints Reservation, a property of the Trustees of Reservations, has a short trail system visiting sedimentary outcrops that contain the tracks of three-toed dinosaurs. Footprints dating back 200 million years and access to the Connecticut River win over guests at this tiny but special site.

General description:	Three short hikes present the appeal of these two reservations.
General location:	West bank of the Connecticut River at Northampton.
Special attractions:	Vistas, Triassic period dinosaur footprints, floral fossils, Eyrie House Ruins, Connecticut River access, mixed forests, mountain laurel, fall foliage.
Length:	Metacomet–Monadnock (M–M) Trail South, 4.5 miles round trip; M–M Trail North, 2.8 miles round trip; Dinosaur Footprints Trail, 0.25-mile round trip.
Elevation:	M–M Trail South, 650-foot elevation change; M–M Trail North, 300-foot elevation change; Dinosaur Footprints Trail, minimal elevation change.
Difficulty:	M–M Trail South, strenuous; M–M Trail North, moderate; Dinosaur Footprints Trail, easy.
Maps:	Mount Tom State Reservation map.

Special concerns: Fee admission to Mount Tom. Tread softly and respectfully. Obey the respective rules for the two sites.

Season and hours: Spring through fall for hiking. Mount Tom, 8:00 A.M. to 6:00 P.M.; Dinosaur Footprints Reservation, dawn to dusk.

For information: Mount Tom State Reservation; the Trustees of Reservations, Western Regional Office.

Key points:

M–M Trail South:

    0.0   Trailside Museum trailhead; head south.

    0.6   Whiting Peak.

    2.2   Mount Tom tower facility; return as you came.

M–M Trail North:

    0.0   From picnic area opposite museum, head north.

    0.3   Goat Peak.

    1.1   Dry Knoll.

    1.4   Eyrie House Ruins; return as you came.

Dinosaur Footprints Trail:

    0.0   U.S. Highway 5 trailhead; explore both forks.

    0.1   Connecticut River; return to US 5.

Finding the trailhead: From Interstate 91, take exit 18 and go south on US 5. In 3.2 miles, find the Smiths Ferry Road entrance to Mount Tom State Reservation on the right. Continue south on US 5 for another 1.7 miles to find the paved turnout for Dinosaur Footprints Reservation on the left.

The hikes: Start the Metacomet–Monadnock hikes near the Trailside Museum off Smiths Ferry Road (1.6 miles west off US 5, 0.1 mile east of its junction with Christopher Clark Road). Find parking opposite the museum.

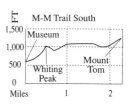

For the **M–M Trail South,** follow the white-diamond- and paint-blazed earthen lane heading south into an area of mature hemlocks, west of the Trailside Museum. In 200 feet, catch a glimpse of the rustic museum off to the left. Birch, mountain laurel, witch hazel, and chestnut interweave the forest. Maple and mixed oak claim the upper canopy. Enjoy a pleasant stroll, chasing the faint blazes.

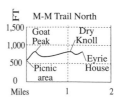

At 0.25 mile, a storage yard is to the right; the Quarry Trail follows the woods road as it veers left; and the foot trail of the M–M continues straight ahead. A sign on the M–M indicates MOUNT TOM 2 MILES. Ascend via a steep root- and rock-bound trail; stone steps and switchbacks advance the ridge assault.

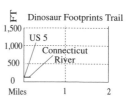

Mount Tom State Reservation–Dinosaur Footprints Reservation

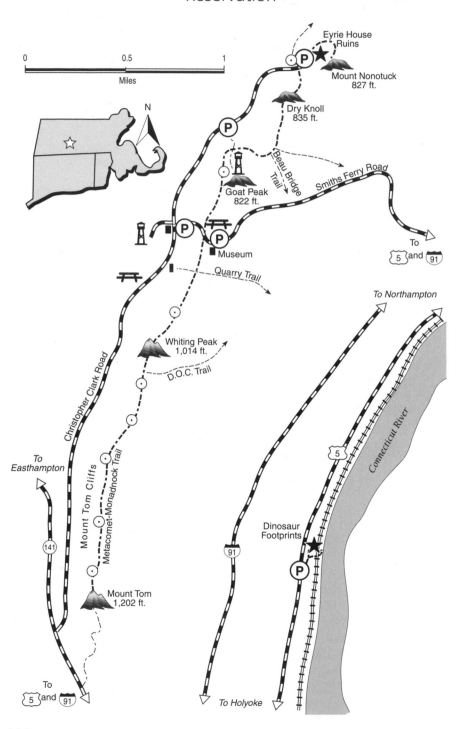

0   0.5   1
Miles

N

Eyrie House Ruins

Mount Nonotuck 827 ft.

Dry Knoll 835 ft.

Beau Bridge Trail

Smiths Ferry Road

Goat Peak 822 ft.

Museum

Quarry Trail

To 5 and 91

To Northampton

Whiting Peak 1,014 ft.

D.O.C. Trail

Christopher Clark Road

Connecticut River

To Easthampton

141

Mount Tom Cliffs

Metacomet-Monadnock Trail

5

Dinosaur Footprints

91

Mount Tom 1,202 ft.

To 5 and 91

To Holyoke

Top the ridgeline (0.4 mile) and continue south, hugging the west rim. A spur soon leads to an impressive rock jut for a grand western perspective of Easthampton, the rural and wooded Connecticut River Valley, and the Berkshires vanishing to the horizon. Continue south for a rolling ridge tour, pocketing better and better views. Ragged breaks and weathered niches create foot- and handholds for mounting the rimrock.

At 0.6 mile, tag Whiting Peak (1,014 feet). Low-stature oak, hickory, and pine cloak the summit ridge. At 0.85 mile, the D.O.C. Trail heads left; keep to the M–M. The fragmented cliff of Whiting and the stirring profile of Mount Tom hold viewers spellbound. Autumn paints an especially pretty landscape.

Before long, pursue the narrow ledge of the vertically fragmented cliff of Mount Tom Ridge. The sheer rock plummets 300 feet to a skirt of jagged scree and the treed slope tapering to the valley floor. This is not a hike for the timid or foolish.

Where a secondary trail rounds inland at 1.3 miles, continue forward, following the white paint blazes for some rock climbing. If you opt to follow the secondary trail, quickly bear right to return to the blazed hike at the scree base of an upper-tiered ledge.

Keep to the west side of the ridge, overlooking pull-apart walls, fractured towers, and pinnacles. Vultures sail the thermals. The brief departures into the woods only amplify the excitement of this otherwise vista-packed tour. At 1.5 miles, overlook a tower station, soon spying the beacon and radio towers atop Mount Tom (elevation 1,202 feet). By 2 miles, add over-the-shoulder looks at Amherst, the University of Massachusetts (UMass), and Summit House crowning the Holyoke Range.

Round the tower facility of Mount Tom, but beware of the hazardous concrete walkway. At the south side of the towers (2.25 miles), enjoy looks at Hartford, Connecticut, and the distinct traprock ridges marching south. Where the M–M starts its descent for MA 141, turn around.

Locate the **M–M Trail North** at the edge of a picnic area opposite the Trailside Museum. Pass north through a boulder barricade, following a paved lane, to take an immediate left uphill. Again, white diamonds and blazes indicate the foot trail. Traverse a low ridge of hemlock and birch. Despite an abrupt western cliff, the ridge offers no views.

Oak, maple, and mountain laurel soon alternate with the hemlocks. At 0.15 mile, veer right for a steep ascent. Where the trail angles left, the grade calms. Top out at a clearing, finding a 180-degree view, and then detour right to top Goat Peak.

Descend, cross a woods road, and climb trail and stairs to Goat Peak (elevation 822 feet). Atop the peak, a three-story platform unfolds a 360-degree view, with Mount Tom, the Connecticut River, Holyoke, and the Holyoke Range. From this tower, bird-watchers conduct an annual hawk count. Return to the clearing at 0.45 mile and resume the M–M northward, rounding the nose of the ridge, passing through a scenic grove of mountain laurel. Next, descend, crossing over the same woods road to round the north flank of Goat Peak.

Mount Tom view, Mount Tom State Reservation, MA.

At 0.75 mile, the blue Beau Bridge Trail heads right; keep to the M–M Trail, passing an easy-to-miss red-blazed trail in 50 feet. Ascend among oak, maple, birch, and witch hazel, finding moderate-to-steep grades before again following the ridge. Small ledge features dot the woods.

From Dry Knoll at 1.1 miles, overlook an oxbow on the Connecticut River, UMass, and Mounts Sugarloaf and Toby. A descent follows, coming out on Christopher Clark Road (1.25 miles). The M–M continues north, but turn right to reach Mount Nonotuck Vista Parking and the trail to Eyrie House Ruins.

To view the ruins, hike from the end of the paved road, contouring up-hill through deciduous woods. Soon the site's rock walls rise above the trail. At 1.4 miles, reach Eyrie House, built into the slope. Find walls 3 feet thick, arched doorways, and collapsed windows; within the central wall, a door-way frames a northwest view. The return is as you came.

The **Dinosaur Footprints Trail** descends from US 5, quickly forking. The boardwalk straight ahead leads to a large canted sedimentary outcrop just below the highway. The soft rock shows pockmarks from weathering and footprints left eons ago by a society of three-toed dinosaurs. While cut-ting the highway, workers discovered this important record of the past.

The right fork descends, crossing the railroad track to reach the Connecticut River shore, where keen eyes may discover more, although generally fainter, dinosaur tracks. The outcrop along shore also bears fossil casts of plants and tree limbs and the ripples from an ancient shallow lake. Spend some time scrutinizing the rock and admiring the water.

To more easily identify the dinosaur tracks, envision a three-toed foot by grouping your fingers in that arrangement. Now hold your hand above the depressions. The outcrops here hold dozens of prints, coming in three sizes. The largest belonged to the *Eubrontes giganteus* (a carnivore 20 feet long). The medium-size ones record the *Anchisauripus silliman;* the small prints, *Grallator cuneatus.* Find some of the best prints in the highway cut, within 10 feet of the boardwalk. Return as you came.

22 Metacomet–Monadnock Trail, Holyoke Range

General description: This fragment of the long-distance Metacomet–Monadnock (M–M) Trail offers a rolling ridge tour, with both challenging and comfortable stretches. It lags bald summits, rocky knobs, and outcrops, rounding up vistas, and passes Horse Caves, an interesting area of overhangs and rock jumbles.

General location: 5 miles north of South Hadley, Massachusetts.

Special attractions: Vistas, varied woods, Summit House, Notch Visitor Center, fall foliage. The flight path for the spring–fall hawk migration passes over the western extent of the range.

Length: 9.5 miles one-way.

Elevation: Find a 721-foot elevation change; reach the high point atop Mount Norwottuck (1,106 feet), the low at the hike's eastern terminus on Harris Mountain Road (385 feet).

Difficulty: Strenuous.

Maps: Holyoke Range/Skinner State Park trail map.

Special concerns: Expect areas of steep pitches and rises, with poor traction; carry plenty of water; no camping. Because the M–M and some of the cross-trails and woods roads traverse isolated private parcels, keep to the official trails, respecting private ownership and heeding notices.

Season and hours: Spring through fall for hiking. Gates close at 7:00 P.M. Summit House, 11:00 A.M. to 5:00 P.M. weekends and holidays.

For information: Skinner State Park.

Key points:
    0.0   Summit House; hike M–M Trail east.
    0.3   Taylor's Notch.
    2.9   Mount Hitchcock.
    3.8   Bare Mountain.
    4.7   Notch Visitor Center.

6.0   Mount Norwottuck.

6.3   Horse Caves.

8.6   Long Mountain.

9.5   End at Harris Mountain Road.

Finding the trailhead: From the junction of Massachusetts Highways 116 and 47 in South Hadley, go north on MA 47 for 3.4 miles and turn right onto Mountain Road. Go 0.4 mile more and bear right to enter Skinner State Park. Reach Summit House Parking in another 1.6 miles (the park road is open early May to November).

For Notch Visitor Center (a central access point), follow MA 116 northeast from the MA 47–MA 116 junction in South Hadley. To find the hike's eastern terminus, continue north on MA 116 past the visitor center, turn east onto Bay Road, and then turn south onto Harris Mountain Road. The trail is on the right.

The hike: This segment of the **M–M** travels the bumpy 9-mile ridge of the Holyoke Range. Start the hike at the Summit House, atop Mount Holyoke (elevation 940 feet), for an eastbound tour.

Climb the steps and round the Summit House veranda for a superb panoramic view, with clear days adding looks at Mount Monadnock in New Hampshire and Mount Snow in Vermont. Closer to home, admire the Connecticut River Valley and Mounts Tom and Toby. Round to the east side of the veranda, descend the steps, and follow the white blazes east across the picnic area.

In 0.1 mile, the trail drops steeply from the crest, passing through an oak–maple complex, reaching Taylor's Notch (0.3 mile). Cross the road and remain on the white-blazed M–M, ascending steeply. Beware—the loose basaltic rock can steal footing. Top out at an open outcrop (0.6 mile) for a 180-degree view north.

The well-marked trail now molds to the rolling line of the narrow ridge, without edit or censure. Expect some steep, precarious pitches, and enjoy pockets of mountain laurel in the deciduous woods. One by one, top the bumps dubbed the Seven Sisters. Songbirds and both red and gray squirrels offer companionship. At 1.5 miles, find a trail register and another overlook of the valley tapestry.

At an open flat at 2 miles, the M–M curves right; ribbons may mark a second trail to the left. The M–M now travels a carriage-width trail, rounding the north face below the crest. Pass among hemlock and birch before angling back to travel the dry ridgetop. At 2.9 miles, claim Mount Hitchcock, finding a reclining beacon of red iron and concrete foundations. The Mount Hitchcock Trail descends away right; keep to the M–M.

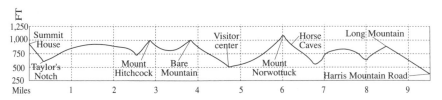

Metacomet–Monadnock Trail, Holyoke Range

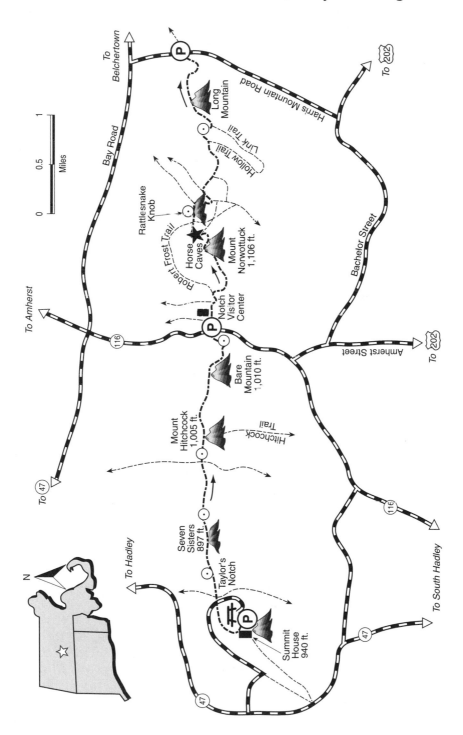

Descend to travel a stand of magnificent mature hemlock, only to ascend sharply from their rich shade. The path now parallels a pair of red pipes. Cross over them, skirt a fenced enclosure, and top Bare Mountain (3.8 miles). Find looks north to the University of Massachusetts (UMass) and south to Springfield, with the Holyoke Range stretching east. A long rocky descent with shallow switchbacks, followed by an easier stretch among the big trees of the lower slope, leads to MA 116 and Notch Visitor Center across the highway (4.7 miles).

Pass through the visitor center parking lot, following the white-blazed M–M along a cabled-off route at the south end of the lot. Skirt the visitor center building to resume the tour east, passing through a maze of well-marked trails. Near the visitor center and Trap Rock Quarry, be alert for several quick direction changes on the M–M.

The orange-blazed Robert Frost Trail (RF) shares the initial distance. Where the shared trail curves left to cross a gravel turnaround beneath utility lines, look for the hike to settle into its ridge-pursuing course. Ascend to a fork; the Robert Frost continues straight, while the M–M bears right on a rootbound tote road, switchbacking uphill.

Follow the woods road and foot trail of the M–M, drifting into the drier forest mix of the upper ridge and reaching the crest (5.5 miles). The interval between paint blazes increases, but the tracked path remains reasonably apparent. At 6 miles, top the rocky summit of Mount Norwottuck, the highest point in the Holyoke Range. Low oaks rim the site and filter looks; best views stretch north.

Follow faint blazes along the outcrop to the next lower tier, and keep right (south). Avoid taking the steep secondary trail down the north flank. The M–M briefly tops the ledge of Horse Caves for a 180-degree eastern perspective, spotlighting Rattlesnake Knob and Long Mountain.

Descend south and east, rounding to the rock jumble and overhangs of Horse Caves for another difficult descent, easing over the rocks. Horse Caves (6.3 miles) traces its name to revolutionary times. It was here, according to local history, that Daniel Shays sheltered the horses for Shays' Rebellion.

An easier segment of trail leads away from the caves; follow the white blazes. Before long, meet up with the orange-blazed Robert Frost Trail, which shares the remainder of the hike east. Regularly blazed, the RF clarifies travel.

Bypass a trail heading left and, in another 0.2 mile, take the 100-foot vista detour left. It follows the ridge of Rattlesnake Knob, ending with a bold look at Long Mountain and a grand window to autumn color. Resume the hike, descending east on the M–M/RF. Where the trail bottoms out, find hemlock and beech. Ahead, bear right along a woods road; the Cliffside Trail descends left to Bay Road in 0.8 mile.

In another 0.1 mile, turn left, still following a woods road, and then stay right as a second trail descends to Bay Road. At 7.25 miles, top a hill with an elevation marker and register. Roll along the ridge and descend to cross the Hollow Trail (8 miles). As the trail next ascends and keeps left, an outcrop to the left offers views of Mount Norwottuck.

Top Long Mountain (elevation 906 feet) at 8.6 miles. Next comes a treacherously steep, boot-skidding descent, crying for a switchback. A tame, relaxing tour follows, passing through a hemlock–hardwood forest with mountain laurel. Arrive at Harris Mountain Road, with its limited trailhead parking, at 9.5 miles. Across the road, the M–M continues its journey toward Mount Monadnock in New Hampshire some 76 miles north.

23   Quabbin Park

OVERVIEW

In the Swift River Valley, a 120,000-acre open space protects Quabbin Reservoir, a 39-square-mile man-made lake providing drinking water for the Boston metropolitan area. In the 1930s, the raised waters claimed four towns. Stone walls, cellars, wells, fruit trees, and roads to nowhere hint at the valley's past. At the lake's south end, Quabbin Park engages hikers with foot trails and abandoned roads. The undisturbed open space hosts a variety of wildlife, with likely sightings of deer, bald eagle, turkey, loon, fox, and beaver.

General description:	Three short hikes provide a peek at the park's offering. Travel mixed woods, top the summit tower, pass cultural remains, and explore the shores of Quabbin Reservoir, Swift River, and Pepper's Mill Pond.
General location:	5 miles west of Ware, Massachusetts.
Special attractions:	Tower vistas, fishing, cultural sites, bald eagles (five nesting pairs, with eighteen remaining year-round), spring wildflowers, fall foliage, fall hawk migration.
Length:	Summit Tower–Reservoir Loop, 3.3-mile loop; Swift River Hike, 1.5 miles round trip; Pepper's Mill Pond Loop, 1-mile loop.
Elevation:	Summit Tower–Reservoir Loop, 500-foot elevation change; Swift River Hike, less than a 50-foot elevation change; Pepper's Mill Pond Loop, virtually flat.
Difficulty:	Summit Tower–Reservoir Loop, easy to moderate; the other two hikes are both easy.
Maps:	Park map, available at visitor center.
Special concerns:	The park is a watershed for Boston's drinking water. Use the provided receptacles for disposing of refuse. No smoking, swimming, wading, horses, dogs, camping, or fires.
Season and hours:	Year-round, daylight hours only; spring through fall for hiking. Visitor center, 8:30 A.M. to 4:30 P.M. weekdays, 9:00 A.M. to 4:30 P.M. weekends.

For information: Metropolitan District Commission, Quabbin Park Visitor Center.

Key points:
Summit Tower–Reservoir Loop:
    0.0   Enfield Lookout trailhead.
    1.0   Quabbin Tower.
    2.3   Hank's Place Picnic Area.
    2.5   Quabbin Reservoir.
    3.3   End loop at Enfield Lookout.

Swift River Hike:
    0.0   Winsor Power Station trailhead.
    0.3   Swift River.
    0.7   Gate near Massachusetts Highway 9 bridge; turn around.

Pepper's Mill Pond Loop:
    0.0   East entrance road trailhead.
    0.4   Cross stream.
    0.8   Cross dam and spillway bridge.
    1.0   End loop at trailhead.

Finding the trailhead: From the junction of MA 32 and MA 9 in Ware, go west on MA 9 for 4.2 miles, finding the east entrance to Quabbin Park and the trailhead to Pepper's Mill Pond on the north side of the highway. Continue west on MA 9 another 1.3 miles to reach the middle entrance, heading north into the park for Winsor Dam, the visitor center, and the other two trailheads. Find the west entrance north off MA 9, 1.6 miles farther west.

    The hikes: For the **Summit Tower–Reservoir Loop,** start at Enfield Lookout, the summit parking lot, or Hank's Place Picnic Area and travel counterclockwise.

    From Enfield Lookout, a popular eagle-watching turnout, locate trail post 23 for the start of the hike, 100 feet south of the turnout on the opposite side of the road. Round the gate and hike uphill on an attractive grassy woods road, touring a slope of white pine, maple, oak, birch, and ash. Huckleberry, fern, and low rock ledges compose the forest floor.

    At the T-junction at 0.1 mile, go left, remaining on woods road, soon entering a grassy clearing with a wooden shed along its southern edge. Traverse the clearing and, at the far side of the building (0.25 mile), turn right. Faint yellow blazes now point hikers into a stand of spruce for foot-trail travel.

    Pass a few abandoned fruit trees to ascend a fern-laced forest of tall hardwoods, replaced, in turn, by the low-stature trees and huckleberry bushes

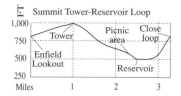

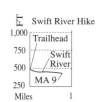

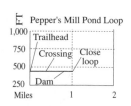

Quabbin Park

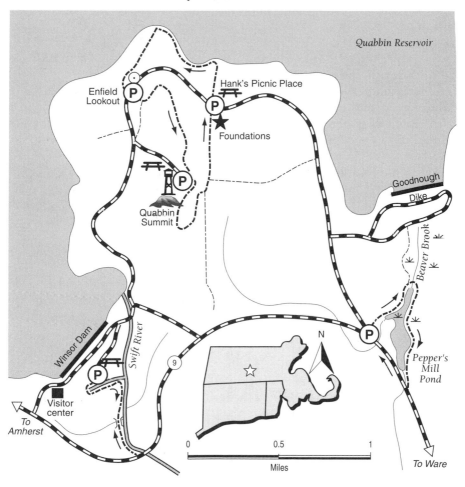

of the upper slope. Filtered lighting, the song of the wind, and a swirl of autumn leaves may contribute to a tour. By 0.9 mile, pass through a stand of teenage trees, skirting a meadow swath to the hiker's left. Come out at the summit parking area, near a picnic table and post that may be missing its number (post 26 on the map).

The loop resumes 100 feet to the left, near the end of the rockwork curb of the summit drive; again look for the faint yellow blazes. But first, cross the summit flat to ascend the paved walk to Quabbin Tower (elevation 1,026 feet). Stairs spiral to the window-enclosed tower loft for views of Quabbin Reservoir, some of its sixty islands, Belchertown, the Berkshires rolling west, and the hilly, wooded Swift River Valley. During the height of hawk migration, some 400 birds a day migrate over the reservoir and past the tower.

Resume the counterclockwise loop at 1.2 miles, skirting the other side of the meadow swath, passing amid oaks. The foot trail descends via lazy sidewinding curves. At 1.6 miles, enter a pine plantation; at 1.7 miles, meet Webster Road (a retired dirt road) and follow it left.

Ahead, big sugar and silver maple, ash, and beech trees line the country lane, as do remnant stone walls. To the right, pass a deer-study enclosure and later a scenic rock border and stone foundation. At post 24 (2.25 miles), cross the park road to follow a northbound paved and gravel lane, skirting the west side of the open lawn of Hank's Place Picnic Area.

Round another gate, passing between thickety hedgerows with fields to either side. Upon reaching the reservoir at 2.5 miles, turn left to round a cove. Travel is either via rocky beach or the deciduous-wooded bank. An unmarked footpath parts the woods and overlooks shore; pines slip into the mix.

At 2.85 miles, find a sunken grade ascending left (south) to Enfield Lookout. Follow the maple-lined corridor uphill, pass another deer-study enclosure, and round the meadow slope below the vista before charging uphill to the park road. Arrive opposite post 23 and turn left for Enfield Lookout (3.3 miles).

At the north end of Winsor Dam, take the side road descending to the base of the dam to reach a picnic area, Winsor Power Station, and the start for the **Swift River Hike.** Park at the picnic area and hike down the paved authorized-vehicle road to Winsor Power Station. In 100 yards, round the fenced enclosure to follow the foot trail heading downstream along the west shore.

Water emerges in a fury from the power station spillway. Mature planted pines clad the steep canyon slope, while riprap shapes an unnatural channel, splashed by the remarkably clear water. Dogwood, bramble, goldenrod, aster, and black-eyed Susan crowd the trail. By 0.2 mile, follow a woods road traversing a broad river bench, with a 10-foot drop to the water. A second path travels the opposite shore.

At 0.3 mile, where the trail curves south, waters from Winsor Dam and the power station merge. Downstream flows a broad, beautiful clear-green river with a natural shore. Because the river offers catch-and-release sport, the dancing lines of fly anglers are commonly spied. Spurs branch to the river for better viewing or access. The woods grow more mixed and offer full shade beyond a power-line corridor. Grassy points and gentle bends add to the river's charm.

At 0.65 mile, find a low grassy point from which to watch the fish. A side brook merges on the right. Downstream, cross a footbridge over this brook; signs caution USE AT YOUR OWN RISK. Next, ascend some 25 feet above the river, where mountain laurel adds to the midstory and river overlooks engage. At 0.75 mile, reach a gate near the MA 9 bridge and turn around.

For the **Pepper's Mill Pond Loop,** find the trailhead on the east entrance road, north of MA 9 before the stone entrance pillars. Post 40 marks the start of this clockwise tour.

Round a gate and proceed east along a grassy woods lane. The hike parallels a drainage, passing amid planted pines and a shrubby understory. In 100 feet, a two-track angles left; continue forward, following the inlet

112

drainage downstream to the pond. Ash, maple, hickory, and chestnut vary the woods, with oaks claiming the upper canopy; beware of poison ivy.

As a foot trail rounds the west shore, lily pads and aquatic grasses decorate the shallows, turtles sun on logs, and fish ripple the water. At 0.2 mile, a grassy point suggests a pause. Vultures make circular passes over the pond, while kingfishers noisily announce their presence. Stranded bobbers rest among the lily pads.

The path—while unmarked—is well trampled, but expect to step over some logs. Sheep laurel colors the banks. Discover the remains of an abandoned beaver lodge, gnawed stumps, and collapsed dens. Despite its proximity, MA 9 only minimally intrudes.

At 0.3 mile, pass beneath a utility line and continue upstream along a beaver-pond outlet. Before long, find a cable stretched between the shores and cross the stream atop some stones. The height of the cable allows only taller hikers to use it to steady their crossing. With the beaver dam breached, a snag-and-meadow marsh has replaced the upstream pond.

Now round the east shore of Pepper's Mill Pond, passing back under the power line. A beaver dam has raised the water of an adjacent bog, creating a second pond, briefly reducing the trail to an isthmus. The water lily bloom or the blush of autumn particularly recommends a tour. Side trails branch to points overlooking Pepper's Mill Pond.

By 0.7 mile, skirt the open water of the outlet cove, crossing the dam and spillway bridge at 0.8 mile. Ascend from the spillway to MA 9 and follow its shoulder west, paralleling the inlet drainage back upstream to the trailhead (1 mile).

24 Purgatory Chasm State Reservation

OVERVIEW

In its 187 wooded acres, this south-central Massachusetts state reservation cradles a picturesque 0.25-mile-long gorge of jumbled rock enclosed by cliffs. The walls, both sheer and jagged, measure from 20 to 70 feet high. A second chasm on the property, Little Purgatory Chasm, captures the drama in miniature and spotlights a scenic grotto and cascade.

General description: Two hikes explore most of the reservation's trails and walkable woods roads. One travels the belly and rim of Purgatory Chasm. The other travels the wooded outskirts, with a side trip to Little Purgatory Chasm.

General location: 10 miles southeast of Auburn, Massachusetts.

Special attractions: Visitor center, a dramatic fissure in solid rock, mixed forests, varied understory, fall foliage.

Length: Chasm Loop Trail, 0.5-mile loop; Charley's Loop–Little Purgatory Hike, 2.6 miles round trip.

Elevation: Trails show less than 100 feet of elevation change.

Difficulty: Chasm Loop Trail, moderate; the Charley's Loop–Little Purgatory Hike is easy.

Maps: State reservation map.

Special concerns: Wear boots and beware of slippery rock. No food or beverages in the chasm. Mountain bikes are prohibited in or around the chasm. Do not climb chasm walls without a permit. Apply for permits at the park, and bring personal climbing gear.

Season and hours: Spring through fall for hiking, daylight hours.

For information: Purgatory Chasm State Reservation.

Key points:

Chasm Loop Trail:
0.0   Chasm Trailhead.
0.2   Devil's Coffin.
0.4   Fat Man's Misery.
0.5   End loop at Chasm Trailhead.

Charley's Loop–Little Purgatory Hike:
0.0   Charley's Loop Trailhead.
0.8   Little Purgatory Chasm Trail.
1.5   Grotto; backtrack to 0.8-mile junction.
2.6   Complete Charley's Loop.

Finding the trailhead: From the junction of U.S. Highway 20 and Massachusetts Highway 146 in North Millbury (south of Worcester), follow MA 146 south for 7.1 miles and turn right (west) onto Purgatory Road. Locate the visitor center on the right in 1.2 miles and trailhead parking on the left in another 0.1 mile.

The hikes: For the **Chasm Loop Trail,** start near the picnic shelter and mapboard. A sign points to the chasm, and blue markers lead the way. Pass into the gorge, negotiating the prescribed route over and between the massive boulders and slabs that litter the chasm floor.

The initial walls rise some 20 feet, with ferns invading the seams and fissures. Lichens and mineral stains accent the cliffs, while hemlock and deciduous trees fringe the rim. Among the rocks, look for etched inscriptions dating to the early 1900s.

The imposing rock shows hues of red, orange, gray, bronze, black, and purple, especially striking when wet. Fissures reveal how the rubble was created; massive overhangs lend drama. After the initial 0.1 mile, dirt trail segments bridge the boulder scrambles, as hikers descend into the chasm's lower bowl. Here, find 70-foot-high sheer walls and named features. Discover the vertical plummet of "Lover's Leap" and the triangular jut of "Devil's Pulpit," both on the right.

As the walls grade lower near the end of the chasm, find "Devil's Coffin" on the right. Aptly named, this feature holds a coffin-shaped rock in the dark recess of a natural mausoleum. A canted slab for a grave marker completes the image. In the drainage at the chasm's mouth grow iris, fern, and grasses.

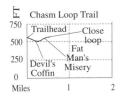

The blue loop then swings left for the return. Skirt the chasm, traveling within a white pine–huckleberry complex, before reaching the rim at "Fat Man's Misery" (0.4 mile). Smooth sides shape this widened fissure, measuring 15 feet deep, 30 feet long, but

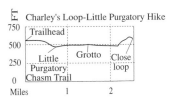

only 18 inches wide. From atop the outcrop, peer into Purgatory Chasm, gaining new perspective. Where the trail next visits the rim, find the boxy opening of "Devil's Corncrib." Complete the hike at the picnic area (0.5 mile).

For the **Charley's Loop–Little Purgatory Hike,** follow the paved lane between the picnic shelter and the stone rest room hut, reaching the cabled-off woods road of Charley's Loop; yellow blazes point the way.

Pass among picnic sites to explore the periphery woods of hemlock, hardwood, and pine, well removed from Purgatory Chasm. Enjoy an attractive lane and comfortable slow descent. Huckleberry, mayflower, twisted stalk, sarsaparilla, and fern contribute to the understory flora. Large boulders offer trailside seating.

At 0.5 mile, turn right, now following yellow and blue markers along a narrow woods road that parts a varied woods. Ignore the unmarked side trails and any errant blazes without trails. At 0.8 mile, reach a multiple junction where a hard right on an old woods road enters Purgatory Chasm near Devil's Coffin, the yellow- and blue-blazed Charley's Loop continues on a footpath angling uphill along the chasm's west rim, and the main woods road proceeds straight for Little Purgatory Chasm and Trail.

Before completing the loop, detour forward on the woods road to visit Little Purgatory Chasm. In less than 0.1 mile, find a junction; the main road ahead is Little Purgatory Trail. Turn left onto the smaller woods road for the actual hike to Little Purgatory Chasm. In 50 feet, turn right onto an unmarked grassy lane entering woods. Before long, a footpath replaces the vegetated lane, paralleling Purgatory Brook upstream.

Step around and between the rocks along the shore, coming to a grotto cupped by 10-foot-high solid rock. There, find a small cascade at the confluence of Little Purgatory and Purgatory Brooks. By climbing the slope to follow Little Purgatory Brook upstream, gain an overlook of this smaller chasm before the trail ends in 200 feet.

Future plans call for a return trail. Meanwhile, backtrack downstream, returning to the 0.8- mile junction at 2.3 miles. Follow the yellow- and blue-marked foot trail uphill to the left to complete the clockwise hike of Charley's Loop.

Travel a rock-studded forest of beech, maple, white pine, and black and chestnut oak, adding hemlock as the trail progresses. At 2.5 miles, overlook

Purgatory Chasm State Reservation

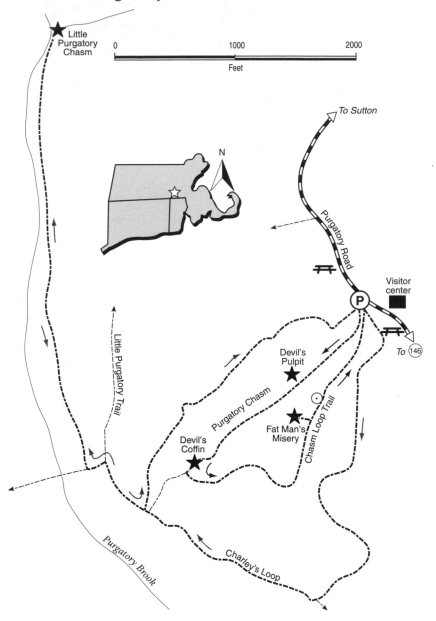

Purgatory Chasm. Top a rise and descend to the picnic area, arriving amid massive outcrops and boulders.

An alternative return travels the woods road of the Little Purgatory Trail north to the woods road of the Old Purgatory Trail. Turn right onto the Old Purgatory Trail and again onto Purgatory Road to return to the picnic area and trailhead for a 3-mile hike; consult the park map.

25 Blackstone River and Canal Heritage State Park

OVERVIEW

Part of a greater national heritage corridor, this 1,000-acre state park celebrates the Industrial Age. Within its borders, find nearly 6 miles of the twisting Blackstone River and some of the best-preserved sections of the 45-mile historic canal that linked Providence, Rhode Island, and Worcester, Massachusetts. The Blackstone River both powered manufacturing and transported the raw material and finished product of the region's eighteenth- and nineteenth-century mills. Its counterpart canal operated from 1828 to 1848, when it was superseded by railroads.

General description:	Two hikes explore the park, traveling multiple-use trails. The Towpath Hike travels a scenic, mostly natural corridor through the old industrial beltway. King Philip's Trail travels the wooded hillside above Rice City Pond, ending at a prominent rock overlook.
General location:	East of Massachusetts Highway 122 in Uxbridge and Northbridge.
Special attractions:	Historical locks, dams, bridge abutments, and foundation; scenic woods and wetland; vistas; wildlife.
Length:	Towpath Hike, 4 miles one-way; King Philip's Trail, 2.6 miles round trip.
Elevation:	Towpath Hike, 50-foot elevation change; King Philip's Trail, 150-foot elevation change.
Difficulty:	Both easy.
Maps:	State park map.
Special concerns:	Come prepared for mosquitoes.
Season and hours:	Year-round; spring through fall for hiking. Daylight hours.
For information:	Blackstone River and Canal Heritage State Park.

Key points:
Towpath Hike:
- 0.0   Southern trailhead.
- 1.0   River Bend Farm.
- 1.2   Hartford Avenue.
- 2.2   Plummer's Trail.
- 4.0   End at Plummer's Landing.

King Philip's Trail:
- 0.0   King Philip's Trailhead.
- 1.3   Lookout Rock; return as you came.

Finding the trailhead: From the MA 122–MA 16 junction in Uxbridge, go east on MA 16 for 0.5 mile and turn left onto Cross Street to find parking for the southern terminus of the towpath behind Stanley Woolen Mill.

For King Philip's Trail and the park headquarters, go 1.2 miles north on MA 122 from its junction with MA 16 and turn right onto Hartford Avenue. Find parking on the left in 1.3 miles. Reach Plummer's Landing, the northern terminus for the Towpath Hike, on Church Street, east off MA 122, 2.4 miles north of Hartford Avenue.

The hikes: The **Towpath Hik**e links the following named park trails: Blackstone Canal and Towpath, Goat Hill Trail, and Plummer's Trail. Northbound, start behind the Stanley Woolen Mill. Built in the early 1850s, this mill processed raw wool into finished dye cloth and supplied American troops with vital blanket and overcoat fabric.

Hike north on Blackstone Canal and Towpath, crossing a footbridge. The levee initially shows an open herbaceous bank, with aspen, oak, maple, birch, sumac, and elm growing at the sides. Travel the east bank of the dark canal water, passing picnic sites on the right.

At 0.2 mile, cross a bridge at a 1917 spillway where the released water slips over bedrock speeding to the flowing river. Woods and marsh woodlands now claim the right-hand side of the levee, lending shade and charm to the corridor. Watch for historic rock constructions along the canal.

The channel broadens near the bridge to River Bend Farm on the west shore (1 mile). The farm's scenic red barn, serenely reflected in the canal waters, holds the park visitor center. Turtles, polliwogs, fish, and herons may suggest a pause.

At 1.2 miles, reach the dike at Gatehouse Lock, with the Blackstone River flowing to the right and a fine reflection of Stone Arch Bridge to the north. Cross the dike and ascend through a picnic area to Hartford Avenue.

Next, cross the road and pass north through an open field, finding a kiosk and a sign for a multiple-use trail. The hike now follows the Goat Hill Trail to the right of the kiosk, traveling an earthen lane along the base of Goat Hill. Hardwoods mostly screen out any eastern looks at Rice City Pond, now mainly a marsh. Builders created the pond in the 1800s for flood control and a low-water reserve. For this hike, forgo the trails ascending left that top Goat Hill; keep to the waterway.

At 1.5 miles, pass below a balanced split rock, finding an open view of Rice City Pond. The trail now rolls and narrows, encountering rock walls. Pass through a breach in one of the walls, coming to a junction at 2.1 miles. Descend right for Goat Hill Lock and the next canal segment. The stone-lined channel of the lock frames a southern look at Rice City Pond.

Cross the canal on cross-laid logs and resume north on Plummer's Trail. The levee passes between a wooded bottomland and canal wetland. At

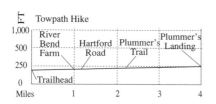

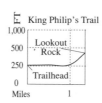

Blackstone River and Canal Heritage State Park

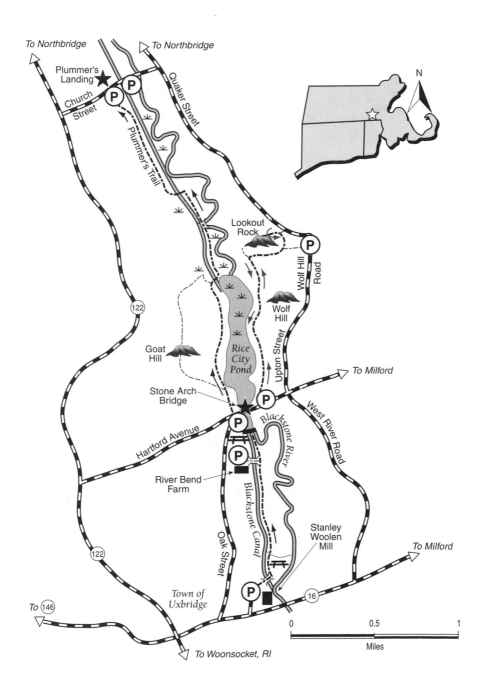

To Northbridge

To Northbridge

Plummer's Landing

Church Street

Quaker Street

Plummer's Trail

122

Lookout Rock

Wolf Hill Road

Wolf Hill

Goat Hill

Rice City Pond

To Milford

Stone Arch Bridge

Blackstone River

West River Road

Hartford Avenue

River Bend Farm

Blackstone Canal

Oak Street

Stanley Woolen Mill

To Milford

122

Town of Uxbridge

16

To 146

To Woonsocket, RI

N

0   0.5   1

Miles

River Bend Farm Visitor Center, Blackstone River and Canal Heritage State Park, MA.

2.5 miles, glimpse the braided glimmer of the Blackstone River as it flows closer to the towpath. Where the trail crosses a woods road that accesses the river, an opening adds looks at an island and the wooded ridge of Lookout Rock. A few azalea adorn the corridor. At 2.7 miles, footbridges span a breach between canal and river.

At the junction post and bench seat at 2.9 miles, turn left, crossing a filled-in portion of the canal to again hike north along the west shore. Pass between field and woods, skirting a big sycamore at 3.4 miles. Soon after, glimpse a breach mingling river flow with canal water. At the junction at 3.75 miles, proceed forward for Plummer's Landing; the path to the right leads to a canoe access and picnic area. On the north side of Church Street, excavated foundations recall the store and commercial hub opened by Israel Plummer in 1837.

For **King Philip's Trail,** start at the parking lot west of the headquarters and hike north on a cable-closed gravel lane. Edge a grassy area below the tree and rock slope of Wolf Hill, passing a couple of picnic tables. Oak, aspen, and planted pine cover the slope, but the trail remains open.

At 0.2 mile, briefly enter a mature pine plantation. The wetland of Rice City Pond claims the foot of the slope, with skunk cabbage, cattail, loosestrife, and sweet pepperbush. The foot trail is thin and canted. At 0.4 mile, traverse a gravel flat; a few blue markers point the way. Spurs branch left toward the pond. A screech can announce the passing of a hawk overhead.

The trail mildly rolls, keeping some 20 feet above the wetland pond. Stay left, passing an abandoned trail uphill to the right. Dip to cross a drainage (1 mile), again touring a pine flat. At 1.1 miles, reach another junction. The worn dirt trail to the left leads to the base of Lookout Rock with its overhangs and myriad scrambles to the top. Follow the woods road ascending to the right between plantation and outcrop for a more tempered approach to the summit.

In 0.1 mile, veer left; the woods road ahead meets Quaker Street. At 1.25 miles, top a rise, finding a second link to this neighborhood street. Here, a short spur to the left tops an outcrop for looks at Goat Hill, Rice City Pond, and Stone Arch Bridge.

Resume the rolling hike toward Lookout Rock and follow either foot trail or woods road arcing left. Mount the rock at 1.3 miles for a grand area overview. Enjoy the meandering glint of the Blackstone River as it parts the wetland meadow of Rice City Pond. Wolf and Goat Hills shape the basin, and soaring vultures add to the overall impression. The return is as you came.

26 Laughing Brook Wildlife Sanctuary

OVERVIEW

Threaded by Laughing Brook and the Scantic River, this 354-acre sanctuary of the Massachusetts Audubon Society engages with woodland, field, riparian, and wetland habitats. The sanctuary also protects the home of Thornton W. Burgess, a children's author who drew from this natural setting for his animal tales. The storyteller's home, a national historic place, dates to 1780.

General description: Four short nature trails examine the sanctuary offering.

General location: In Hampden, Massachusetts.

Special attractions: Bird- and wildlife-watching; brook, pond, and river; wildflowers; fall foliage.

Length: Burgess House Trail–Crooked Little Path, 0.7-mile round trip (1.2 miles adding the Big River Loop–Red Pine Trail, when the Scantic River can be forded safely); Storyteller's Trail–Neff Loop, 2.5 miles round trip; Green Forest Trail, 1.2 miles round trip; Smiling Pool Path–Jimmy Skunk Loop, 0.5-mile round trip.

Elevation: Burgess House Trail–Crooked Little Path and Smiling Pool Path–Jimmy Skunk Loop, less than a 40-foot elevation change; Storyteller's Trail–Neff Loop, 200-foot elevation change; Green Forest Trail, 100-foot elevation change.

Difficulty: All easy.

Maps: Sanctuary trail map.

Special concerns: Per-person admission fee or Massachusetts Audubon Society membership; obey posted rules. Find the characteristic Audubon blazing, with blue heading away from the trailhead, yellow returning.

Season and hours: Year-round, Tuesday through Sunday and Monday holidays. Grounds, dawn to dusk; nature center, 10:00 A.M. to 4:00 P.M. Tuesday through Saturday, 12:30 P.M. to 4:00 P.M. Sundays and Monday holidays.

For information: Laughing Brook Education Center and Wildlife Sanctuary.

Key points:

Burgess House Trail–Crooked Little Path:
- 0.0 Education center trailhead.
- 0.2 Crooked Little Path loop junction.
- 0.3 Scantic River seasonal crossing.
- 0.5 Close loop; backtrack to trailhead.

Storyteller's Trail–Neff Loop:
- 0.0 Education center trailhead.
- 0.1 Storyteller's Trail junction.
- 0.6 Neff Trail loop junction.
- 1.9 Close Neff Trail loop; backtrack to trailhead.

Green Forest Trail:
- 0.0 Education center trailhead.
- 0.2 Loop junction.
- 0.4 Split boulder.
- 1.0 Complete loop; backtrack to trailhead.

Smiling Pool Path–Jimmy Skunk Loop:
- 0.0 Education center trailhead.
- 0.2 Jimmy Skunk Loop junction.

0.3   Close Skunk Loop; turn right onto Smiling Pool Path.

0.5   End at education center trailhead.

Finding the trailhead: From the junction of Massachusetts Highways 220 and 83 in East Longmeadow, go south on MA 83 toward Hampden, Massachusetts, and Somers, Connecticut. In 1.5 miles, turn left onto Hampden Road, go 2.6 miles, and turn right onto Somers Road at the sign for Laughing Brook. Go 0.2 mile, turn left onto Main Street, and continue 2 miles more, turning left off Main Street into the sanctuary's parking lot. Start all trails behind the education center at the fee and map station.

The hikes: For the **Burgess House Trail–Crooked Little Path,** head left on Smiling Pool Path and in 100 feet take the Burgess House Trail left downstream along East Brook. Within its shady corridor of maple, oak, hornbeam, elm, and witch hazel, this laughing brook speaks in babbles and is scenic, dark, and clear.

Cross the footbridge, skirt behind a building, and bear left past the Storyteller's House to cross Main Street at a crosswalk; exercise caution at the crossing, supervising youngsters. At the edge of a meadow starts the Crooked Little Path, a loop; bear left for clockwise travel. The footpath enters a tanglewood of elm, maple, and grapevine, still pursuing East Brook downstream. At 0.25 mile, a spur breaks to the stream as the tour bears right.

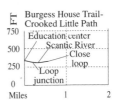

At 0.3 mile, at the site of a former bridge, view the Scantic River, a designated scenic river referred to as the Big River in the stories of Thornton Burgess. The Big River Loop–Red Pine Trail network occupies the opposite shore and is accessible when low water levels allow a safe, but wet crossing. The Crooked Little Path continues downstream along the river and across the meadow to complete its loop. Return to the crosswalk at 0.5 mile and the education center at 0.7 mile.

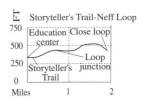

When the Scantic can be forded, a 0.5-mile clockwise tour joining the Big River Loop and Red Pine Trail passes through woods of white and red pines and deciduous trees and has a boardwalk option through wetland woods. It ends in a spruce plantation before returning hikers to the fording site.

For the **Storyteller's Trail–Neff Loop,** retrace the start of the last hike, following Smiling Pool Path left to the Burgess House Trail and crossing East Brook. Turn right onto the Storyteller's Trail at the junction behind the building east of the Storyteller's House. This trail ascends the west ridge above East Brook. Spruce and maple cloak the slope. At 0.3 mile, bear left. As the ridge widens to a plateau, oak, pine, and hickory fill out the woods. Enjoy a relaxing woods meander.

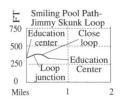

123

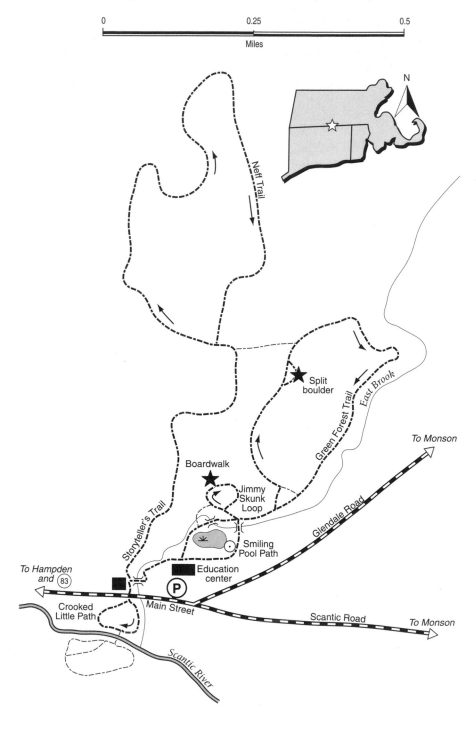

Laughing Brook Wildlife Sanctuary

0   0.25   0.5
Miles

N

Neff Trail

Split boulder

East Brook

Green Forest Trail

To Monson

Boardwalk

Jimmy Skunk Loop

Storyteller's Trail

Smiling Pool Path

Glendale Road

To Hampden and (83)

Education center

P

Crooked Little Path

Main Street

Scantic Road   To Monson

Scantic River

At 0.6 mile, bear left onto the Neff Trail; the Storyteller's Trail continues right. Ahead, reach the loop junction and again bear left. Alternately pass among pines and mixed woods on this rolling trail; in autumn, find a pleasant leaf shuffle.

By 1 mile, ascend through a dark hemlock woods, keeping a sharp eye out for blue blazes. In places, mountain or sheep laurel, club moss, and huckleberry adorn the woods, and a few aspen enliven the canopy. Step over and through stone walls. Grouse, deer, fox, chickadee, and toad may be spied. At 1.3 miles, yellow markers indicate the halfway point and the start of the return. Now look for a few exceptionally big trees. Close the loop and return to the Storyteller's Trail at 1.9 miles. Backtrack to the education center (2.5 miles).

From the trailhead, the **Green Forest Trail** follows Smiling Pool Path to the right, past a deck overlooking the small wildlife pond, with willows contributing to its thickly wooded rim and catfish and minnows in the dark water. Shortly after, pass the Meadow Training Station on the right.

Cross the bridge over East Brook and keep right along the brook for the Green Forest Trail. Seasonal offerings enhance travel and suggest repeat visits. Discover hawk and butterfly migrations in fall, snow fleas in winter, wildflowers in spring, and cicadas in summer.

Pine–deciduous woods shade the hike where it parallels East Brook upstream. At the loop junction (0.2 mile), bear left for clockwise travel and a mild ascent. Hemlocks bring a richer shade. Keep left where the Lone Little Path cuts the loop. At 0.4 mile, a fork to the right offers a 100-foot side trip to a 9-foot-high cleanly split boulder.

Proceed forward past the Storyteller's Trail, journeying among pines. Gradually, yellow replaces blue as the guiding color. Along a sturdy rock wall, find a 3-foot-diameter pine and Great Oak, monarchs of the woods. Next, overlook an S-bend of East Brook and a vernal pool. Again keep left at the cut-across path to bring the loop to a close at 1 mile. Return to the trailhead (1.2 miles).

For the **Jimmy Skunk Loop,** follow the **Smiling Pool Path** right, crossing over East Brook. At the upcoming junction, proceed northwest off the pool path for the Jimmy Skunk Trail. Walk past the Tree Platforms, coming to the loop junction (0.2 mile). Turn left for a clockwise tour, keeping right where a second access spur approaches the loop. The hike travels the site's Oak Forest Boardwalk and tops attractive tiered platforms for sanctuary overlooks. A wild turkey vulture may circle overhead. Complete the loop and return to the Smiling Pool Path, turning right to explore the west shore back to the trailhead (0.5 mile).

Eastern Massachusetts Trails

This region features the foothills and flatter reaches of the state, including the white-sand beaches and wildlife lands of the northern coast and the inspired landscapes of Cape Cod peninsula. Even near the cosmopolitan center of Boston, prized open spaces offer solitude, natural discovery, and adventure. Lowland woods, meadows, ponds, swamps, rocky hilltops, the sleepy Charles River, pristine dunes, and coastal and bay shores vary travel.

27 Parker River National Wildlife Refuge

OVERVIEW

This 4,662-acre national wildlife refuge occupies the southern two-thirds of Plum Island, a classic Atlantic barrier island. Drumlins (low hills left behind by the last retreating glacier) gave rise to the island, collecting ocean-deposited sand and silt that later fused into a single land mass. The refuge encompasses a dune–beach complex, tidal flat, freshwater marsh, stunted pines, and cranberry bogs.

Piping plovers, which nearly vanished in the 1800s, nest at the seaward toe of the dunes. Because beachgoers inadvertently threaten the bird's success, the refuge closes its beach to the public during the crucial summer nesting season.

General description: Short nature trails explore the various habitats and offer refuge overlooks. When open, the beach offers 6.5 miles of uninterrupted strolling.

General location: South of Newburyport, Massachusetts.

Special attractions: Nesting piping plovers and migrating shorebirds and waterfowl; summer-flocking swallows; plum and cranberry picking (from the Tuesday after Labor Day through October 31); clamming; surf fishing; observation platforms and blinds.

Length: Hellcat Swamp Nature Trail, 1-mile loop, with option to extend; Pines Trail, 0.4 mile round trip; Beach Hike, 6.5 miles one-way.

Elevation: Hikes are flat or show minimal elevation change.

Difficulty: All easy.

Maps: Refuge map.

Special concerns: Entrance fee; when parking lots fill, the refuge closes its gates. Visitors may pick one quart of plums and/or cranberries per person per day. Otherwise, there is no collecting of natural objects, and no collecting of beach-stranded fishing gear. Leave pets at home, keep off the dunes, and carry insect repellent. Green-headed flies and mosquitoes can annoy, even on the beach.

Season and hours: Year-round, sunrise to sunset. The beach is closed April 1 through mid- to late August. (Any beach segments unclaimed for nests are gradually opened to the public starting July 1.)

For information: Parker River National Wildlife Refuge.

Key points:

Hellcat Swamp Nature Trail:
- 0.0 Hellcat Swamp Trailhead.
- 0.1 Marsh Loop.
- 0.4 Observation blind.
- 0.9 Close loop; return to trailhead.

Pines Trail:
- 0.0 Pines Trailhead.
- 0.1 Loop junction; keep left.
- 0.2 Barricade/marsh overlook; backtrack to trailhead.

Beach Hike:
- 0.0 Parking Area 1 trailhead.
- 0.6 North Beach, Parking Area 2.
- 5.1 South Beach.
- 6.5 End at Parking Area 7 and observation platform.

Finding the trailhead: In Newburyport, go north on U.S. Highway 1/Massachusetts Highway 1A and bear right onto Water Street prior to the Merrimack Bridge. Follow Water Street south, turning left (east) onto Sunset/Plum Island Turnpike to enter the refuge on the right. From the entrance station, drive south

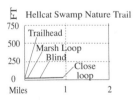

through the refuge, finding Beach Parking Area 1 in 0.1 mile, Hellcat Swamp Nature Trail in 3.6 miles, the Pines Trail in 4.4 miles, and Parking Area 7 in 6.5 miles. Enter Sandy Point State Reservation south of Parking Area 7. Respect posted slow speeds, and park only in designated sites.

The hikes: For the **Hellcat Swamp Trail**, round the gate, following the wide lane north from Parking Area 4. Pass through a corridor of honeysuckle, wild rose, wild plum, bayberry, Virginia creeper, poison ivy, and poison sumac. Watch your step as a multilevel boardwalk advances the tour.

In 100 yards, the trail forks. The right fork crosses the refuge road for a 0.3-mile boardwalk tour of the dunes (subject to summer closures for nesting birds). Proceed forward for an elevated-boardwalk tour of the freshwater marsh. At 0.1 mile, reach the Marsh Loop and head left (clockwise).

Loosestrife, sensitive fern, grasses, and cattails grow in the marsh. Drumlins and treed islands break the flatness of the wetland terrain. Swallows

127

Parker River National Wildlife Refuge

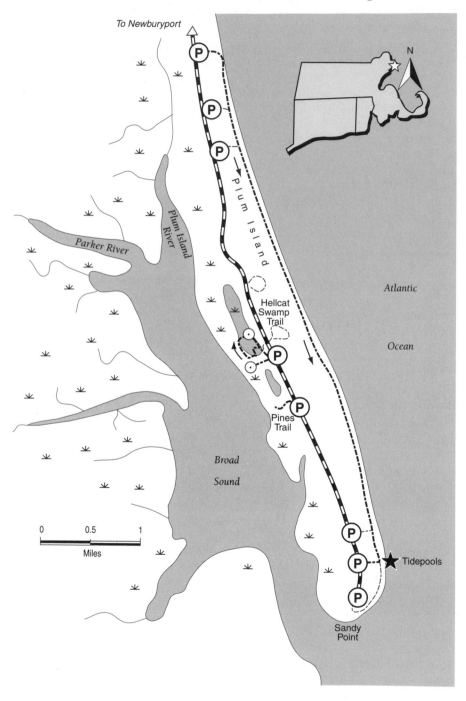

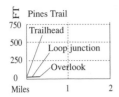

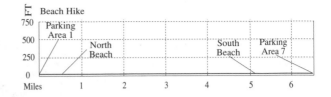

flock over the marsh, while a hawk hunts low to the rushes. At 0.4 miles, a spur heads left to an observation blind.

A wetland woods ushers hikers to this open-air, three-sided blind. Peering through the viewing slots, locate deer, hawks, gulls, geese, ducks, and other wildlife. Resume clockwise travel at 0.7 mile, remaining among wetland trees and shrubs. Close the loop at 0.9 mile, and retrace the initial 0.1 mile to the trailhead.

To extend the tour, hike west from Parking Area 4 on gravel lane and footpath, reaching a dike beyond the rest rooms. Travel atop the dike to a three-flight observation tower. The platform overlooks the channeled waters of the freshwater marsh and Broad Sound estuary. Watch for geese, gulls, shorebirds, and raptors, with snowy egrets in August. When ready, return to the parking area (0.25 mile).

Just north of Parking Area 5, the **Pines Trail** journeys west through a stand of runty pitch pine and thick shrub; a loose-sand path leads the way. Wintering owls favor this site. Beach plum and bayberry contribute to the congestion of shrubs. At 0.1 mile, find a loop junction; stay left as the path to the right becomes severely pinched and overgrown with poison ivy. End the hike at the wooden barricade at 0.2 mile, enjoying a marsh look. Return as you came to the trailhead.

The **Beach Hike** travels 6.5 miles between Parking Areas 1 and 7. A broad crystalline-sand beach spreads between the tideline and the toe of the dunes. On a north–south journey, the natural beach of the refuge quickly replaces the civilized beach of town. The close-breaking waves create a cant along the lower beach. When churned by Atlantic storms, find a dazzling show of fury.

Farther south, the tide-washed beach loses its cant for easier strolling, and the waves flatten for a calmer aspect. Boardwalks accessing the parking areas, a breakwater, and Emerson Rocks mark off distance. For the length of the tour, dunes back the beach. Dune grass, false heather, wild rose, and beach plum stabilize the shifting sands. You may be tempted to explore more deeply, but respect this delicate area by traveling only along the boardwalk accesses.

Seaweed, buoys, lobster pots, clamshells, and drift logs capture beachcombers' attention, while the rocky tidepools at the south end of the tour draw the curious to their knees. Discoveries include barnacles, sea stars, crabs, and snails. In January and February, harbor seals sun on the main beach. Hikers may extend the walk south via the adjoining Sandy Point State Reservation, rounding to a treed point.

Tidepool rocks, Parker River National Wildlife Refuge, MA.

28 Crane Memorial Beach Reservation

OVERVIEW

Once the summer retreat of Chicago industrialist Richard T. Crane, this property of the Trustees of Reservations unites Castle Neck, a white-sand barrier beach backed by spectacular rolling dunes, and Castle Hill, a mansion estate overlooking the natural oceanscape. The Agawam Indians first occupied this area, harvesting fish and shellfish. In 1633, John Winthrop established the first organized settlement here.

General description: The hikes explore Castle Neck, traveling ocean and bay shore and rolling across dunes. Mileage markers and numbered stakes aid in navigating trails.

General location: About 4.5 miles southeast of Ipswich, Massachusetts.

Special attractions: Nesting piping plovers and least terns; areas of both wild and bathing beach; dunes; salt marsh; stunted forest; cranberry bogs; ocean, bay, and Castle Hill views.

Length: Crane Beach–Essex Bay Hike, 6 miles round trip; Dunes Loop, 4.1 miles round trip, with opportunities to shorten.

Elevation: Crane Beach–Essex Bay Hike, 30-foot elevation change; Dunes Loop, 70-foot elevation change.

Difficulty: Both moderate (due to loose sands).

Maps: The Crane Properties map.

Special concerns: Separate admission fees apply for Crane Beach (Castle Neck) and the Castle Hill site; phone before visiting Castle Hill. No dune play. Although hikers may roam the dunes, keep to the prescribed trails to preserve this special landscape. Rangers regularly patrol the area to police inappropriate behavior. Respect nesting closures, granting the endangered birds a wide safety margin. Beware of poison ivy and ticks, which can carry Lyme disease. Carry water.

Season and hours: Year-round, 8:00 A.M. to sunset.

For information: The Trustees of Reservations, Northeast Regional Office.

Key points:
Crane Beach–Essex Bay Hike:
- 0.0   Crane Beach Access.
- 1.5   Loop junction; continue south on beach.
- 2.7   River mouth/end of Castle Neck.

3.7 Follow yellow trail into dunes.

4.5 End loop at Crane Beach; backtrack north.

Dunes Loop:

0.0 Dunes Trailhead.

0.1 Loop junction.

0.9 Wigwam Hill.

1.8 Marsh view.

4.0 Complete loop; return to trailhead.

Finding the trailhead: From the junction of Massachusetts Highways 1A and 133 at the South Ipswich village green, go east on Argilla Road for 4.2 miles to enter Crane Beach.

The hikes: For the **Crane Beach–Essex Bay Hike,** cross to the beach on the boardwalk behind the information and first-aid station and turn right (southeast). Dune grass and beach pea anchor the shifting sands, while a broad bathing beach spans the width of the parking area. Most people linger within comfortable reach of the bathhouse, leaving hikers a long open-beach invitation.

Low tides unveil an expansive braided beach that stretches well into Ipswich Bay. The cutoff shallow pools and trickling channels isolate bars and islands of rippled sand for an eye-pleasing mosaic. The compressed sand offers easy strolling. High tides reveal an even-width strand of blinding white sand meeting the brilliant blue ocean. Waves break mildly to shore. Above the high-tide line, encounter beach closures (April through August) protecting the nests of the piping plover and least tern. Confine strolling to the tide-washed sands.

For the first 0.5 mile, a flat grassy plain grades to the dune hills behind the beach. Beyond the 0.5-mile mark, find abutting dune banks, with swallows nesting in the more stable seams. Looks south applaud Cape Ann, over-the-shoulder looks the "Great House" atop Castle Hill.

Drying seaweed and uprooted dune grass scatter the upper edge of the beach. Beginning at 0.9 mile, color-coded trails pass between beach and dunes. When using these, keep to the narrow travel aisles and pass swiftly to avoid scoldings from the nesting tern colonies.

A gull dropping a clam from 50 feet high, terns bathing in a standing pool, or a piping plover darting across the sand may enhance a journey. The dunes variously reveal grass-capped mounds, bald swayback ridges, and turrets of compacted sand. The yellow trail emerging from the dunes at 1.5 miles marks the return from Essex Bay.

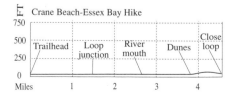

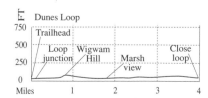

Crane Memorial Beach Reservation

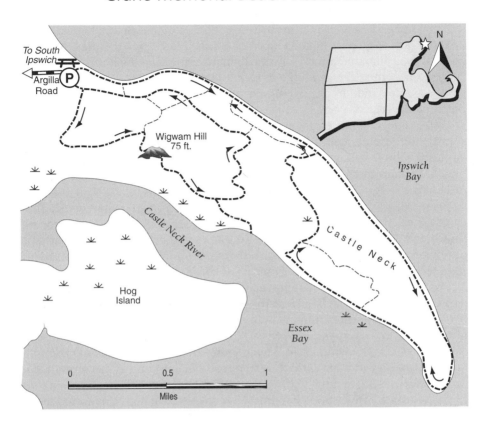

Keep to the ocean beach. Near the end of Castle Neck (2.65 miles), the dunes flatten out. Round the broad beach curvature, now overlooking the spot where Castle Neck River meets the mouth of Essex Bay. Gray numbered stakes point the way. Hog Island, a wildlife refuge owned by the Trustees, commands the views. The bay-shore sand displacing underfoot provides a workout.

Bypass the first yellow-marked trail entering the dunes at post 10 and continue rounding the pinched bay shore, overlooking a tidal marsh with cordgrass and other salt tolerant species. Beach pea dresses the dune. Look for herons and egrets within the marsh. Beyond the marsh, the beach opens up. Low dunes build between the gray stakes and bay.

At 3.75 miles, turn right onto the yellow trail, mounting the dunes for a rolling tour back to the beach. At 3.9 miles, where the yellow spur arrives from post 10, bear left. Low undulations, steep sandy ascents, and beach–bay glimpses highlight the hike's dune segment. Pockets of aspen, black cherry, beach plum, bayberry, and poison ivy claim the swales; false heather, with its fleeting yellow bloom, mats the slopes. At 4.25 miles, skirt a natural cranberry bog.

At 4.4 miles, where the blue trail continues the journey through the dunes, follow the yellow trail out of the dunes and onto the beach. Turn left on the beach at 4.5 miles, and hike back to the parking area (6 miles).

The **Dunes Loop** leaves the southern end of Crane Beach Parking Area next to a large sign posting the reservation rules. This open trek ties the green and red trails into a counterclockwise loop (backtracking the numbered posts).

Pass through a tree-shaded corridor and turn right at 0.1 mile, following a 4-foot-wide sandy track, edging the forested dunes. False heather spreads between trail and woods.

At 0.6 mile, approach a segment of wooden fence, briefly traveling an open stand of pitch pine, wild plum, red oak, and birch. In places, shifting sands engulf the lower branches of the pines, and winds cause the aspens to tremble. An open dune follows. Bear right onto the red trail (0.8 mile) for the 4-mile loop; the green trail heads left for a shorter tour.

Round a bowl and top Wigwam Hill (elevation 75 feet) for an overlook of Castle Neck, Essex Bay, Hog Island, and the ocean. With a steep descent, find afternoon shade among some red maple and cherry trees, but beware of poison ivy. More forest and shrub thickets follow as the trail ascends and rolls to the next bay view, overlooking a salt-marsh plain.

Dip bayside and find a junction at 1.5 miles. To the right, a 0.7-mile round-trip detour tags the bay shore at the marsh. Solitude and fine views of the bay and Hog Island recommend the detour, but high tides can steal much of the tidal flat.

Now resume the counterclockwise loop through Castle Neck Dunes, enjoying a tapestry of open sand, forest, shrub pockets, and beach grass. Deer, red foxes, harriers, and the yellow-rumped warblers of fall may grace a tour. In winter, snowy owls have been known to take refuge in the protected dunes habitat.

At 2.6 miles (post 14), continue straight ahead, still backtracking the red numbers; the red-marked spur to the right accesses the yellow and blue trails and, ultimately, the beach. The trail next rolls, topping a series of dune rises for ocean overlooks. At 3.25 miles, again proceed forward as spurs branch to the beach and across the dunes.

Green-colored posts serve as guides, as the trail traverses and rolls up the sides of open sand bowls. At the 3.5-mile fork, bear right, and at 3.7 miles bypass another spur to the beach. As the loop nears the parking area and recreational beach, respect closures that protect the nesting birds and the integrity of the dunes. Close the loop at 4 miles; reach the parking area at 4.1 miles.

29 Bald Hill Reservation

OVERVIEW

This joint-agency open space at the town intersect of Boxford, Andover, and Middleton, Massachusetts, offers tranquil woods strolling, wetland ponds, and a historical farmsite. Bald Hill Reservation encompasses 867-acre Boxford State Forest, the 390-acre J. C. Phillips Wildlife Sanctuary, and nearly 370 acres of the Essex County Greenbelt Association. The site boasts a varied flora, both familiar and rare. Cobbles host hepatica, bloodroot, and columbine; bogs feature rose pogonia and swamp azalea; and the woods seclude yellow wood sorrel, violet, and lady's slipper.

General description:	Within the reservation's interlocking trail system, multiple round-trip and loop hike options exist; the selected loop unveils the typical discovery. Carry a map to plot travel and negotiate the numbered trail junctions.
General location:	2 miles southwest of Boxford.
Special attractions:	Mixed forest, wetland, ponds, historical farmsite, wildflowers, wildlife, fall foliage.
Length:	7.7 miles round trip, with spur to Bald Hill.
Elevation:	Find a 100-foot elevation change.
Difficulty:	Easy to moderate.
Maps:	Bald Hill Reservation map (generally available at trailhead); Boxford State Forest map.
Special concerns:	No hiking off the trail in the wildlife sanctuary between April 1 and July 1. Overnight camping is by special permit only. Look for metal posts or wooden number tags on nearby trees to identify junctions.
Season and hours:	Spring through fall; the area closes thirty minutes after sunset.
For information:	Boxford State Forest; Essex County Greenbelt Association.

Key points:

0.0 Middleton Road trailhead.
0.4 Crooked Pond vantage.
0.7 Loop junction (post 13).
1.3 Bald Hill.
1.8 Russell Hooper farmhouse ruins.
4.9 Willis Woods.
7.0 Close loop (post 13); backtrack to trailhead.

Finding the trailhead: From Interstate 95, take exit 52 and follow Topsfield Road west to Boxford (1.2 miles). From the town triangle in Boxford, go west on Main Street for 0.3 mile and turn left (south) onto Middleton Road. Find marked parking for Bald Hill Reservation on the right in 1.6 miles. Be

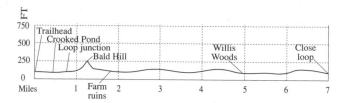

alert, because this small parking lot—adequate for three to five vehicles—is tucked away among the woods and a neighboring residence.

The hike: Hike the gated dirt fire lane of Bald Hill Road west into J. C. Phillips Wildlife Sanctuary, touring a hemlock woods with dispersed oak, pine, and birch. Skunk cabbage dots a drainage to the left. Cross a small dam to a shallow pond and marsh, coming to junction 17 at 0.25 mile.

Stay on Bald Hill Road as it traverses the reservation east to west. Beyond post 16, find the shrubby outer limits of Crooked Pond, a popular birding site. A 20-foot detour left at 0.4 mile (post 15) provides the only open look at the scenic dark oval, with its lily pads, still-water reflections, and backdrop of stately hemlocks. Beware, though; the log fragments that provide dry footing have a tendency to shift and settle, stealing balance. Enjoy a marvelous harmony of bird cheeps and frog ribbits.

Later, white pines replace the hemlocks, and snags rise near the pond. At an inlet crossing, look for turtles. Remain on Bald Hill Road, passing post 14 and bearing left at post 13 (the loop junction). Gently ascend to leave the wildlife sanctuary at post 12 (1.1 miles). Here, a 0.2-mile detour to the right tops Bald Hill, a 247-foot drumlin (glacial hill). Although the grassy summit rimmed by trees is pleasant, it lacks views.

Resume the clockwise loop from post 12 at 1.5 miles; white blazes occasionally mark the tour. Where the trail parallels a rock wall dividing grassy plots (beyond post 11), look for the stone fireplace, chimney, and flooring recalling the old Russell Hooper farmhouse (1.8 miles); sumac and rhododendron grow near the site. Hike behind the sign identifying the farm to observe the foundation and floor of the old barn (1784 to 1946).

From the farmstead, locate the continuation of Bald Hill Road at junction post 10 downhill to the left. Stay on Bald Hill Road, counting down the numbers to post 6 (3.7 miles) for a pleasant rolling woods stroll. More snags pierce the woodland of pine, oak, and maple. At 2.5 miles, cross a dark-spilling brook, its bank sprinkled with wildflowers. At 2.9 miles, skirt a marshy woods.

Upon reaching post 6, turn right onto a secondary woods road, leaving Bald Hill Road; a rock wall parallels this secondary route. At post 6A (4.1 miles), take a sharp right, resuming the rolling meander, skirting seasonal ponds.

At junction 30 (4.8 miles), opt for either fork; each travels the wooded outskirts of a marsh to meet at post 18. For this description, continue straight (bear right), touring the regimented pine plot of Willis Woods before turning left at post 31 to reach 18. (Note that in this area, the numbers seen in the field and those on the agency maps may not correspond completely. The numbers cited represent the actual numbers seen on the trail.)

136

Club moss, Bald Hill Reservation, MA.

Bald Hill Reservation

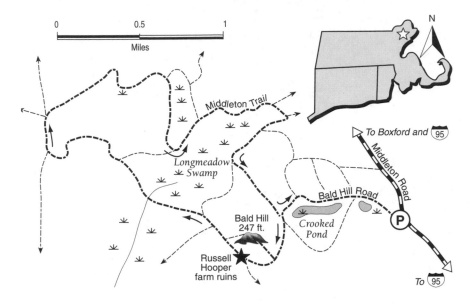

At junction 18, bear right onto the woods road of the **Middleton Trail** (it would be a left for hikers who chose to go left at junction 30). Shagbark hickory now adds to the woodland. Ahead, skirt the northern extent of Longmeadow Swamp, turn right onto a foot trail at post 19, and keep right at posts 20 and 21.

At an unmarked junction at 6.4 miles, stay left on the same path/woods road. At junction 26, bear left to close the loop at post 13 (7 miles). Back-track on Bald Hill Road through the wildlife sanctuary, reaching the trail-head at 7.7 miles.

30 Breakheart Reservation

OVERVIEW

At this Metropolitan District Commission (MDC) property, outcroppings and rocky topped hills, freshwater lakes, mixed woods, and an interlocking network of trails engage hikers. Long ago, this site drew Native Americans, offering food, shelter, and stone for tools. Colonial settlers worked the land as farms, and at the turn of the twentieth century, a private hunting and fishing reserve occupied what is now Breakheart. Lore traces the name to the 1860s, when lonely, brokenhearted Civil War soldiers trained at this then far-off site.

General description: Two short hikes, one traveling along lakes, the other along ridges, present the area offering.

General location: 5 miles northwest of Saugus, Massachusetts.

Special attractions: Vistas of the Boston skyline, central Massachusetts, and New Hampshire; spring- and summer-flowering shrubs and flora; fall foliage; fishing; wildlife-watching.

Length: Lakes–Eagle Rock Hike, 3 miles round trip (2.2 miles when summer parking is available at Silver Lake); Ridge Trail–Hemlock Road Loop, 2.7-mile loop.

Elevation: For each, find less than 200 feet of elevation change.

Difficulty: Both moderate.

Maps: Reservation map.

Special concerns: Keep dogs leashed. Swim only at the designated beach at Pearce Lake.

Season and hours: Year-round, dawn to dusk for walk-in traffic; vehicle access in summer only.

For information: Breakheart Reservation.

Key points:

Lakes–Eagle Rock Hike:
  0.0   Silver Lake Trailhead.
  0.2   Pearce Lake shore.
  1.1   Top Eagle Rock.
  1.7   Underpass.
  2.2   Complete loop at Silver Lake picnic area.

Ridge Trail–Hemlock Road Loop:
  0.0   Headquarters trailhead.
  1.3   Castle Rock.
  1.6   Hemlock Road.
  2.7   Headquarters trailhead.

Finding the trailhead: From Interstate 95, take exit 44 for U.S. Highway 1 South/Massachusetts Highway 129 West and go south on US 1 for 2.5 miles. Take the Lynn Fells Parkway exit, go 0.3 mile, and turn right onto Forest Street. In another 0.3 mile, find year-round parking at the headquarters and summer access to the site's 2-mile one-way Pine Tops Road. Start trails from the headquarters parking lot year-round. In summer, hikers may choose to start the Lakes–Eagle Rock Hike from Silver Lake.

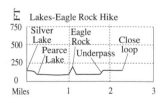

The hikes: For the **Lakes–Eagle Rock Hike,** hike Pine Tops Road counter to traffic, starting left (west) of the headquarters. In 0.4 mile, reach Silver Lake parking; look for a signed blue-blazed trail heading left, north of the parking area entrance. The Breakheart Hill Trail leaves the opposite side of Pine Tops Road.

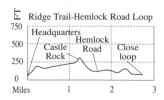

Zero the pedometer and hike counterclockwise along the wooded north shore of Silver Lake. Initially, find the trail wide with a wood-chip surface, passing among oak, sassafras, pine, highbush blueberry, and sweet pepperbush. Rock outcrops open the shoreline, allowing access and viewing of this Q-shaped lake, with its tree–rock shore and scenic island.

The trail then narrows, and hemlocks appear where it curves left. Because unmarked side trails and a grassy road branch off the lake circuit, keep to the shoreline. On the west shore before a small dam and spillway bridge, turn right at a green post to descend a wide improved trail toward Pearce Lake. Discover attractive stonework, small pools, a flume, and a bench; the

Breakheart Reservation

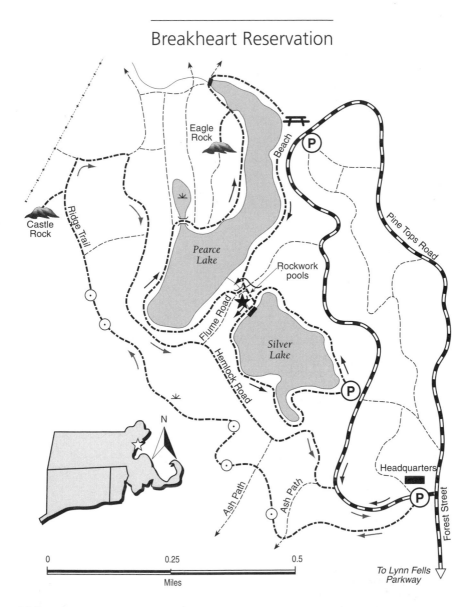

0   0.25   0.5

Miles

structures hark back to the days of the private hunting and fishing reserve and the Civilian Conservation Corps camp. Jewelweed, goldenrod, cattail, and joe-pye weed adorn the small wetland.

Next ascend steps, cross the bridge, and descend to reach the Pearce Lake shore; you may also access this shore via an underpass. Turn left for a clockwise tour of this large, claw-shaped water; blue blazes continue to guide hikers. Travel is on a thin, rolling footpath. At 0.3 mile, an outcrop slopes 20 feet to the water. Again enjoy a picturesque rock–woods shore and treed islands; reflections, tints of fall, and heron and osprey heighten the beauty.

Along the west shore, pass below scenic cliff outcrops. Upon crossing a footbridge spanning the neck of a small cove, continue straight to resume the shoreline trek; other blue routes branch left. Cross-lake views find the designated swimming area.

At 1 mile, a wooden post indicates Eagle Rock to the left; for the lakes hike alone, continue straight. A side trip to Eagle Rock follows blue paint blazes up the outcropping, topping the high point for a 360-degree panorama. Admire Pearce Lake, Castle Hill, the wooded reservation, Boston's city skyline, and the surrounding towers, silos, and steeples. Graffiti alone mars the aloof point. Return to Pearce Lake (1.2 miles) and turn left.

Cross the spillway, round the developed beach, and resume the wooded shoreline hike, enjoying cross-lake views of Eagle Rock. At 1.7 miles, parallel a small flume upstream to the underpass and return to Silver Lake. Back at Silver Lake, turn right, crossing the dam and spillway. Dogwood, aspen, sheep laurel, and sweet pepperbush accent the tour. Round the outcrop-narrowed bay arm to conclude the loop at the picnic area at 2.2 miles.

For the **Ridge Trail–Hemlock Road Loop,** hike Pine Tops Road west from the headquarters (counter to traffic) and turn left near the start to follow the white-blazed Ridge Trail. Oak, hop hornbeam, maple, hazelnut, fern, and berry bushes contribute to the rolling tour, with oak soon winning dominance.

At 0.3 mile, cross Ash Path and top an outcrop for views of the Boston skyline, ocean harbors, and woods. Bearberry and circular lichen mottle the ridge outcrop. Descend and again cross Ash Path for the full 2.7-mile tour; a right turn onto Ash Path shortens the loop. The Ridge Trail rolls back uphill to traverse a ridge of low-stature oaks, with open outcrops broadening the previous view.

On the next descent, traverse a red maple swamp via boardwalk, only to return to the rocky ridge (0.8 mile). At 1.1 miles, the Ridge Link Trail heads right, offering another opportunity to shorten the loop; continue straight ahead.

Ascending to the rocky crest at 1.2 miles, curve right with the white blazes; avoid taking the wide, unmarked trail to the left. At 1.25 miles, find a junction post. To the left, faint yellow blazes mark an old road leading to the top of Castle Rock and a sweeping overlook. The power-line corridor below the rocky outpost both opens and intrudes on the view.

Resume the loop in 0.1 mile, passing between Castle Rock and another outcrop rise. Descend to a T-junction with a dirt road (Spruce Path) and turn right, still pursuing the white blazes. At 1.6 miles, meet and turn right onto

Forest learning.

Hemlock Road (a closed paved route, now a pedestrian way) for a pleasant, rolling tree-framed return.

At 1.9 miles, Ridge Link Trail merges on the right as hikers glimpse Pearce Lake. Hemlocks now alternate with the high-canopy hardwoods. At 2.25 miles, Ash Path arrives on the right. Glimpse Silver Lake and pass Ash Path a second time, meeting Pine Tops Road at 2.5 miles. Turn right to close the loop and return to the trailhead at 2.7 miles.

31 Broadmoor Wildlife Sanctuary

OVERVIEW

At this 600-acre sanctuary of the Massachusetts Audubon Society, a fine network of nature trails explores pond, marsh, red maple swamp, field, forest, and the Charles River shore. Within each microenvironment, find signature plant and wildlife discoveries. Seasonal variations enrich the tours.

> **General description:** Three short hikes applaud the site's diversity and tranquility. Visit pond, marsh, and river; explore a red maple swamp; and top a glacial-deposit hill.
> **General location:** In South Natick and Sherborn, Massachusetts.
> **Special attractions:** Spring-, summer-, and fall-flowering annuals, shrubs, and aquatics; mixed forests; wildlife sightings.

Length:	Mill Pond/Marsh–Charles River Hike, 3 miles round trip; Blueberry Swamp Hike, 2.4 miles round trip; Indian Brook–Glacial Hill Hike, 3 miles round trip.
Elevation:	All show less than 60 feet of elevation change.
Difficulty:	Easy.
Maps:	Sanctuary trail map.
Special concerns:	Per-person admission fee or Massachusetts Audubon Society membership. Maps are available for loan or purchase and should be carried to negotiate the maze of interlocking trails. Blue blazes travel away from the visitor center, yellow ones return to the center, and white ones mark the connecting trails. No dogs, bikes, or picnicking.
Season and hours:	Year-round, Tuesday through Sunday and holidays that fall on Monday, but generally spring through fall for hiking. Trails, dawn to dusk; visitor center, 9:00 A.M. to 5:00 P.M. weekdays, 10:00 A.M. to 5:00 P.M. weekends and holidays.
For information:	Broadmoor Wildlife Sanctuary.

Key points:
Mill Pond/Marsh–Charles River Hike:
- 0.0 Visitor center trailhead.
- 0.2 Broadmoor Bridge.
- 1.0 Loop junction.
- 1.5 Charles River.
- 2.0 Complete loop; backtrack to trailhead.

Blueberry Swamp Hike:
- 0.0 Visitor center trailhead.
- 0.2 Broadmoor Bridge.
- 0.4 Glacial Hill Trail.
- 0.8 Blueberry Swamp Loop.
- 1.6 Complete loop; backtrack to trailhead.

Indian Brook–Glacial Hill Hike:
- 0.0 Visitor center trailhead.
- 0.1 Indian Brook Trail.
- 0.6 Glacial Hill Trail.
- 1.2 Loop junction.
- 1.4 Top glacial hill.
- 1.8 Complete loop; backtrack to trailhead.

Finding the trailhead: From the center of South Natick, go 1.7 miles west on Massachusetts Highway 16 and turn left (south) to enter the sanctuary. From the MA 16–MA 27 junction at Sherborn, go 1.5 miles east on MA 16 and turn right. Start hikes at the visitor center, descending the gravel lane south into the sanctuary.

The hikes: For the **Mill Pond/Marsh–Charles River Hike,** descend from the visitor center, hiking the gravel lane of the Marsh Trail framed by pine, oak, and maple. Poison ivy flourishes, climbing the tree trunks. Keep to this

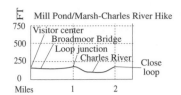

Mill Pond/Marsh-Charles River Hike

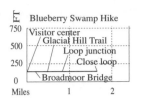

Blueberry Swamp Hike

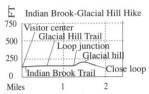

Indian Brook-Glacial Hill Hike

lane until the bridge crossing. Alternatively, hikers can follow the wheelchair-accessible trail from the visitor center down to the marsh, meeting the Marsh Trail soon after the Indian Brook Trail junction. At the marsh, birch and beech join the ranks, as do sweet pepperbush, cinnamon fern, and mayflower.

At 0.2 mile, split-level Broadmoor Bridge spans a watery neck of Mill Pond and has a viewing deck for admiring the marsh of Indian Brook. Areas of open water, pond lilies, arrow arum, duckweed, cattail, and a dense expanse of the pervasive purple loosestrife contribute to the tapestry. Mink, muskrat, frog, heron, and dragonfly cause fingers to point. Departing the bridge, find a scenic tree-shaded outcrop, with azalea scenting the early-summer air.

Wood chips and pine needles soften the trail as it turns left at the junction at 0.3 mile and rolls east along the south shore of the marsh. Dense berry bushes and low maples can steal the marsh views. At 0.5 mile, come to and cross the next bridge. Geese frequent the open water and sometimes the rock outcrops in the woods. White pond lilies decorate the water in mid-July.

Keep right at the start; avoid taking the Boundary Trail. To the sides of the trail are the sites of a 1700s sawmill and a gristmill; a pair of grinding stones mark where the gristmill stood. Cross a stone dam and proceed forward at the four-way junction. At the second four-way junction, turn left (east) and then keep right to travel a tree-shaded lane, edge a field overlooking the pond, and pass beneath some nice shade maples.

At 0.75 mile is a monument noting the Stillman family's generosity. Soon after, parallel a rock wall to the South Street crossing. At 1 mile is the loop junction; go left (clockwise), touring a complex of pine, oak, and huckleberry. This rolling semishaded tour leads to the Charles River (1.5 miles). Enjoy a few open overlooks as the trail continues along the wide, sleepy canoe water. Duckweed colors the edge, while the screech of an osprey draws eyes skyward. Sweet pepperbush, azalea, and tupelo hug the shore. At 1.9 miles, draw away from the river to bring the loop to a close at 2 miles. Return as you came, reaching the visitor center at 3 miles.

For the **Blueberry Swamp Hike,** retrace the start of the first hike, crossing over the main bridge, but turn right at 0.3 mile. Pass through a pine–maple woods with poison ivy, huckleberry, and fern. Wood chips soften the wide trail.

At the junction at 0.4 mile, turn right onto the Glacial Hill Trail, exploring a pine–oak corridor with similar understory vegetation. At 0.8 mile, find the Blueberry Swamp Loop. The paths to the left and straight ahead shape the loop; the right fork continues the Glacial Hill Trail and leads to the Indian Brook Trail.

Go left for a clockwise tour of the swamp, traveling a mixed-hardwood

144

corridor with sweet pepperbush. Squirrels leap through the treetops. By 0.9 mile, round the red maple swamp; the ground often dries by summer. High-bush blueberry contributes to the vegetation, as does a fickle showing of skunk cabbage. At 1 mile, bear right, continuing the swamp circuit; the Quacking Frog Trail heads left.

Then, at 1.15 miles, bear left, easing gently upslope away from the swamp. Soon after, bear right as an unmarked trail arrives on the left. At the 1.3-mile junction, near the boundary, keep right; to the left is a gate. A board-walk now crosses the swamp for a closer look. Travel mixed forest to close the loop at 1.6 miles; return to the visitor center at 2.4 miles.

For the **Indian Brook–Glacial Hill Hike,** descend the gravel lane from the visitor center, turning right onto the Indian Brook Trail at 0.1 mile. Cross a service road and skirt a field, traveling on an exposed mowed track. Aspen, oak, maple, and a dense shrub border of honeysuckle, wild grape, sumac, and Virginia creeper add to the hike. Looks left find the maple-lined drainage of Indian Brook. Oak woods then embrace the journey to the T-junction at 0.6 mile.

Go right onto the Glacial Hill Trail to add the Glacial Hill Loop, ascend-ing a grassy woods road; the incline soon flattens. Oak, hickory, pine, and maple compose the woods, while glimpses over the left shoulder spotlight a snag-filled wetland of Indian Brook. Beaver-raised waters claimed the trees. At 1.2 miles, find an unmarked T-junction and turn left, still traveling a woods road, now rounding a red maple swamp with highbush blueberry.

Broadmoor Wildlife Sanctuary

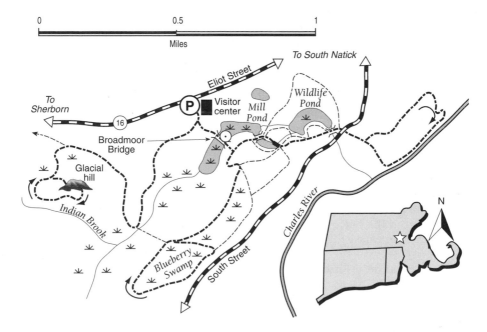

Lily pads, Broadmoor Wildlife Sanctuary, MA.

At 1.25 miles, reach the loop; go left for a clockwise tour of the doughnut-shaped glacial-deposit hill. Ascend an oak–maple flank, top the hill at 1.4 miles, and encircle the depression; leafy branches screen out views. With a dip to the center, find vernal pools giving rise to cinnamon ferns and other greenery. The trail then returns to the rim, with yellow blazes guiding the way. Descend to find overlooks of the swamp before closing the loop at 1.75 miles. Return to the trailhead at 3 miles.

32   Blue Hills Reservation

OVERVIEW

At this 7,000-acre open space south of Boston proper, some 100 miles of interlocking trails offer visitors a plethora of hike options. The skyline hills prove natural destinations and centerpieces for loop travel. The selected three hikes hint at the discovery and challenge found at this superb urban wild—a Metropolitan District Commission (MDC) property.

     General description: Three day hikes of varying length and difficulty
                                          explore key features of the Blue Hills chain.
         General location: 10 miles south of downtown Boston.

Special attractions:	Vistas, observation towers, historic weather station, diverse forest, rock features, wildlife sightings, fall foliage.
Length:	Great Blue Hill–Skyline Loop, 4.5 miles round trip; Tucker Hill Loop, 2.9 miles round trip; Chickatawbut Tower Loop, 0.8 mile round trip.
Elevation:	Great Blue Hill–Skyline Loop, 400-foot elevation change; the other two hikes each show a 140-foot elevation change.
Difficulty:	Great Blue Hill–Skyline Loop, strenuous; Tucker Hill Loop, easy; Chickatawbut Tower Loop, moderate.
Maps:	Reservation map; purchase at Trailside Museum or from the map dispenser on the front porch of the headquarters.
Special concerns:	There is an admission fee to Trailside Museum (a Massachusetts Audubon facility). Keep pets leashed. Carry a map to sort out the numbered trail intersections and unnamed trails and to track the progress of the color-blazed trails.
Season and hours:	Year-round; spring through fall for hiking. Trails, dawn to dusk; Trailside Museum, 10:00 A.M. to 5:00 P.M. Tuesday through Sunday.
For information:	Blue Hills Reservation Headquarters or Blue Hills Trailside Museum.

Key points:

Great Blue Hill–Skyline Loop:
- 0.0   Trailside Museum trailhead.
- 0.6   Eliot Tower and loop.
- 1.8   Houghton Hill.
- 2.0   Hillside Street.
- 2.8   Hemenway Hill.
- 3.4   Wolcott Hill.
- 3.8   End loop at Eliot Tower; backtrack to trailhead.

Tucker Hill Loop:
- 0.0   Houghtons Pond Trailhead.
- 0.6   Loop junction.
- 2.3   Close loop; backtrack to trailhead.

Chickatawbut Tower Loop:
- 0.0   Chickatawbut Trailhead.
- 0.1   Observation tower and loop.
- 0.3   Nahanton Hill.
- 0.7   Complete loop at tower; descend to trailhead.

Finding the trailhead: From Massachusetts Highway 93, take exit 2B and go north on MA 138 for about a mile, finding the signed entrance to the Trailside Museum on the right. For Houghtons Pond Parking (Tucker Hill Loop), again proceed north from exit 2B on MA 138, but turn right (east) at the light onto Blue Hills River Road, and continue 1.2 miles to the parking area.

Blue Hills Reservation

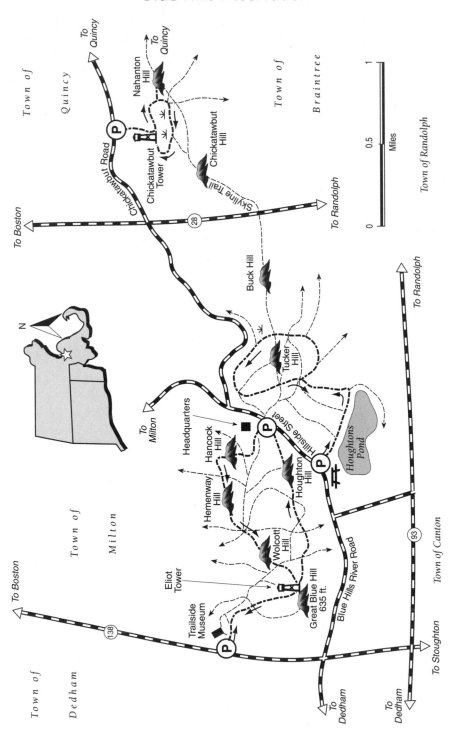

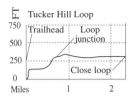

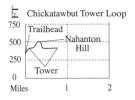

For the headquarters and Chickatawbut Tower Loop, continue east on Blue Hills River Road, which becomes Hillside Street as it bears north. Look for the headquarters on the left in another 0.25 mile, next to the state police offices. For Chickatawbut Tower, continue 0.5 mile past the headquarters, bear right at the split on Chickatawbut Road, and stay on it for about 2 miles, crossing MA 28. The trail heads south opposite the turnout for Chickatawbut Overlook.

The hikes: For the **Great Blue Hill–Skyline Loop,** start at the Trailside Museum Parking Lot, south of the museum. Follow the red dot trail that mounts the stairs on the west flank of Great Blue Hill heading for Eliot Tower and the weather observatory. Great Blue Hill, elevation 635 feet, is the highest point on the Atlantic Coast south of Maine. Mixed deciduous trees and evergreens clad the slope.

At 0.1 mile, top a granitic outcrop among the small birch, and find seasonal looks at the ski area to the south. Cross over Summit Road (an alternative approach to the peak), ascending among outcrops and pines. At 0.5 mile, the trail swings right; keep a sharp eye out for blazes.

At a concrete post, turn left to reach the observation tower in 100 feet. The attractive stone tower has an open deck, covered breezeway, fireplace, and a spiral staircase to its top. Long, rectangular open-air windows offer views in all four directions. Admire the wooded open space, Boston city skyline, Houghtons and Ponkapoag Ponds, the castlelike top of the weather observatory, and the bumpy Blue Hills skyline.

Continue rounding Eliot Tower in a clockwise direction, hiking past the red Coon Hollow Trail, which returns to the museum. Near a stone walkway/bridge erected in 1904, in honor of the landscape architect and key preservationist Charles Eliot, find the North Skyline Trail (the loop's return) descending at post 1063. Cross the bridge to reach the South Skyline Trail at post 1066, and follow it off the hill for a counterclockwise tour of the Skyline Loop. Blue rectangular blazes mark the Skyline Trail.

Find a sharp descent, rocky and wooded. Deer, red fox, and grouse can divert the eye; so can the views east and south across the reservation. At 1 mile, a dirt road arrives on the left; a detour along it leads to a small pond and a Wolcott Hill loop. For this hike, continue straight, following a spring runoff downhill. At 1.3 miles, squeeze through a jumble of big granite boulders. Oak and beech shade the tour as the trail flattens.

Cross a dirt road at 1.5 miles and bypass junction 1123, crossing a log over a small drainage; skunk cabbages dot the woodland. The South Skyline Trail now rolls, crossing over Houghton Path to mount Houghton Hill. Top Houghton Hill, a round-topped bump with glacier-planed rock, at 1.8 miles. Branches

149

restrict views; blueberries offer sweet summer tastes.

At junction 1152, bear right, following a rocky road uphill, and at junction 1156 again bear right for a steep, rocky downhill pitch to Hillside Street and the state police offices (2 miles). For the loop, hike north along the shoulder of Hillside Street, going past the MDC Ranger Stables to pick up the **North Skyline Trail** near the reservation headquarters; again look for the blue rectangular blazes.

The North Skyline Trail reveals a similar rugged persona, touring pine–oak woods and rocky slopes. It bears north for a steep ascent of Hancock Hill (elevation 510 feet). Although burned in 1987, the succession of young trees already has claimed some of the view. Looks extend seaward and north to Boston.

With an abrupt down and up, top Hemenway Hill for southern views and an admiration of the wooded terrain. Now descend steeply, cross the dirt road of Wolcott Path, and begin a rolling, rocky woods ascent of Wolcott Hill (elevation 470 feet). A summit rock outcrop with a lone-standing pine provides a fine vantage for viewing Eliot Tower and Great Blue Hill. With another rocky pitch and climb, the North Skyline Trail reaches Eliot Tower (3.8 miles). Bear right to return as you came, or hike Coon Hollow Trail downhill to the Trailside Museum (4.4 miles).

For a long-distance Skyline Hike (9 miles one-way), instead of taking the Skyline Loop, cross Hillside Street at 2 miles to pick up the Skyline Trail as it proceeds east across the reservation. It continues much as it did, touring full woods and topping rocky hills. Pitch pine and scrub oak claim the dry hilltops, and the dips and climbs become less sharp. End near St. Moritz Ponds in Quincy.

For the **Tucker Hill Loop,** park at Houghtons Pond and hike toward the beach, bearing left (east) to round the pond. Travel a yellow- and green-blazed dirt lane, passing behind the bathhouse (0.1 mile). At 0.3 mile, the green Tucker Hill Trail continues forward (east), no longer paralleling shore. The surface briefly changes to pavement as hikers tour a mixed woods interspersed by dogwood. Reach the loop junction at 0.6 mile and go left.

A few spruce enter the mix as the loop crosses over the Skyline Trail. American beech suffer the inevitable carving of initials, and Canada mayflowers adorn the woods floor. At 1.25 miles, curve right, paralleling above Chickatawbut Road. At 1.4 miles, tour slightly higher up the flank of Tucker Hill. Where the trail follows a narrow shaded lane at 1.5 miles, find the slope of Tucker Hill more pronounced, with big granite boulders at its base.

Ascend steadily, touring a dark hollow woven by some beautiful big trees. At 1.7 miles, cross the Skyline Trail as it descends from Tucker Hill and proceeds east. Soon after, cross the Massachuseuck Trail. Then, at 1.9 miles, bear right in a scenic grove of white pines to close the loop at 2.3 miles. Retrace the paved and dirt roads past Houghtons Pond to the trailhead at 2.9 miles.

For **Chickatawbut Tower Loop,** ascend the stairs heading south opposite the turnout for Chickatawbut Overlook; yellow dots mark the tour. Reach a stone picnic shelter with the stone observation tower set back from it at 0.1

mile. When open, the 50-foot tower overlooks the treetops for a fine panorama. When the tower is closed, take the Nahanton Hill detour for the view.

Go left at the tower for a clockwise loop, but watch closely for the faint yellow blazes, because the popularity of the area has introduced a lot of pretenders to the trail. After a short descent, the loop curves right. Here, detour left, ascending the rock stairs to the summit of Nahanton Hill (0.3 mile). The summit's low, rounded northern outcrops offer a grand view of Boston, its harbor and harbor islands, and a distant New Hampshire peak rising above the haze.

Return to the loop at 0.4 mile and resume the clockwise tour, going right at junctions. Pass between a couple of granite knobs and skirt a wetland woods before closing the loop at the tower at 0.7 mile. Descend to the trailhead at 0.8 mile.

33 Ponkapoag Pond Trail

General description:	This trail encircles a large pond south of the Blue Hills chain and offers a close-up look at a bog.
General location:	Blue Hills Metropolitan District Commission Reservation, 10 miles south of Boston, Massachusetts.
Special attractions:	Scenic open-water pond and enfolding bog, rare Atlantic white cedars, bog boardwalk, spring and summer wildflowers, carnivorous plants, wildlife.
Length:	4 miles round trip.
Elevation:	Find an 80-foot elevation change.
Difficulty:	Easy to moderate.
Maps:	Blue Hills Reservation map; purchase at the Trailside Museum (1 mile north of Massachusetts Highway 93 at exit 2B) or from the headquarters at 695 Hillside Street (take exit 3 off MA 93 and go north for Houghtons Pond; find the headquarters west off Hillside Street, 0.25 mile north of Houghtons Pond).
Special concerns:	Keep pets leashed. Carry insect repellent, and be respectful of the sensitive bog habitat.
Season and hours:	Year-round; generally spring through fall for hiking. Dawn to dusk.
For information:	Blue Hills Trailside Museum or Blue Hills Reservation Headquarters.

Key points:
- 0.0 Trailhead.
- 0.2 Loop junction.
- 0.6 Ponkapoag Boardwalk.
- 2.3 Fisherman's Beach.
- 3.8 Close loop; return to trailhead.

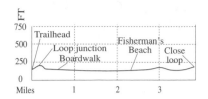

Finding the trailhead: Locate the trail on the south side of MA 93 at exit 3. Start at the gated road heading south off the exit ramp at Blue Hills River Road. Find parking for four vehicles; do not block the gate. Alternatively, hikers can park at the west or south lots at Houghtons Pond (north of MA 93), and hike south on Blue Hills River Road to the trailhead.

The hike: For this green dot tour, hike south uphill on the closed dirt road passing through a pine–oak woods with some big trees. Canada mayflower dresses the floor in early spring. At 0.25 mile, reach the loop junction (intersection 5241) and bear right for a counterclockwise tour.

Reach the loop's high point, isolated by woods, and descend to lake level. At junction 5176 near a YMCA camp, a detour left leads to the cedar bog; the path straight ahead continues the loop.

For the detour, pass through a small open area and bear left to reach a stone marker and signboard for the bog trail (0.6 mile). Lots of blue butterflies flit about in early May. Built originally in 1947, the Ponkapoag Boardwalk traverses a national environmental study area—a unique spongy landscape, in between a solid and a liquid. Sphagnum moss, carnivorous plants, Atlantic white cedar, leatherleaf, cranberry, and highbush blueberry contribute to the bog anatomy. Blue flag iris and sheep laurel add floral accents.

Chained end to end, the 15-inch-wide planks offer a narrow walkway across the bog. Beneath the planks, spy the original corduroy boardwalk. Walk gingerly and limit your party to one hiker per plank, because the walkway gives with the liquid-land. Sometimes the coffee-steeped water laps over the plank edges. In a few areas, paired planks allow for passing. In the open sphag-

Ponkapoag boardwalk, Blue Hills Reservation, MA.

Ponkapoag Pond Trail

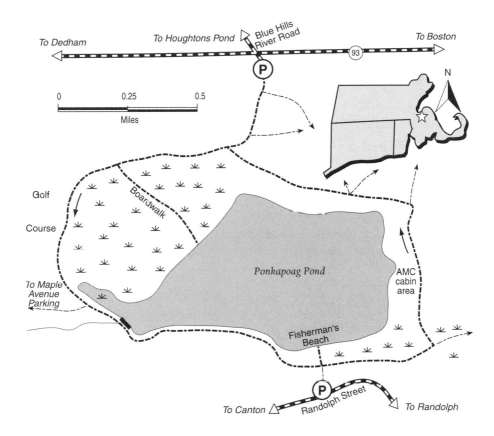

num bog, geese rear their young while sunlight glints off the open-water channels. At the end of the boardwalk, find the first open view of Ponkapoag Pond.

Retrace the boardwalk and resume the pond loop at 1 mile, bearing left. Before long, round a gate to travel the woodland buffer to Ponkapoag Golf Course; the bog commands views to the left. Flickers, blue jays, robins, mourning doves, Canada geese, and red-winged blackbirds enliven the setting. At 1.6 miles, round a second gate, leaving behind the golf course to find the Maple Avenue entry on the right.

The woods–bog tour continues, with occasional gaps in the vegetation affording open looks at Ponkapoag Pond. Cross a small spillway framed by birch, and travel the woods below a residential area. Violet, trout lily, jack-in-the-pulpit, marsh marigold, and buttercup sprinkle springtime color.

At 2.3 miles, find the Randolph Street access and a spur to Fisherman's Beach, a 100-foot-long beach offering a view of Great Blue Hill. The pond circuit continues, now following a dirt road through a more varied woodland.

At 2.8 miles, the route curves left, continuing to round the pond. At 3 miles, skirt the overnight cabins of the Appalachian Mountain Club (AMC), available by reservation only. Descend away from the cabins, pass through the AMC parking lot, and follow the orange and green blazes west, again on foot trail.

Cross a small brook at 3.4 miles and stay with the green blazes, continuing west along a rise to close the loop at 3.75 miles. Return to the trailhead at 4 miles.

34 Borderland State Park

OVERVIEW

Managed from the start for wildlife and nature appreciation, the 1906 estate of botanist Oakes Ames and his artist wife, Blanche, offers present-day travelers a fine natural arena to explore. Within its 1,772 acres, find ponds, a cedar swamp, field, woods, and rocky hills, as well as a superb system of short trails, suggesting a variety of hikes.

General description:	Two hikes incorporate many of the trails, applauding the area's varied habitats and overall relaxation. One features the ponds, the other the wooded rocky hills.
General location:	5 miles south of Sharon, Massachusetts.
Special attractions:	Stone mansion; old quarry; scenic ponds; spring-flowering trees, shrubs, and wildflowers; Atlantic white cedar swamp; wildlife-watching; fishing; fall foliage.
Length:	Leach Ponds Loop, 4-mile loop (3.5 miles for the shorter loop); Northern Trails Hike, 7.4 miles round trip.
Elevation:	Leach Ponds Loop, 30-foot elevation change; Northern Trails Hike, 100-foot elevation change.
Difficulty:	Leach Ponds Loop, easy; the Northern Trails Hike is moderate.
Maps:	State park map.
Special concerns:	Fee area. The mansion is shown by guided tour.
Season and hours:	Year-round, 8:00 A.M. to sunset.
For information:	Borderland State Park.

Key points:
Leach Ponds Loop:
- 0.0   Mansion trailhead.
- 0.2   Stone lodge/Leach Pond.
- 1.7   Mountain Street.
- 2.1   Puds Pond dam.
- 4.0   Mansion trailhead.

Northern Trails Hike:

0.0   Visitor center trailhead.
1.1   Loop junction.
2.2   Quarry Trail loop.
3.1   Moyles Quarry.
6.3   Close loop at Northwest Trail; return to trailhead.

Finding the trailhead: From Interstate 495, take exit 10 and go east on Massachusetts Highway 123 for 3.4 miles. There, turn left onto Poquanticut Avenue, following signs for the park. Go 1.3 miles and turn left onto Massapoag Avenue to reach the entrance on the right in another 2 miles. Start the Leach Ponds Loop at the lower parking lot near the mansion or at the visitor center parking lot (follow signs for pond and lodge); start the Northern Trails Hike at the visitor center.

The hikes: Starting the **Leach Ponds Loop** at the lower parking lot, hike the wide surfaced path past a small information station to cross the groomed lawn stretching before the 1910 English-style stone mansion, an ivy-clad square fortress with rooftop bell. The site's formal landscaping shows a circular hedge with fountains.

Leach Ponds Loop

At the T-junction (0.1 mile), a right leads to the mansion; go left for Leach Pond. A second junction quickly follows. Here, a left leads to the visitor center and West Side Trail; a right leads to the pond, lodge, and all other trails. Go right.

Hike a closed gravel road through hardwood forest, going left at the fork. Either prong reaches the single-room stone lodge that overlooks picturesque Leach Pond at 0.25 mile. White pine, birch, and red maple shade the shore of this large pond, while white pond lilies decorate the mosaic of red and green pads atop the shallow water. Frog, heron, and sunfish may be spied. Swallows roost in the eaves of the building. For the loop, go left on the carriage road, returning via the Pond Edge Trail to the right.

The carriage road offers a relaxing stroll, with spurs to pondside benches. Many of the named trails branch left from this key travel artery. Pass a small side pond. Dogwoods accent the leafy branch-draped corridor, and glacial erratics scatter the woods. Along the shore, azalea, sweet pepperbush, sheep laurel, and highbush blueberry add floral cheer. Created in 1825, Leach Pond allowed then-owner Colonel Leach to manipulate the water level in the cedar swamp downstream on Poquanticut Brook.

Past the junction with the Northwest Trail, find a pond loop option (1 mile). The path to the right travels the beltway between Leach Pond and Upper Leach Pond for a 3.5-mile tour, while the carriage road ahead travels the perimeter of both ponds for the full 4-mile tour. Both offer looks at Upper Leach Pond. Go forward for the longer tour.

Upper Leach Pond, the smaller of the two, shows more open water, with an attractive rim of birch. Pass the left-bound spurs to the Granite Hills Trail, still enjoying the mixed forest and occasional pond glimpses. Where the car-

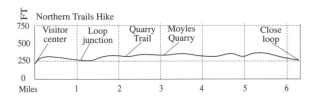
Northern Trails Hike

riage road meets Mountain Street (a public road) at 1.7 miles, turn right. The hike then resumes on the right in 200 feet.

Follow a grassy two-track south through woods, skirting Puds Pond to the east. Keep to the doubletrack. A small dam extends the first (and last) open view of Puds Pond, which has minimal aquatic vegetation and a private residence across the way; no swimming. At 2.25 miles, the spur from the shorter loop arrives on the right to share the remainder of the tour.

Continue south, edging a field decorated in daisy and clover to meet a dirt park road (accessed off Bay Road) near the park's white farmhouse. Turn right; mature sugar maples now usher hikers to a gate (2.8 miles) for the return leg of the hike. Round the gate to once more admire Leach Pond.

At 3 miles, locate Pond Edge Trail to the right. It offers a pleasing 0.75-mile shoreline stroll back to the lodge (from there, backtrack the start of the hike). The carriage road offers an easier stroll and thus faster return to the mansion area. Both returns cover 4 miles and offer glimpses of the Atlantic white cedar swamp and Poquanticut Brook. Side trails branch between the two return trails.

For the second hike, the **Northern Trails Hike,** start at the west side of the visitor center, following the marked West Side Trail. Beyond the small manicured lawn, travel a carriage-width path through beech–oak woods with sassafras, witch hazel, and huckleberry. At 0.2 mile, bear right, keeping to the West Side Trail. Maples crowd the moister pockets as plank boardwalks span the wet reaches.

At 0.5 mile, go left on the French Trail to explore the northern park. This rock-studded foot trail passes among multiton boulders. Ahead, a spur tops an outcrop while the French Trail rounds the rock's base. Sun penetrates the woods. Generally the trails go unblazed, but a few markers guide hikers through the outcrop areas. At 0.9 mile, go left on the cart path of the Northwest Trail, passing beneath a fuller umbrella of leaves.

Pass Split Rock Trail on the right (the loop's return) at 1.1 miles and a nearly hidden pond on the left. At 1.5 miles, turn right onto the Ridge Trail, an undulating footpath weaving among low-growing oaks and open rocks. Atop the ridge, encounter a few false paths created by mountain bikers; most are brief and soon merge with the prescribed trail.

At 2.2 miles, reach a multiple junction: The left and middle forks shape the Quarry Trail loop; the right fork continues the Ridge Trail. Go left for a clockwise tour of the Quarry Trail, traveling a scenic narrow footpath through a lush mixed woods with a moister understory. Keep right at junctions. At 3.1 miles, reach Moyles Quarry on the right. A sign marks this tree-filled gap, which provided stone for a viaduct on the Boston & Providence Railroad in the early 1800s. At a map post at 3.2 miles, turn left for the Morse Loop.

Pass through a gap in a rock wall and skirt a small pond on the left, coming

156

Borderland State Park

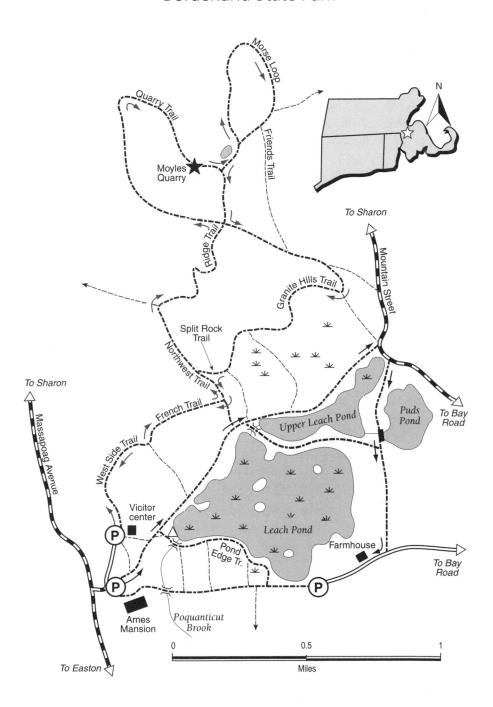

N

To Sharon

Morse Loop

Quarry Trail

Moyles Quarry

Friends Trail

Mountain Street

To Sharon

Ridge Trail

Granite Hills Trail

Split Rock Trail

Northwest Trail

French Trail

To Sharon

Massapoag Avenue

West Side Trail

Upper Leach Pond

Puds Pond

To Bay Road

Visitor center

P

Leach Pond

Farmhouse

To Bay Road

Pond Edge Tr.

P

P

Ames Mansion

Poquanticut Brook

To Easton

0   0.5   1

Miles

to the loop junction. Clockwise, walk among young pines, full oaks, and a hemlock grove. Keep to the main trail, because side spurs either branch to area streets or dead-end. At 3.9 miles, continue straight, and in another 200 feet bear right, forgoing the Friends Trail. Upon closing the loop, turn left, return to the Quarry Trail, and again go left.

Where hikers return to the Ridge Trail (4.4 miles), resume left. At 5 miles, pass the southern end of the Friends Trail, arc around a room-size boulder, and turn right to reach the Granite Hills Trail at its upper loop. Go right, touring mixed woods and outcroppings, passing the junctions for the upper and lower Granite Hills loops. Soon after a pair of footbridge crossings, turn right onto the Split Rock Trail (6 miles).

Skirt a split boulder cracked like an egg and the trail's acclaimed Split Rock, incorporated into a rock wall. The fissure of the latter measures several feet wide. Follow the rock wall to close the loop at Northwest Trail (6.3 miles). Go left, backtracking the Northwest, French, and West Side Trails to the visitor center (7.4 miles).

35 Cape Cod Canal

OVERVIEW

The building of this canal eliminated 135 miles of open-ocean navigation around the isthmus of Cape Cod, and in doing so opened up a fine recreation corridor for bicycle rides, family strolls, exercise walks, fishing, and nature study. Scenic paved lanes travel both banks of the canal, with nearby hiker trails visiting a Native American council grounds, a World War II fortification, and the canal's past.

Miles Standish first proposed the canal in 1623. In 1772, George Washington ordered a construction survey, but not until 1918 did Cape Cod Canal become a reality.

General description: Parallel bike-and-pedestrian ways travel the canal's north and south shores much of the way between Cape Cod Bay and Buzzards Bay. On the north shore, find the Bournedale Interpretive Trail and Sagamore Hill Trail, two short trails that introduce the area's history.

General location: At the neck of Cape Cod, Massachusetts.

Special attractions: Fishing, bird-watching, historical sites, spring flowers, azalea, multiple accesses (some with comfort stations).

Length: Northern Bike-and-Pedestrian Way, 7 miles one-way; Southern Bike-and-Pedestrian Way, 6.5 miles one-way; Bournedale Interpretive Trail, 0.8-mile loop; Sagamore Hill Trail, 0.7 mile round trip.

Elevation:	Bike-and-Pedestrian Ways, flat; Bournedale Interpretive Trail, 20-foot elevation change; Sagamore Hill Trail, 50-foot elevation change.
Difficulty:	All easy.
Maps:	Cape Cod Canal Recreational Guide.
Special concerns:	Scusset Beach State Reservation at the east end of the northern pathway and the site of the Sagamore Hill Trail charges a seasonal entrance fee. Be mindful of poison ivy, and beware of slippery canal riprap. Keep pets leashed.
Season and hours:	Year-round. Recreation areas, 9:00 A.M. to dusk; field office, 9:00 A.M. to 4:00 P.M. weekdays.
For information:	U.S. Army Corps of Engineers, Cape Cod Canal Field Office.

Key points:

Northern Bike-and-Pedestrian Way:

   0.0   Scusset Beach State Reservation trailhead (eastern terminus).

   2.4   Sagamore Recreation Area/Sagamore Bridge.

   3.4   Herring Run Recreation Area.

   5.8   Bourne Bridge.

   7.0   End at Buzzards Bay below rail bridge.

Southern Bike-and-Pedestrian Way:

   0.0   Sandwich Marina Recreation Area trailhead.

   2.0   Sagamore Bridge.

   5.2   Bourne Recreation Area.

   6.5   End at Tidal Flats Recreation Area.

Bournedale Interpretive Trail:

   0.0   Herring Run Recreation Area trailhead.

   0.2   Loop junction.

   0.6   Close loop; return to trailhead.

Sagamore Hill Trail:

   0.0   Sagamore Hill Trailhead.

   0.3   Summit of Sagamore Hill; return to trailhead.

Finding the trailhead: In the Bourne–Sagamore area, find the canal bounded by U.S. Highway 6/Canal Road to the north, US 6A/Sandwich Road to the south.

From east to west, access the Northern Bike-and-Pedestrian Way at Scusset Beach State Reservation, at Sagamore and Herring Run Recreation Areas, and at Buzzards Bay below Railroad Bridge. Locate the field office at Buzzards Bay off Academy Drive. The Bournedale Interpretive Trail heads west from Herring Run Recreation Area, and the Sagamore Hill Trail heads north within Scusset Beach State Reservation.

From east to west, reach the Southern Bike-and-Pedestrian Way at Sandwich Marina, Bourne Recreation Area, and Tidal Flats Recreation Area.

The hikes: The **Northern and Southern Bike-and-Pedestrian Ways** extend similar linear tours overlooking the long straightaways and gentle cur-

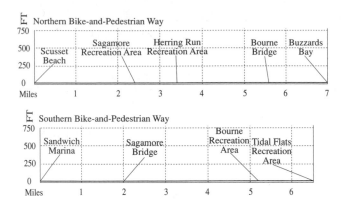

FT
Northern Bike-and-Pedestrian Way
750
500 | Scusset   Sagamore   Herring Run   Bourne   Buzzards
       Beach   Recreation Area Recreation Area   Bridge   Bay
250
0
Miles   1   2   3   4   5   6   7

FT
Southern Bike-and-Pedestrian Way
750
500 | Sandwich   Sagamore   Bourne
       Marina   Bridge   Recreation Tidal Flats
250   Area   Recreation
                                                            Area
0
Miles   1   2   3   4   5   6

vature of Cape Cod Canal. The eastern extreme of the southern pathway has a strong industrial flavor, with a power plant, tanks, and the close proximity of a parallel rail line. The elongated campground at Bourne Scenic Park abuts a 0.5-mile stretch of the northern bikeway.

For the most part, though, wooded buffers and an abrupt slope isolate the canal trails from the residential and town areas. Find the northern pathway more open for continuous canal and cross-canal views. An intermittent thick tree–shrub border along the southern pathway affords more shade. The enfolding terrain gradually rises east to west.

Three attractive bridges span the corridor, contributing to views and serving as benchmarks: From east to west, find Sagamore Bridge, Bourne Bridge, and the vertical-lift rail bridge. The channel lights are numbered and can be used to track progress. Multiply the number on the light by 100 feet to determine the distance to or from the canal's east entrance.

Steep riprap banks dip to the tide-influenced canal water. Saltwater anglers often occupy the rocks. Seaweed and algae color the submerged rocks, while mussels, barnacles, snails, and starfish cling to the splashed jumble. Gulls, herons, and cormorants pass above the canal, as yellow warblers and jays pulse between the hillside shrubs. The parallel routes have benches for reflecting, feeling the breeze, and admiring the amiable canal host.

On the canal's north shore, the **Bournedale Interpretive Trail** starts at the west end of Herring Run Recreation Area (located west of Sagamore Bridge off US 6). Descend the stairway and turn right. Just beyond a thin drainage, locate the sign for the self-guided loop.

Ascend the steps and bear west, traveling a foot trail contouring the wooded slope between the bikeway and MA 6. Pine, oak, red cedar, cherry, sumac, azalea, milkweed, greenbrier, and sweet fern dress the slope and enrich the tour. At 0.2 mile, reach the loop.

Bear left, enjoying frequent canal views before returning to the woods and shrubs. Overlook the bikeway, the canal, and the boats moving through the channel. Plaques describe the canal's reconstruction in 1937 and the original digging from 1911 to 1914.

FT
Bournedale Interpretive Trail
750 | Herring Run Recreation Area
500 | Loop junction
250 | Close loop
0
Miles   1

FT
Sagamore Hill Trail
750 | Trailhead
500
250 | Sagamore
          Hill
0
Miles   1

At 0.4 mile, find a three-way junction. Here, the loop swings right, returning along a higher contour; the Bournedale Hill Trail continues west along the

Cape Cod Canal

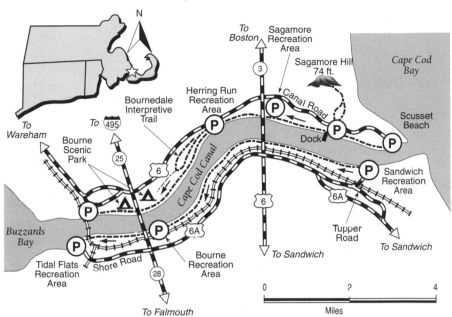

wooded slope, reaching a gate at Bourne Scenic Park in another mile. Stairs descend to the bikeway for an alternative loop return. Keep to the interpretive trail loop.

Oak, pine, maple, and beech shield the trail from the road as more interpretive plaques mark the way. One identifies a glacial erratic (a boulder surfed here on a sheet of ice, thousands of years ago). Return to the trailhead at 0.8 mile.

East of the small rotary at the entrance to Scusset Beach State Reservation, look for the unmarked **Sagamore Hill Trail** as it heads north at the gate opposite the parking lot for the fishing pier and a bait and snack shop. Park at the lot and cross the park road for the trail.

Round the gate, following the mowed fire lane north. Signs explain the cultural significance of this site as an Indian council ground and World War II artillery encampment. A congestion of shrubs and small trees frame the corridor; plaques identify fox grape, greenbrier, and tupelo.

At 0.25 mile, the overgrown path to the right offers an uneventful woods return for a loop. Proceed forward across a clearing that records the encampment site of the 241st Coastal Artillery Battery C. Now keep to the main groomed trail as it bears left and up the hill to a ready room and a Panama gun mount. Recessed in the slope, the ready room has a steel arched entry. If you duck inside, beware of the downward-hanging bolts.

From here, stairs ascend to the bald summit of Sagamore Hill (0.35 mile), where the Wampanoag and other local tribes came together for discussion. Views extend east, featuring Cape Cod Bay; interpretive panels mark the summit. Return as you came.

36   Wellfleet Bay Wildlife Sanctuary

OVERVIEW

On the forearm of Cape Cod, this 1,000-acre sanctuary of the Massachusetts Audubon Society (MAS) occupies a prized location on Wellfleet Bay and Harbor. In 1928, the land supported the private Austin Ornithological Research Station. Today, the sanctuary owes much of its diversification to Dr. Austin's efforts to sculpt the land and promote vegetation that would attract birds. Salt marshes, spring-fed waters, upland pine–oak woods, and field and edge communities compose the sanctuary's vital jigsaw puzzle.

General description:	Interlocking loops explore the property, with three hikes incorporating much of the trail system.
General location:	Cape Cod at South Wellfleet.
Special attractions:	Bird-watching, an observation blind, a salt-marsh boardwalk, spring-flowering shrubs.
Length:	Silver Spring Trail, 0.6-mile loop; Goose Pond–Try Island Hike, 2 miles round trip; Bay View–Fresh Brook Hike, 1.6 miles round trip.
Elevation:	Trails show a maximum 30-foot elevation change.
Difficulty:	All easy.
Maps:	Sanctuary map. Purchase a guide for the Goose Pond Trail at the nature center.
Special concerns:	Per-person admission fee or MAS membership. Obey posted rules; no pets. Beware of poison ivy. Because high tides can claim the boardwalk and the access to Try Island (note the name), be alert to the tides and allow sufficient time for travel both to and from these sites.
Season and hours:	Year-round. Trails, 8:00 A.M. to dusk daily; nature center, 8:30 A.M. to 5:00 P.M. Tuesday through Sunday (daily, Memorial Day through Columbus Day).
For information:	Wellfleet Bay Wildlife Sanctuary.

Key points:

Silver Spring Trail:
- 0.0   Nature center trailhead.
- 0.3   Cross Silver Spring Brook bridge.
- 0.6   End at trailhead.

Goose Pond–Try Island Hike:
- 0.0   Nature center trailhead.
- 0.2   Goose Pond loop junction.
- 0.4   Marsh Cabin; detour to Try Island and boardwalk.
- 1.8   Close Goose Pond loop; return to trailhead.

162

Bay View–Fresh Brook Hike:

0.0   Nature center trailhead.
0.5   Fresh Brook Pathway loop junction.
1.1   Close Fresh Brook Pathway loop; return to trailhead.

Finding the trailhead: In South Wellfleet, just north of the Eastham town line, turn west off U.S. Highway 6, entering the wildlife sanctuary. Look for the blue and white MAS sign.

The hikes: All trails start near the nature center.

The **Silver Spring Trail** encircles Silver Spring Brook where a small dam broadens the channel. Head south away from the nature center on a wood-shavings path, bearing left at a sign for Silver Spring.

Pitch pine and deciduous shrubs line the path leading to a bench over-looking the dark, silty pool on Silver Spring Brook. Red-winged blackbirds enliven the air. Red maple, highbush blueberry, sheep laurel, sweet pepperbush, and winterberry grow along the pond. Painted turtles rest on the logs, and pond lilies decorate the surface in summer.

Circle the pond in a clockwise direction. A small dock provides up- and downstream views. In places, thick splotches of algae claim the water's edge. Reach the south shore via a footbridge for a walk along the low pine-clad ridge. Pine needles soften the trail, and a woodpecker may telegraph its location.

At 0.5 mile, meet and bear right on the Goose Pond Trail, crossing over the earthen dam. A cattail marsh and salt meadow capture the spill water; looks span to the bay. Where the Bay View Trail heads left, proceed on the Goose Pond/Silver Spring Trail, returning to the center at 0.6 mile.

The **Goose Pond–Try Island Hike** explores the southern sanctuary. Hike south on the wood-shavings path, bearing right at the information board. Be alert; the numbered attractions occur in rapid-fire succession. Pass the Bay View Trail on the right, cross the earthen dam to Silver Spring Brook, and keep south, avoiding the Silver Spring Trail on the left.

A broad pine-needle-strewn trail leads the way. As it swings right, overlook Goose Pond to the left, the matted marsh meadow of Silver Spring Brook to the right. Phragmites (plumed reeds) and cattails edge and protrude into the water. A secluded birding blind is on the pond's left shore.

Cross the outlet via boardwalk and, at 0.25 mile, go right (counterclockwise) to pursue the interpretive numbers in sequence. An observation deck adds views of wooded Try Island and the bay. Travel a transition habitat, reaching the open estuary and a junction at 0.4 mile. Among the red cedars to the left is Marsh Cabin.

When tides allow, turn right to visit both Try Island Trail and the boardwalk; bear left for the Goose Pond Trail alone. Opting for the island-boardwalk

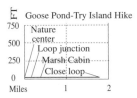

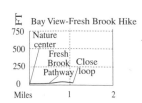

detour, find the first access to the Try Island Trail on the right just past the junction; the second approach is on the right at the start of the boardwalk. Bypass both to hike the boardwalk.

Fish riffle the channels, while the soft earth records the tracks of birds and deer. The boardwalk allows for a close scrutiny of the estuary and its workings. Fiddler crabs poke out from holes and threaten one another with their single oversize claw. The walk ends at a small, quartz-sand barrier beach; sun-dried mussel, snail, and clamshells strew the sands. Gulls and shorebirds often occupy the area. Beware of the sinking sand closer to the water.

Return on the boardwalk and take the first left to add the Try Island Trail. On the loose-sand rise, find mats of lichen, stunted red cedar, beach plum, oak, and pignut hickory. Benches offer area overlooks. Exit the woods, cross a salt meadow, and resume the Goose Pond Trail at 1.2 miles.

Bear right, edging the marsh, discovering sea lavender and glassworts; beach homes across the way steal from the site's wildness. The trail then curves to travel a low wooded rise. At 1.6 miles, turn left; here, the sandy trail parts a patch of bearberry, drawing into an open area. Woods again claim the tour

Wellfleet Bay Wildlife Sanctuary

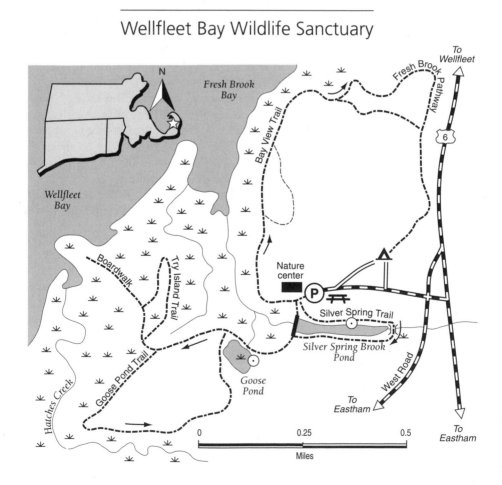

as it approaches Goose Pond. Close the loop at 1.75 miles, retracing the first 0.25 mile to the trailhead.

The **Bay View–Fresh Brook Hike** explores the northern extent of the property. Go south on Goose Pond Trail, quickly turning right (north) on the Bay View Trail. Edge the saltwater marsh, touring below a low pine rise. Bearberry pushes through the grassy forest mat. Expansive marsh views reward hikers.

At 0.2 mile, veer into the woodland, now composed of mixed deciduous trees and beach plum, coming to a junction. From April 15 to July 15, an active osprey nest may close the right fork; the two forks rejoin farther north. In 200 feet, the left fork reaches a gap that allows a peek at the osprey nest. The trees on the rise stand no more than 10 to 15 feet tall.

More marsh views follow as the trail totters from salt-marsh edge to pine upland. Upon crossing a corner of the marsh (0.5 mile), reach benches and a junction. Bear left for a clockwise tour of Fresh Brook Pathway; the right completes the Bay View Loop.

On a clockwise tour of the pathway, travel a pine–oak upland at the northern perimeter; benches overlook the textured marsh drainage of Fresh Brook. Mosses turn the sides of the rolling trail green, as taller oaks frame the path. Where a side trail heads left, bear right for the loop.

At 0.9 mile, turn right onto the Bay View Trail to complete the Fresh Brook Pathway loop at 1.1 miles, and return as you came along the marsh for a 1.6-mile hike. Or follow the Bay View Trail left, paralleling US 6 south, passing through woods and the site's tent campground to reach the nature center at 1.4 miles.

37 Cape Cod National Seashore: Beach Hike

General description:	Between the narrow spit of Coast Guard Beach in Eastham and Race Point Beach in Provincetown, to the north, the national seashore unfurls an unrivaled 25-mile-long invitation to discovery. Pass through monitored areas for swimming, wading, and sunbathing and little-traveled natural areas for reverie.
General location:	Cape Cod, Massachusetts.
Special attractions:	Nesting piping plovers and terns; clean crystalline sands; multiple access points, some with rest rooms and water; wildlife sightings; beachcombing (no collecting).
Length:	23 of the seashore's 25 miles (excluding the 2-mile spit stretching south at Coast Guard Beach).
Elevation:	The hike is flat.
Difficulty:	Easy to strenuous, depending on length.
Maps:	Cape Cod National Seashore Official Map and Guide.

Special concerns: Fee area(s). Keep off the abutting sandbank and dunes; cross only at designated sites. Seasonally, expect to encounter some daytime oversand vehicle use between Head of the Meadow Beach and Race Point (consult the oversand vehicle brochure for time and stretches). All oversand drivers must secure a permit, and all beach users must respect private property and the closed areas protecting nests and sensitive dunes. Carry water.

Season and hours: Year-round, 6:00 A.M. to sunset.

For information: Cape Cod National Seashore, Park Headquarters.

Key points:

  0.0   Coast Guard Beach.
  1.0   Nauset Light.
  3.2   Marconi Beach.
  5.2   LeCount Hollow Town Beach.
 11.0   Ballston Town Beach.
 15.5   Head of the Meadow.
 17.0   High Head.
 23.0   End at Race Point Beach.

Finding the trailhead: On Cape Cod, go north from Eastham on U.S. Highway 6 East; multiple marked turns lead to the national seashore east off the highway. Find Salt Pond Visitor Center off US 6 in Eastham; there, pick up a map to plot travel.

The hike: Glacial activity formed the cape. Its southern beaches are backed by a low, continuous sandbank or bluff, replaced by wind-sculpted dunes north of Head of the Meadow. Throughout its length, a light-colored sand sweeps to the ocean. An occasional thunderclap of surf peppers the otherwise constant ocean roar.

Traveling the forearm and raised fist of Cape Cod peninsula, a south–north stroll of the national seashore begins at Coast Guard Beach (1.8 miles east of Salt Pond). Start below the retired Nauset Coast Guard Station, a charming, weathered white building with green shutters and a red roof.

A thin fingerlike spit stretches south 2 miles, separating the tidal flat of Nauset Marsh from the ocean. From this spit, hikers can overlook the longer spit of Nauset Beach, isolated to the south. Cross-marsh looks find Fort Hill. In 1927, author/naturalist Henry Beston built a cottage on the sands overlooking this estuary and there led a solitary life for a year; his Cape Cod impressions are recorded in *The Outermost House*.

Northbound from Coast Guard Beach, encounter an uninterrupted avenue of glistening sand. In about a mile, pass below Nauset Light, a maritime bea-

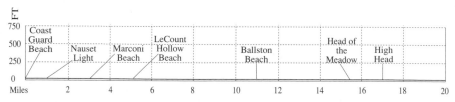

FT
750
500
250
0
Miles   22

Race
Point
Beach

con with its upper third painted red, set back in the low pines. The breeze whips a white spray from the crests of the long waves breaking near shore. Patches of pebbles with bits of white shell alter the look of the beach; farther north, cobbles strew the shore. Both tide and season may influence discovery.

Due to riptides and an unpredictable ocean floor, rangers encourage hikers to confine their wading to protected beaches at Coast Guard, Nauset Light, Marconi, Head of the Meadow, and Race Point. Lobster pots, buoys, skate egg cases, and clamshells divert the eyes, as do feeding terns, harbor seals, and raucous gulls. At 3.25 miles, find the Marconi Beach stairway, where sands drift over the lower steps and wild roses top the 30-foot bluff. Farther north sits Marconi Station, site of the first transatlantic cablegram.

LeCount Hollow Town Beach (5.25 miles) and White Crest Town Beach (6 miles) mark off distance; for each, a steep sandy slope serves as access. In places, the slope to the water becomes more pronounced. Grasses now claim the slip face at the foot of the cliff. Find the town beach facilities more primitive and seasonal in availability; some offer no sanitary facilities at all. Despite the bluffs grading higher, rooftops sometimes peek over their tops.

The town beaches of Cahoon Hollow (7 miles), Newcomb Hollow (8.5 miles), and Ballston (11 miles) sound off progress. At Ballston Beach, snow fences line the bluff, ushering hikers to the sanctioned access gap. Round a wetland to reach its parking area; loose sand taxes the legs. More homes top the headland.

A broad U-shaped gap in the bluff signals the access at Longnook Beach at 12.5 miles. The bluffs now measure 70 feet high, and loose sand hints at

Nauset Coast Guard Station, Cape Cod National Seashore, MA.

Cape Cod National Seashore: Beach Hike

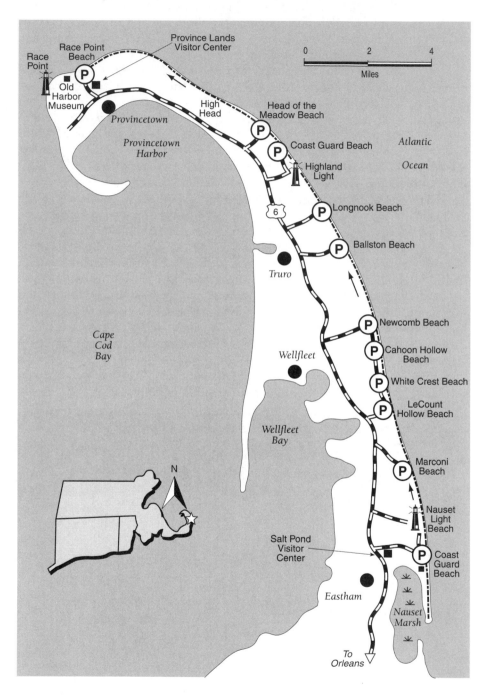

the dune character farther north. Beware of these sliding, unstable cliffs.

A flat, narrow strand welcomes carefree strolling as a long, remote beach stretches north. At 14 miles, find the next landmarks, radar station domes and the stained white-brick tower of Highland Light, the first lighthouse on Cape Cod, built 1798 and replaced in 1857. It rises 183 feet above sea level and remains active. Reach Coast Guard Town Beach in about a mile.

At Head of the Meadow (15.5 miles), find the start of the 10-foot-high dunes, with the beach curvature accounting for a slightly different wave action. A seaward cant again meets the ocean, seabirds bob in the water, and horse-shoe and spider crabs wash to shore. At times, the sand takes on a pink hue. Seasonally, oversand vehicles or their telltale tracks can be spied. At High Head (17 miles), passing ducks may hint at a marsh and Pilgrim Lake cradled in the dunes.

Eventually, looks west across the dunes find the profile of a stone tower, Pilgrim Monument in Provincetown. Inland from Race Point Beach (23 miles), find Province Lands Visitor Center and the Old Harbor Museum Boardwalk, an interpretive trail relating facts about shipwrecks and the early life-savers, and about some possible marine mammal sightings. The northern beach shows a coarser-grained sand that easily displaces beneath the foot. Facing mostly north, the beach receives less punishment from the Atlantic, offering milder waters for the frolic of youngsters. End at the visitor center or at the tip of Race Point.

38 Cape Cod National Seashore: Northern Nature Trails

OVERVIEW

The national seashore extends a varied collection of nature trails that examine the cultural and natural history and early commerce of the area. Explore cranberry bog, cedar swamp, and migrating dunes and visit the site of a spring where Pilgrims first tasted the sweet water of the New World.

General description:	Ten short nature trails (five in Eastham; see hike 39) are dispersed throughout Cape Cod National Seashore; find the featured trails north of Eastham at Wellfleet, Truro, and Provincetown.
General location:	Cape Cod, Massachusetts.
Special attractions:	Historical sites; a rare Atlantic white cedar swamp; estuarine, pond, and seashore vistas; spring-flowering annuals and shrubs; fall foliage; bird-watching.
Length:	Featured hikes range between 0.5 and 1.25 miles in length.

	Elevation:	Find less than a 100-foot elevation change.
	Difficulty:	All are easy to moderate.
	Maps:	National seashore map; pick up interpretive brochures at the park visitor centers or trailheads.
	Special concerns:	Fee area. No pets. Carry insect repellent, and beware of poison ivy. Hikers may purchase a plant identification guide at the visitor center; it identifies plants seen at numbered sites along the park trails.
	Season and hours:	Year-round, 6:00 A.M. to sunset.
	For information:	Cape Cod National Seashore, Park Headquarters.

Key points:

Atlantic White Cedar Swamp Trail:

- 0.0 Trailhead.
- 0.5 Cedar swamp.
- 0.7 Old Wireless Road.
- 1.2 End at trailhead.

Pamet Valley Trail:

- 0.0 Trailhead.
- 0.2 Abandoned Bog House; return as you came.

Small's Swamp Trail:

- 0.0 Trailhead.
- 0.1 Loop junction.
- 0.2 Wetland boardwalk.
- 0.6 Close loop; return to trailhead.

Pilgrim Spring Trail:

- 0.0 Trailhead.
- 0.3 Pilgrim Spring.
- 0.7 End at trailhead.

Beech Forest Trail:

- 0.0 Trailhead.
- 0.3 Beech Forest Loop.
- 0.5 Pond Loop.
- 1.0 End at trailhead.

Finding the trailhead: Locate the trailheads east off U.S. Highway 6 in Wellfleet, Truro, and Provincetown; brown signs mark the turns. First, however, stop at Salt Pond Visitor Center east off US 6 in Eastham to pick up a map and plot your travel.

The hikes: The Wellfleet area serves up an award-winning nature trail, the Atlantic White Cedar Swamp Trail. Hikers seeking a longer trek in this area should ask about the Great Island Trail.

The premier **Atlantic White Cedar Swamp Trail** travels 1.25 miles and invites a slow and appreciative investigation. To access it, turn east off US 6 for Marconi Station and proceed 1 mile to the station parking lot. West off the parking lot loop, find the hike's loop junction in 50 feet. Go left for a

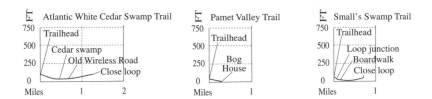

clockwise tour, passing through dwarf woods, mature pines, and black oaks to cross a single-lane dirt road, reaching the cedar swamp (0.5 mile).

A scenic boardwalk meanders through the picturesque dense cedar stand, but beware: The boardwalk can be slippery when wet. A wonderful aura of mystery clings to the site on gray, foggy days. Mossy mounds add to the texture. Historically, the trees measured 4 feet in diameter, but those fell to harvest long ago. Turnout benches serve admirers.

Reach the boardwalk's loop junction at 0.6 mile and go left. The forest opens up, losing the intermingling deciduous trees and shrubs. Discover knotted cedars, intriguing branchworks, and moss-and-lichen-reclaimed stumps. At 0.7 mile, the right fork completes the boardwalk loop for a backtracking return to the parking lot. Go left for a loop return to the trailhead, tracing Old Wireless Road, the 1903 route to Marconi Station. From the oak and sheep laurel outskirts of the swamp, ascend steadily via the sandy road, rediscovering the same woods habitats encountered on the descent; midway is a bench. The hike ends at 1.25 miles.

Three nature trails begin in the Truro area: Pamet Valley, Small's Swamp, and Pilgrim Spring Trails.

For the **Pamet Valley Trail,** turn east onto North Pamet Road in Truro, go 1.5 miles, and park in the small lot below the environmental education center. Cross North Pamet Road to start this 0.5-mile trail, passing among pine and beach plum; bearberry is the ground cover. The trail rolls, with reinforced steps advancing the tour. At 0.1 mile, look for the long arm of a pine that bowed to the ground, rerooted, and again shot skyward. Overlook the bog and descend to round it.

A boardwalk framed by highbush blueberry and various other shrubs and grasses leads to the sometimes soggy remnant of a cranberry bog. Bogs of American cranberry naturally thrive in kettle depressions in the dunes; in the 1800s, such bogs were cultivated into a commercial enterprise. Berries typically ripen in September and October. Reach the abandoned Bog House at the end of the boardwalk and return as you came.

For the **Small's Swamp** and **Pilgrim Spring Trails,** go east at the sign for Pilgrim Heights and proceed to the interpretive center at the end of the road. The shelter overlooks the site toured by the Small's Swamp Trail.

For the 0.75-mile **Small's Swamp Trail,** pass through the shelter, descending log-braced steps to the loop junction (0.1 mile). Stay left alongside a rustic rail fence, passing among pitch pines and black oaks; grass,

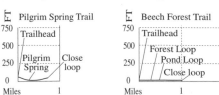

Cape Cod National Seashore: Northern Nature Trails

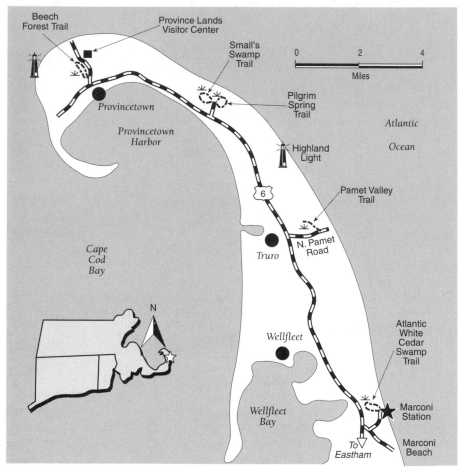

bearberry, and fern patch the floor. A dense woodland thicket then claims the flat. At 0.25 mile, a boardwalk skirts a wetland area. Ascend in a shower of white spring blooms to a vista with interpretive signs.

Below stretches Salt Meadow, a salt grass meadow threaded by a dark-water channel isolated from the ocean by dunes. This site marks the demarcation between the glacial headland and the wind-formed Provincetown Hook. Offshore in 1778, the wreck of the *Somerset*, a British man-of-war, allowed the colonists to capture the British sailors. From the second interpretive sign, the trail curves back into a pitch pine woods to close the loop and return to the trailhead (0.75 mile).

The 0.7-mile **Pilgrim Spring Trail** begins to the right of the shelter, entering a stand of 25-foot-tall pines; needles soften the path. At 0.2 mile, draw into the open, coming to a vista with interpretive panels. The view spans Salt Meadow. Archaeological discoveries date a Native American presence here to 2,000 years ago.

Next, descend a set of steps and travel a passage through woods and scrub thicket to reach the small monument citing the Pilgrim discovery of the freshwater spring on November 16, 1620. Led by Miles Standish, the first Pilgrims followed the tracks of Indians and deer to locate this water. Near the site, find a table and the paved bike path. Resume the clockwise loop, ascending back toward the parking area. Cross a pine-clad hilltop, traverse the picnic area, and round past a seasonal rest room, returning to the interpretive shelter.

Near Provincetown, reach the last nature trail, the **Beech Forest Trail,** 0.5 mile north off US 6 on Race Point Road. This figure-8 trail unites a 0.75-mile pond loop and a 0.25-mile beech forest loop. The hike skirts Beech Forest Pond, a wildlife pond pinched at the middle by marsh grass; pond lilies decorate the dark stillness.

From the marked trailhead, pass through a mixed woodland on a log-bordered path of loose sand. Canada mayflower and flowering trees and shrubs recommend a spring tour. Small birds animate the treetops; geese and meadowlarks sound from nearby. Before long, the trail rolls along a tree-reclaimed dune. Dense vegetation denies pond views.

At 0.3 mile, bear right for the Beech Forest Loop. The signature tree abounds as the trail travels a "canyon" passage among the dune rises; most of the beech trees have escaped the degradation of initial-carvers. A boardwalk briefly advances the trail. At 0.4 mile, begin the rolling return, ascending and descending log-braced steps, traversing the wooded dunes. Sassafras, oak, and pine intermingle with the beech.

At 0.55 mile, meet the Pond Loop and bear right for an outer-perimeter tour of this figure-8 trail system. The trail mildly descends to round Beech Forest Pond. Where the trail again ascends, gain a pond overlook. The pitch pines create a more open border for stealing pond glimpses; shrubby islands mark the glacial kettle pool. Pass the rest room to end the hike at 1 mile.

39   Cape Cod National Seashore: Eastham-Area Nature Trails

OVERVIEW

The national seashore boasts a superb assembly of short nature trails that introduce both the cultural and natural history of the area. Journey to the past, visiting sites that hark back to the Native Americans, the Pilgrims' arrival, colonial settlement, and maritime history. Explore kettle ponds, marsh, red maple swamp, and coastal forest.

General description:	Ten short nature trails are dispersed the length of Cape Cod National Seashore. Five lie within easy reach of Eastham/Salt Pond Visitor Center; locate the others to the north at Wellfleet, Truro, and Provincetown (see hike 38).
General location:	Cape Cod, Massachusetts.
Special attractions:	Historical sites; marsh, pond, and coastal vistas; spring-flowering shrubs; bird-watching.
Length:	The featured hikes range between 0.2 and 2 miles in length.
Elevation:	Find less than a 100-foot elevation change.
Difficulty:	All are easy to moderate.
Maps:	National seashore map; pick up interpretive brochures at the park visitor center or at the trailheads.
Special concerns:	Fee area. No pets. Carry insect repellent, and beware of poison ivy. Hikers may purchase a plant identification guide at the visitor center; it describes the vegetation seen at the numbered posts along park trails.
Season and hours:	Year-round, 6:00 A.M. to sunset.
For information:	Cape Cod National Seashore, Park Headquarters.

Key points:

Red Maple Swamp–Fort Hill Nature Trail Hike:
- 0.0   Shared trailhead.
- 0.2   Red Maple Swamp.
- 0.7   Skiff Hill.
- 1.2   Fort Hill.
- 1.9   Penniman House.
- 2.0   End back at trailhead.

Buttonbush Trail:
- 0.0   Salt Pond Visitor Center trailhead.
- 0.2   End loop at visitor center.

Nauset Marsh Trail:
- 0.0   Salt Pond Visitor Center trailhead.
- 0.4   Salt Pond footbridge and dike.
- 1.2   End loop at trailhead.

Doane Loop Trail:
- 0.0   Doane Rock/Doane Loop Trailhead.
- 0.2   Homesite of Deacon Doane.
- 0.5   Complete loop at trailhead.

Finding the trailhead: Locate the trailheads east off U.S. Highway 6 in Eastham; brown signs mark the turns. Also find Salt Pond Visitor Center in Eastham; there pick up a national seashore map.

The hikes: At the southernmost trail site, the **Red Maple Swamp** and **Fort Hill Nature Trails** interlock, suggesting a single 2-mile tour. Reach

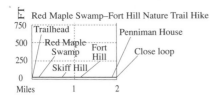
Red Maple Swamp–Fort Hill Nature Trail Hike

Buttonbush Trail

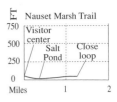
Nauset Marsh Trail

the common trailhead by way of Governor Prence Road. Find parking on the left in 0.3 mile, east past the historic Penniman House.

From the northeast corner of the parking lot, edge field and woods, with cross-field looks at the coast. At 0.1 mile, the swamp and Fort Hill trails go their separate ways; go left, touring the wishbone-shaped **Red Maple Swamp Trail** first. Pass through a corridor of eastern red cedar and bear left. Log-braced earthen stairs then descend to the flat of the Red Maple Swamp, where a curving boardwalk continues the tour. Mosses clump at the feet of shrubs, and a thick mat of algae and decaying leaves caps the standing water.

At 0.25 mile, the left fork allows hikers to shorten the swamp loop; stay right for the full tour. Catbrier and raspberry entangle the trail's sides; soggier reaches can be especially buggy. Woodpecker, robin, chickadee, and blue jay may divert attention as another scenic boardwalk leads the way. Netted chain fern and snags contribute to the woods.

At 0.5 mile, the cutoff arrives on the left; again bear right. Interpretive plaques identify highbush blueberry, fox grape, winterberry, and sweet pepperbush. Just ahead, a left leads to Hemenway Landing, a small boat launch on the estuary; go right for Skiff and Fort Hills. Find broken-shell and paved surfaces, as the trail rounds a seasonally open rest room.

At 0.7 mile, three benches overlook Nauset Marsh, with its low-tide mosaic of open water and salt meadow grass. The paved trail then returns to a red cedar corridor, coming out at Skiff Hill (0.75 mile). Here, find a covered open-sided interpretive kiosk and a relocated twenty-ton boulder. Look for the distinctive grooves that record where Nauset Indians sharpened their implements on this abrasive metamorphic rock.

Now follow the **Fort Hill Trail** as it heads seaward near the kiosk. By 0.8 mile, traverse a low bluff, edging a rolling field partitioned by rock walls. Continue to enjoy overlooks of Nauset Marsh. Rabbits and bobwhites favor the field. At a large stone at 1.1 miles, enjoy a final view of the marsh as it opens to the sea. Pass and ascend through a field, topping Fort Hill at a parking area (1.2 miles) for an admiring look at the rock, field, and woods terrain.

Pass through a gap in the fence, descending through field and amid black locust trees to encircle the Penniman House, a picturesque two-story Second French Empire mansion topped by a cupola. Swallows dart from the open basement. A whalebone archway hints at how Penniman made his fortune at sea. Orange lichens mottle the bone. End at the parking area at 2 miles.

Start both the **Buttonbush** and **Nauset Marsh Trails** at Salt Pond Visitor Center.

Cape Cod National Seashore: Eastham-Area Nature Trails

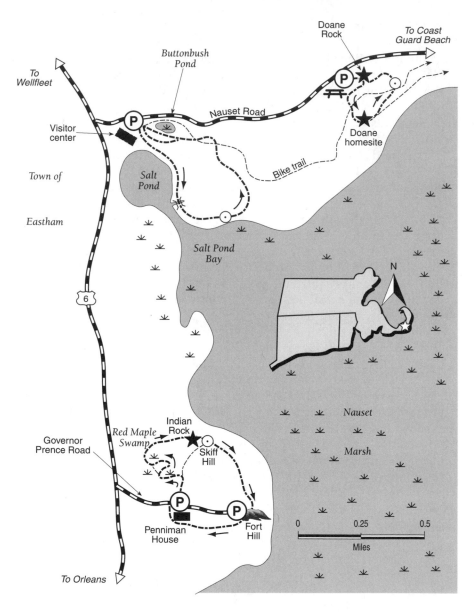

To Wellfleet

Buttonbush Pond

Doane Rock

To Coast Guard Beach

Nauset Road

Visitor center

Doane homesite

Town of

Eastham

Salt Pond

Bike trail

Salt Pond Bay

6

N

Red Maple Swamp

Indian Rock

Skiff Hill

Nauset

Governor Prence Road

Marsh

Penniman House

Fort Hill

0   0.25   0.5

Miles

To Orleans

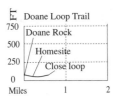

The 0.2-mile Buttonbush Trail serves blind and low-vision visitors with guide ropes, touch cues for signaling steps, and large-type and Braille interpretive plaques.

Below the parking area, head east from the amphitheater, bearing left for a clockwise loop. This circuit travels to a boardwalk overlooking Buttonbush Pond, a kettle pond about 2 feet deep left behind by receding glaciers some 18,000 years ago. Winterberry, wild rose, and grape adorn the area. In spring, cream floral balls top the 3-foot-tall buttonbush, aiding in its identification. Midway, pass the Nauset Marsh Trail. Beach plum and bayberry edge the trail. At 0.2 mile, complete the loop.

Reach the 1.2-mile **Nauset Marsh Trail** east of the visitor center and to the right of the amphitheater. Descend toward the open shore of Salt Pond. On Sunday, a kayaker or clammer may be encountered. Road noise from US 6 intrudes.

This classic freshwater kettle pond became brackish when breached by tide. Salt grass, seaside lavender, and cordgrass accent its shore, while beach plum and oak claim the slope rising above the wide hiking lane. Keep to shore, reaching the outlet and tidal channel; cross a footbridge; and tour the dike. Do not stray from the trail—private property lies to the right.

Enter woodland, crossing over a two-track, following signs to the right. Stairs ascend to an overlook bench at 0.6 mile; low tides reveal a scenic mudflat. A gull feeding on crabs or clammers armed with rakes and buckets hint at the food-rich habitat. The circuit continues through open cedar, coming to a junction: To the right is Doane Memorial; the path ahead continues the loop.

A more mixed woods frames the open aisle of the foot trail. Round a small wetland with lilies and buttonbush before the trail again rolls uphill. Twice cross the bike path, meeting the Buttonbush Trail at 1.1 miles. Go left with the traffic flow to end at the amphitheater.

Go 0.9 mile east from Salt Pond Visitor Center to reach the 0.5-mile **Doane Loop Trail,** a wheelchair-accessible route at Doane Picnic Area.

Start from the first parking area, following the wide paved path away from the designated wheelchair-accessible parking space. Doane Rock sits to the left; the loop is to the right. Detour left a short distance to discover the largest glacial erratic deposited in the park. Glaciers carried Doane Rock to this site an estimated 12,000 years ago. Some 18 feet of its height point skyward, while another 12 feet remain locked in the ground. The boulder spans 45 feet.

The loop bypasses the rest room and crosses the park road at a crosswalk to travel a mixed pine–oak woods. Cross a second road and a paved bike trail to reach a sign for Doane Memorial at 0.2 mile. View the homesite of Deacon Doane across the roadway. A foundation and a stone marker commemorate the settlement of Nauset/Eastham by seven Pilgrim families who broke from the Plymouth majority, coming here in 1644.

Bypass a trail branching to the beach, following Doane Loop as it bends left. Cross back over the bike trail, finding a spur to a vista bench. Sights include the Nauset Coast Guard Station, the marsh, and ocean. Return to the picnic area at the second parking lot and return to the start.

Fern, Red Maple Swamp Trail, Cape Cod National Seashore, MA.

40 South Cape Beach State Park

OVERVIEW

A relative newcomer to the Massachusetts Forests and Parks system and part of Waquoit Bay National Estuarine Research Reserve (NERR), this 401-acre park has all the earmarks of an up-and-coming star. The Department of Environmental Management (DEM) has slated improvements for facilities, trails, and roads, but even as the park struggles through infancy, hikers find enjoyable discovery. Crystalline-sand beaches; vital ponds and wetlands; nesting piping plover, tern, and osprey; and an off-season wilderness solitude all recommend a look. A visitor center serving the area can be found at Waquoit Bay NERR.

General description: An inland nature trail and pair of beach hikes explore the park offering.

General location: Southwest corner of Cape Cod, Massachusetts.

Special attractions: Coastal and bay beaches; estuarine and freshwater ponds; marsh, coastal shrub, and woods habitats; bird-watching; surf fishing; beachcombing (no collecting).

Length: Great Flat Pond Trail, 1-mile loop (plans call for redesign and expansion of this trail); Dead Neck Beach–Waquoit Bay Hike, 3.7 miles round trip; Eastward Beach Hike, 1.6 miles round trip.

Elevation: All are flat.

Difficulty: Great Flat Pond Trail and Eastward Beach Hike, both easy; the Dead Neck Beach–Waquoit Bay Hike is moderate.

Maps: South Cape Beach map (generally available in a map box at the start of the Great Flat Pond Trail).

Special concerns: Vehicle admission fee in summer; no dogs. Respect nesting sites, granting birds a wide margin of safety. Note that future plans call for a developed trail along Sage Lot Pond.

Season and hours: Year-round, daylight hours.

For information: South Cape Beach State Park; Waquoit Bay NERR.

Key points:
Great Flat Pond Trail:
  0.0   State park trailhead.
  0.1   Loop junction.
  0.9   Close loop; return to trailhead.

Dead Neck Beach–Waquoit Bay Hike:
  0.0   State park beach boardwalk access.
  0.1   Town beach.

1.5   Jetty.
3.7   End at beach boardwalk.

Eastward Beach Hike:
0.0   State park beach boardwalk access.
0.8   Cobbled end of second point; return as you came.

Finding the trailhead: From the Mashpee Rotary on Massachusetts Highway 28, take Great Neck Road south. In 2.6 miles, where Main Road curves right, continue forward on Great Oak Road, following signs for the park. In another 2 miles, turn left onto the unpaved entrance road. Within a mile, find a paved road heading left; it leads to the state park's parking lot and beach boardwalk. The dirt road continues, ending at a town beach parking area.

The hikes: All hikes start from the state park parking area.

Find the circuit of the **Great Flat Pond Trail** north of the parking area. Pass through forest of pitch pine and oak and follow a narrow sandy footpath parting waist- to chest-deep shrubbery, skirting a vast salt-marsh meadow and pond—Great Flat Pond. Huckleberry, highbush blueberry, azalea, sheep laurel, bracken fern, and greenbrier compose much of the floral congestion. The loop twice crosses the paved park road. In the woods, beware of poison ivy and look for lady's slipper.

Although obstructed side trails branch toward Great Flat Pond and marsh overlooks, keep to the primary loop, traveling foot trail, berm, and boardwalk. Where the loop does allow for open views, admire the head-tall grasses of Great Flat Pond. When wet or frosty conditions exist, be especially careful on the plank boardwalks.

For the **Dead Neck Beach–Waquoit Bay Hike** and **Eastward Beach Hike,** start at the state park's beach boardwalk. Hikers who choose to start at the town beach 0.1 mile west need to adjust the mileages accordingly.

Turn west (right) upon reaching the south-facing beach for the **Dead Neck Beach–Waquoit Bay Hike;** views span Vineyard Sound to Martha's Vineyard. Travel loose, light-colored crystalline sands, passing below low dunes trimmed in wild rose, dune grass, and poison ivy. The strand measures some 40 feet wide, depending on tide. A filament of dark seaweed often records the tideline.

Lifeguard perches mark the town beach, where anglers cast their lines in the off-season. Terns, cormorants, and shorebirds commonly divert attention. At 0.4 mile, a beach-access trail leads to Sage Lot Pond; keep to the beach.

Off-season visits promise wonderfully wild walks, with discoveries of crab claws and carapaces, snails, and slipper shells, as well as a rainbow spec-

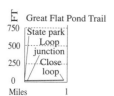

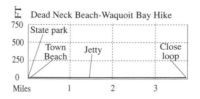

South Cape Beach State Park

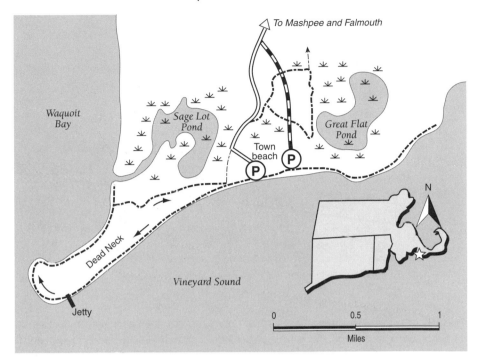

To Mashpee and Falmouth

Waquoit Bay

Sage Lot Pond

Great Flat Pond

Town beach

P   P

Dead Neck

Vineyard Sound

Jetty

N

0   0.5   1

Miles

trum of seaweed: tubular, leafy, or stringy. At 0.6 mile, a spur accesses the closed dirt track that links Sage Lot Pond with the jetty area to the west. Proceed on beach; the sinking sands work the calf muscles.

Before long, skirt the fragile nesting sites of the piping plovers, staying well below the mesh enclosures. If tides prohibit doing that, turn back. The well-being of the plovers supersedes any rights or wishes of the hiker. At 1.5 miles, reach a rock jetty capped by flat rocks, walkable when storms and seas allow.

The beach tour continues, now rounding Waquoit Bay and offering admiring looks at Washburn Island, the beautiful bay curvature, and Waquoit Bay National Estuarine Reserve on the far shore. Find small estuarine pools and a finer, compressed sand for easier strolling; moonshells, clams, and scallops dot the white sand. Signposts rise in the flat to the right, and dunes swell to 6 feet tall.

At 2.5 miles, before reaching the estuarine grasses and open-water mouth of Sage Lot Pond, find a path heading inland to a jeep road, this hike's loop return. But first detour along the bay 0.1 mile farther to view the pond's outlet. Discoveries may include weathered snags and posts providing roosts for seabirds; a fishing boat marooned in the mud; and swans, ducks, and cormorants sharing the sheltered water.

Return to the 2.5-mile junction and hike inland, following the jeep trail as it curves left to Sage Lot Pond; to the right leads back to the coastal shore

South Cape Beach, South Cape Beach State Park, MA.

(avoid taking during nesting season). The jeep track offers grand overlooks of Sage Lot Pond. Red and white shore roses, daisies, and beach peas sprinkle seasonal color as a reclaimed flattened dune stretches right. At 3.2 miles, take the foot trail to the right, return to the beach, and turn left (east) to end at the boardwalk (3.7 miles).

For the **Eastward Beach Hike,** turn left (east) upon reaching the south-facing beach. Here, hikers again find areas of the leg-taxing, sparkling sands. What differentiates this hike are the 5- to 6-foot-tall dunes backing the strand. At 0.15 mile, a gap in the dunes offers a peek at Great Flat Pond, its open water, and marsh shore.

At a broad sandy point at 0.3 mile, pebbles crunch beneath your shoes. Before long, snow fences collect and hold the sand as hikers pass below a golf course. Keep to the beach; a second point of land comes into view. The cobbly end of this second point at 0.8 mile signals the turnaround, because residences rise above the beach to the east, further stealing its wildness. Views west find Woods Hole, Elizabeth Islands, and Martha's Vineyard.

Western Connecticut Trails

The Connecticut River forms a natural divide, slicing Connecticut into east and west halves. West of the river, find the rugged, steep, and hilly terrain of Litchfield Hills and the traprock ridges rising from the Connecticut River Valley. A flatter coastal plain meets Long Island Sound to the south.

Typically, southern hardwoods with hemlock groves and pine plantations shade travel. Red maple swamps splash intense red splendor on the autumn landscape, while mountain laurel (the state flower) grows with abandon, heralding spring and early summer. Tulip poplar is showy in both bloom and size. Stone walls, charcoal sites, and Native American and colonial history spice travel. Explore forest, hilltop, rocky ledge, brook, pond, swamp, and a Housatonic River reservoir; roam a giant's anatomy; and hide with the exiled British judges who ordered the execution of Charles I.

41   Peoples State Forest

OVERVIEW

This 3,000-acre forest, purchased by public subscription in the 1920s, stretches east from West Branch Farmington River in northwest Connecticut. It contains a diverse forest with stately trees, one of the best overlooks in the state, and Barkhamsted Lighthouse, a historic Indian settlement. Touring the forest, find a splendid system of interlocking trails; the described loop incorporates several of them.

General description:	This rolling day-hike loop passes amid relaxing woods and showers of mountain laurel, snaring a pair of prized overlooks and passing historic sites.
General location:	5 miles north of New Hartford, Connecticut.
Special attractions:	Historic Indian cemetery, cellar holes, diverse woods, vistas, bird-watching, fall foliage.
Length:	6.1 miles round trip (this is the loop measurement alone; it excludes a spur distance to Chaugham cabin, because hikers have options of routes to take).
Elevation:	The loop shows a 550-foot elevation change.
Difficulty:	Moderate.
Maps:	State forest brochure (generally available at the site).
Special concerns:	A fee is charged weekends, Memorial Day weekend through Columbus Day weekend. Pets must be leashed. Find the trails color-coded; blazes either show the actual color or a dot of the specified color on a blue background.

Season and hours: Year-round; spring through fall for hiking, 8:00 A.M. to sunset; Stone Museum, Sunday afternoon, Memorial Day through Columbus Day, with Saturday hours added July and August.

For information: Peoples State Forest.

Key points:

    0.0   Robert Ross Trailhead.
    0.1   Stone Museum.
    0.2   Loop junction.
    1.6   Jessie Gerard Trail and approach to Chaugham cabin site/Indian cemetery.
    2.4   Chaugham Lookout.
    3.5   Beaver Brook Recreation Area.
    5.9   Complete loop; return to trailhead.

Finding the trailhead: From New Hartford, go west on U.S. Highway 44 for 1.4 miles, and turn north onto Connecticut Highway 181. In 1 mile, turn right to cross the Farmington River. Upon exiting the bridge, turn left onto East River Road. You will pass Greenwoods Road on the right in 0.8 mile; it travels north through the heart of the forest, accessing trails and recreation areas. In another 0.2 mile, turn left off East River Road for Matthies Grove Recreation Area and trailhead parking.

The hike: This loop travels the Robert Ross, Jessie Gerard, Charles Pack, and Agnes Bowen Trails, all named for benefactors of Peoples State Forest. From the information board and map box at Matthies Grove Recreation Area, cross East River Road and hike east on the blue-blazed Robert Ross Trail, passing between a pair of posts.

Ascend on the soft bed of an old road grade, touring a white pine–deciduous woods. At 0.1 mile, find Stone Museum, a small, seasonally open natural history museum. Skirt it, veering left across a gravel parking lot to resume the hike.

Pass beneath some head-tilting big trees and bear left at the 0.2-mile junction with Agnes Bowen Trail (the loop's return). Foot trail now continues the tour, ascending in a mixed forest with mountain laurel, maple-leaved viburnum, fern, and sarsaparilla; a few tulip poplar grace the woods.

The blue trail discards its climbing mode at 0.6 mile to descend through a picturesque laurel corridor. Pass the occasional rock sporting a squirrel's acorn harvest. At 0.8 mile, bear right, following a woods road to the King Road turnaround; there angle left into forest. Where the trail forks, bear right, staying with the blue blazes for a similar rolling trek through relaxing woods.

At 1.3 miles, angle uphill, crossing the Agnes Bowen Trail. Now, a defined slope drops west to the Farmington River. The terrain grows rockier below an outcrop crest displaying rounded cliffs and sharp-edged breaks. Descend steeply for a short distance, meeting the yellow

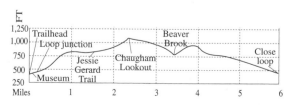

Peoples State Forest

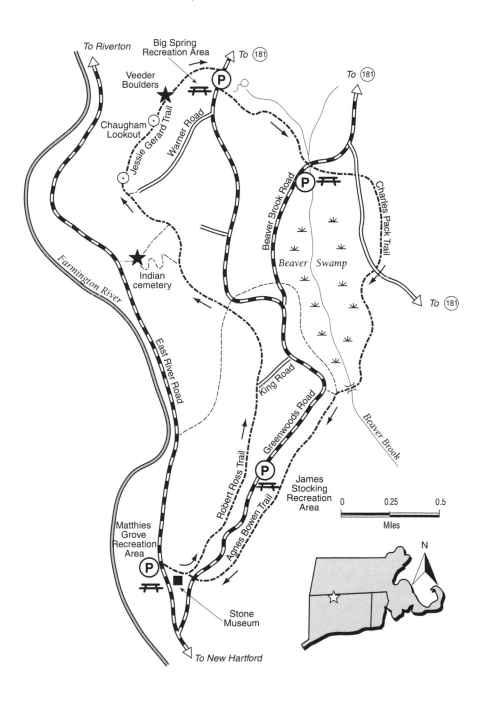

To Riverton

Big Spring Recreation Area

To (181)

Veeder Boulders

To (181)

Chaugham Lookout

Warner Road

Jessie Gerard Trail

Farmington River

Beaver Brook Road

Charles Pack Trail

Indian cemetery

Beaver Swamp

East River Road

To (181)

King Road

Greenwoods Road

Beaver Brook

Robert Ross Trail

James Stocking Recreation Area

0   0.25   0.5

Miles

Agnes Bowen Trail

Matthies Grove Recreation Area

Stone Museum

N

To New Hartford

Jessie Gerard Trail at its southern access spur (1.65 miles). A descent left on it leads to what is dubbed Barkhamsted Lighthouse (the Chaugham cabin site), as well as an Indian settlement cemetery, with primitive head- and footstones. This southern spur comes out at East River Road in 0.25 mile. Chaugham, a Native American, married the rebellious daughter of an American colonist. At night, the light from his cabin shown like a beacon, alerting stagecoach travelers that New Hartford was within 5 miles.

For the loop, follow a shared segment of the Robert Ross/Jessie Gerard Trail uphill to the right. At 1.8 miles, locate the northern access spur of the Jessie Gerard Trail. It offers an alternative descent of 299 stone steps to the Chaugham cabin site; bear left (south) where it forks to view the cellar hole and graves.

For the loop alone, continue climbing at 1.8 miles. In autumn, skeins of honking geese pass south over the Farmington River. At 2 miles, where the blue trail heads right to Warner Road, stay on the yellow Jessie Gerard Trail for a treacherously steep ascent over stone steps and canted outcrops. Reach the first of two overlooks at 2.1 miles for a mostly wild southern view out the Farmington Valley. When dressed in fall foliage, the landscape inspires. Top the ridge and hike north through forest to Chaugham Lookout (2.4 miles) for a northwestern perspective with the rural charm of Riverton.

The loop resumes north, still following yellow blazes for a slow descent among hemlocks. Beyond the bookend multiton Veeder Boulders (2.5 miles), the descent quickens. Soon, bear right onto a woods road to reach Greenwoods Road, the main forest artery. Turn right to resume the loop on the yellow Charles Pack Trail (2.9 miles) as it heads left just past Big Spring Recreation Area.

Pass the rock-rimmed circular pool of Big Spring and descend along Beaver Brook, touring rich hemlock–hardwood forest. Despite a rocky forest floor, the trail remains relatively rock-free. Cross a side brook on hewn logs to reach little-used Beaver Brook Road. Go left, cross the brook on the road bridge, and turn right, following blazes through Beaver Brook Recreation Area, a small, rustic picnic site.

Ascend through similar forest on lightly tracked path, now relying on blazes. At 3.65 miles, cross Pack Grove Road, a dirt woods road, to contour the hemlock slope above it. Proceed over a scenic rock wall and descend to cross Pack Grove Road a second time. Big hemlocks continue to embellish the tour; find more rock walls and foundations. At the fork at 4.65 miles, bear right and descend to cross a footbridge over Beaver Brook.

As the trail ascends, it skirts Beaver Swamp, betrayed only by a change of lighting in the forest. At 4.8 miles, leave the Charles Pack Trail and pursue the orange Agnes Bowen Trail, heading left to close the loop.

Enjoy a scenic rolling course, once again in greater concentrations of mountain laurel. Skirt the edge of James Stocking Recreation Area to descend a rocky, rootbound foot trail beside a drainage. Tulip trees inspire. At 5.8 miles, cross the drainage via stones to cross Greenwoods Road. Close the loop back at the 0.2-mile junction (5.9 miles) and backtrack the blue Robert Ross Trail to Matthies Grove Parking.

42   Sharon Audubon Center

OVERVIEW

In northwest Connecticut, this 684-acre wildlife sanctuary of the National Audubon Society offers 11 miles of foot trail that meander past brook, pond, and bog, across wooded ridge, and through unkempt fields dotted with wildflowers. The Lucy Harvey Multiple-use Interpretive Area near the museum offers an easy 0.3-mile trail explaining the area's natural and cultural history.

General description:	Two hikes stitch together several named trails, exploring the east and west halves of the sanctuary. The east hike visits two ponds and tours woods and field. The west hike remains primarily in woods, basking in solitude.
General location:	3 miles south of Sharon, Connecticut.
Special attractions:	Bird- and wildlife-watching, ponds, gardens, historical sites, spring maple sugaring, fall foliage.
Length:	East Loop, 2.5 miles round trip, including a side trip on the Woodchuck Trail; West Loop, 1.7 miles round trip.
Elevation:	East Loop, less than a 100-foot elevation change; West Loop, 250-foot elevation change.
Difficulty:	Both moderate.
Maps:	Sanctuary map (available at the trailhead mapboard or center office); borrow a brochure for the Lucy Harvey walk at the office.
Special concerns:	Per-person admission fee or National Audubon Society membership; obey posted rules. No pets.
Season and hours:	Year-round; spring through fall for hiking. Trails, dawn to dusk; visitor center/nature store, 9:00 A.M. to 5:00 P.M. Monday through Saturday, 1:00 P.M. to 5:00 P.M. Sunday.
For information:	Sharon Audubon Center.

Key points:

East Loop:
- 0.0   Trailhead.
- 0.1   Loop junction at Ford Pond.
- 0.5   Add Woodchuck Trail.
- 1.9   Bog Meadow Pond vista.
- 2.4   Close loop; return to trailhead.

West Loop:
- 0.0   Trailhead; cross Herrick Brook.
- 0.1   Explorer's Hut.
- 0.6   Third bridge crossing of Herrick Brook.

1.4   Bog Meadow Road.

1.7   End loop at trailhead.

Finding the trailhead: From the junction of Connecticut Highways 4, 41, and 343 at the southern outskirts of Sharon, go east on CT 4 for 2.2 miles and turn right (south) to enter the sanctuary. From the CT 4–U.S. Highway 7 junction in Cornwall Bridge, go west on CT 4 for 5.2 miles to reach the sanctuary entrance.

The hikes: Loop hikers encounter multiple junctions. Because not all of them have signs, carry a map. The West Loop receives less traffic, which for some of us is a plus, but when the leaves obscure the trails in autumn, be especially alert for the few markers and any natural clues to the trail. Both hikes start from the mapboard at the south end of the parking lot.

For the **East Loop,** pass behind the mapboard and turn left, following the Lucy Harvey Multiple-use Area Trail upstream along a ditch and Herrick Brook. The ditch and Ford Pond (just ahead) supplied water to Handlin Mill, a saw- and cider mill that formerly stood behind what is now the center office. Maple, sumac, witch hazel, and wild grape edge the corridor.

In 100 yards, reach the grassy cart path of Bog Meadow Road (the old town road) and turn right, leaving the Lucy Harvey tour. Cross a small bridge, pass the rustic Ice House, and veer left on a foot trail ascending the earthen levee along Ford Pond. This large pond shows a filmy surface and vegetated shallows, enfolded by grasses, shrubs, and woods. When autumn paints the brim and summons arrows of honking geese, the setting becomes electric.

At the pond's southwest corner, find the loop junction: To the left travels the Fern Trail; ahead lies the Hendrickson Bog Meadow Trail. Follow the Fern Trail left as it hugs the south shore of Ford Pond. Hemlock groves and stands of maple, ash, and birch claim the shore, with at least six species of fern at their feet. A tulip tree drops showers of blooms in spring and its unique leaves in fall. Encounter some rocks and roots.

Keep to shore, avoiding a connecting spur to the Hendrickson Bog Meadow Trail. Beaver-girdled and fallen trees open the tour. Soon after, overlook the cattail reaches of the upper pond. Oaks fill out the canopy. As the trail draws away from Ford Pond, reach a junction (0.4 mile). This time, go left on the Hendrickson Bog Meadow Trail to continue clockwise on the East Loop; the Fern Trail continues straight ahead.

Cross a boardwalk and tour a marsh–woods habitat with maple, ash, and birch. At 0.5 mile, go left to add a tour of the Woodchuck Trail; go right for the loop alone.

For this "see-the-sanctuary" tour, go left, traveling a grassy path through multistory forest, paralleling some deep drainage cuts. At 0.75 mile, reach the loop junction for the Woodchuck Trail.

Clockwise, travel a faint road grade through younger forest and bear left, finding some scenic

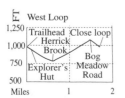

Sharon Audubon Center

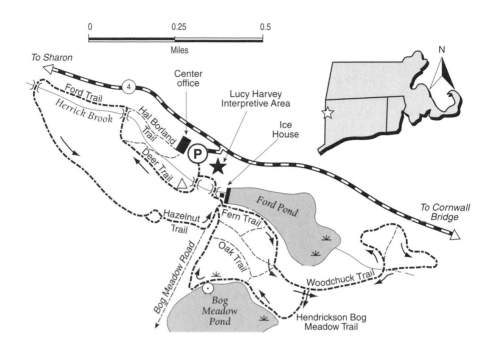

old maples. Next, traverse a couple of meadowy fields, adorned in fall by goldenrod, aster, Queen Anne's lace, and milkweed. At 1.1 miles, meet a two-track, follow it right for 30 feet, and then turn left, entering a third field. Grouse may sound in the distance; birdhouses mark the field. Ascend steadily before finding the fifth field near the boundary; enjoy a northwest view, looking down the field and through a notch. Bear right and descend. At 1.4 miles, bear left, entering woods to close the Woodchuck Loop in 100 yards. Go left, returning to the junction with Hendrickson Bog Meadow Trail (1.7 miles). There, turn left for the East Loop.

Pass through shady forest and round the base of a rocky slope, arriving at the grassy bank of Bog Meadow Pond, another big open pond with a shrub shore, backed by snags and forest. Here, geese sometimes stop over. Along the boardwalk, find highbush blueberry, bog grass, buttonbush, and loosestrife. At 1.9 miles, a boardwalk spur heads left for 100 feet, reaching a platform at the edge of the pond for a farewell look.

Resume the hike, reentering woods now isolated from the pond. At the next junction, continue forward; the path to the right accesses the Oak and Fern Trails. Soon, the Hendrickson Bog Meadow Trail curves right beneath pines to travel a small field enlivened by crickets; bear right at the upcoming fork. Return to woods, staying on the Bog Meadow Trail, passing the Oak Trail on the right. On the left, Bog Meadow Road parallels the route. After a mild ascent to a field, find a slow descent through mixed woods. Exit a hemlock grove to close the loop at the Fern Trail (2.4 miles); return to the trailhead at 2.5 miles.

For the second sanctuary tour, **West Loop,** pass behind the mapboard, bear right, and descend to cross Herrick Brook on a footbridge. Next, round behind the Explorer's Hut and turn right onto the Deer Trail, contouring the slope downstream. Maple, birch, oak, and hemlock provide shade; mossy boulders pierce the forest duff. Where the trail grows obscure, maintain a contour line slightly higher than the hut. A few remaining interpretive numbers might offer clues to the trail.

An old road grade clarifies travel as the trail contours and mildly descends, paralleling Herrick Brook downstream. At 0.25 mile, the Deer Trail ends at the blue Hal Borland Trail. Bear left onto the Borland Trail, remaining on the road grade for a sharp descent. Cross a footbridge over the scenic 10-foot-wide brook and bear right, ascending to a junction in 50 feet. The Borland Trail continues right, while the Ford Trail heads left, advancing the West Loop.

The Ford Trail passes amid hemlocks, touring the wooded slope below CT 4; roadway sounds provide hikers with another bearing. Deer commonly add to a tour. Travel a rolling course paralleling Herrick Brook downstream to the next footbridge, at 0.65 mile. After crossing, head upstream 50 feet to locate an arrow pointing out a steep ascent alongside a stone wall.

As the trail angles left, settle into a comfortable rolling tour along the upper slope. Striped maple, witch hazel, and hazelnut form the midstory. At 1.2 miles, find the Hazelnut Trail junction; either way continues the tour. To the right, follow a faint road grade masked by leaves with a few huckleberry and oak reclaiming the bed. At 1.35 miles, the forks merge; continue forward, still following a road grade.

Descend to the sunken grade of Bog Meadow Road and follow it left downhill to Ford Pond. Pass below the levee and Ice House and turn left to return to the trailhead (1.7 miles).

43   Burr Pond State Park

OVERVIEW

The centerpiece of this Connecticut state park, eighty-eight-acre Burr Pond dazzles travelers with its clear waters. In the 1850s, this watery impoundment powered early industry, including the world's first condensed-milk factory. The encircling trail travels the pond's richly wooded rim and visits quiet coves, a peninsula, and a rock cave. A second trail originates in the park, the Muir Trail; it offers a wooded journey south through Paugnut State Forest to Sunny Brook State Park (2.5 miles northwest of Torrington).

General description:	The Pond Loop may be toured alone or joined with the Muir Trail for a longer day hike.
General location:	5 miles north of Torrington, Connecticut.
Special attractions:	Attractive pond, diverse forest, mountain laurel and wildflowers, memorials, wildlife, fall foliage.
Length:	Pond Loop, 3.2-mile loop; Pond Loop–Muir Trail Hike, 8.1 miles round trip.
Elevation:	Pond Loop, less than 100 feet in elevation change; Pond Loop–Muir Trail Hike, about 400 feet in elevation change.
Difficulty:	Pond Loop, easy; the Pond Loop–Muir Trail Hike is moderate.
Maps:	State park map; Torrington and West Torrington 7.5-minute USGS quads; John Muir Trail/Paugnut State Forest map from the *Connecticut Walk Book.*
Special concerns:	Fee area.
Season and hours:	Year-round; spring through fall for hiking. Open 8:00 A.M. to sunset. Off-season visits focus on nature.
For information:	Burr Pond State Park.

Key points:
Pond Loop:
    0.0   Beach area trailhead.
    1.0   Memorial rock.
    1.7   Big Rock Cave.
    2.2   Peninsula.
    2.5   Muir Trail junction; stay on loop.
    3.2   Complete loop at picnic area.

Pond Loop–Muir Trail Hike:
    0.0   Beach area trailhead; review first 2.5 miles of Pond Loop.
    2.5   Muir Trail junction; hike south.
    3.4   Cross Buttrick Road.
    4.2   Top Walnut Mountain.
    5.1   Sunny Brook State Park; return to Burr Pond.
    7.4   Resume Burr Pond Loop.
    8.1   End at picnic area.

Finding the trailhead: From Connecticut Highway 8, take exit 46 for Burrville, head west on Pinewoods Road for 0.5 mile, and turn left. In 1 mile, turn right onto Burr Mountain Road for the park. Find the entrance on the left in 0.5 mile. Start the hikes from the beach area.

The hikes: At the developed swimming beach, bear right for a counterclockwise tour of the **Pond Loop,** finding the trail as it enters the woods

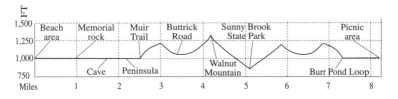

beyond the paddleboat/canoe rentals. Briefly tour the lower edge of a picnic area, enjoying beautiful still-water reflections of both the treed rim and a scattering of shoreline boulders. Hemlock, birch, maple, beech, pine, witch hazel, and showy mountain laurel shape an attractive passage. Noteworthy big trees slow hikers' strides.

Where the trail gets pinched by Burr Mountain Road, find ash and basswood shadowing the wetland shrubs and jewelweed drainages. Pass through the boat-launch parking area to resume the woods stroll. Vulture, duck, grouse, owl, and kingfisher may suggest that you raise the binoculars. At 0.6 mile, find a rock seat at the water's edge; nearby grow wild grape, dogwood, and arrowhead.

Before long, pass through a boggy area; boardwalks and footbridges advance the trail. On the right at 1 mile, find a memorial on a cabin-size boulder; it honors an area forester (1886 to 1945). A former beaver pond now stretches right, while mountain laurel dresses the pond's edge.

Pass under a utility line, contouring the slope farther above the pond. At 1.65 miles, an unlabeled blue trail heads right, accessing the Muir Trail; forgo this spur, keeping to the Pond Loop. Upon descent, look left to find Big Rock Cave, a skyward-tilted boulder with a blackened overhang.

Again pass through a shrubby utility corridor, reaching a peninsula spur at 2 miles. Follow the spur left through laurel and hemlock, reaching the outcrop nose of the peninsula for pond viewing and lazing in the sun. Resume the counterclockwise Pond Loop at 2.3 miles, rounding beneath hemlock and birch.

At 2.5 miles, reach the labeled Muir Trail, heading right. For the 3.2-mile Pond Loop alone, continue rounding shore, returning to the picnic area via the footbridge below the dam. For the longer **Pond Loop–Muir Trail Hike,** go right.

Opting for this longer hike, ascend through similar forest, weaving amid the rocks, soon passing a scenic split boulder. Chestnut, maple, and oak join the ranks as the hike turns right onto an old woods road. At 2.75 miles, cross the width of a utility corridor, gaining looks out the cut notch, and in another 0.1 mile turn left to again follow foot trail. Pines, many of them with multiple trunks, now intersperse the hardwoods.

Descend, bearing left to skirt a meadow and snag area, likely a reclaimed beaver pond given the girdled trees in the area. The added light from the clearing brings a burst of mountain laurel. At 3.4 miles, cross Buttrick Road, a dirt forest road, and angle left, traversing an open pine forest of evenly spaced tall straight trees. The trail contours, enters a scenic stand of beech, and crosses pallets at a muddy stretch.

In another 0.25 mile, find back-to-back crossings of a woods road and Guerdat Road; the trail remains well blazed. Next, ascend from the upper drainage of Walnut Mountain Brook and bear left onto a road grade (3.8 miles). At the junction at 3.95 miles, a right turn leads to Walnut Mountain, a left turn leads to Guerdat Road, and the path ahead completes the Muir Trail.

Detour right, ascending a winding cobbled road. On a rock at 4.1 miles, a faint red arrow points out a tree-framed view overlooking the crowns of

Burr Pond State Park

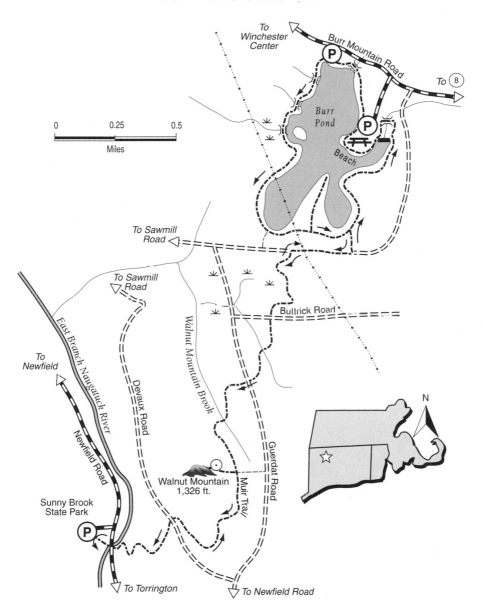

the immediate hardwood forest toward the next rise. A tree-ringed grassy circle marks the top (elevation 1,326 feet). Return to the Muir Trail at 4.35 miles, and turn right (south).

Round along the ridge of Walnut Mountain, traversing an outcrop; cairns help point the way. Next, descend sharply, touring amid the boulder and rock slabs of the lower slope to cross Devaux Road. Beyond a beech grove and wet area, turn right, descending beside the cobbly East Branch Naugatuck River.

Past a memorial to the area trail builder, ascend the rocky embankment of Newfield Road, cross the road bridge, and descend left through forest to the parking lot of Sunny Brook State Park, a primitive park (5.15 miles). Backtrack to Burr Pond and the loop trail, (7.4 miles).

Go right to conclude the counterclockwise tour, exploring the bay arm where the dam is located. At the dam and spillway (7.85 miles), continue forward along the outlet, bearing left onto a woods road. Cross a footbridge and turn left, following the outlet upstream past the dam, to return to the picnic area at a gate behind the rest room building (8.1 miles).

44 Metacomet Trail, Talcott Mountain

General description:	This segment of the long-distance Metacomet Trail tours the rolling ridge of Talcott Mountain, topping rock outcrops and visiting Heublein Tower for vistas.
General location:	3 miles west of Bloomfield, Connecticut.
Special attractions:	Heublein Tower, diverse woods, vistas, mountain laurel, wildflowers, fall foliage, hawk migration.
Length:	9.75 miles one-way.
Elevation:	Find a 650-foot elevation change.
Difficulty:	Moderate to strenuous.
Maps:	Talcott Mountain State Park map; Avon 7.5-minute USGS quad; Metropolitan District Talcott Mountain Reservoir Area map (purchase from the Metropolitan District Commission administration building, north off Farmington Road/Connecticut Highway 4 at the Farmington–West Hartford town line).
Special concerns:	No food, drink, or pets in Heublein Tower. Keep pets leashed while hiking. Obey respective rules for Metropolitan District Commission (MDC) and state park lands.
Season and hours:	Spring through fall, 8:00 A.M. to sunset. Heublein Tower, usually 10:00 A.M. to 5:00 P.M. Thursday through Sunday, mid-April through August, and daily Labor Day through October, but because staffing can alter tower hours, phone the park office before visiting.
For information:	Penwood and Talcott Mountain State Parks.

Key points:
- 0.0   Southern trailhead.
- 1.4   Leave reservoir.
- 2.7   Heublein Tower.

4.2	Cross CT 185 to Penwood State Park.
6.2	Lake Louise.
6.5	The Pinnacle.
7.5	Wilcox Park.
9.5	Bartlett Tower ruins.
9.7	End at Mountain Road.

Finding the trailhead: With multiple access points, the Metacomet allows for various-length round trips, as well as shuttle hikes. Find the southern terminus at MDC's Hartford Reservoir 6; turn north off U.S. Highway 44, 2.2 miles east of CT 10. Central to the tour, find entry roads to Penwood and Talcott Mountain State Parks diagonal to one another off CT 185, 3 miles west of Bloomfield.

For undeveloped Wilcox Park to the north, go 1.1 miles northwest on CT 185 from Penwood State Park and turn right onto Terrys Plain Road. Go 2.7 miles and turn right onto Wintonbury Road, following it 0.3 mile to the dead end. Round the barricade to find the blazes of the Metacomet Trail in 20 feet.

Shuttle hikers should refrain from using Mountain Road (reached south off CT 315 just west of the CT 315–CT 189 junction) to spot a vehicle, because it is narrow with minimal road shoulder. For hikers who do use it, opt instead for a drop-off or pickup arrangement and avoid blocking driveways or clogging the turnaround.

The hike: The Talcott Mountain leg of the Metacomet Trail traverses MDC land, Talcott Mountain and Penwood State Parks, and the open space of Wilcox Park. Northbound, start along the gated woods road, touring the west shore of Hartford Reservoir 6. The blue-blazed Metacomet Trail arrives from the left to follow the reservoir road. Avoid the two-track bearing right toward the dam.

Along the road, discover an uncommon diversity of trees, including mixed oak, spruce, pine, maple, hemlock, beech, birch, dogwood, basswood, hickory, ash, and tulip poplar. The glare from the reservoir filters through the thick mesh of hemlock, adding to the hike's serenity. Where secondary trails branch left, keep to the dirt road. After a mile, cross a pair of drainages with scenic stone bridge rails. Near the end of the reservoir (1.45 miles), angle left uphill, pursuing blue blazes.

Low boulders riddle the forest floor, as the woods remain diverse and soothing. Enjoy a meandering tour of mild gradient, coming to a T-junction with a second woods road at 1.95 miles. Go left and take a quick right, ascending via foot trail. Next, cross a woods road to ascend a shrubby power- and gas-line corridor. From the corridor, bear left on woods road, still plodding

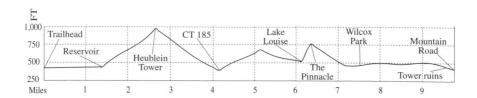

uphill, still touring beautiful woods. A massive chestnut oak rises to the left at 2.35 miles.

Angle right across a paved lane to travel the Talcott Mountain ridge. Round a radio tower, and travel the rock outcrop of the western rim. Below a picnic pavilion, overlook the abrupt western slope toward Simsbury. Oak, laurel, and cedar favor the rim; look below for a breakaway pinnacle.

Reach the 165-foot-tall Heublein Tower at 2.7 miles. When open, its observation room provides a panoramic view spanning an estimated 1,200 square miles. Locate Mount Monadnock in New Hampshire and the blue sliver of Long Island Sound. Historic displays and re-created rooms also suggest a look. In fall, enjoy the foliage and hawk migration.

Northbound, round west below Heublein Tower, enter a hemlock pocket, and turn left onto the Tower Trail, a woods road descending toward the entrance of Talcott Mountain State Park. In 100 yards, the blue-blazed Metacomet Trail turns right (north) to travel King Phillip Mountain; the Tower Trail travels the west rim below the mountain.

The Metacomet now rolls from laurel corridor to outcrop knoll, until 3.4 miles, where it descends on an old road grade through tall forest. In 0.25 mile, turn right onto a footpath; stay attentive, because quick directional changes follow.

Angle right across a utility corridor, reaching a woods road heading toward some residences. At the road, take a quick left, briefly edging the shrubby utility corridor before veering right through hemlock–birch woods. Cross (or wade) a brook, and cross CT 185 to enter Penwood State Park (4.25 miles).

Hike north through the lower parking area and up the park road, skirting Gale Pond (no access). At 4.45 miles, turn left off the park road, ascending a wooded slope returning to the rolling ridge of Talcott Mountain. A select cut has removed the large hemlocks that once presided between CT 185 and the Pinnacle to the north, altering the forest appearance. Where the trail enters the sag, avoid the spur heading left. Where the trail rises out of the sag, a brief detour left reaches a high point for a seasonal glimpse at the Farmington Valley. Resume the Metacomet Trail as it descends north, traveling along a wide earthen lane. At its junction with a red-blazed trail (5.4 miles), go left.

Coming off a small rise, veer right and then left, ascending among mountain laurel to top an outcrop and follow the ridge north. Pass a stone pedestal 50 feet off the trail and descend to the park road at Lake Louise (6.2 miles), finding a dock and tables.

Bear right to round the shrubby east bank of the lake, touring a marshy maple woodland. Pass below a retained scree slope, coming to a junction at 6.35 miles. A left continues the lake basin tour; the Metacomet heads straight, only to turn uphill to the right in 50 feet.

Follow foot trail and a steep stone stairway, top the ridge at a picnic flat, and bear left, still ascending. Next, tag The Pinnacle for views west at Simsbury, the Farmington River Valley, and the hazy ridges disappearing west. To the south, locate Heublein Tower. At the concrete foundations of an old lookout tower, a white-blazed trail heads right; stay north.

Metacomet Trail, Talcott Mountain

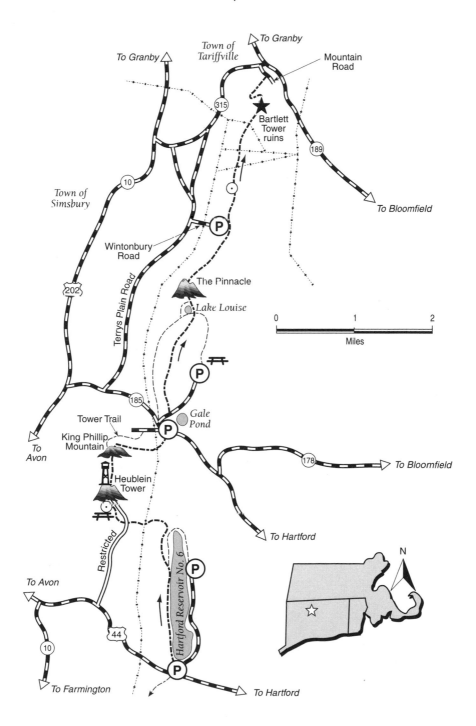

At 6.65 miles, bypass an alternate red dot trail that descends left. The ridge hike continues in woods, rounding and topping rocky knolls and dipping through sags, but gaining no views. Often near the rocky knolls, well-tracked side paths bypass the more challenging blazed route. At 7.35 miles, begin the steep descent; look for a switchback, and watch your footing. Reach the closed dirt road in Wilcox Park east of the barrier on Wintonbury Road (7.5 miles). Shuttle hikers may end here.

The Metacomet, however, continues north. It skirts a private residence and ascends a cedar–deciduous slope to a birch flat. A rolling ascent then leads to an open outcrop (8 miles), which overlooks a utility corridor in the woods below and the Farmington Valley beyond. A vibrant burst of autumn foliage helps hikers forgive the intrusion of power lines.

At 8.25 miles, pass through the first of three utility corridors. Yellow blazes join the blue ones. Descend east from the crest, come to a woods road, and turn left, staying with the blue blazes of the Metacomet Trail; the yellow trail heads right on the woods road. Next, pass through a dark hemlock grove, descend the width of another utility corridor, and cross a red-blazed woods road. Draw back west atop the ridge, finding some grand big trees, snags, and split trunks. At 9.1 miles, cross the final utility corridor with looks east and west out its clearing.

Again roll between knoll features, passing from foot trail to carriage road at 9.45 miles. Descend 250 feet, finding the Bartlett Tower ruins on the right. The 40-foot-tall redbrick chimney and stone fireplace recall a recreational development and signal a turnaround for round-trip hikers. Seasonally, swallows pepper the skies.

Northbound travelers should descend the carriage road, turning right onto a foot trail at 9.6 miles. Pass through a mixed woods to emerge at Mountain Road at 9.75 miles, the northernmost point for this description.

45 Macedonia Brook State Park

OVERVIEW

Originating with a gift of land from the White Memorial Foundation of Litchfield, Connecticut, this 2,300-acre Connecticut state park nudges the New York State border. Split in half by the clear-skipping waters of Macedonia Brook, the park offers exciting ridgeline tours, vistas, peaceful woods, and stonework from the past. During the Revolutionary War, some one hundred Scatacook Indian volunteers manned signal fires atop these and other area ridges of the Housatonic Valley.

General description: A demanding loop travels the east and west ridges framing the Macedonia Brook drainage.

General location: 4 miles northwest of Kent, Connecticut.

Special attractions: Vistas, ridge and valley forests, spring wildflowers, mountain laurel, wildlife, fall foliage.

Length: Ridge Loop, 6.8-mile loop.

Elevation: Find a 700-foot elevation change.

Difficulty: Ridge Loop, strenuous. The East Ridge Hike is moderate; the West Ridge Hike, rigorous.

Maps: State park brochure.

Special concerns: Fee for campground only; keep pets leashed. Note that a brief difficult rock descent and climb on the west ridge may be unsuitable for children and novice hikers. Use your hands, and beware of difficult footing and the likelihood of scrapes.

Season and hours: Year-round; spring through fall for hiking. Open 8:00 A.M. to sunset.

For information: Macedonia Brook State Park.

Key points:

Ridge Loop:

    0.0   East Ridge Trailhead.
    2.4   Cross Keeler Road bridge.
    3.7   Cross dirt Chippewalla Road.
    4.6   Cobble Mountain.
    6.8   End at small picnic area.

Finding the trailhead: From the junction of U.S. Highway 7 and Connecticut Highway 341 in Kent, go west on CT 341 for 1.7 miles and turn right, following the sign for Macedonia Brook State Park. Go 0.8 mile, reaching the park at the junction of Macedonia Brook and Fuller Mountain Roads. Follow Macedonia Brook Road into the park, reaching the trailhead at the bridge in 0.5 mile, the headquarters in 0.9 mile, and the campground in 1.3 miles.

The hike: Start the **Ridge Loop** where the park road crosses over Macedonia Brook, 0.4 mile south of the headquarters; park at the small picnic area at the northwest corner of the bridge. For a counterclockwise tour, follow the blue-blazed trail as it heads east from the south side of the bridge, making a steady assault on the east ridge (the milder of the two framing ridges). The west ridge entices with vistas and mountain laurel, but has a complicated rock passage.

Travel a mixed-age, multistory forest with a wildflower-sprinkled floor, soon viewing the rocky crest. By 0.2 mile, trace the ridgetop north, still ascending.

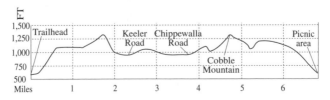

199

Macedonia Brook State Park

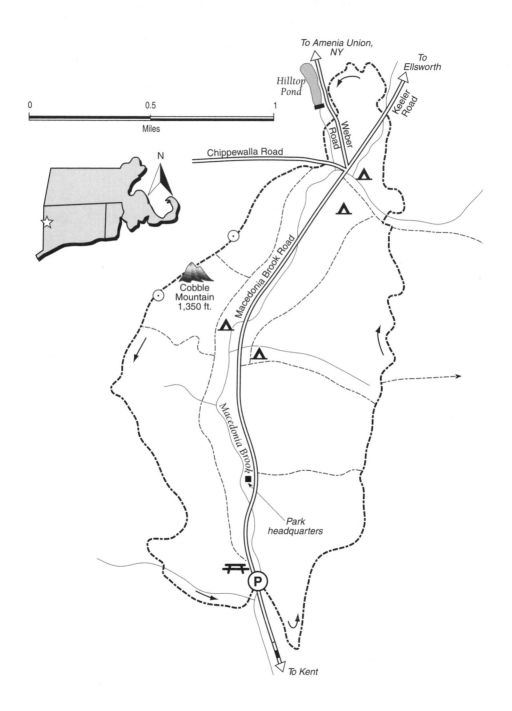

To Amenia Union, NY

To Ellsworth

Hilltop Pond

Keeler Road

Weber Road

Chippewalla Road

Macedonia Brook Road

Cobble Mountain 1,350 ft.

N

0   0.5   1

Miles

Macedonia Brook

Park headquarters

P

To Kent

Mixed oaks favor the top. Enjoy the companionship of deer, gray squirrel, chipmunk, woodpecker, scarlet tanager, and passing geese. At times, veils of fog rise from the valley drainages. Where a yellow-blazed trail descends left to the park core, stay with the blue-blazed trail. Stone walls now intersect the path, while birch, maple, and hickory mix with the oaks.

The Ridge Loop next crosses over the green-blazed trail that links the campground (left) with Fuller Mountain Road (right). At 1.5 miles, descend sharply and watch your footing, especially when the path is masked by leaves or rain-soaked. A scenic fern floor awaits at the bottom. Contour the east slope, coming out on a woods road. Follow it left for a spell, descending above a headwater of Macedonia Brook. At 2 miles, turn right onto a footpath to cross the rocky brook. False hellebore, skunk cabbage, and moss accent the watery ribbon.

Ascend and gently roll, now touring along the western base of the east ridge, finding a congested, leafy woods. At 2.4 miles, meet Keeler Road (a dirt road), cross the road bridge, and enter the woods on the other side of Macedonia Brook. Or, you can detour south on Keeler Road to reach a water pump and pit toilet before continuing the loop.

Follow the marked trail between the brook and a rock wall before turning left to pass through a gap in the wall. Yellow violet and jack-in-the-pulpit grow near the brook. The complement of big trees offers little clue that in 1848, the demand for charcoal fuel virtually denuded these slopes. Ahead, enter a sharp descent marked by steep short pitches and a riddling of rocks. Hemlocks cloak the moister slope.

At 3 miles, the right fork leads to a view of Hilltop Pond, a private dammed water with a pretty birch shore. The Ridge Loop bears left, paralleling the wooded slope just above Weber Road. At 3.25 miles, cross Weber Road to follow a gated, grassy woods road back into the park; a garter snake may slither by. At 3.7 miles, cross dirt Chippewalla Road, keeping to the same woods road. In 200 feet, hike the foot trail, heading right for a sashaying woods climb.

Patches of mountain laurel precede the ridgetop. At 4.2 miles, travel a rounded bald outcrop among the low oaks, glimpsing neighboring ridges. Descend south along the west ridge, finding an open view atop a steep, slanted rock face. Here, admire the Macedonia Brook drainage with its ever-

Frog, Macedonia Brook State Park, CT.

Jack-in-the-Pulpit, Macedonia Brook State Park, CT.

green treetops piercing the leafy canopy and gain looks at Cobble and Chase Mountains. Be careful when descending, because the footholds are few and the rock surface is boot-polished.

At 4.4 miles, reach a thin drainage where the green trail descends left to the campground. Ahead stretches a treacherous ascent, tracing a thin, canted ledge along a tiny chasm, followed by a challenging rock scramble. Although the ascent is difficult, downhill hikers protest even more loudly—some scooting down on their backsides. Formerly this route tested the mettle of the Appalachian Trail hiker, until designers rerouted the national scenic trail.

Top the ridge at 4.6 miles, hiking across the lichen-mottled outcrop of Cobble Mountain for western views. At 4.75 miles, gather the most expansive view, overlooking a broad New York valley, the cliff-sided ridge below, and the distant Catskills and Taconics. Vultures soar the thermals.

Now descend, coming to a junction with the white trail. It continues the steep descent left to the campground, while the blue Ridge Loop bears right for a rolling, contouring trek amid mountain laurel and rich hardwood forest. Enjoy a taller, fuller forest than that on the rocky crest. At 6 miles, the descent accelerates; bear left just before a side drainage. The trail remains in rich woods and twice crosses the side brook via stones to end at the small picnic area at 6.8 miles.

46 White Memorial Foundation: Nature Trails

OVERVIEW

Snuggled in the Berkshire foothills of northwest Connecticut, this 4,000-acre private reserve offers the public some 35 miles of trail and woods road to explore. Devoted to conservation, education, research, and suitable recreation within a natural arena, the foundation has set aside 600 acres as a "natural area," where the land and habitats can change and prosper free from intervention. Ten acres of old-growth forest, a premier boardwalk, Bantam Lake and River, mixed woods, marsh, and ponds further endorse the area.

General description: Three short hikes present the reserve's diversity, visiting lakeshore, swamp, and hilltop.

General location: In Litchfield and Morris, Connecticut.

Special attractions: Boardwalks and observation platforms, bird and wildlife sightings, spring and summer wildflowers, old-growth trees, fall foliage, museum/nature center.

Length: Lake Trail, 1 mile round trip; Little Pond Boardwalk Hike, 3.2 miles round trip; Apple Hill Trail, 3.4 miles round trip (with marsh detour).

Elevation: Lake Trail, 20-foot elevation change; Little Pond Boardwalk Hike, virtually flat; Apple Hill Trail, 200-foot elevation change.

Difficulty: Lake Trail and Little Pond Boardwalk Hike, both easy; the Apple Hill Trail is moderate.

Maps: Foundation map (purchase at museum).

Special concerns: Admission fee for the museum; the trails are free. Obey posted rules. Purchase a map to learn the reserve's blazing scheme and sort out trail options. Expect some soggy reaches.

Season and hours: Year-round, generally spring through fall for hiking. Trails, dawn to dusk. Museum, 9:00 A.M. to 5:00 P.M. Monday through Saturday, noon to 5:00 P.M. Sunday (May through October); 8:30 A.M. to 4:30 P.M. Monday through Saturday, 9:00 A.M. to 4:00 P.M. Sunday (November through April).

For information: White Memorial Conservation Center.

Key points:
Lake Trail:
- 0.0   Carriage House area trailhead.
- 0.1   Loop junction.
- 0.7   Bantam Lake observation tower.
- 0.9   Close loop; backtrack to trailhead.

Little Pond Boardwalk Hike:
- 0.0   Museum area trailhead.
- 0.5   Cross Bissell Road.
- 1.0   Loop junction (elevated boardwalk).
- 2.2   Complete loop; backtrack to trailhead.

Apple Hill Trail:
- 0.0   Northern trailhead.
- 0.3   Laurel Hill.
- 0.6   Bog boardwalk.
- 1.7   Apple Hill; return to northern trailhead.

Finding the trailhead: From the Connecticut Highway 63–U.S. Highway 202 junction in Litchfield, go southwest on US 202 for 2.1 miles and turn left onto Bissell Road, followed by a right onto Whitehall Road to reach White Memorial Conservation Center in 0.5 mile. There, begin the Lake Trail and Little Pond Boardwalk Hike.

For the Apple Hill Trail, continue east on Bissell Road from its intersection with Whitehall Road for 0.6 mile, and turn right onto Whites Woods/Alain

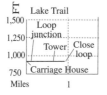

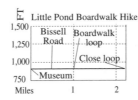

Little Pond Trail, White Memorial Foundation, CT

White Road. In 1.6 miles, turn right onto East Shore Road. Find the gated north trail terminus on the left in 0.7 mile; reach a southern terminus in another 0.9 mile. Park roadside, and do not block the gates.

The hikes: For the yellow-blazed **Lake Trail,** start below the Carriage House in the conservation center area, following a dirt road along the back side of a stone wall and bearing right. Ancient sugar maple adorn the start. At 0.1 mile, reach the loop junction and go right, following a woods road. Impressive gnarled oak and tamarack now contribute to the tour. Stay with the yellow blazes where side trails branch or cross the route.

Descend to a marsh woodland and, at 0.3 mile, go left on a narrow foot trail through fuller forest. Roots snake across the path, while poison ivy scales the tree trunks. Cross a duckweed-coated channel, gaining glimpses of Bantam Lake. At 0.7 mile, find concrete pilings and a boardwalk leading to a lake observation tower. Overlook the marshy edge of North Bay, with Marsh Point across the water. Goldfinches, swallows, ducks, and swans may add to the scene.

Continue the counterclockwise tour, staying briefly along shore before bearing left through marshy woods. Parallel a rock wall and pass through a break in an intersecting wall to close the loop and return to the trailhead at 1 mile.

For the **Little Pond Boardwalk Hike,** start on the Self-guiding Nature Trail (brochure sold at museum). Follow the unsurfaced road heading east just north of the museum. At 0.25 mile, turn left, traveling an attractive marsh meadow; the slow, glassy Bantam River flows along the opposite side. Where the nature trail turns left, continue forward, crossing Bissell Road at 0.5 mile. A few old-growth trees punctuate the journey.

A pine–hemlock forest next houses the way; travel is on a scenic needle-strewn

White Memorial Foundation: Nature Trails

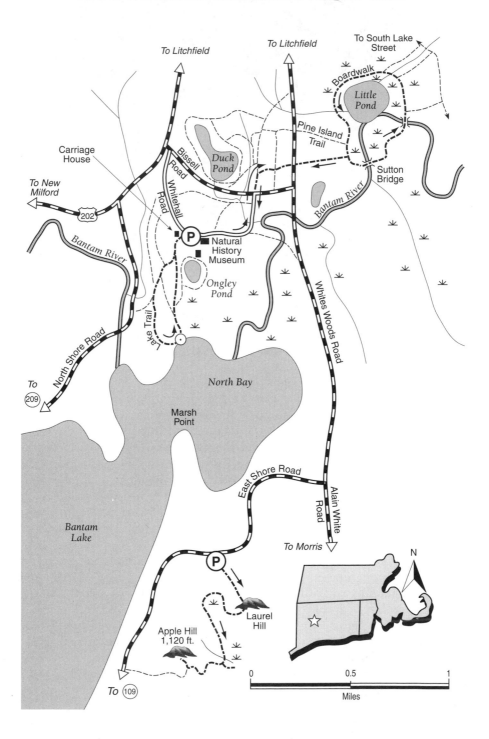

To Litchfield

To Litchfield

To South Lake Street

Boardwalk

Little Pond

Pine Island Trail

Carriage House

Bissell Road

Whitehall Road

Duck Pond

Bantam River

Sutton Bridge

To New Milford

202

Bantam River

P

Natural History Museum

Ongley Pond

Whites Woods Road

Lake Trail

To 209

North Shore Road

North Bay

Marsh Point

Bantam Lake

East Shore Road

Alain White Road

To Morris

P

Laurel Hill

Apple Hill 1,120 ft.

To 109

N

0   0.5   1

Miles

lane. At 0.6 mile, meet Little Pond Trail, blazed with a black square within a white square, and follow it right through choked forest. Cross Whites Woods Road at 0.75 mile, tour a mixed evergreen–deciduous woods, and bear left, rounding an open field. After the route changes to foot trail, find the loop junction (1 mile).

Go right for a counterclockwise tour, traveling the site's acclaimed elevated boardwalk, passing through woods and a dense stand of 8-foot-tall phragmites (plumed reeds). Cross the Bantam River via Sutton Bridge. Lily pads top the margins of the glassy stream; canoeists part the waters.

Standing water, tufted marsh grass, and cattails bring a rich texture to the marsh. In places, shrubs shape a tight, humid corridor. Again cross the Bantam River and pass a side trail branching right, toward the boundary. Maple, pine, skunk cabbage, and fern now dress the tour.

At 1.4 miles, overlook a horseshoe river bend shaded by grand old willows. Ahead, enjoy open looks at the marsh-bordered Little Pond. Keep to the pond circuit where a side trail branches right to South Lake Street. Lily, arrowhead, cattail, bog grass, and dark pools provide exceptional viewing. Geese, swallows, and beavers may draw attention.

Depart the boardwalk and, at 2.1 miles, prior to closing the loop, find the red triangles marking the Pine Island Trail. This trail travels a deep woods to encircle Duck Pond, aided by the Mattatuck Trail. For hikers seeking a longer tour, Duck Pond offers a logical extension; consult your map. For Little Pond alone, continue forward, closing the loop at 2.2 miles. Turn right and retrace the hike to the museum at 3.2 miles.

Apple Hill, White Memorial Foundation, CT.

On a north–south tour, the blue-blazed **Apple Hill Trail** ascends a grassy woods road bordered by tall thin trees that weave a full canopy. In 0.1 mile, veer left as indicated by an arrow; here, mountain laurel foreshadows the ascent of Laurel Hill. Upon skirting a gnarled split-branched oak, a foot trail replaces the old road. Leaves and fallen birch nearly hide a collapsed rock wall lining the tour.

Descend, crossing some soggy reaches; generally there are enough stones and roots to allow a dry hopscotch travel. Skunk cabbage, wood anemone, purple violet, starflower, and jack-in-the-pulpit shout in springtime, and the forest becomes more mixed, both in variety and in age. At 0.6 mile, a narrow boardwalk passes through a bog with highbush blueberry, hellebore, tufted grasses, duckweed, and moss. Laurel showers the exit. Chickadee, pileated woodpecker, scarlet tanager, and warbler delight travelers.

At 1 mile, pass a small circular dark-water pond with a larger marshy water beyond the trees to the left. Noisy ducks and geese betray its location. At 1.1 mile, find a junction; here, a 0.2-mile round-trip detour left adds a view of the snag-riddled marsh. A right resumes the hike to Apple Hill.

En route to the hill, pass a marshy patch and an oak old-timer. The climb briefly intensifies before reaching the brushy top. Follow the grassy swath, bearing right at the junction; the trail branch heading left leads to the southern trailhead. Reach the one-story summit observation tower at 1.5 miles (1.7 miles with wetland detour). Vistas span Bantam Lake, the rolling forested hills, and area farms. Return as you came.

47 White Memorial Foundation: Five Ponds Hike

General description:	This sampling of the Mattatuck Trail travels an isolated corner of the White Memorial Foundation property, visiting five ponds of unique personality.
General location:	In Litchfield and Morris, Connecticut.
Special attractions:	Bird and wildlife sightings, spring and summer wildflowers, fall foliage, museum/nature center at main area of foundation property.
Length:	5.5 miles round trip with Teal Pond Loop; add 1.2 miles if you include the side loops at Heron and Fawn Ponds as well.
Elevation:	The trail shows a 150-foot elevation change.
Difficulty:	Moderate.
Maps:	Foundation map (purchase at museum).
Special concerns:	Admission fee for the museum; the trails are free. Obey posted rules. Purchase a map to learn the reserve's blazing scheme and sort out trail options. Expect some soggy reaches.

Season and hours: Year-round; generally spring through fall for hiking. Trails, dawn to dusk. Museum, 9:00 A.M. to 5:00 P.M. Monday through Saturday, noon to 5:00 P.M. Sunday (May through October); 8:30 A.M. to 4:30 P.M. Monday through Saturday, 9:00 A.M. to 4:00 P.M. Sunday (November through April).

For information: White Memorial Conservation Center.

Key points:
- 0.0 Northern trailhead.
- 0.3 Heron Pond.
- 0.9 Plunge Pool overlook.
- 1.0 Fawn Pond.
- 1.2 Add Teal Pond side trip.
- 3.0 Beaver Pond dam; return north to trailhead (5.5 miles).

Finding the trailhead: From the Connecticut Highway 63–U.S. Highway 202 junction in Litchfield, go southwest on US 202 for 2.1 miles and turn left onto Bissell Road, followed by a right onto Whitehall Road to reach White Memorial Conservation Center in 0.5 mile, which is where the museum is located and where maps can be purchased.

For the Five Ponds Hike, from US 202 in Litchfield, turn south onto CT 63 (Straits Turnpike) and go 2.2 miles to locate the trailhead on the left. Parking is on the right just south of the trailhead at the South Farm Entrance. A southern terminus is reached by following CT 63 south and turning left (east) onto Isaiah Smith Lane, following it to its end near Beaver Pond (consult map).

The hike: The blue rectangles of the Mattatuck Trail guide the Five Ponds hikers east along a woods road, ascending through a mixed forest of pine, maple, and some oak. In marshy areas, marsh marigold, mayflower, and fern can be spied. At 0.3 mile, the trail levels off at Heron Pond. A small stone dam marks the side traveled by the Mattatuck Trail. On approaching the pond, discover a foot trail heading right for a 0.6-mile shoreline tour at the forest edge with frequent views. A beaver lodge rests along the pond's west edge. The loop returns at the other end of the small dam.

For this hike description, forgo the loop. Large birch trees accent the woods beyond Heron Pond. The climb resumes. Some huge pines, interestingly split snags, and showings of mountain laurel contribute to the forest. White Memorial Foundation characteristically has more big trees and snags on its property than seen elsewhere in western Connecticut. Keep to the Mattatuck Trail.

At 0.8 mile, reach the high point and descend to an overlook of Plunge Pool (0.9 mile). Aptly named, Plunge Pool sits some 80 to 100 feet below the trail at the base of a vertical, vegetated slope. The big pear-shaped pond is showy, with rimming maple and mountain laurel and a punctuation of woodpecker snags.

At about 1 mile, follow the yellow-blazed trail heading right to visit Fawn Pond. This side

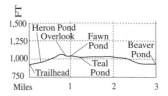

209

White Memorial Foundation: Five Ponds Hike

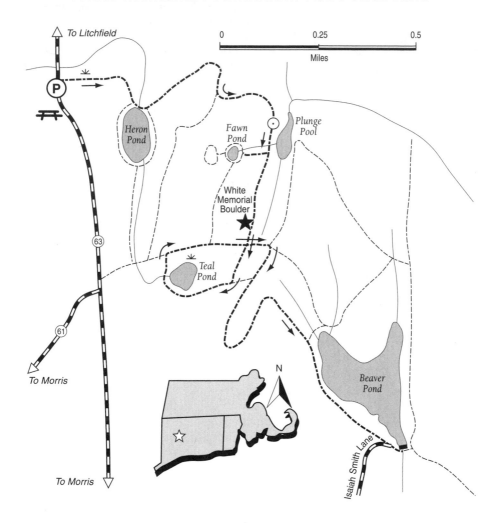

trail climbs from the Mattatuck Trail, passing along a drainage to meet the shore in 100 yards. Fawn Pond is postcard pretty, with a pond lily mosaic, bog grass island, and isolated silver logs. Frogs and dragonflies animate the scene. Again, a 0.6-mile loop encircles the pond and a wet area. For this hike, forgo the loop and return to the southbound Mattatuck Trail (1.1 miles).

Next, come upon a moist bottom meadow with ferns and a memorial to Alain and May White, the brother and sister whose love for nature prompted the saving of these thousands of acres of quiet woods. The tribute is a sheer-faced boulder in keeping with the setting and their values.

At 1.2 miles, turn right for the Teal Pond Trail. Follow the white rectangle blazes only to turn left in a matter of feet to follow the orange-blazed pond circuit in a clockwise fashion. The trail rounds through forest to over-

Memorial stone, White Memorial Foundation, CT.

look the marsh-reclaimed end of the pond with its mossy mats and inter-mingling open water. Red-winged blackbirds favor this site. Bear right to con-tinue rounding the pond, gathering views of its open-water portion. View the small dam on the outlet and beaver-fallen trees before crossing the dam, passing the beaver lodge, and meeting the white-blazed trail. Turn right to complete the loop and return to the blue Mattatuck Trail (1.75 miles); again turn right.

Find a final look at Teal Pond where the Mattatuck crosses a woods road. As the trail descends, a tilted rock outcrop shapes its side. At 1.9 miles, be alert, because the Mattatuck Trail hooks right; the white trail proceeds for-ward. The Mattatuck continues to roll out a mixed-forest tour on woods road. At 2.3 miles, a dark hemlock area houses travel. Afterward, hemlocks have an alternating presence with the leafy trees. On the descent to Beaver Pond, snare pond glimpses between the trees.

At 2.7 miles, keep to the Mattatuck where the white-blazed foot trail merges from the left. Beaver Pond, much larger than the others, approximates a lake in size. It is popular with anglers, some of whom port in canoes from the Isaiah Smith access. The lake enjoys a pristine wooded shore. At 2.9 miles, pass the gated Isaiah Smith access on the right to end this hike at the stonework dam and outcrop shore for a fabulous pond view (3 miles). Re-turn north via the Mattatuck Trail alone.

48 Sessions Woods Wildlife Management Area

OVERVIEW

In its 455 acres, the Sessions Woods Wildlife Management Area (WMA) demonstrates various land management and wildlife enhancement practices, explained by two self-guiding loops. Explore mixed woods and small meadow clearings; brook, marsh, and vernal pond; laurel thicket; and a backyard wildlife habitat. Sightings of deer, fox, beaver, wild turkey, cardinal, heron, and pileated woodpecker may add to a tour; carry binoculars.

General description:	Two short loops explore the WMA.
General location:	In Burlington, Connecticut.
Special attractions:	Bird- and wildlife-watching, marsh/beaver pond, observation tower, waterfall, diverse woods, spring-flowering shrubs.
Length:	Beaver Pond Trail, 2.6-mile loop, with an additional 0.7 mile of side spurs; Deer Sign Trail, 0.6-mile loop.
Elevation:	Beaver Pond Trail, 200-foot elevation change; Deer Sign Trail, 40-foot elevation change.
Difficulty:	Both easy.
Maps:	WMA map, generally available at trailhead register.
Special concerns:	Keep pets leashed. No collecting, and no feeding of wildlife. Beware of ticks and poison ivy.
Season and hours:	Year-round, but generally spring through fall for hiking. Sunrise to sunset.
For information:	Sessions Woods Wildlife Management Area.

Key points:
Beaver Pond Trail:
- 0.0 Entrance trailhead.
- 1.0 Spurs to blind and observation tower.
- 1.3 Waterfall.
- 2.7 Summer House.
- 3.3 Close loop at parking area.

Deer Sign Trail:
- 0.0 Education center trailhead.
- 0.6 Complete loop.

Finding the trailhead: From the junction of Connecticut Highways 4 and 69 in Burlington, go south on CT 69 for 3.3 miles and turn right to enter Sessions Woods WMA.

The hikes: Both trails welcome "Sunday" strolling, with seasonal discoveries bringing hikers to their knees or tilting their heads skyward. Gravel- or cinder-surfaced service roads host travel.

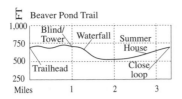

Look for the start of the **Beaver Pond Trail** on the right-hand side of the entrance road as you turn into the parking lot. This counterclockwise, mildly rolling tour travels rich hardwood forest of maple, oak, hickory, black cherry, and birch, with a varied shrub understory of bramble, brier, sassafras, and chestnut. Near the start, the blue Tunxis Trail arrives on the right and briefly shares the way. Interpretive signs introduce vegetation and explain management practices.

In clear-cut openings, wildflowers abound. In the forest and wooded swamps, mountain laurel, sheep laurel, azalea, and pond lily up the ante. Benches along the tour suggest pauses. In stillness, the wildlife often comes to you. At about 0.25 mile, the Tree ID Trail heads left to follow along East Negro Hill Brook; it comes out at Digger Dam for a shorter loop option. Stay on the Beaver Pond Trail for the selected hike. In another 0.25 mile, a side trail branches left to a berry patch and soon after, the Tunxis Trail departs to the right.

Next, pass some big pines, arriving at the beaver pond and marsh (0.75 mile), where a spur leads to a waterfowl blind. The vast snag-filled pond particularly captivates when capped with pink and white pond lilies, when reflecting its autumn-tinted rim, or when a family of deer drinks at its edge. Managers artificially manipulate the water level, making use of pipes and beaver instinct. When pipes draw down the water, the beaver return to action, raising the pond level. The feathered occupants of an osprey nesting platform may divert attention.

Beyond the main pond, a quick spur left leads to a vernal pond and its observation platform, rimmed by mountain laurel. Salamander and frog may be spied. More wetland, some rock outcroppings, and hemlocks now mark the loop. At just over a mile, spurs branch right to a viewing blind and left to the 25-foot-tall observation tower (elevation 756 feet). The crow's nest of the three-story tower puts hikers above the trees for views stretching from Avon to Meriden.

Back on the loop, quickly come upon the waterfall spur. This 0.25-mile detour descends to the right via footpath and earthen stairs, reaching the waterfall on bouldery Negro Hill Brook. The drainage shows massive boulders and slabs. In rivulets, the falls spills through rock crevices. After heavy rains, a more lively falls courses over and through the rocks.

Resume the counterclockwise loop at 1.6 miles. Side trails branch to Digger Dam (a fish enhancement weir) on Negro Hill Brook, where the Tree ID Trail comes out. The primary trail remains mainly wooded, with occasional meadow openings. At 2.4 miles, keep to the service road, touring a scenic pocket of white pine. At 2.7 miles, a spur heads left to Summer House, a

Sessions Woods Wildlife Management Area

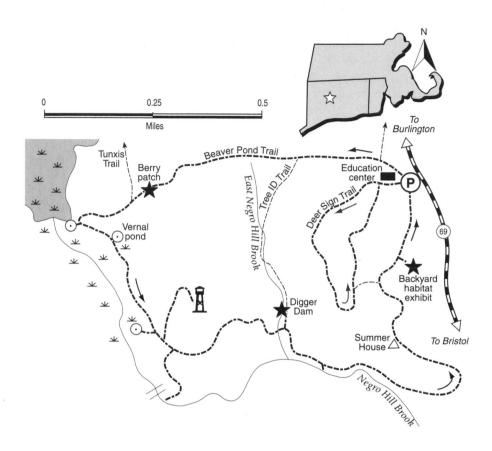

covered pavilion with benches and vistas of the ridges to the south. Soon after, a second spur to the left leads to the outdoor classroom.

At 3 miles, turn right to explore the fenced backyard wildlife habitat, with identified plantings and a frog pond. Butterflies, dragonflies, and songbirds animate the enclosure. From the backyard habitat, return to the service road. Close the loop, rounding a maintenance building to exit at the parking lot (3.3 miles).

Find the trailhead for the **Deer Sign Trail** to the left of the education center. Round the gate and follow the service road to the right for a counterclockwise tour. The circuit passes through forest and meadow. Look for a bat shelter that can support 300 bats, nesting boxes and platforms, and brush piles for wildlife shelter. A few large boulders punctuate the tour. Along the trail, interpretive plaques explain how the management of each microcosm promotes wildlife. Midway, a bench suggests a more reflective appreciation. Close the loop at 0.6 mile.

49 Ragged Mountain Preserve Trail

General description:	Within this 563-acre open space acquired through the Land and Water Conservation Fund, a demanding loop journeys through restful mixed woods and traverses a stirring cliff rim.
General location:	In Berlin, Connecticut.
Special attractions:	Vistas, an exciting tiered and broken ridge, mixed woods, wildlife sightings, fall foliage.
Length:	6.1-mile loop.
Elevation:	Travel from a trailhead elevation of 230 feet to a summit elevation of 761 feet atop Ragged Mountain.
Difficulty:	Strenuous.
Maps:	Meriden and New Britain 7.5-minute USGS quads.
Special concerns:	Use caution along the rim. Boots are recommended to protect your ankles. Be especially careful after rain, frost, or heavy dew. Avoid during times of snow and ice. Copperheads occur here, so be attentive when reaching, sitting, or stepping.
Season and hours:	Year-round, as weather allows.
For information:	Conservation Commission, Berlin Town Hall.

Key points:

- 0.0 West Lane/Wigwam Road trailhead.
- 0.1 Loop junction; bear left.
- 1.7 Metacomet Trail and Ragged Mountain.
- 3.1 Junction; leave Metacomet Trail on preserve trail.
- 4.0 Wooded edge of Panther Swamp.
- 6.0 Close loop; return to trailhead.

Finding the trailhead: At the junction of Connecticut Highways 372 and 71A in Berlin, go south on CT 71A for 1.2 miles and turn right (west) onto West Lane. Go 0.6 mile, reaching the trailhead where West Lane ends at Wigwam Road. Find roadside parking for up to a dozen vehicles. When arriving from the Berlin junction of CT 71 and CT 71A, go 1.1 miles north on CT 71A and turn left onto West Lane, proceeding to the trailhead.

The hike: At the trailhead, a boulder plaque commemorates the acquisition of Ragged Mountain Memorial Preserve. Enter the conservation land and follow the blue blazes with the red dots, bearing left for a clockwise loop. A narrow woods road hosts travel, ascending amid hemlock, oak, maple, beech,

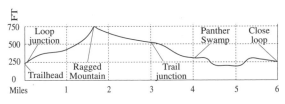

and birch. Huckleberry and only a handful of other understory species pierce the leaf duff.

At 0.3 mile, go right on a footpath for a slow,

Ragged Mountain Preserve Trail

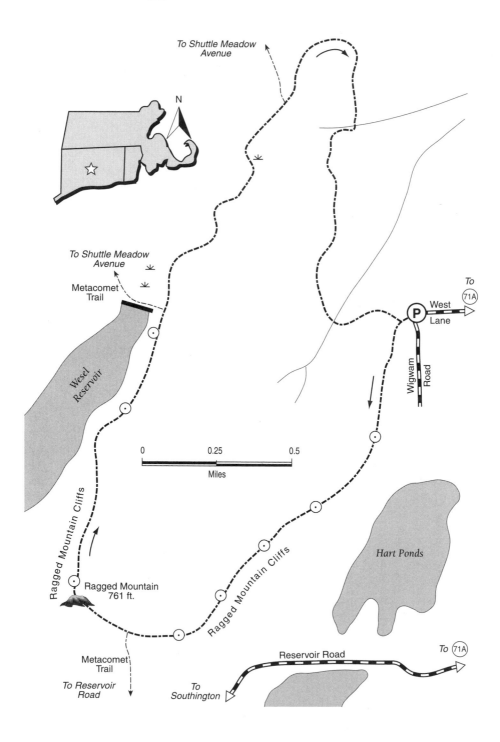

To Shuttle Meadow Avenue

N

To Shuttle Meadow Avenue

Metacomet Trail

Wesel Reservoir

Ragged Mountain Cliffs

0   0.25   0.5
Miles

Ragged Mountain Cliffs

Ragged Mountain 761 ft.

Metacomet Trail

To Reservoir Road

To Southington

P   West Lane

To 71A

Wigwam Road

Hart Ponds

Reservoir Road

To 71A

gradual ascent. Poison ivy caps the rocks and spirals skyward on the trunks of trees. The trail grows more rocky and rolling. Blazes appear at regular intervals, cluing hikers to the subtle direction changes.

By 0.5 mile, begin traversing among outcrops and along the rim. As the low cliffs grade higher, gaps in the woods afford southeastern glimpses. Where the cliffs plummet some 100 feet, views sweep Hart Ponds and the wooded terrain; swans ply the water. Rain cloud, fog, or excessive humidity can bring an uneasy aura of mystery.

Wild rose, blueberry, strawberry, and meadow grass accent the dark-rock realm. The trail mostly hugs the edge, with brief lapses into the woods. Red eft, toad, slug, turtle, and spotted salamander may entertain the curious. But be on guard; the area is known to have copperheads.

Mounting the next rim level, look for a pull-apart section of cliff isolated from the main wall by a deep fissure. Survey Hart Ponds, as well as the Hanging Hills of Meriden. Some Indian pipe and prince's pine lend floral accent. Where the trail dips, enjoy a fuller maple woods; low oaks dress the open rock.

Soon after a fissure dishes up a southwestern view and a chance to admire the vertical-cliff profile, reach the Metacomet Trail (1.7 miles). Bear right onto the Metacomet for the loop, now following blue blazes across the summit of Ragged Mountain. Find more spurts of climbing, some that require hand assists, and gain better views trending west.

By 2 miles, hear rock climbers shouting instructions from the cliffs below and hike past a steep climber's trail with wire-mesh steps that descends left. More hemlocks shade the trek. Where the trail splits, take either fork, because they soon merge. To the right, pass through woods, emerging atop an outcrop at 2.4 miles. Keep to the blue-blazed route.

A short detour left from the trail at 3 miles reaches the rim rising directly over Wesel Reservoir for a dizzying look over the cliff. One early summer, a spotted turtle had chosen this forbidding site for laying her eggs. Grant all wildlife a wide safety and comfort margin.

At the junction at 3.1 miles, depart the blue Metacomet Trail and leave the ridge, once again following the blue blazes with the red dots and once again following woods road. In the next few tenths of a mile, look for the trail to take a couple of turns, all well blazed. Hemlock, hickory, oak, and maple weave a relaxing tour.

At 4 miles, turn right off the woods road, taking a footpath through a dark hemlock–oak stand. The hike now passes along the wooded edge of Panther Swamp and rolls over low hilly bumps. The woods grow more mixed. Stay with the blue blazes with the red dot.

The spur heading left at 4.4 miles leads to Shuttle Meadow Avenue; keep right, returning to woods road. Both the spur and the main trail have the same blazing scheme. Descend steadily, remaining in woods and skirting a privately owned grassy flat. American basswood and birch join the mix, with bigger-diameter trees enhancing the scene.

At 5.1 miles, turn right, following a foot trail, ascending a rocky slope near an often dry drainage, with a seasonal falls. Traverse a man-made rock wall before topping out at 5.3 miles. After a brief descent, contour the wooded slope and again descend. At 5.8 miles, turn right onto a woods road, still following blazes. Close the loop at 6 miles and turn left, reaching the trailhead on West Lane at Wigwam Road at 6.1 miles.

50 Southford Falls State Park

OVERVIEW

At this charming 120-acre Connecticut state park, find scenic picnic lawns with big shade trees, Papermill Pond, a cascading falls tumbling through a small gorge, the sparkling tannin-colored waters of Eight Mile Brook, and a covered bridge. Although short, the trail system visits each of these features and travels a wooded hillside reaching a low tower, now mostly enclosed by trees. Historically, the racing falls powered various mills, including an early match factory.

General description:	With easy-to-moderate grades, this loop travels downstream along Eight Mile Brook, ascends the hill rising east of the brook, and returns along Papermill Pond.
General location:	4 miles southeast of Southbury, Connecticut.
Special attractions:	Pond, falls, and brook; hemlock–hardwood forest; covered bridge; millstones, a steam-engine foundation, and remnant sluice pipe; mountain laurel; fall foliage.
Length:	1.5-mile loop.
Elevation:	Find a 300-foot elevation change.
Difficulty:	Moderate.
Maps:	State park map.
Special concerns:	No camping; keep pets leashed.
Season and hours:	Year-round, spring through fall for hiking. Open 8:00 A.M. to sunset.
For information:	Southford Falls State Park.

Key points:
0.0 Papermill Pond trailhead.
0.1 Southford Falls.
0.8 Tower.
1.5 Complete loop at upper bridge.

Finding the trailhead: From Interstate 84, take exit 16 and go south on Connecticut Highway 188, passing through Southford to reach the park on the left in 2.9 miles.

The hike: From the parking area at Papermill Pond, hike the wide gravel lane heading south along the west shore to reach the falls and the core of the park. Papermill Pond reflects its wooded shore, but the wake of a muskrat can distort the watery image. In 200 feet, reach the upper bridge above the dam and falls, the loop junction. Forgo crossing, continuing south (downstream) along the west shore, maneuvering over the open rock outcrop to view Southford Falls.

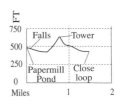

Natural outcrops and attractive stonework shape the racing multidirectional cascades of Southford Falls. The longest drop of this 12-foot-high waterfall measures 6 feet. Find a beautiful juxtaposition of black rock and tiered white streamers. From the falls, Eight Mile Brook slips through a narrow rocky gorge, dropping in stages, exciting eye and ear.

Downstream at the covered bridge (0.15 mile), find a gently riffling brook. Painted red with white trim, this Burr-arch bridge (built in 1972) replicates a circa-1804 design. Nearby, locate the stones and other evidence of the site's milling heritage. Pass through the bridge. On the east shore, turn left for the falls loop alone, gaining new perspectives on it and the gorge before crossing the upper bridge at 0.3 mile. For the longer loop to the tower, turn right, following the east shore of Eight Mile Brook downstream; red blazes mark the way.

Enjoy a rich woods of maple, birch, aspen, tulip, elm, and hemlock. At 0.25 mile, bypass a spur on the left that offers yet another loop option. Where a small boardwalk traverses a moist bottomland, find the tannin-tinted waters of Eight Mile Brook within easy striking distance. Just beyond the walk, look for the red-blazed trail to head left uphill, leaving the brook behind (0.4 mile).

Southford Falls, Southford Falls State Park, CT.

Southford Falls State Park

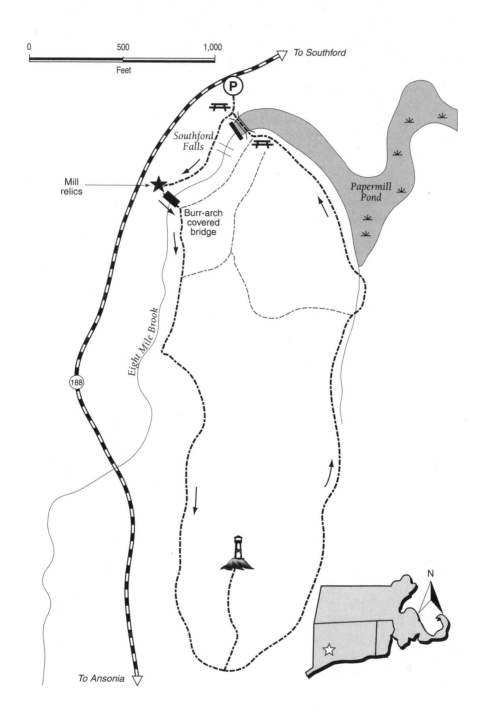

0   500   1,000
Feet

To Southford

Southford Falls

Mill relics

Burr-arch covered bridge

Eight Mile Brook

188

Papermill Pond

To Ansonia

N

Laurel, witch hazel, beech, and tall oak crowd the west-facing slope. As the trail rounds behind an outcrop knoll for a contouring ascent, hear the rising drone of CT 188. A few hazelnut and maple-leaved viburnum vary woods views. With another uphill pulse, top a small outcrop overlooking the wooded slope. Now round left, coming to the tower junction at 0.75 mile; a sign points out the turn for clockwise travelers. Go left for the tower, right to continue the loop.

On the tower spur, ascend left in oak and laurel, reaching the two-story platform at 0.85 mile. Trees enfold three sides, but hikers earn a southwestern glimpse of a neighboring ridge and a rural scene, pretty in autumn flush. A secondary trail crosses the summit to descend the east slope via a laurel thicket, but for this hike, backtrack to the loop junction and turn left.

Travel the upper reaches of the eastern slope among oaks and tall mountain laurel. Below an outcrop crest, maples fill out the forest, just as mountain laurel wanes from the mix. Soon pass through a hilltop depression where outcrops sweep up both sides of the bowl. Here tulip poplar and aspen add their signature leaves.

Veer right up the side of the bowl, again in mountain laurel, coming to a plank walk and junction at 1.3 miles. To the left lies Eight Mile Brook for an alternative return. Bear right to complete the loop near the pond.

Reach the marshy end of Papermill Pond in 200 feet. Scenic boulders mark the far shore, while greenbrier, highbush blueberry, and sweet pepperbush crowd the immediate bank. Traverse the open lawn, passing between a shelter and the pond shore to close the loop at the upper bridge (1.5 miles). From the bridge, search for pickerel among the aquatic vegetation. Often a heron stalks the shallows for shimmery minnows.

51   Kettletown State Park

OVERVIEW

Occupying the east shore of Lake Zoar, a long lake impoundment on the Housatonic River, this 605-acre Connecticut state park offers lake, brook, woods, and crest discovery. The name, legend has it, refers to the actual price colonists paid the Pootaluck Indians for the hunting and fishing rights in this area—a brass kettle. In 1919, the raised lake waters swallowed the site of the historic Indian village, erasing all record of this farming people, who operated a sophisticated drum communication system that could relay a message 200 miles in just two hours.

General description: Three day hikes of varying difficulty incorporate the area's nature and hiking trails, presenting the park's natural merit. Each offers lake overviews, but only the Pomperaug–Oxford Loop accesses Lake Zoar.

General location:	5 miles south of Southbury, Connecticut.
Special attractions:	Lake Zoar overlooks and access, small waterfall, picturesque Kettletown Brook, rich hemlock–hardwood forests, flowering dogwood and mountain laurel, fall foliage.
Length:	William Miller Trail, 0.5 mile round trip to vistas (1.75-mile loop); Pomperaug–Crest Loop, 3.7 miles round trip; Pomperaug–Oxford Loop, 6.5 miles round trip.
Elevation:	William Miller Trail, 100-foot elevation change. For both the Pomperaug–Crest Loop and the Pomperaug–Oxford Loop, find a 450-foot elevation change.
Difficulty:	William Miller Trail, easy. Pomperaug–Crest Loop, moderate. Pomperaug–Oxford Loop, strenuous.
Maps:	State park map.
Special concerns:	The state park and Jackson Cove Recreation Area to the south both charge seasonal vehicle fees. Hikers must keep pets leashed; no trail camping, no fires.
Season and hours:	Year-round, spring through fall for hiking. Open 8:00 A.M. to sunset.
For information:	Kettletown State Park.

Key points:

William Miller Trail:
- 0.0 William Miller Trailhead.
- 0.2 Vistas; backtrack to trailhead.

Pomperaug–Crest Loop:
- 0.0 Bathhouse trailhead.
- 0.1 Cross Kettletown Brook to loop junction.
- 1.6 Hulls Hill.
- 1.9 Crest Trail junction.
- 2.6 Lake Zoar view.
- 3.6 Complete loop; return to bathhouse.

Pomperaug–Oxford Loop:
- 0.0 Bathhouse trailhead.
- 1.9 Crest Trail junction; keep to Pomperaug Trail.
- 2.5 Jackson Cove.
- 2.6 Oxford Loop junction.
- 3.2 Pomperaug Trail; turn left.
- 3.9 Close Oxford Loop; backtrack on Pomperaug the entire way, or take Crest Trail at 4.6 miles.

Finding the trailhead: From Interstate 84, take exit 15 and head south on Kettletown Road, following signs for the park. In 3.5 miles, turn right onto George's Hill Road to find the entrance on the left in 0.8 mile. Start all hikes from the day-use areas.

To access the Pomperaug Trail at Jackson Cove Recreation Area, forgo taking the right-hand turn onto George's Hill Road at 3.5 miles; instead, con-

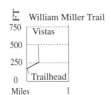

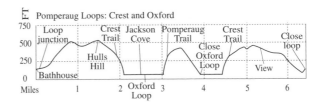

tinue south another 1.3 miles on Maple Tree Hill Road, and then proceed forward on Jackson Cove Road for 0.2 mile.

The hikes: For the **William Miller Trail,** take the park road toward the Youth Group Camp to find this blue-blazed trail (a barricaded woods road) heading north to the right of a kiosk; look for it where the road forms a loop. In a setting of hemlock, oak, birch, beech, hickory, dogwood, and tulip poplar, ascend, bearing left at the trail's loop junction in 100 feet. Seasonally, leaves soften the appearance of the woods road.

Above the trail to the left, admire the outcrop crest of a small hill. Before long, a spur marked by an orange dot on a blue blaze journeys left to top the hill. Where the vista spur branches at 0.2 mile, either fork leads to a view. The left vista overlooks a more natural lake setting, featuring the steep tree-mantled drainage. The vantage to the right has a wilder cliff aspect but overlooks a more developed shore.

Return as you came (0.5 mile), or opt for the 1.75-mile clockwise loop. The well-blazed loop tours time-healed woods road and foot trail through diverse woods. Stay left, forgoing two cut-across spurs that shorten the loop. Be attentive to blazes. Jay, deer, and grouse may be spied.

For better parking, start the **Pomperaug–Crest Loop** below the bathhouse at the beach, hiking the paved and gravel-surfaced lane following Kettletown Brook upstream. Come to a footbridge and a sign for the nature trails at 0.1 mile. Cross the bridge and turn left (upstream) onto the Brook and Boulder Nature Trail.

Meander between boulders overlooking the rushing cascades of Kettletown Brook; hemlocks contribute a soothing darkness. Bear left, following blue blazes to the Pomperaug Trail on the opposite side of the park road (0.3 mile). A sign marks the trail, but there is nearby parking for only a couple of vehicles.

Follow the blue-blazed Pomperaug Trail, encountering a couple of quick direction changes before settling into a steady line of travel. A foot trail leads through the hemlock–birch forest, passing remnant rock walls. The ascent grades from moderate to steep before the trail tops and traverses a low ridge (0.8 mile).

With a rolling descent, reach the 1-mile junction. The spur to the right (blazed with a white dot on blue background) leads to the campground and Crest Trail, allowing hikers to shorten the loop. Stay left. The Pomperaug Trail dips to a moist bottom with sweet pepperbush, then ascends amid oak and birch. Outcrops and boulders riddle the woods. At 1.4 miles, find a rush of mountain laurel. At 1.65 miles, top the outcrop summit of Hulls Hill for a framed view east.

Kettletown State Park

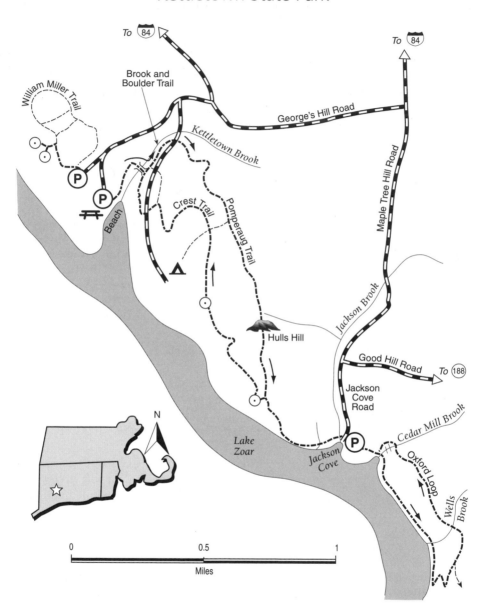

To 84

To 84

William Miller Trail

Brook and Boulder Trail

George's Hill Road

Kettletown Brook

Crest Trail

Pomperaug Trail

Maple Tree Hill Road

P

P

Beach

Hulls Hill

Jackson Brook

Good Hill Road

To 188

Jackson Cove Road

Lake Zoar

Cedar Mill Brook

Oxford Loop

P

Jackson Cove

Wells Brook

N

0   0.5   1

Miles

Next, descend along the sparkling mica-rich outcrop and through woods, reaching a junction and locator map at 1.9 miles. Here, the blue Pomperaug Trail continues straight for Jackson Cove Recreation Area and the Oxford Loop. To complete the Pomperaug–Crest Loop, bear right onto the Crest Trail, marked by a white dot on blue background.

The Crest Trail mounts a low rocky knoll for a limited seasonal view; it then descends the knoll, circling back on itself, contouring the hemlock slope.

With a brief steep climb, top the ridge rising above Lake Zoar (2.1 miles). At 2.3 miles, a short spur leads to a restricted lake view. Briefly pull away from the rim before returning to the western crest for better views at 2.6 miles. Mountain laurel has a sketchy presence in the high-canopy forest.

Descend a hemlock slope, crossing over a stone wall to reach a junction at 3 miles. Here, the Pomperaug–campground connector from the 1-mile junction arrives on the right; the campground is to the left. Proceed forward to return to the nature trails and your vehicle. Blue blazes again lead the way.

Ascend the ridge above the campground, passing behind a huge boulder. Now angle downhill, taking a switchback before coming to a set of wooden steps descending left; a foot trail continues right. Either way returns to the trailhead; right returns via the Brook and Boulder Trail.

For this hike, descend left on the Upland Nature Trail. It angles left across the park road and descends more steps, coming out at the Hemlock Trail. Glimpse the beach across the way and follow the Hemlock Trail to the brook footbridge, returning to the trailhead at 3.7 miles.

For the **Pomperaug–Oxford Loop,** follow the preceding trail description to the 1.9-mile Crest Trail junction, but this time, remain on the blue-blazed Pomperaug Trail for a steep 0.25-mile descent to the Lake Zoar shore. At the lake, the trail curves left, following the shoreline south. Dogwood, hemlock, maple, birch, and upper-canopy oak frame the way. Where clearings offer open lake views, beware of poison ivy. Round a small cove and cross a brook on a rickety hewn log to contour the slope some 30 feet above shore. Dogwoods remain bountiful, showy in spring bloom, dashing in autumn red.

A steep pitch leads to the rock-hopping crossing of Jackson Brook and the boat launch at Jackson Cove Recreation Area (2.5 miles). Traverse the gravel parking lot, picking up the trail at the southeast corner. Clinging seeds of the bordering weeds are a nemesis in late summer and fall. Enter the woods, coming to the loop junction at Cedar Mill Brook (2.6 miles).

Here, the blue-blazed Pomperaug Trail heads upstream to the left; the white dot Oxford Trail continues forward along the shore. Stay along shore for a counterclockwise tour; beautiful maples fill in the drainage, while a sycamore rises near the junction. Contour 10 feet above the shore, again finding dogwoods in the mix. At 2.95 miles, come to an open flat with rocks extending into the water. Hemlocks next shade travel.

Cross Wells Brook and ascend some log-recessed steps to travel a higher contour. Wells Brook shows a rocky drainage with pretty cascades. Just beyond, find an old millrace (a flume for washing logs down to the lake/river for milling). Climb via switchbacks, reaching the Pomperaug Trail at 3.15 miles. Turn left to close Oxford Loop and return to the trailhead. To the right, the Pomperaug Trail continues south for another 1.5 miles.

On the Oxford Loop, contour the upper slope shaded in hemlock, descending briefly to cross Wells Brook. Where the trail forks at 3.3 miles, take the higher road/path; the woods become more mixed. Reach the tour's rocky high point at 3.55 miles. Although you could discover garnet crystals in the area rock, you will certainly find a seasonal view.

Again descend amid hemlock, with a steep descent along Cedar Mill Brook at 3.75 miles. An 8-foot rock face interrupts the stream, seasonally hosting a racing falls. At 3.9 miles, close Oxford Loop and backtrack the Pomperaug Trail, returning to its junction with the Crest Trail at 4.6 miles, returning to the trailhead at 6.5 miles.

52 Sleeping Giant State Park

OVERVIEW

The trails of this state park travel the anatomy of one of south-central Connecticut's most prominent landmarks—Sleeping Giant. Rising 700 feet and sprawling over 2 miles, the Giant serves up grand panoramas. In 1977, the entire trail system won national recreation trail distinction. Color-coded blazes identify the six east–west trails, while red geometric shapes point out the five north–south routes. Together, they suggest multiple hiking loops; obtain a brochure from the ranger or from a map box at the information board near the entrance.

General description:	The two hiking loops chosen to represent this award-winning trail system travel mixed hardwood forest and picturesque mountain laurel groves, topping rocky outcrops and cliffs for grand overlooks.
General location:	8 miles northeast of New Haven, Connecticut.
Special attractions:	Stone observation tower; vistas of Long Island Sound, West Rock Ridge, and the northern traprock ridges; dramatic cliffs and bald outcrops; June-flowering mountain laurel; bird- and wildlife-watching.
Length:	Tower Path–Blue Trail Loop, 3.6-mile loop; White Trail–Violet Trail Loop, 6-mile loop.
Elevation:	Each loop shows a 650-foot elevation change.
Difficulty:	For the Tower Path–Blue Trail Loop, find the Tower Path easy; the Blue Trail (part of the Quinnipiac Trail) is strenuous. For the White Trail–Violet Trail Loop, find the White Trail strenuous and the Violet Trail easy.
Maps:	State park brochure (usually available at entrance station or at the entrance information kiosk).
Special concerns:	Seasonal day-use fee. Expect steep grades, rocky terrain, and sections requiring hand assists.
Season and hours:	Spring through fall, 8:00 A.M. to dusk. Icy conditions make ledges and cliffs too treacherous for travel.
For information:	Sleeping Giant State Park.

Key points:
Tower Path–Blue Trail Loop:
- 0.0   Picnic area trailhead.
- 1.6   Mount Carmel/stone tower.
- 1.9   Giant's Waist.
- 2.5   View from Chin.
- 3.1   Quarry.
- 3.6   Complete loop at picnic area.

White Trail–Violet Trail Loop:
- 0.0   Picnic area trailhead.
- 0.6   Top Giant's Chest.
- 1.1   Right Hip.
- 2.3   Hezekiah's Knob.
- 2.9   Kiosk near Chestnut Lane.
- 3.9   Rocky ridge of Giant's Left Hand.
- 5.5   Cross Red Diamond Trail near Quarry.
- 6.0   Close loop at picnic area.

Finding the trailhead: From the junction of Connecticut Highways 10, 68, and 70 in Cheshire, go south on CT 10 for 5.3 miles and turn left (east) onto Mount Carmel Avenue. Reach the park entrance on the left in 0.3 mile.

The hike: The **Tower Path–Blue Trail Loop** joins two of the park's most popular—although leagues apart in difficulty—trails; stay on the Tower Path for an "easy" round trip.

From the east side of the picnic area parking lot, take the wide, graveled Tower Path marked PEDESTRIANS ONLY. Maple, oak, hemlock, birch, beech, and dogwood weave a canopy of texture and full shade, while a vibrant mid-story of young trees and mountain laurel engages the eye. Where chestnut oaks claim the canopy, more sun penetrates.

At the many junctions, keep to the gravel tower road, switchbacking ever higher for a steady, moderate climb. By 0.8 mile, tree-filtered views present the cliff and boulder rubble shaping the Giant's Chin. Ahead, a monument honors a leader in preserving the park.

Cross to the other side of the mountain, encountering more boulders. Near its intersection with the Blue Trail (1 mile), the road briefly flattens. Cross the Blue Trail a second time to top Mount Carmel (the Giant's Left Hip) at 1.6 miles, reaching an attractive four-story stone tower with arched observation windows at each level. Ramps ascend the summit tower; vistas applaud the surrounding forest, rounded ridges, and basalt features and sweep the New Haven skyline to Long Island Sound. Backtrack on the Tower Path, or return via a rugged descent on the Blue Trail.

For the more challenging return west, find the first blaze of the Blue Trail on the southwest corner of the tower; avoid following the blue blazes that head northeast. Travel a rocky terrain, passing through similar woods, with a few azaleas in the mix.

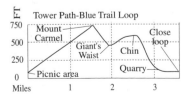

227

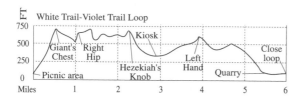

White Trail-Violet Trail Loop

Upon crossing the Tower Path, sharply ascend to and then steeply pitch from the Giant's Waist, staying on the Blue Trail. At 2.2 miles, again cross the Tower Path for a calmer tour along the north side of the Giant's Chest—only to charge up the rocky back side of the Chin, which elsewhere presents a conspicuous cliff profile.

Where the trail levels, enjoy views. After a steep 20-foot rock descent (requiring hands), a short spur leads to an overlook of the dizzying vertical cliffs forming the Chin; views span to the Giant's Chest. After 2.6 miles, find a grueling descent through low-stature forest and over canted rock faces, skirting an abandoned quarry. Road noise echoes up the Elbow, as hemlocks fill out the forest. The trail bottoms out at the quarry. At the base of the hill, follow the Mill River downstream and turn left before reaching CT 10. Close the loop at the picnic area at 3.6 miles.

For the second hike, the **White Trail–Violet Trail Loop,** follow the more difficult White Trail first, returning on the calmer violet-blazed route for a counterclockwise circuit.

Find the White Trail heading north from the picnic area loop. Cross a footbridge and ascend, contouring the slope. Maple, beech, American basswood, oak, and hickory lace over the trail. Pass below a talus slope, soon ascending the rocky base. Overhead loom dramatic reddish brown cliffs, crags, and overhangs, partially veiled by leaves.

Summit tower, Sleeping Giant State Park, CT.

228

Sleeping Giant State Park

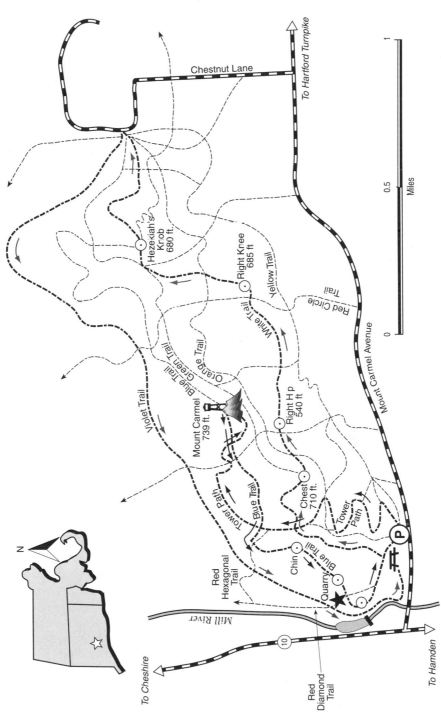

Mountain laurel, Sleeping Giant State Park, CT.

At 0.3 mile, the White Trail crosses over the wide Tower Path to resume its twisting ascent, advancing via rock stairs and passing showy displays of mountain laurel. Contour below the fissured cliff and breakaway blocks of the Giant's Chest before topping the heaving rise at 0.6 mile. Chestnut oaks and shrubs vegetate the rises. Find an open view of the Chin and a ledge overlooking the campus of Quinnipiac College before descending to contour a wooded slope.

Across the Orange Trail, the descent steepens. Ahead, contour the talus base of the Right Hip (1 mile). Ledges provide toeholds for the scramble to the top of the Hip (1.1 miles). Gain more views of the south-central Connecticut neighborhood.

Resume the rigorous workout, migrating down the Giant's anatomy. Cross the Red Circle Trail to ascend a rocky slope, topping the Right Knee (1.75 miles). Again cross the Orange Trail for a rolling tour among mountain laurel to claim Hezekiah's Knob (2.3 miles); at times, storm clouds enfold the Giant. Descend through woods and laurel and skirt an outcrop of pillow basalt before descending the Giant's Right Foot.

Pass the Green and Yellow Trails, reaching a kiosk near a limited access on Chestnut Lane (2.9 miles). In the vicinity of the kiosk, find seven blazed trails radiating outward; several suggest alternative returns. For this hike, pursue the violet blazes, returning along the left side of the Giant.

By contrast, the Violet Trail offers a sleepy woods walk. Large oak and tulip poplar punctuate the forest; the fallen orange-and-green blooms of the tulip tree may decorate the leaf mat. Encounter low rock walls and logs or stepping-stones at muddy sites. Hemlocks join the mix as hikers approach the rocky ridge of the Giant's Left Hand (3.9 miles); mountain laurel showers this low ridge. With a rocky descent, hike below a similar ridge feature.

At 4.2 miles, cross the Red Circle Trail, resuming an easier undulating tour in mature forest and mountain laurel. At 5 miles, hear the first drone of CT 10; until this time, the hike has been remarkably insulated. The laurel show pretty twisted trunks as the route crosses the Red Hexagonal Trail.

At 5.5 miles, cross the Red Diamond Trail near the abandoned quarry, a red-rock cliff and scar to the left. A concrete shell is to the right. Descend steeply along a rockwork wall and a second ruin where an eroding staircase advances the trail. Arches mark some of the standing walls, as poison ivy and Virginia creeper reclaim the ruins. Follow the gravel lane away from the ruins to reach a foot trail, which contours and descends above the pond impoundment on the Mill River.

Cross the end of the breached dam and pursue the river downstream. The Red Diamond and Blue Trails briefly merge and depart. Now turn left away from the river to enter the west side of the picnic area near the Dumpsters. Close the loop at 6 miles.

53 Zoar Trail

General description: In Lower Paugussett State Forest, on the west shore of Lake Zoar, this blue-blazed loop applauds lake and woods, with a side trip to a waterfall. The first 2.4 miles have been designated a scenic trail by the Department of Environmental Protection.

General location: 1 mile north of Stevenson, Connecticut.

Special attractions: Lake Zoar access and vistas, waterfall, diverse woods, wildlife, fall foliage.

Length: 6.5-mile loop (5.1-mile loop when a seasonal trail closure is in effect).

Elevation: Find a 500-foot elevation change.

Difficulty: Moderate.

Maps: Southbury 7.5-minute USGS quad; Lake Zoar Area Trails, *Connecticut Walk Book.*

Special concerns: Respect the seasonal trail closure on the loop. During hunting season, avoid hiking here or take the necessary precautions, including bright orange clothing.

Season and hours: Spring through fall, daylight hours.

For information: Paugussett State Forest.

Key points:
- 0.0 Great Quarter Road trailhead.
- 1.2 Tiny beach.
- 1.6 Prydden Brook/falls detour.
- 1.7 Seasonal bypass junction.

2.4 End of scenic trail section; turn left.
3.4 Meet up with woods road (seasonal bypass).
3.6 Cross Prydden Brook.
5.9 Great Quarter Road.
6.5 End at trailhead.

Finding the trailhead: From Interstate 84, take exit 11 and follow the signs to Connecticut Highway 34. Turn east onto CT 34, heading toward Stevenson, Derby, and New Haven, for 4.9 miles. There, turn left onto Great Quarter Road and follow it northeast 1.3 miles to where it ends at a turnaround and parking area. Westbound CT 34 travelers find Great Quarter Road 0.2 mile west of the CT 34–CT 111 junction in Stevenson; turn right.

The hike: Round the rock barrier and follow the blazes north along a closed woods road, passing through the hemlock–hardwood forest. Avoid the shoreline here; it is private property. With the exception of side paths branching away to skirt a fallen tree or a badly eroded spot, the woods road guides travelers the first 0.25 mile, crossing a wooded flat above the steep treed slope to sparkling Lake Zoar. Maple-leaved viburnum, fern, and sassafras decorate the understory.

The grade becomes pathlike, ascending the steep lakeside slope. By 0.5 mile, descend toward the water. Tulip poplar appear among the hemlock and birch. Within striking distance of shore, find cross-lake views of Jackson Cove Recreation Area as well as north–south views of this long impoundment of the Housatonic River.

The trail rolls along the slope, tracing a onetime route to the town of Stevenson before following a recessed woods road to the water's edge. The rising lake waters resulting from the dam's completion in 1919 created several roads to nowhere. Find rockier travel ahead, as the trail vacillates from 10 to 100 feet above shore. At 0.9 mile, a bouldery lake slope offers cross-lake views of the steep, treed eastern ridge and a plunging outcrop. Autumn colors particularly recommend the view.

Remain close to the water, finding a thin sandy beach with stump seating at 1.2 miles. Maple, oak, and ash line the shore. From the beach, ascend a woods road, placing a low rise between the trail and the lake. Cross a drainage and bear left. Before long, glimpse Prydden Falls below the trail.

Where the trail comes to the Prydden Brook crossing (1.65 miles), hikers may wish to postpone crossing and instead bear right, following the unmarked side trail beside the brook downstream to the falls. Tulip poplar grow near the brook. At the falls, a series of cliff and rock jumbles are adorned with white streamers and weeping moss. This side path also accesses the shore. The waterfall proves a satisfying destination for an alternative 3.5-mile round-trip hike.

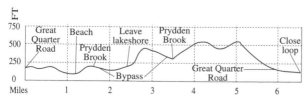

Keeping to the primary trail alone, cross Prydden Brook and continue uphill on an old road grade. At 1.75 miles is a junction.

232

Zoar Trail

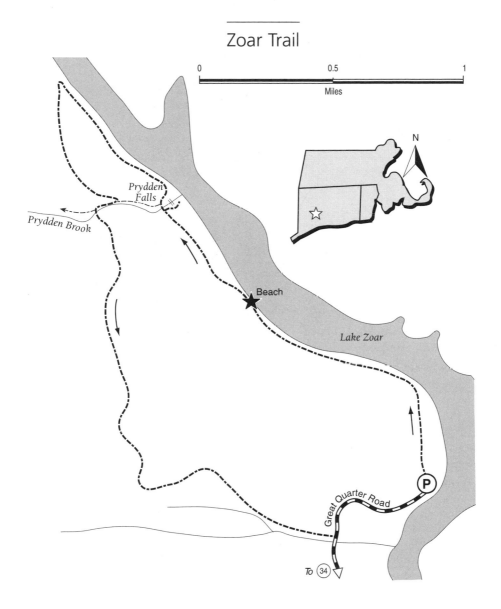

Travel the footpath to the right from August 15 to April 15. Remain on the woods road (blazed blue/yellow dot) from April 15 to August 15. Because the loop's footpath travels a sensitive nesting area, respect the posted wildlife closure.

When permissible, though, follow the blue blazes right along the sometimes faint foot trail, traversing a hemlock–hardwood plateau and rounding the slope above shore. Gradually descend to a junction at 2.4 miles, just beyond a jut overlooking the lake. This marks the end of the scenic trail section; a sign for southbound travelers shows they are now entering SCENIC TRAIL NEXT 2.4 MILES.

Fall leaves.

At 2.4 miles, the Zoar Trail turns left; paint blazes and a small sign indicate the turn. Avoid the path straight ahead that leads to private land. The Zoar Trail steeply sidewinds and angles upslope, topping the ridge at 2.7 miles. Travel through choked hemlock stands and deciduous woods. At a T-junction with another path, go left. Round below a rocky knoll, keeping the knoll to your left, then veer right, descending among hemlocks to merge with a woods road (the blue/yellow dot alternative route from the 1.75-mile junction) at 3.4 miles.

The remainder of the hike is common to both loops. April through mid-August hikers reach this point by following the woods road uphill for 0.25 mile, paralleling and overlooking the Prydden Brook drainage.

Turn right onto the woods road (continue forward if already on it). It presents a beautiful passage framed by tulip poplar, maple, beech, oak, and birch, with mountain laurel, sweet pepperbush, and witch hazel. In about 0.1 mile, look for the blue-blazed Zoar Trail to turn left off the woods road. Because this narrow footpath is easily missed, cued only by a small ribbon and paint blazes on a tree offset from the road, be alert.

Cross Prydden Brook via stones to ascend in an area of laurel and beech. The hike rolls from outcrop knoll to outcrop knoll. Deer, woodpecker, and hawk are possible sightings. Atop the rocks, Lake Zoar becomes but a distant gleam; the focus of this leg is woodland. Rock tripe and green lichen adorn the rocks, as do flecks of mica, seams of quartz, and garnet nodes. Stay with the blue blazes.

At 4.2 miles (summer hikers subtract 1.4 miles from the recorded distances), start the descent. Laurel continues to decorate the rolling, contouring route. In a wooded bottom at 4.75 miles, come to the first of two back-to-back junctions with a lightly traveled trail blazed by a blue dot on a yellow background; keep to the blue-blazed Zoar Trail.

Find one last ascent of a rocky rise before descending via a rock-reinforced woods road and leafy footpath; at times, muddy pockets riddle the trail. Traverse a flat outcrop for looks across the immediate forest, and descend, skirting private property to the right. Exit onto Great Quarter Road near a NO OUTLET sign at 5.9 miles, turn left, and hike 0.6 mile on Great Quarter Road to close the loop at the trailhead.

54 Cockaponset State Forest

OVERVIEW

In south-central Connecticut, this state forest offers hikers a tranquil woods retreat and access to Pattaconk Reservoir. The forest boasts a fine trail system, well blazed and with numbered junctions that correspond to the state forest map and posted field mileages. Find incremental and cumulative mileages listed on the back of the state forest map.

General description:	The selected two hikes incorporate most of the forest trail system, exploring pond, woods, laurel groves, and low rock ledges. To reach the reservoir, hike north on the Pattaconk Trail.
General location:	5 miles south of Haddam, Connecticut.
Special attractions:	Scenic reservoir, mixed hardwood forest, mountain laurel and rare orchids, wildlife, fall foliage.
Length:	Circuit Walk, 3.3-mile loop; Pattaconk to Cockaponset–Wildwood Loop, 9.7 miles round trip.
Elevation:	Circuit Walk, 150-foot elevation change; Pattaconk to Cockaponset–Wildwood Loop, 300-foot elevation change.
Difficulty:	Circuit Walk, easy. Pattaconk to Cockaponset–Wildwood Loop, moderate.
Maps:	State forest map.
Special concerns:	Bring water.
Season and hours:	Spring through fall for hiking, 8:00 A.M. to sunset.
For information:	Cockaponset State Forest.

Key points:
Circuit Walk:
    0.0   Pattaconk Lake trailhead.
    1.6   Cross abandoned Filley Road.
    3.3   Emerge at southern parking lot.

Pattaconk to Cockaponset–Wildwood Loop:
    0.0   Pattaconk Lake trailhead.

1.0 Cross Pattaconk Brook.
1.2 Junction 6; follow Cockaponset Trail.
2.2 Old County Road/junction 8.
3.1 Loop junction; go counterclockwise.
5.2 Junction 14; follow Wildwood Trail.
6.6 Close loop; backtrack to trailhead.

Finding the trailhead: From Connecticut Highway 9, take exit 6 and go west on CT 148 for 1.7 miles. There, turn right (north) onto Cedar Lake Road (east of the CT 148–CT 145 junction), go 1.6 miles, and turn left at the sign for Pattaconk Lake State Recreation Area. Find large dirt parking lots on either side of the road before reaching the barricade in 0.3 mile.

The hikes: Start both hikes by rounding the barrier and following the blue blazes to the right. Bear right at the fork, coming to a four-way junction at 0.1 mile.

For the **Circuit Walk,** head left (south) on the Pattaconk Trail, following the blue blaze with a red dot. Pass through mixed woods, with beech, witch hazel, maple, oak, and mountain laurel, ascending a low ridge with a rocky crest. Among the rocks, find mossy shelves and fern caps, with chestnut oaks favoring the ridgetop.

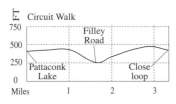

Descend for a rolling tour, crossing over secondary trails and woods roads. The heart of the woodland reveals oak and beech. At 1.1 miles, start a long, steady descent, cross a drainage, and, at 1.45 miles, curve left. To the right lies private property. At the upcoming brook, find two blazed crossing sites; take your choice and turn left upon crossing. Mossy rocks adorn the brook.

Cross abandoned Filley Road (a paved road), reaching junction 2 at 1.65 miles. To the right lies CT 148; bear left onto the blue Cockaponset Trail to complete the Circuit Walk, touring a mature, multistory forest. Initially, the trail shows a less refined bed, with more roots and rocks.

From an impressive beech grove, cross a brook to tour an eskerlike low, flat ridge, where tulip poplars find a niche. Deer, grouse, woodpecker, and mouse may surprise travelers. When the trail begins a long steady climb, it improves in quality. Cross a faint jeep track and a rocky drainage, ascending to end at the southern parking lot at 3.3 miles.

For the **Pattaconk to Cockaponset–Wildwood Loop,** go right at the four-way junction at 0.1 mile, hiking north on the Pattaconk Trail (blue with red dot). The wide hiker avenue travels the west shore of Pattaconk Reservoir, a scenic pond displaying an irregular shoreline. Spurs branch to the canted sandy bank. Sweet pepperbush, azalea, and witch hazel dot the shore. At 0.25 mile, pass a natural stone sofa overlooking

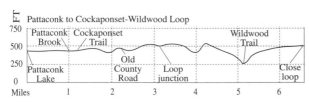

Cockaponset State Forest

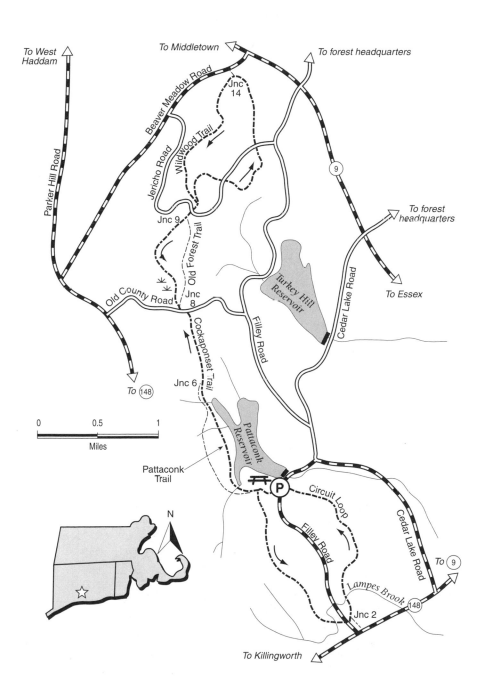

the water. Yellow and white pond lilies spangle the shallows.

Ahead, the trail rolls along the wooded, rocky slope, briefly drawing away from the pond to cross a sometimes muddy inlet. Pass a split rock, touring a bouldery site to resume north along shore where a congested leafy bank masks a lily-pad-coated cove. Cross a second rocky inlet atop flat stones, leaving the reservoir (0.8 mile).

Cross rocky Pattaconk Brook at 1 mile. Here, the blue Cockaponset Trail pinches toward the Pattaconk Trail. Keep right, following the red dot blazes for a relaxing woods stroll; both trails again meet at junction 6 (1.25 miles). This marks the end of the Pattaconk Trail. Continue north on the Cockaponset Trail, passing among scenic large-diameter trees.

Travel a wooded tier between ledges, reaching little-used Old County Road (a dirt road) at 2 miles. Turn left on it, finding the blue blazes heading north in 0.15 mile. Reach junction 8. The old woods road to the right is the Old Forest Trail; stay on the blue Cockaponset footpath, now ascending. The trails again meet at junction 9.

Before long, the Cockaponset Trail overlooks an extensive marsh of phragmites (plumed reeds) and snags. Cross a low rockwork dam to round the marsh via a snug green aisle of sweet pepperbush, sassafras, oak, and junglelike mountain laurel. A scenic outcrop rise with ledges and overhangs overlooks the trail (2.5 miles).

Honeycombed, folded, and fractured outcrop rises continue to frame travel. Small clearings hint at the forest management. At 2.75 miles, reach junction 9, continuing north on the Cockaponset Trail. Turn right onto Jericho Road at 3 miles. Where the trail reaches Jericho Road, look for a tiny plot of rare orchids staked off to the right; admire, but do not touch.

Cockaponset Trail, Cockaponset State Forest, CT.

Via the roadway, cross a small drainage, turning left in 100 feet; again find a passage characterized by tight laurel and rock outcroppings. Just ahead, reach the loop junction. Stay on the blue Cockaponset Trail, returning via the red dot Wildwood Trail on the left.

On the Cockaponset, ascend and round amid outcrops, edging a standing dead forest of pines, where the polelike trunks tower over the young hardwoods reclaiming the site. Top an outcrop overlooking a wooded draw and pass the footings of an old lookout (3.5 miles). The trail now rolls, snakes, and twists back on itself, passing from outcrop ridge to draw and back. Scenic rock steps advance the trail.

At 4 miles, come to Jericho Road a second time, turn left for 50 feet, and pick up the trail on the right. Here, tall laurel shapes a forest within a forest. At 4.5 miles, look for a couple of quick direction changes, coming out at the clearing of an old camp.

Cross Jericho Road one last time (4.75 miles), finding the continuation of the blue Cockaponset Trail to the left of a trail marked only by two wooden posts. Slowly descend to junction 14 (5.25 miles). Here, the red dot Wildwood Trail continues the loop straight ahead; the Cockaponset Trail bears right (north) to Beaver Meadow Road.

Follow the Wildwood Trail into an inviting hemlock grove and ascend to a woods road. Hike right along the woods road, and take a quick left, returning to a foot trail to reach and travel a ridge where mountain laurel thins. Again hike among pine snags and some striking outcrops to close the loop at 6.65 miles; backtrack to the trailhead at 9.7 miles.

55 Regicides Trail

General description:	In south-central Connecticut, this hike combines two rolling tours along West Rock Ridge, an elongated traprock mountain with rust-colored cliffs.
General location:	West Rock Ridge State Park, northwest of New Haven.
Special attractions:	Historic Judges' Cave, vistas, mid-June to July mountain laurel blooms, evergreen–deciduous woods.
Length:	13.6 miles total. It is 0.8 mile round trip to reach the Regicides Trail at Buttress Gap. From Buttress Gap, Judges' Cave (southbound) is 1.2 miles round trip; north from the gap stretches an 11.6-mile round trip.
Elevation:	Find a 400-foot elevation change.
Difficulty:	Moderate, with uneven rocky footing.
Maps:	Regicides Trail, *Connecticut Walk Book;* New Haven 7.5-minute USGS quad.
Special concerns:	Carry water; none is available along the trail.

Season and hours: Spring through fall, 8:00 A.M. to dusk; nature center, 10:00 A.M. to 4:00 P.M. Monday through Friday, closed holidays.
For information: West Rock Ridge State Park.

Key points:

- 0.0   Nature center parking.
- 0.4   Buttress Gap; hike south.
- 1.0   Judges' Cave; hike north.
- 1.6   Buttress Gap.
- 4.0   North Summit Trail junction.
- 7.4   End at Baldwin Parkway; return to parking (13.6 miles).

Finding the trailhead: From the corner of Fitch Street and Whalley Avenue (Connecticut Highway 63) in New Haven, go north on Fitch Street for 0.6 mile and turn left onto Wintergreen Avenue; brown signs for West Rock Ridge State Park mark the turn. Keep to Wintergreen Avenue, turning left onto Brookside/Wintergreen Avenue at 0.9 mile. Find the state park on the left in 0.5 mile; locate West Rock Nature Center and trail parking on the right 0.1 mile farther.

The hike: A divided trail travels the western escarpment rim and crest of West Rock Ridge, touring rock outcrop, mixed woods, and mountain laurel stands, snaring select views along the way. The southern 1.2-mile round trip visits a page from seventeenth-century English–American history at Judges' Cave.

Reaching the **Regicides Trail** is anything but straightforward. From the nature center parking lot, cross Wintergreen Avenue and follow the paved foot trail beyond a pair of wooden posts to enter West Rock Ridge State Park. Traverse its abandoned parking lot to exit at the rock barrier, coming out near the entrance station (0.1 mile). There, turn right onto Baldwin Parkway (closed due to budget cuts). Where the road forks ahead, bear left and keep a sharp eye out for a wide, unmarked earthen trail ascending the slope to the right (0.1 mile from the station).

Follow this trail, passing through a maple–mountain laurel corridor to reach the blue-blazed Regicides Trail at Buttress Gap (0.4 mile). A left leads to the Judges' Cave in 0.6 mile; a right offers the primary tour.

To the left (southbound), closely watch the blazes, because they point away from the initial trailbed and up the slope in 200 feet. Maple, oak, and hickory frame the way, replaced by an oak-studded top. Rounded outcrops present city views to the west, as the trail journeys over the tunnel for Wilbur Cross Parkway. At 0.9 mile, blue blazes point right, but the forks come together at the oak-shaded picnic site and Judges' Cave. A former park road likewise accesses the site.

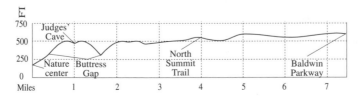

Regicides Trail

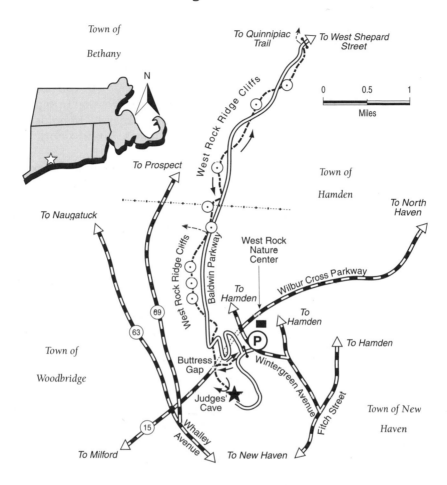

Within the barn-size boulder jumble, overlapping rocks create cavelike entries, overhangs, and short passages. At this spot, American colonists shielded Judges Edward Whalley and William Goffe, two of the three regicides who had issued the death warrant for Charles I and became fugitives themselves with the restoration of Charles II to the British throne. Hiding here, they eluded royal agents for three months before escaping to Massachusetts. Also of historical note is a nearby outcrop with meticulously carved names dating to the mid-1800s.

When through exploring this area, return to Buttress Gap (1.6 miles) for the trek north. Northbound from the gap, blue blazes point out a quick, steep, rocky ascent. If you can steel yourself to make the grade, you will find the rest of the hike gently rolling. Earthen segments bridge rocky stretches.

West Rock Ridge, a volcanic dike that eroded free, towers 400 feet above the valley floor. Atop its western escarpment (1.7 miles), oaks, eastern red cedar, and berry bushes grow among the outcrops, boulders, and crags. Beware of poison ivy; a roadway drone echoes up slope.

Drifting away from the escarpment and past an airplane beacon, the trail briefly follows a gravel service road. Stay alert for the blazes, which point out a descent to the right in 200 feet. Maple, hickory, and dogwood enfold the way.

At 2 miles, cross forsaken Baldwin Parkway (the first of six crossings) and pass three radio towers, returning to woods. Mountain laurel threads beneath the chestnut, white, and red oaks. A second parkway crossing brings a return to the western escarpment, with limited looks at marshy Konolds Pond and cross-valley views of a wooded ridge. Open views trending north now occur about every 0.2 mile.

Oak and hemlock stands now alternate with the mountain laurel groves. Although both obscure views, the smoother trail allows for easier walking. At 4 miles, the red-blazed North Summit Trail heads left as the Regicides Trail approaches and crosses a former vista turnout on the parkway. When next at Baldwin Parkway, follow it left a few hundred feet before returning to the rim for a partial view of Lake Dawson. Deer, owl, grouse, and woodpecker can surprise hikers. More views follow, as do more parkway crossings.

The crossing at 5.7 miles puts hikers on the east side of the ridge in an oak–rocky meadow habitat. Where the trail slips back west, find a 180-degree view lauding the bumpy spine of West Rock Ridge. The trail withholds an eastern perspective until 6.7 miles, where views encompass a field-rimmed pond, city skyline, and woods.

As the trail curves away west, it tags Baldwin Parkway one last time (at 7.4 miles). For the Regicides tour alone, return to the gap (13.2 miles) and retrace the initial 0.4 mile to the parking lot. For a less demanding return, loop back along tree-shaded and time-softened Baldwin Parkway. The blue-blazed route continuing north offers a shuttle option to hikers who spotted a vehicle at the start of the Sanford Trail (consult *Connecticut Walk Book*), or a long-distance trek on the state's Quinnipiac Trail.

56   Devil's Den Preserve

OVERVIEW

In southwestern Connecticut, this 1,720-acre preserve owned by The Nature Conservancy (TNC) contributes to a critical open space measuring nearly 10 square miles. Combined with adjoining town, trust, and water company lands, the reserve provides habitat that encourages wildlife breeding and diversity. The Den boasts some 20 miles of interlocking trails for a variety of hiking tours, exploring woodland, swamp, rock ledges, and ravines. Cultural sites enhance the journey.

General description: A broad-swinging loop travels several of the named trails, touring much of the preserve; side spurs visit granite ledges and a bouldery ravine.

General location: In Weston and Redding, Connecticut.

Special attractions: Rich hardwood forest, historical sites, granite ledges, limited vistas, wildflowers (including fourteen species of violet), flowering shrubs, fall foliage, wildlife.

Length: Den Loop, 5-mile loop (7.2 miles with the suggested side trips).

Elevation: Travel from a trailhead elevation of 250 feet to a ledge elevation of 550 feet.

Difficulty: Moderate.

Maps: Preserve map.

Special concerns: Donation suggested; register at the map/information board at the parking lot. No pets, no bikes, no smoking, no picnicking, no fishing, and no swimming. The preserve has its own blazing scheme: Red indicates a woods road, yellow indicates a foot trail, and white indicates a trail that is part of the greater Saugatuck Valley trail system. Find junctions numbered in correspondence with the map, aiding in navigation and trail selection. Most junction posts display an arrow pointing the way back to the parking lot. The Den offers no amenities.

Season and hours: Year-round, spring through fall for hiking. Sunrise to sunset, with gates locked promptly at sunset.

For information: Devil's Den Preserve.

Key points:

0.0 Preserve trailhead; follow Laurel Trail.
0.4 Godfrey Pond.
1.5 Sawmill ruins.
2.6 Deer Run Trail detour.
3.4 Redding Great Ledge.
5.6 Ambler Gorge Trail detour.
7.2 End loop at parking area.

Finding the trailhead: From Connecticut Highway 15 (the Merritt Parkway), take exit 42 and travel north on CT 57 for 4.8 miles. There, turn right (east) onto Godfrey Road, go 0.5 mile, and turn left onto Pent Road. The route changes to dirt, entering the preserve. With the Den located within 35 miles of New York City, the parking lot can fill on weekends.

The hike: The suggested Den Loop begins on the Laurel Trail; locate it over your left shoulder as you look at the preserve map-information board. A carved sign and post 21 mark its start. Round the log gate, following the red- and white-blazed wood-shavings lane into the preserve.

Slowly ascend, touring a rich woods of oak, maple, and beech, with witch hazel, mountain laurel, and sweet pepperbush filling out the midstory. A scenic stone wall briefly lines the trail. At 0.2 mile, reach a collier's mound ex-

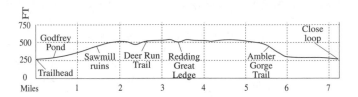

hibit, a conical stack of wood with interpretive signs. Charcoal burning was a chief Weston industry in the 1800s; more than forty charcoal burn sites or remnant collier huts riddle the Den.

Pass through a gap in a stone wall at post 22, turn right, and then keep right at an upcoming junction. Stone walls and large boulders accent the woods. Tulip poplar, hickory, and birch all contribute to this visually rich tour, bathed in relaxation. At 0.4 mile (post 31), bear left onto the Godfrey Trail and then detour left at the next post.

The detour leads to the Godfrey Pond Sawmill Site, with a restored dam and historical ruins dating from the eighteenth century. Resume the loop, reaching the top of the dam to view the attractive pond, shaped like a painter's palette. Stay with the red and white blazes, rounding the leafy south rim of Godfrey Pond.

At post 34, a spur branches to the pond; bear right for the loop, traveling near the east boundary. Fall litters the lane with a vibrant collage of shape and color. At 0.6 mile (post 35), bear left, staying on the Godfrey Trail; the Perry Trail journeys right. Where a yellow trail branches left, again keep to the Godfrey Trail, enjoying the towering tulip poplars and attractive beech.

At 1.2 miles, pass a split rock on the right, and in another 200 feet, look right for what might be a reclaimed charcoal mound. Sinewy hornbeam and dogwood contribute to the woods. At 1.5 miles, find a rusted steam boiler, tiger engine wheel, smokestack, and flywheel from a portable sawmill that operated here from the late 1800s to the early 1900s. A 30-foot-deep stone-lined well likely supplied water. Rustic interpretive panels blend with the setting.

Stay on the red and white Godfrey Trail, passing Sap Brook Trail on the left. Soon after, pass through a breach in a rock wall to find the Aspetuck Trail, arriving at an angle on the right (post 64, 2.1 miles). The Aspetuck, together with the Perry Trail, offers a shorter loop return. Bear left for the full tour, now following the Bedford Trail.

In a few feet, the Godfrey/Pillars Trail descends right, reaching a stone-pillar entry off CT 53 in 1.1 miles. En route, it tours inviting woods, passes extensive stonework, and affords a glimpse of Saugatuck Reservoir. Keep to the Bedford Trail for the loop, descending and contouring the base of a hill, traveling a marshy site.

At 2.6 miles, as the Bedford Trail curves left, be alert for an easy-to-miss, although marked, junction (post 54). Detour right on the yellow-blazed Deer Run Trail to reach both Great Ledge and Redding Great Ledge.

With a rolling ascent, in 0.25 mile, cross through a gap in a stone wall, arriving at post 55. Bear right; the Redding Trail arrives on the left. After the Dayton Trail arrives on the right, round a stone wall at post 56 and again

Devil's Den Preserve

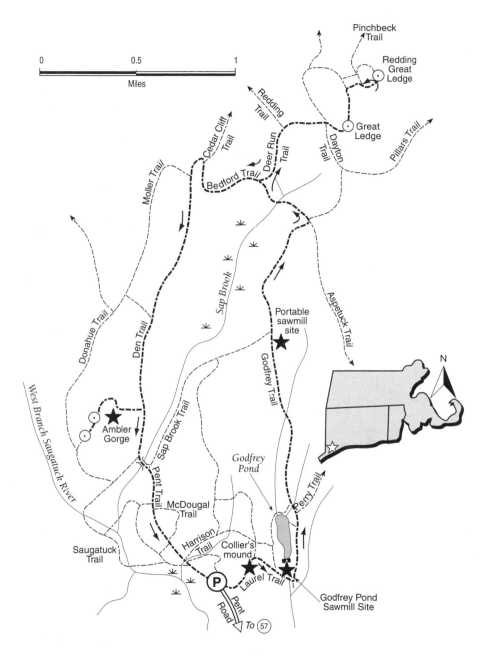

0   0.5   1
Miles

Pinchbeck Trail

Redding Great Ledge

Redding Trail

Cedar Cliff Trail

Moller Trail

Deer Run Trail

Bedford Trail

Dayton Trail

Great Ledge

Pillars Trail

Sap Brook

Portable sawmill site

Aspetuck Trail

Donahue Trail

Den Trail

West Branch Saugatuck River

Godfrey Trail

N

Ambler Gorge

Sap Brook Trail

Godfrey Pond

Perry Trail

Pent Trail

McDougal Trail

Harrison Trail

Collier's mound

Saugatuck Trail

P

Laurel Trail

Godfrey Pond Sawmill Site

Pent Road

To 57

bear right for the ledges. Travel a sun-drenched woods of oak, maple, and a few hickory, arriving at Great Ledge, a long granite ledge with a 70- to 100-foot cliff. This featured ledge offers both open and tree-framed looks across the Saugatuck Valley woodland and distant flat ridges.

Flywheel, Devil's Den Preserve, CT.

Traverse Great Ledge and descend through woods, passing the marker for the Weston–Redding town line. Ahead, the yellow blazes to the left lead to the Pinchbeck Trail; continue forward on the white trail for Redding Great Ledge.

At the T-junction (a loop junction), go right to top Redding Great Ledge (3.4 miles), finding an open look at Saugatuck Reservoir with its treed point and islands. Tall, twisted laurel accent the tour; deer frequent the woods. Backtrack (or complete the white loop and backtrack) to the Bedford Trail at post 54 (4.2 miles); bear right, resuming the counterclockwise tour.

Bypass the yellow Cedar Cliff Nature Trail and the Moller Trail, both on the right, slowly ascending to a plateau of red and chestnut oaks. With a gradual descent, again find a mix of birch, beech, maple, and tulip poplar. Where the Donahue Trail heads right at post 49 (5.2 miles), continue forward, now on the Den Trail.

Round below outcrop ledges and cliffs, coming to the yellow-blazed Ambler Gorge Trail. Detour right on this trail, still rounding the outcrop, descending to a bouldery bowl and jumble-rock ravine. Seasonally, a cascade graces the jumble. Books of muscovite (a kind of mica) glisten in the granite. Cross the hewn log with its chicken-wire wrapping and ascend to two modest vistas, tagging the second one at 5.9 miles. Although the trail continues, retrace your steps and resume the Den Loop back at post 44 (6.2 miles).

The counterclockwise circuit now descends, passing amid a high-canopy forest. At post 10, bear left, crossing a footbridge over Sap Brook. Stay with the red and white blazes, rounding toward the parking lot, now on the Pent Trail. (The Bedford, Den, and Pent Trails are but a single route; only the name changes.) Do not veer from this main woods road.

Ahead, the tour rolls and skirts outcrop hills, with the McDougal Trail, Saugatuck Trail, and Harrison Trail all branching off this final leg of the hike. At 7 miles, pass junction post 5, finding a pair of sentinel tulip trees. Soon after, reach an overlook to the right; it presents the marshy drainage of West Branch Saugatuck River at Saugatuck Refuge. Reach the parking area at 7.2 miles.

Eastern Connecticut Trails

Eastern Connecticut holds a gentler terrain, a landscape of mild undulations, glacier-flattened ridges, and picturesque outcrop hills. The region cradles the largest forest in the state and a stretch of undeveloped shore along Long Island Sound. Travel rolling woodlands of southern hardwoods, eastern hemlock, and planted pine; enjoy splendid displays of mountain laurel; explore remote ponds; and tour a rare rhododendron and Atlantic white cedar swamp.

57 Bigelow Hollow State Park

OVERVIEW

Near the Massachusetts border, this Connecticut state park boasts large ponds, deep woods, and tranquility. The ponds invite tours. Circuits explore Bigelow and Breakneck Ponds and visit Mashapaug Pond. Nipmuck State Forest abuts the park, expanding open space and wildlife habitat.

General description:	Three pond circuits of varying difficulty introduce this state park, its water, wildlife, and forest.
General location:	20 miles northeast of Vernon, Connecticut.
Special attractions:	Picturesque ponds with secluded coves, peninsulas, and shrubby islands; deep hemlock woods; conifer–hardwood forests; mountain laurel; beaver sites; fall foliage.
Length:	Bigelow Pond Loop, 1.8-mile loop; Mashapaug Pond View Trail, 5.1-mile loop; Breakneck Pond Loop, 6.4 miles round trip.
Elevation:	Bigelow Pond Loop, 30-foot elevation change; Mashapaug Pond View Trail, 200-foot elevation change; Breakneck Pond Loop, 100-foot elevation change.
Difficulty:	Bigelow Pond Loop, easy to moderate; Mashapaug Pond View Trail, moderate; Breakneck Pond Loop, strenuous.
Maps:	State park map (park personnel encourage hikers to carry a copy of the current map/trail guide).
Special concerns:	Seasonal fee area. No camping. Selective logging in the area can impact the appearance and modify the location of trails.
Season and hours:	Year-round, generally spring through fall for hiking. Open 8:00 A.M. to sunset.
For information:	Bigelow Hollow State Park.

Key points:
Bigelow Pond Loop:
    0.0   Bigelow Pond Trailhead.
    0.7   Along Connecticut Highway 171.
    1.1   Peninsula.
    1.8   End at trailhead.

Mashapaug Pond View Trail:
    0.0   Bigelow Pond Trailhead.
    0.1   Loop junction.
    0.8   Mashapaug Pond Picnic Area.
    1.1   Spur to peninsula and beaches.
    4.2   Top pine hill.
    5.0   Close loop; return to trailhead.

Breakneck Pond Loop:
    0.0   Bigelow Pond Trailhead.
    1.0   Loop junction at Breakneck Pond.
    3.2   Cross outlet.
    5.4   Complete loop; return to trailhead.

Finding the trailhead: From Interstate 84, take exit 73 for Union, and go east on CT 190 for 2 miles. Turn right (east) onto CT 171, go another 1.4 miles, and turn left to enter the park. All trails start from Bigelow Pond Picnic Area at the north end of Bigelow Pond (about 0.75 mile into the park).

    The hikes: For the **Bigelow Pond Loop** and the **Mashapaug Pond View Trail,** start to the left of the regulations sign, following the blue-and-white blazes through the picnic area. Turn right near the pond's shore, cross a boardwalk over the inlet brook, and reach a trail fork (0.05 mile). Here the Mashapaug Pond View Trail heads uphill to the right; the Bigelow Pond Loop follows the yellow blazes left for a counterclockwise tour.

    Go left for the **Bigelow Pond Loop,** touring a boulder-studded woods, enjoying full shade. Pass between a regal hemlock and gargantuan boulder, rounding the west shore of this elongated pond sculpted by small islands and points. Boughs overhang the water; shrubs crowd the shore. Enjoy mountain laurel, sweet pepperbush, and fern, but watch your step on this rocky, rootbound trail.

    At 0.75 mile, travel along the guardrail of CT 171 to reach the east shore. The highway bank acts as a dam. Ahead, turn left off a gravel fire lane before coming to a gate to resume on foot trail. Hemlock and pine needles offer a cushiony bed for the east-shore trail, which rounds some 15 feet above shore. Openings provide anglers with pond access.

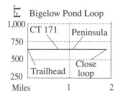

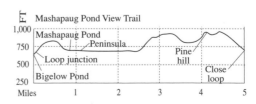

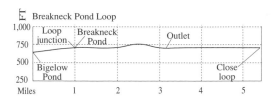

Breakneck Pond Loop

At 1 mile, veer right, coming to a junction below a wooden gate. Although the yellow loop continues right, take the 0.1-mile spur left out to a mushroom-shaped peninsula, with a scenic outcrop, picnic table, and deep drop-off. To the north, the peninsula shapes a shallow bay. Return to the loop, hiking north through the boat launch/picnic area and across a peninsular rise to end at Bigelow Pond Picnic Area at 1.8 miles.

From the 0.05-mile junction, beyond the inlet boardwalk, go right, ascending the hill for the blue-and-white-blazed **Mashapaug Pond View Trail.** At 0.1 mile is the loop junction. Go straight for the Mashapaug Pond Parking Lot and boat launch, returning via the fork on the left. Be attentive to blazes.

This rolling ascent passes through woods of hemlock, maple, birch, and oak, interrupted by pockets of fern. Descend and cross a closed service road before reaching the picnic area shore and turning left (0.8 mile). Find a water pump and pit toilets at Mashapaug Pond Picnic Area.

Mashapaug Pond is a vast, deep pond with a forested edge and private property bordering much of its shore to the north. This trail travels its wild southern extreme. The clear water and gravelly bottom entice swimmers and waders. At 1.1 miles, a yellow-blazed spur to the right reaches a large peninsula. Where the spur forks, find picnic tables and small beaches. Oak, white pine, and laurel clad the point. Here, too, gain a better perspective of the pond's size.

Return to the loop (1.25 miles) and turn right, touring a hemlock shore; avoid the yellow trail on the left. Laurel thrives where pines and oaks win a stronghold. At the end of a second peninsula, find two small islands linked by a barely submerged sand spit. The trail next skirts a long lake arm, staying in woods. At 1.75 miles, continue forward to return to Bigelow Pond; a left returns to Mashapaug Pond's parking and boat launch.

Cross a small inlet, still paralleling the shore north. At 2.4 miles, draw away from Mashapaug Pond for a pleasant hemlock–hardwood forest stroll. At a T-junction, turn left uphill, avoiding the abandoned yellow-blazed trail to the right. At 2.75 miles, stay with the blue-and-white blazes, again forgoing a yellow-blazed trail on the right.

Meander through alternating groves of hemlock and laurel, then enter the more open woods of a select cut. Cross a woods road and top a low pine-clad hill, finding a 3-foot-tall stone wall. Descend and roll through fuller forest, closing the loop at 5 miles. Return to the trailhead at 5.1 miles.

For the **Breakneck Pond Loop,** cross the park road to a kiosk and mapbox and follow the white-blazed East Ridge Trail right; the Ridge Trail (blazed blue with an orange bar) heads left. Upon meeting a closed logging road, bear left (north) for Breakneck Pond, still following the white blazes through a deep hemlock woods intermixed with white pine, oak, and black cherry. At the fork (0.2 mile), stay left.

Bigelow Hollow State Park

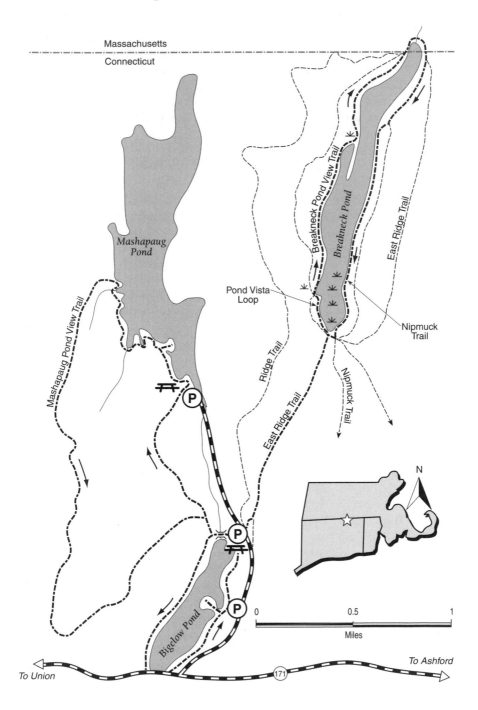

Massachusetts
Connecticut

Mashapaug
Pond

Mashapaug Pond View Trail

Breakneck Pond View Trail

Breakneck Pond

East Ridge Trail

Pond Vista
Loop

Nipmuck
Trail

Ridge Trail

East Ridge Trail

Nipmuck Trail

N

Bigelow Pond

0   0.5   1

Miles

To Union

171

To Ashford

At 1 mile, bear left to reach the marshy southern end of Breakneck Pond and the loop junction. Here, the East Ridge Trail heads right, leading to the blue Nipmuck Trail (the return); go left on the Breakneck Pond View Trail (white dot on blue blaze) for a clockwise loop.

In a few feet, veer right onto the orange-blazed Pond Vista Loop to travel closer to shore, passing amid mountain laurel, hemlock, pine, and beaver-gnawed trees. After rounding a knoll, view lily pad waters and gain an open look seemingly down the length of Breakneck Pond. Rolling wooded ridges enfold the water.

At 1.2 miles, return to the Breakneck Pond View Trail, following it right. Beaver-raised waters may require a brief reroute to a logging road. A few feet ahead, turn right off the rocky logging road back onto footpath; be alert for this key blaze.

The rugged, undulating footpath of the Breakneck Pond View Trail now hugs the shoreline, following it north. Enjoy kingfisher, heron, and wood-pecker. Open water and shrubby islands characterize the pond. At 2.1 miles, cross a beaver dam, discovering that what had appeared to be the pond's end was actually an island-pinched channel. This long water stretches north, lapping into Massachusetts.

At 2.7 miles, pass below a cluster of boulders adorned in rock tripe lichen to travel a low ridge clad in hemlock and hardwoods. Toward the lake sits a marsh. Before the pond's outlet (3.2 miles), reach a junction. To the left is the Ridge Trail (blue with orange bar). Stay on the Breakneck Pond View Trail, cross the outlet, and bear right onto a logging road to continue the shore-line tour southward on the blue-blazed Nipmuck Trail.

Pass the Massachusetts–Connecticut state line monument, where the white-blazed East Ridge Trail angles upslope. Keep toward the pond, reaching a scenic point with towering pines overlooking a mat of aquatic blooms. At 3.6 miles, bear right off the roadway, still following the blue blazes, rolling but never straying far from shore. Abundant mountain laurel weaves through the forest. Next, traverse a glacial deposit of rocks and boulders.

Cross a picnic flat (4.75 miles), finding rougher trail. A second flat shows buttonbush and highbush blueberry, frogs and whirligig beetles. At 5.1 miles, cross-pond views present a beaver lodge. At the upcoming junction, the orange-blazed trail (right) stays closer to the pond, closing the loop at 5.4 miles. If you stay on the blue-blazed trail, turn right where it meets the white-blazed East Ridge Trail to close the loop at 5.5 miles. Retrace the East Ridge Trail south to end at 6.4 or 6.5 miles.

58 Mashamoquet Brook State Park

OVERVIEW

Mashamoquet *(mushmugget)* Brook, meaning "stream of good fishing," flows west to east across this 1,000-acre northeast Connecticut state park composed of rolling wooded terrain, natural rock features, and picturesque swamp. A pair of interlocking loops explore the rolling woods, while a simple nature trail introduces the swamp habitat. Stone walls web the park, hinting at its early settlement; an old gristmill, maintained as a museum, recalls the milling past.

General description:	The two selected day hikes capture the relaxation of the woods and the richness of the wetland.
General location:	15 miles northeast of Storrs, Connecticut.
Special attractions:	Fishing, bird-watching, swamp, mixed woodland, outcrop ledges and natural rock features, spring flora and fall foliage, mountain laurel.
Length:	Wolf Den Swamp Nature Trail, 0.5-mile loop; Blue Loop, 4.4 miles round trip.
Elevation:	Wolf Den Swamp Nature Trail, minimal elevation change; Blue Loop, 400-foot elevation change.
Difficulty:	Wolf Den Swamp Nature Trail, easy; the Blue Loop is moderate.
Maps:	State park map.
Special concerns:	Seasonal fee area, weekends and holidays only. To avoid a fee, park at the visitor center for free.
Season and hours:	Year-round; generally spring through fall for hiking. Open 8:00 A.M. to sunset.
For information:	Mashamoquet Brook State Park.

Key points:
Wolf Den Swamp Nature Trail:
    0.0   Park office trailhead.
    0.5   Complete loop.

Blue Loop:
    0.0   Picnic area trailhead.
    0.2   Loop junction.
    1.2   Pass park office (alternative start).
    2.1   Indian Chair.
    2.5   Wolf Den.
    4.2   Complete loop; return to trailhead.

Finding the trailhead: At the U.S. Highway 44–Connecticut Highway 97 junction in Abington, go east on US 44, finding Mashamoquet Brook Campground on the right in 1 mile; the main day-use entrance and the trailhead for Blue Loop on the right in 1.2 miles; and CT 101 in 2 miles. Turn right

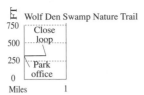

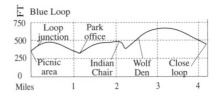

onto CT 101, go a few yards, and turn right onto Wolf Den Drive to reach the park office/visitor center, Wolf Den Campground, and nature trail.

The hikes: Find the start of the **Wolf Den Swamp Nature Trail** on the east side of the park road opposite the park office. At this time, no brochure pairs with the interpretive trail. Begin rounding a broad open lawn where a three-story white birdhouse shelters swallows. The trail then tours the shore of the snag-pierced swamp, with skunk cabbage, tufted grasses, arrowhead, cattail, and phragmites (plumed reeds). Geese, red-winged blackbirds, woodpeckers, fish, frogs, and turtles enliven the swamp; at times, insects annoy. Travel the narrow wooded buffer between swamp and lawn, reaching a dock and bench before drifting through a pine plantation to close the loop at 0.5 mile.

For the **Blue Loop,** start at the picnic area, crossing the footbridge over Mashamoquet Brook, downstream from Old Red Mill. Near the bridge, a diversion rejoins the main brook, shaping a long wooded island. Large boulders rim the clear, tannin-colored water.

On the south shore, a 0.2-mile upstream spur leads to Mashamoquet Brook Campground (sites 11 and 12); campers wishing to join the hike will arrive via this spur. To reach the Blue Loop, follow the yellow blazes away from the brook to the base of a ridge and angle uphill to the right on a wide rock-studded lane. Soggy patches may mar travel after snowmelt or rain. The framing woods consist of hemlock, oak, and birch.

Top the ridge, meeting the Blue Loop at 0.2 mile; go left for a clockwise hike. The sounds of nature replace the roadway hum. Follow a 4-foot-wide earthen lane, coming to a junction with the Red Trail in 100 yards. Stay left for the blue tour, traveling a shared section of trail. Snapped trees can hint at harsh weather, while scenic stone walls intersect the trail. Enjoy a canopy of dancing leaves. In late fall and winter, the bare branches may reveal nests or perhaps an owl.

At 0.6 mile, the Blue Loop bears left, while the Red Trail continues ahead. Mountain laurel appears as the trail descends steadily to cross a footbridge over a thin tributary of Mashamoquet Brook (1 mile). Find maple, hemlock, and false hellebore here. The relaxation of the woods invites thoughts as well as feet to wander. At 1.1 miles, reach the paved road to the park office and Wolf Den Campground. Turn right, following blazes.

At 1.2 miles, look for the Blue Loop to head uphill to the right, reentering woods beyond the park office/information center. The Wolf Den Swamp Nature Trail begins on the opposite side of the road. A single big pine stands at the gateway to the Blue Loop, and a white barn sits uphill to the right.

Pass through a gap in a 3.5-foot-tall stone wall, returning to hemlock–oak habitat. In places, the stone wall incorporates the natural outcrop ledge. The trail rolls, topping exposed bedrock, where hikers can admire the woodland and wait for wildlife to come to them. Laurel again interweaves the forest; solitude abounds in the off-season.

The trail grows narrower, with rocks studding the path. At 1.7 miles, descend from the main outcrop area to cross a footbridge over a small brook supporting a false hellebore wetland. A spring-drained rocky area follows; jack-in-the-pulpits favor this moist site.

Topping an outcrop at 2.1 miles, look for a yellow arrow pointing out the ledge that holds Indian Chair, a natural rock sofa complete with back- and armrest. The seat offers a squirrel's-eye view of the woodland, with vultures soaring by.

Continue clockwise on the Blue Loop, touring woods with a fuller midstory. The Red Trail again merges as hikers descend to a drainage boardwalk, where marsh marigolds complement the dark water. Now climb steeply, reaching Wolf Den at 2.5 miles; look for the impression of a former plaque. Here, rock ledges shape a boxy opening leading to a crawlspace, 30 feet long. In 1742, Israel Putnam crept into this den and shot a wolf that had annoyed area farmers.

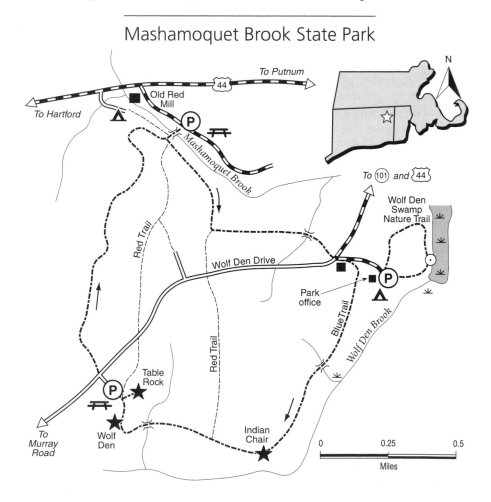

Mashamoquet Brook State Park

Hiker bridge, Mashamoquet Brook State Park, CT.

In another 0.1 mile, reach a three-pronged junction where a 200-foot spur to the right leads to Table Rock—an elevated 10-foot by 20-foot natural slab. The Red Trail heads straight, and the Blue Loop heads left, passing through dense laurel to rustic Wolf Den State Park Picnic Area (2.7 miles). From the picnic area, hike out the graveled access road, reaching Wolf Den Drive in 0.1 mile. Look right to locate the Blue Loop as it heads north off Wolf Den Drive.

Resume the hike north through similar forest, finding dense laurel where the roadway opening brings added light. Enjoy a mildly descending, relaxing woods stroll. At 3.9 miles, bear right, avoiding the closed path ahead; yellow arrows may point out the reroute. Close the Blue Loop at 4.2 miles, and hike the **Yellow Trail** downhill, ending at the bridge (4.4 miles).

59   James L. Goodwin State Forest

OVERVIEW

Abutting 13,000-acre Natchaug State Forest, this 2,171-acre forest contributes to a vital open space and wildlife habitat in northeast Connecticut. Hikers find a fine network of blazed trails. Ponds, swamps, rolling hardwood forests, meadows, tree plantations, and an abandoned rail line vary travel.

General description: A broad swinging loop travels foot trail and woods road through forest and plantation, exploring Pine Acres Pond and Swamp and visiting Black Spruce Pond. The loop incorporates part of the long-distance Natchaug Trail.

General location: 10 miles southeast of Storrs, Connecticut.

Special attractions: Goodwin Conservation Center and arboretum; observation blind; bird- and wildlife-watching; guided nature walks; rhododendron, laurel, azalea, and pond lily blooms; diverse woods; fall foliage.

Length: Pine Acres Pond Loop, 5.1-mile loop.

Elevation: Find a 200-foot elevation change.

Difficulty: Moderate.

Maps: State forest map.

Season and hours: Year-round; generally spring through fall for hiking. Dawn to dusk.

For information: Goodwin Conservation Center.

Key points:
Pine Acres Pond Loop:
- 0.0 Pine Acres Pond Trailhead.
- 1.2 Detour to Governors Island.
- 2.0 Esterbrook Road.
- 2.8 East shore Black Spruce Pond.
- 3.2 Follow Natchaug Trail south.
- 4.6 Cross Airline State Park Trail (railroad grade).
- 5.0 Observation blind.
- 5.1 End at trailhead.

Finding the trailhead: From the junction of U.S. Highway 6 and Connecticut Highway 169 in Brooklyn Center, go west on US 6 for 7.3 miles and turn right (north) onto Potter Road for the state forest. Find parking on the right in 0.2 mile. Arriving from the west, go 3 miles east on US 6 from its junction with CT 198 in South Chaplin and turn left onto Potter Road.

The hike: For the **Pine Acres Pond Loop,** go past the information board, hiking toward the boat launch on a gravel access road. In 200 feet, take the yellow-blazed trail to the right, rounding a gate to follow a woods road to the southern end of Pine Acres Pond, a 133-acre lake built in 1933. Planted white pine and Norway spruce, rhododendron, bramble, poison ivy, jewelweed, and red maple frame the corridor. For a brief spell, the trail travels near US 6, separated by a thin row of cedar, spruce, and hemlock.

At 0.2 mile, where the yellow-blazed trail drifts from the pond, follow the mowed swath along the shore to cross the dam and spillway footbridges. Enjoy open looks at the dark-water pond, its mats of pond lily, arrowhead, and rimming trees. From the second bridge, follow the white blazes to tour the pond's east shore. Travel spruce

256

plantation and hardwood forest, finding sweet pepperbush, azalea, and high-bush blueberry on shore, and scenic showings of tall fern in the woods.

Travel a mostly flat, rootbound trail, with spurs branching to shore. At 0.6 mile, a gap reveals the snag-pierced pond, a watery "bed of nails." Spy a beaver lodge, geese and ducks, cormorants drying their wings, and likely a heron. Beyond a beech-clad rise, an old woods road leads to shore for open views of the pond's lily pad blanket, treed islands, and cattail swamp to the north. Keep to the white-blazed trail, journeying north.

At the 1.2-mile junction, a red blaze at the right points out a shorter return; to the left, a white spur leads to Governors Island; ahead, the primary trail, also blazed white, continues north. Take the island detour, following an attractive levee edged by small pine and dense herbs and forbs, fragrant in early summer. A loop then explores the island, reaching an observation deck and a second viewpoint, overlooking the surrounding bog. Travel in pine–oak woods and mountain laurel. Then, return to the 1.2-mile junction (1.5 miles) and follow the white blazes north.

The thick woods severely limit swamp views. By 1.9 miles, follow a woods road away from Pine Acres Swamp, paralleling a stone wall through a pine plantation. In another 0.1 mile, follow the foot trail left, passing through a breach in the stone wall to reach Esterbrook Road. Hike 100 feet to the right to resume the white trail on the opposite side of the road, now touring a scenic recessed woods road.

At 2.3 miles, veer right into a stand of spruce and then descend sharply left, hiking a sunken grade along the abandoned rail line of the Airline State Park Trail. Before long, angle right to pass over the gravel railroad bed and resume in a lovely hardwood forest graced by ferns.

Cross 11th Section Road at 2.75 miles. The white blazes now lead along the east shore of Black Spruce Pond, but a dense shrub border denies views.

White oak, James L. Goodwin State Forest, CT.

James L. Goodwin State Forest

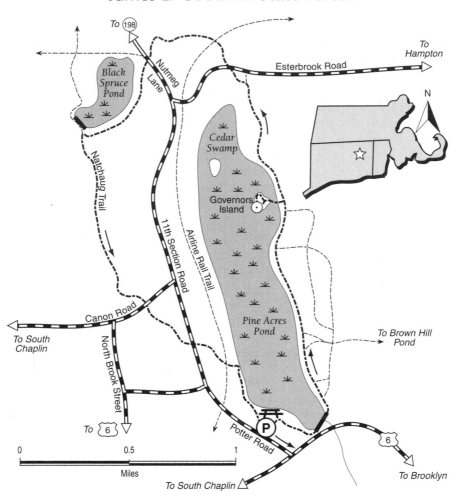

Find the trail rocky and sometimes muddy. Azalea and both mountain and sheep laurel decorate the area in early summer. Travel a corduroy and go right onto an attractive leaf-littered woods road. Here, papery wasp nests may be found in late summer. Glimpse the outline of the pond and its snag-filled waters.

In a stand of pines at 3.25 miles, meet the blue-blazed woods road of the Natchaug Trail and follow it left (south) for the loop. A 250-foot detour right leads to the earthen dam for an open look at Black Spruce Pond, its beaver lodge, lily pads, and many snags.

Ascend south and, at the fork, bear right onto the narrower woods road. Grasses invade the bed, and ferns dress the shoulder as the Natchaug Trail parts hardwood forest and conifer plantation. Because the blue blazes occur less frequently, be alert for the direction change that occurs at 3.95 miles. Here, the Natchaug follows a foot trail to the left, passing through a plantation with dispersed deciduous trees and crossing stone walls. On paved Canon Road, turn left to pick up the southbound trail past a blazed utility pole on the right.

A similar trek leads to 11th Section Road. Angle right across 11th Section Road, descending once more through conifer plantation. The unruly bramble grabs at hikers. At 4.6 miles, cross back over Airline State Park Trail, touring a maple wetland. Boardwalks and corduroys allow hikers to escape the soggiest reaches, as the trail nears Pine Acres Pond.

As the trail traces the west shore, multiple spurs branch to views. Pass an upturned pine, a beaver scent mound, and a beaver lodge before reaching the observation blind (5 miles). Beyond the blind, turn right, ascending the slope to come out near the privies below the parking area (5.1 miles).

60   Gay City State Park

OVERVIEW

At this 1,569-acre east-central Connecticut state park, explore peaceful woodlands, the Blackledge River, swamps and ponds, and the historical remains of an eighteenth-century settlement, Gay City. Started by an isolationist religious sect in 1796, Gay City's early success centered on its mill—originally a sawmill, later a woolen and paper mill. The blockades in the War of 1812, the Civil War deaths of the town's young men, and fire each played a role in the demise of Gay City.

General description:	Two circuits explore the park's woods, wetlands, and history, traveling both woods road and foot trail.
General location:	5 miles southeast of Manchester, Connecticut.
Special attractions:	Historical mill ruins, ditches, cellar holes, cemetery, and stone walls; azalea; hardwood forest; wetlands; wildlife; fall foliage.
Length:	Pond Loop, 2.6-mile loop; Outer Loop, 5-mile loop.
Elevation:	Each trail shows about a 100-foot elevation change.
Difficulty:	Both easy.
Maps:	State park map.
Special concerns:	Fees collected weekends and holidays from Memorial Day weekend through Labor Day weekend; pets must be on a leash.
Season and hours:	Year-round, generally spring through fall for hiking. Open 8:00 A.M. to sunset.
For information:	Gay City State Park.

Key points:
Pond Loop:
- 0.0 Gay City Trailhead.
- 0.2 Pond Loop.
- 0.4 Cross earthen dam.
- 1.3 Cross Blackledge River.
- 2.6 Close loop.

Outer Loop:
- 0.0 Gay City Trailhead.
- 1.0 Cross Blackledge River.
- 2.4 Lily pond spur.
- 3.6 Cross old rockwork dam.
- 5.0 Complete loop.

Finding the trailhead: Find the park 3 miles south of Bolton off Connecticut Highway 85. From Interstate 384 (eastbound access only), take exit 5, and go south on CT 85 for 4.5 miles, turning right (west) to enter the park. Also, find a marked route to the park starting off U.S. Highway 6; watch for signs to guide you at junctions.

Start both hikes on the blue-blazed Gay City Trail, a westbound gated woods road 0.3 mile into the park. Park in the lots just before the trailhead or at a small picnic area just beyond it.

The hikes: Round the gate on the blue-blazed Gay City Trail, hiking the dirt road toward the Youth Group Camp, passing amid tall oak, birch, and maple. At the road fork in 100 feet, the red-blazed Outer Loop heads left. Stay right on the blue trail, passing the youth camp and descending between scenic old-growth maples. Meet the white-blazed **Pond Loop** before the bridge over the Blackledge River at 0.2 mile, and turn right (upstream). The Gay City Trail continues across the bridge to reach the Shenipsit Trail in 2 miles.

For the Pond Loop, hike upstream along the east bank of the brook-size Blackledge River. Muddy banks may reveal where it once held a beaver pond. Follow white blazes along foot trail and woods road, paralleling the river. Soon cross a bridge over the rockwork canal from the old woolen and paper mill. Glimpse the stone legacy of the mill at the head of the canal. Virginia creeper and fern poke through the rock crevices, while frogs favor the murky standing pools.

Continue upstream, now passing between the river and a ditch that carried water to the mill. The stairs to the right ascend to the upper beach parking area. Reach Gay City Pond at 0.4 mile and turn left to cross its earthen dam. This small reservoir shows a stark shore, a small treed island, and mats of pond lily. Look for water snake, frog, or mink.

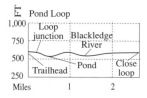

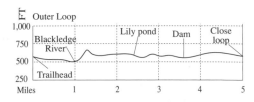

260

Gay City State Park

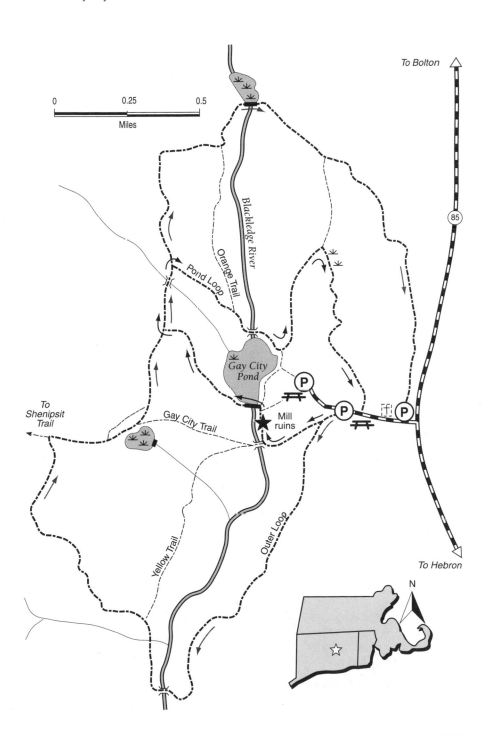

0   0.25   0.5

Miles

To Bolton

85

Blackledge River

Orange Trail

Pond Loop

Gay City Pond

P

P

P

To Shenipsit Trail

Gay City Trail

Mill ruins

Outer Loop

Yellow Trail

To Hebron

N

From the dam, follow the old woods road touring above the pond. Avoid the secondary path along shore. Oak, maple, birch, and hemlock shade the way, while colorful fungi protrude from the leaf mat, attracting the eye. Enjoy a restful, rolling woods meander.

At the fork at 0.65 mile, bear left, soon merging with the red-blazed Outer Loop. Continue north (right), crossing a drainage bridge. Rock walls add to the woods. Stay right at 0.95 mile, leaving the red-blazed trail and descending on an old woods road likely echoing back to Gay City. Be careful when descending, because fallen leaves can easily steal footing.

Cross a footboard over a tiny drainage, ascending to meet the Orange Trail at a T-junction. Turn right; a few azalea now add to the tour. Red maple, fern, highbush blueberry, and sweet pepperbush herald the Blackledge River crossing at 1.3 miles; plank ramps lead to and from the bridge. Now go left, following a foot trail along Gay City Pond, overlooking beaver lodge, island, and beach. At 1.5 miles, stay left for the loop; the right fork leads to the beach.

Pass lower beach parking and a cellar depression, returning to a woods road for a pleasant ramble. Turn right upon meeting the Orange Trail for a second time. Overlook a former beaver pond, now a snag-filled meadow, again enjoying floral shrubs. A woodland tour then leads to the park road; come out opposite an open field. Detour left 200 feet to view the old cemetery, where thin tablets mark graves from the 1800s. Go right (west) to close the loop at 2.6 miles.

For the **Outer Loop,** a popular weekend trail, head left off the Gay City Trail in 100 feet, touring amid large maples and a full rich forest with birch, ash, oak, and hickory. Ferns dress the floor. Upon meeting a second woods road at 0.3 mile, bear right. Rock walls now contribute to the woodland serenity. A slight descent leads to Blackledge River at 1 mile. Sweet pepperbush

Family hike, Gay City State Park, CT.

and azalea adorn the riverbanks, while branches overlace the water.

Cross the bridge and ascend away from the river, turning left past an old foundation where a yellow-blazed connector now heads forward. At 1.9 miles, a short spur leads to a boulder; follow the red blazes.

Next, come to a T-junction with the blue-blazed Gay City Trail. Westbound (going left at the junction), the Gay City Trail reaches the Shenipsit Trail in 1.3 miles. For the Outer Loop, follow the blue and red blazes to the right, cross a small drainage, and slowly descend, traveling parallel to a woods road.

At another small drainage (2.3 miles), bypass an alternate trail marked by a red A, which heads left. At 2.4 miles, a short spur heads right to a large lily pond. Look for night herons, swallows, and other birds; frogs abound. In another 200 feet, the red and blue blazes part; again follow the red-blazed Outer Loop, going left. Soon the alternate trail rejoins on the left.

The Outer Loop's red blazes briefly join the white blazes of the Pond Loop. After they separate, watch for the red-blazed trail to descend right on a wide footpath. Reach the wetland forest of the river drainage and stay left, merging with the Orange Trail for a spell. At 3.6 miles, cross an old rockwork dam. A beaver dam now blocks the spillway, creating a pond. Look for a lodge on shore to the left. At 3.8 miles, the Orange Trail leaves on the right.

At 4 miles, depart the woods road, heading right on a foot trail, touring a wetter forest near CT 85. Here, ash joins the mix. Cross the winter parking lot to reach the park road near the entrance (4.7 miles), and turn right, hiking 0.3 mile along the park road to close the loop.

---

61 Shenipsit Trail, Southern Segment

General description:	This hike focuses on the southern (Great Hill) segment of the nearly 33-mile-long Shenipsit Trail, which journeys north from Meshomasic State Forest through Shenipsit State Forest to halt within 2 miles of the Massachusetts state line. This hike passes between Great Hill Road and Del Reeves Road at the Glastonbury town line.
General location:	1.5 miles north of Cobalt, Connecticut.
Special attractions:	Outcrop vistas, mixed woods, mountain laurel, fall foliage.
Length:	6.5 miles one-way.
Elevation:	This segment has about a 500-foot elevation change.
Difficulty:	Moderate.
Maps:	Shenipsit Trail, *Connecticut Walk Book;* Middle Haddam and Glastonbury 7.5-minute USGS quads.
Special concerns:	Meshomasic State Forest is open daylight hours only; no camping.

Season and hours: Spring through fall for hiking.
For information: Connecticut Department of Environmental
Protection, Bureau of Outdoor Recreation.

Key points:
0.0   Great Hill Road trailhead.
0.3   Great Hill.
2.0   Cross Woodchopper Road.
3.1   Bald Hill.
6.5   End at Del Reeves Road.

Finding the trailhead: From the junction of Connecticut Highways 66 and
17A in Portland (1.2 miles east of CT 9, at exit 16), head east on CT 66 to its
junction with CT 151 in Cobalt. There, head north on Depot Hill Road and
stay on it for 0.8 mile. Turn right onto Great Hill Road/Gadpouch Road, which
changes to dirt, and proceed 0.5 mile to reach the trailhead on the left, with
a small parking turnout on the right. Another larger parking turnout sits just
a bit farther east.

The hike: The characteristic blue blazes of the Connecticut blue trail system point the way north into a varied forest of hemlock, maple, ash, tulip,
birch, sassafras, oak, and beech. Among the woodland flora, find hog peanut,
fern, and poison ivy. The hike begins with a moderate climb that adds the seasonal dressy accents of mountain laurel and bouldery reaches of Great Hill.

Upon topping the ridge, take the white-blazed trail heading left to add a
vista. This 0.1-mile descent leads to a quartzite outcrop and 90-degree southwestern view with Middletown, Great Hill Pond, the Connecticut River, and
the rolling woodland and boxy traprock ridges of the neighborhood. Although
pitch pines and oaks encircle the outcrop, they do not intrude on the view.
Noisy geese gathered in flight or on the pond add to the overall impression.

Resuming the Shenipsit Trail at 0.5 mile, continue north along the ridge.
In a matter of strides, find an eastern outcrop that allows restricted views
of the rolling wooded expanse. Pass through a beech-clad sag at 0.7 mile to
find a slow descent of the broadening ridge.

At 1.5 miles, be alert where the trail turns right to mount a rocky knoll;
blazes may be faint. A slow descent mostly on tote road leads to a state forest road crossing (Woodchopper Road, 2 miles).

Where the trail emerges from young woods, bear left on woods road. Before long, blazes point the way across a flat to the foot of rubble slope and
a cairn at the base of the rock cliff. At the quarry to the right, tourmaline (a
fragile black crystal) was extracted. Imperfect crystals and mica can still be
spied. The trail rolls along, passing among oaks and laurel. At the T-junction
at 2.25 miles, turn
left for a descent on
tote road. The woods
become more mixed.

Hikers may en-
counter some trail

Shenipsit Trail, Southern Segment

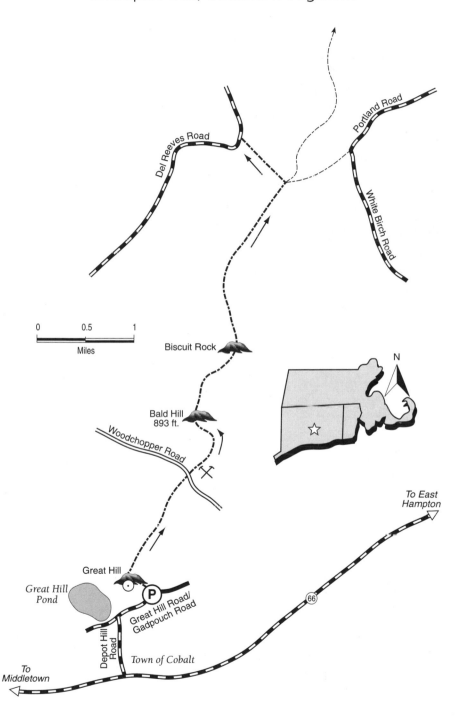

Great Hill, Meshomasic State Forest, CT.

damage resulting from the illegal use of off-road vehicles. Where the trail ascends at 2.6 miles, look for it to turn left. Although rocks and roots are a part of this terrain, the trail is generally good. Logs typically span the drainages at crossings. Sweet pepperbush and fern may dress the banks.

With a fairly steep climb at 3.1 miles, the trail tops Bald Hill (elevation 893 feet), but the name no longer applies to this oak-clad summit. As the trail again descends to woods road, bear right, following blazes. Discover pockets of beech and areas of rock. At 3.5 miles, bypass a yellow trail that heads left to arrive at a T-junction, meeting a woods road at a curve (3.7 miles); bear left. The trail again bears left at a wetland bypass in another 0.1 mile.

A more open woods with thicket sides then hosts travel. Pass along a rock wall and, at 4.4 miles, head left on a larger woods road. At a pine plantation in the woods, the pines are mostly dead, with snag tops, but lady's slipper can add delicate beauty to the woodland floor. Throughout this hike, the tall, mixed forest enchants.

At the T-junction at 5.1 miles, turn right to continue north. A few boulders dot the sides of the road. At 5.9 miles, reach a four-way junction with a white trail. Follow the white trail, descending west to reach the limited trail parking along Del Reeves Road at the Glastonbury line (6.5 miles). This trail, too, tours varied forest and passes an old cellar and foundation before emerging at Del Reeves Road. By instead following the white trail east at 5.9 miles, descend 0.5 mile to the intersection of White Birch and Portland Roads in Marlborough (1.25 miles west of CT 2).

62   Salmon River Trail

General description:	Passing entirely on state land, this lasso-shaped hike explores the river watershed of the Salmon River State Forest and Day Pond State Park.
General location:	Colchester, Connecticut.
Special attractions:	An old Comstock covered bridge, a Salmon River access and view, Day Pond, rock walls and cellar ruins, mixed woods, fall foliage.
Length:	6.9 miles round trip.
Elevation:	This trail shows about a 350-foot elevation change.
Difficulty:	Moderate.
Maps:	Salmon River Trail, *Connecticut Walk Book;* Moodus 7.5-minute USGS quad.
Season and hours:	Spring through fall for hiking.
For information:	Connecticut Department of Environmental Protection, Bureau of Outdoor Recreation.

Key points:
- 0.0   Comstock Bridge Trailhead.
- 2.0   Salmon River Loop; turn right.
- 2.6   Day Pond State Park.
- 3.4   Top forested knob.
- 4.0   Old homestead site.
- 4.9   Close loop; backtrack to trailhead.

Finding the trailhead: From the junction of Connecticut Highways 16 and 196 (south of East Hampton), proceed east on CT 16 for 5.4 miles, then turn left onto Comstock Bridge Road to reach trail parking on the right at the covered bridge.

The hike: Pass through the historic weathered-wood covered bridge that dates to 1791 and spans the shallow Salmon River. Swing a U-turn left, following the blue blazes pointing out this addition to the Connecticut blue trail system. Sycamores contribute to the river shore. The attractive, slow-moving rocky-bottomed river hosts juvenile Atlantic salmon.

The woods enfolding the trail display maple, hemlock, oak, and witch hazel. At the 0.25-mile trail junction, head left, uphill, away from the Salmon River (avoid the path heading upstream), and soon take another left on woods road. Because the trail zigzags between woods roads as it climbs, keep a careful watch for blazes. Full shade graces travel.

Bear right at the Y-junction at 0.5 mile and soon find a river view spanning a steep meadow of goldenrod. The full forest of the opposite slope is especially pretty in fall attire. Where the

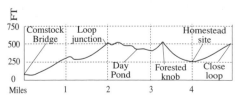

Salmon River Trail

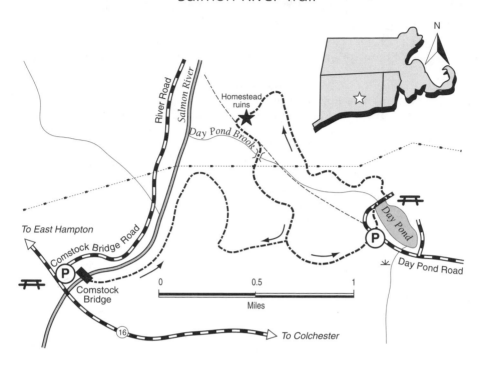

trail flattens atop a rise at 1 mile, American beech have a strong presence, and there are areas of young trees. Before reaching the utility corridor ahead, the trail turns right, uphill, through a full forest with mountain laurel in its midst. At 1.2 miles, the trail tops out and begins a slow descent as it meanders along the ridge.

Discover a rock wall ornamented by encrusting lichen; the trail and woods roll out a relaxing sojourn. More rock walls add to travel. At 2 miles, reach the Salmon River Loop junction and turn right for a counterclockwise exploration. Again the setting is signature Connecticut forest. After passing a 15-foot-high boulder (a glacial erratic) on the right, begin a relaxing descent, cross a woods road at 2.5 miles, and, at 2.6 miles, enter Day Pond State Park with its picnic area, pit toilets, and parking. Day Pond may call for a delay, with its sandy beach and attractive lily mats.

From the state park, follow the blazed Salmon River Trail left, crossing the rockwork dam of Day Pond via gravel park road, and immediately reenter the forest on the left. At 2.75 miles, cross a woods road, bearing slightly left, and soon after pursue Day Pond Brook downstream. An abundance of ferns and the song of the brook add to the hike's tranquility. At the 3.1-mile junction, the Salmon River Trail heads right, upslope, and crosses a utility-line corridor.

At 3.4 miles, the trail crosses over a forested knob before resuming its meandering course. Outcrops coated with lichen and moss vary viewing. Eventually, the trail pairs with a drainage, heading downslope. Cross the drainage past an old dam site (4 miles) to arrive at a homestead ruin, marked by cellar holes and rock walls.

At 4.2 miles, come to a T-junction with a woods road and turn left. In another 0.1 mile, turn right, following Day Pond Brook upstream, passing more rock walls, remnant foundations, and cellar depressions. At 4.3 miles, cross the bridge over Day Pond Brook and head uphill. Hemlocks are well represented. Cross a

Mushroom, Salmon River State Forest, CT.

utility corridor (4.4 miles) and, at 4.9 miles, complete the loop. Turn right to return to the Comstock Bridge Trailhead (6.9 miles).

63 Pachaug State Forest

OVERVIEW

In southeast Connecticut abutting Rhode Island, Pachaug State Forest represents the largest state-held forest in Connecticut, covering some 30,000 acres. The hikes discussed in this write-up originate from the headquarters area and incorporate portions of two long-distance trails: the Pachaug and Nehantic. Discover a rare rhododendron–white cedar swamp, stocked ponds, a rocky brook, and natural and planted forests.

General description:	Three hikes make up this forest sampler. Visit the rhododendron–white cedar swamp, top a high point for a vista, and explore along brook and pond, touring foot trail and woods road, hardwood forest and conifer plantation.
General location:	12 miles northeast of Norwich, Connecticut.
Special attractions:	Rhododendron Sanctuary, Atlantic white cedar swamp, stocked fishing ponds, historical cellar holes and stone walls, wildlife-watching, fall foliage.
Length:	Rhododendron Sanctuary Walk, 0.5 mile round trip; Nehantic Trail to Mount Misery, 1.6 miles round trip; Phillips Pond Loop, 12.5 miles round trip (can extend or shorten).
Elevation:	Rhododendron Sanctuary Walk, flat; Nehantic Trail to Mount Misery, 170-foot elevation change; Phillips Pond Loop, 280-foot elevation change.

	Difficulty:	Rhododendron Sanctuary Walk, easy; Nehantic Trail to Mount Misery, moderate; Phillips Pond Loop, strenuous.
	Maps:	State forest map; Nehantic Trail–Pachaug Trail map, *Connecticut Walk Book.*
	Special concerns:	High water can make portions of the Rhododendron Sanctuary impassable.
	Season and hours:	Year-round, generally spring through fall for hiking. Open 8:00 A.M. to sunset.
	For information:	Pachaug State Forest.

Key points:
Rhododendron Sanctuary Walk:
- 0.0   Cut-off Road trailhead.
- 0.2   Hike's loop.
- 0.3   End loop; return to trailhead.

Nehantic Trail to Mount Misery:
- 0.0   Start on Cut-off Road.
- 0.2   Nehantic Trail.
- 0.8   Mount Misery; backtrack to trailhead.

Phillips Pond Loop:
- 0.0   CCC area trailhead.
- 1.3   Lowden Brook Picnic Area.
- 2.3   Cross Lowden Brook.
- 3.1   Loop junction; continue forward.
- 3.9   Cross Hell Hollow Road.
- 5.4   Quinebaug Trail.
- 7.0   Cross Hell Hollow Road.
- 8.6   Phillips Pond dam.
- 9.4   Close loop; backtrack to trailhead.

Finding the trailhead: From Interstate 395, take exit 85 and go east on Connecticut Highway 138 to Voluntown (5.8 miles). Continue east on CT 138/CT 165 for 0.8 mile and turn north onto CT 49. Go 0.6 mile on CT 49 and turn left (west) onto Headquarters Road. Trailheads radiate from the road fork in 0.7 mile. Locate the Rhododendron Sanctuary and Nehantic Trail to Mount Misery off Cut-off Road to the left. Start the Phillips Pond Loop on the right at the CCC Youth Group Camp Area.

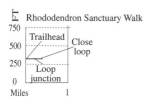

The hikes: The **Rhododendron Sanctuary Walk** starts on the north side of Cut-off Road 0.1 mile west of the Headquarters Road fork. It is marked by a blue Nehantic Trail blaze and a sign, and sits opposite an open field and the Mount Misery Campground. On cushiony trail, pass through an area of hemlock, oak, maple, and pine, bearing right to round an island of trees. Azalea, mountain laurel, sweet pepperbush, highbush blueberry, and

270

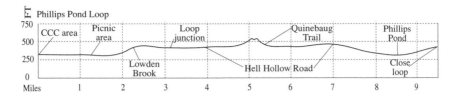

Phillips Pond Loop

750	CCC area	Picnic area			Loop junction			Quinebaug Trail		Phillips Pond	
500											
250			Lowden Brook				Hell Hollow Road			Close loop	
0											
Miles	1	2	3	4	5	6	7	8	9		

red maple announce the swamp.

Ahead, travel a levee in a wetland forest consisting of cedar, sphagnum moss, bog grass, and a captivating jungle of rhododendron, growing 40 feet tall, sporting 8-inch leaves, and, in July, brandishing glorious floral pom-poms. Twisting skyward through the cedar–hemlock canopy, the rhododendron shape a brief but exciting passageway of texture and shape. Corduroys aid passage. The sanctuary walk ends with a small loop at 0.2 mile.

From this loop, three sets of hewn logs head west into the cedar swamp for views of yet another interesting habitat with standing water, stringy cedar trunks, elevated root islands, moss, and ferns. For this hike, keep to the sanctuary walk. When conditions are sufficiently dry, hikers may continue through the swamp and left on woods road, taking the Nehantic Trail to Mount Misery.

Generally, though, Mount Misery hikers should forgo this "swamp connection," and instead hike 0.2 mile west along Cut-off Road from the Rhododendron Sanctuary entrance. Watch for the blue blazes of the Nehantic Trail crossing the road just past a gated woods road on the right. Because this woods road parts the Atlantic white cedar swamp, it offers an alternative viewing access when floods submerge the sanctuary walk.

From Cut-off Road (0.2 mile west of the Sanctuary Trailhead or 0.4 mile via the sanctuary and swamp), head left (south) following the **Nehantic Trail to Mount Misery.** Hemlock, pine, oak, and mountain laurel frame this well-marked, well-traveled trail. Pockets of fern, some rock studding, and sheep laurel bring visual interest. Soon, turn right onto the relocated trail for a switchbacking ascent of the slope; avoid the abandoned erosion-causing trail ahead.

Top a rise and round over an outcrop, encountering oak, twisted pine, and a more open cathedral with limited outward looks. Where the trail descends to a drainage, be careful on the loose gravel. Snags reach skyward with imploring arms. At 0.6 mile, bear right for another switchbacking ascent.

At 0.8 mile, mount a rock outcrop marked by patches of pitch pine and scrub oak for a 180-degree eastern perspective of glacier-planed ridges and lowland forest, with pines towering above the leafy crowns. Backtrack or hike the Nehantic Trail over the summit of Mount Misery (elevation 441 feet), descending its slippery outcrop side to Firetower Road (0.9 mile).

For the **Phillips Pond Loop,** start at the CCC area, following the blue-blazed Nehantic Trail east up the grassy slope from the stone pillars on Headquarters/Trail Road. Enter the pines, coming to the Nehantic–Pachaug Trail junction (0.1 mile). Turn left (north) onto the Pachaug Trail, also blazed in blue, to make a broad-swinging loop around Phillips Pond. The Nehantic Trail continues east to Beachdale Pond Picnic Area in 0.75 mile.

Northbound, the Pachaug Trail contours the wooded slope east of Head-

Pachaug State Forest

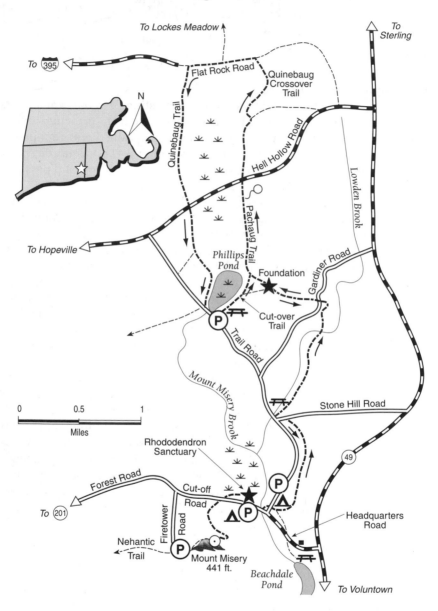

To Lockes Meadow

To (395)

To Sterling

Flat Rock Road

Quinebaug Crossover Trail

Quinebaug Trail

N

Hell Hollow Road

Lowden Brook

Pachaug Trail

To Hopeville

Phillips Pond

Foundation

Gardiner Road

P

Cut-over Trail

Trail Road

Mount Misery Brook

0   0.5   1
Miles

Stone Hill Road

49

Rhododendron Sanctuary

Forest Road

Cut-off Road

To (201)

Firetower Road

Nehantic Trail

P

Mount Misery 441 ft.

P

P

P

Headquarters Road

Beachdale Pond

To Voluntown

quarters/Trail Road. Look for deer, raccoon, and woodpecker, and be ready for quick direction changes wherever the trail meets woods roads. Drainages can muddy the going.

Near an old ruin, meet a woods road and turn left for a birch-lined passage ending at a boulder barrier. Pass through the barrier and hike left, reaching Trail Road south of Lowden Brook Picnic Area (1.35 miles). Turn right and pass between the boulders on the right to resume hiking on the Pachaug Trail.

272

Hike northeast past some picnic tables. The rocky footpath leads through a mixed woods of maple, hickory, ash, beech, pine, hemlock, and birch, following Lowden Brook upstream. Mountain laurel and sweet pepperbush favor the drainage. Lowden Brook shows dark mossy boulders and sparkling cascades. Muddy sites record recent wildlife visits. The trail is rugged and ankle-testing in this riparian stretch, with faint blazes for guides.

Veer upslope from the brook, passing stone walls, before swinging left and finding easier footing. Return brookside at 2.35 miles, cross the brook, and enter a spruce plantation. Next, angle right across Gardiner Road, following a gated woods road toward Phillips Pond. Grasses push up through the roadbed, while ferns shower the shoulders.

Be alert as the trail zigzags through a selection of woods roads. At 2.75 miles, near an impressive stone foundation, the blue-blazed Pachaug Trail turns right, touring a plantation, while a white-blazed trail continues forward to Phillips Pond. Stay on the Pachaug Trail.

At 3.1 miles, the Cut-over Trail (red dot on blue) arrives from Phillips Pond; again keep to the Pachaug Trail, which continues forward for a counterclockwise loop. Blazes now occur at regular intervals.

The hike alternates between hardwood forest and conifer plantation, passing a spring and catch basin on the right at 3.85 miles. Angle right, across paved Hell Hollow Road at 3.9 miles, to follow a wide foot trail through a spruce grove. Stone walls now partition the plantations. At the 4.3-mile fork, bear right for the Pachaug Trail, contouring a rocky slope. At the T-junction in 0.1 mile, turn left onto the yellow-blazed Pachaug–Quinebaug Crossover Trail for the loop; the Pachaug Trail heads right.

Follow the yellow blazes downhill, turning right in 20 feet to contour an oak–birch hillside, with sassafras, chestnut, and huckleberry weaving an understory. Where the trail traverses a wooded plateau, find a scenic beech grove. At 5.15 miles, turn left onto singletrack, dirt Flat Rock Road (closed to vehicles here), following yellow blazes to meet the blue-blazed Quinebaug Trail in 0.2 mile. Go left (east) on the Quinebaug Trail to continue the loop, or detour right (north) about 0.5 mile to find Lockes Meadow, a wetland meadow and popular birding site.

East, the Quinebaug Trail starts out on rocky, exposed roadbed, passing Devils Den, an assemblage of rocks on the left. After 5.7 miles, descend and look for the trail to bear left on a narrower woods road prior to where Flat Rock Road changes to pavement.

Here, the rolling tour temporarily regains its country-lane charm, with draping branches of dogwood, ash, maple, birch, and beech. Beyond a pine plantation, find the trail more cobbled, more exposed, and scarred from illegal vehicle use. Next, round a gate (7 miles), hike right on Hell Hollow Road for 100 feet, and resume the trail on the left.

Descend amid hardwoods, soon passing a stand of mature white pine on this more inviting stretch of the Quinebaug Trail. Where the trail turns left at 7.5 miles, snipped huckleberry shoots can poke through the trailbed. Meander pine plantation and mixed forest, slowly descending. By 8.3 miles, glimpse a red maple swamp, hinting at Phillips Pond. At 8.6 miles, arrive at

Rhododendron Sanctuary, Pachaug State Forest, CT.

the pond near the dam, departing the Quinebaug Trail, which now turns right.

Cross the earthen dam and footbridge, viewing picturesque Phillips Pond with its limited open water, vegetated islands, and aquatic plants. Pass through the picnic area and turn left near the information sign, following the Cut-over Trail (red dot on blue) at 8.7 miles. (Find a water pump and privies in the vicinity of Phillips Pond.)

Round the barrier, touring a maple-draped trail, skirting the pond's marshy outskirts. At 8.85 miles, hikers have the option of returning to the Pachaug Trail via the white-blazed trail to the right, shaving 0.3 mile from the total distance, or keeping to the red-dot-marked crossover. In each case, upon closing the loop, pursue the Pachaug Trail's blue blazes south to return to the trailhead. By following the red dot blazes, reach the Pachaug Trail at 9.4 miles and turn right, retracing the initial 3.1 miles to the CCC area.

64   Devil's Hopyard State Park

OVERVIEW

At the heart of this 860-acre Connecticut state park, find the tumbling streamers and dark-rock escarpment of 60-foot Chapman Falls. (The myth that gives the park its name says the potholes at the foot of the cliff were burned into the rock by the Devil's hooves as he hopped about to avoid the falling water—hence the "hopyard.") Brook-size Eight Mile River, a charming covered footbridge, and loop trails through mature and varied forest complete the offering. Dogwood, mountain laurel, and azalea herald spring; in autumn, enjoy the contrast of the green eastern hemlock spires and the colorful hardwood crowns.

General description: The Chapman Falls Trail and three loop trails explore much of the park: The Witch Hazel Trail visits the southwest corner of the park above Muddy Brook; the Vista Trail circles from the Eight Mile River to a ridgetop vista and back; and the Loop Trail tours a hillside forest.

General location: 8 miles east of East Haddam, Connecticut.

Special attractions: Waterfall and cascades, attractive river and side brooks, mature hemlock, spring floral showcase, bird and wildlife sightings, fishing, fall foliage.

Length: Chapman Falls Trail, 0.2 mile round trip; Witch Hazel Trail, 2.2 miles round trip; Vista Trail, 2.75-mile loop; Loop Trail, 0.8-mile loop.

Elevation: Chapman Falls Trail, 80-foot elevation change; Witch Hazel Trail, 250-foot elevation change; Vista Trail, 300-foot elevation change; Loop Trail, 200-foot elevation change.

Difficulty: Chapman Falls Trail, easy; Witch Hazel and Loop Trails, moderate; Vista Trail, strenuous.

Maps: State park map.

Special concerns: Fee area; keep pets leashed. Boots are recommended.

Season and hours: Year-round; spring through fall for hiking. Open 8:00 A.M. to sunset.

For information: Devil's Hopyard State Park.

Key points:
Chapman Falls Trail:
- 0.0 Falls Trailhead.
- 0.1 Chapman Falls; return as you came.

Witch Hazel Trail:
- 0.0 Picnic area trailhead.
- 0.4 Loop junction.
- 0.6 Baby Falls.
- 1.8 Complete loop; return to trailhead.

Vista Trail:
- 0.0 Covered bridge trailhead.
- 1.0 Ridgetop junction/vista spur.
- 2.7 Complete loop at bridge.

Loop Trail:
- 0.0 Covered bridge trailhead.
- 0.2 Loop junction.
- 0.6 Complete loop; return to bridge.

Finding the trailhead: From the small village of Millington (6 miles east of East Haddam), go east on Haywardville Road, following signs for the park. In 0.7 mile, turn right (south) onto Connecticut Highway 434 (Hopyard Road). In 0.75 mile, turn left for the falls; go another 0.25 mile south, turning left for the picnic area and loop trailheads.

The hikes: For the **Chapman Falls Trail,** cross the road from the parking area and descend the stairs and a short side path angling left to reach a rock outcrop with boulder seating for viewing the three-tiered 60-foot drop. Here, lacy waters curve around and spill over the escarpment of reddish-hued Scotland schist. Stepped ledges, eroded potholes, and a dark plunge pool contribute to viewing, as does the enfolding woods of maple, oak, birch, azalea, dogwood, and mountain laurel.

The potholes, eroded cylindrical holes ranging from a few inches deep to several feet in diameter and depth, are among the finest of their kind in New England. Contrary to myth, they are caused by the persistent abrasion of stones caught and swirled by the stream's eddies. Return as you came (0.2 mile).

For the **Witch Hazel Trail,** park in the first riverside picnic area (the southernmost one), and hike the gated woods road located near the picnic area entrance.

Follow red blazes, hiking downstream along the Eight Mile River on a woods road framed by eastern hemlock, towering oak, maple, dogwood, and mountain laurel, with a sprinkling of violet and wild geranium. Across the Muddy Brook footbridge, the lane narrows to trail width and bears right to cross CT 434. On the west side of CT 434, locate the yellow-blazed loop (0.4 mile), and go straight for a counterclockwise tour.

Hike upstream on a woods road along the hemlock-filled drainage of Muddy Brook. A few big birch accent the woods. Soon turn left onto a footpath, passing closer to the brook to reach Baby Falls, a ledge drop with a pretty 3-foot cascade (0.6 mile). Climb steadily, passing from eastern hemlock to a deciduous forest bursting with fern and dotted by huge boulders. Next, enter a passageway of 10-foot-tall mountain laurel, vibrant even when not in bloom.

Top out at a huckleberry flat (1.1 miles) and descend, backtracking through a laurel grove, fern–deciduous woods, and a hemlock stand. Watch your footing. Close the loop at 1.8 miles, returning to the picnic area at 2.2 miles.

For both the orange-blazed **Vista Trail** and the blue-blazed **Loop Trail,** start at the covered pedestrian bridge located at the picnic area. The scenic bridge spans the Eight Mile River, has rustic wood siding, and sports beam-framed windows for viewing the waterway's rich hemlock drainage and draping deciduous trees.

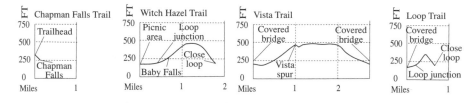

276

Devil's Hopyard State Park

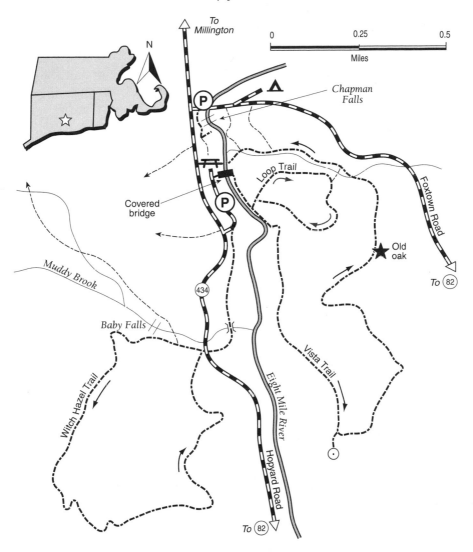

Cross to the east shore and turn right (downstream) for a counterclockwise hike on the orange-blazed **Vista Trail** and to reach the blue Loop Trail (a left) in 0.1 mile. The wide-surfaced trail travels amid mature hemlock, white pine, and hardwood. Laurel and azalea border the brook-size river. After 0.1 mile, the orange-blazed trail narrows to a footpath, rolling up and over the rocks of the lower slope to reach the riverbank at 0.3 mile. Fern and moss complement the tannin-darkened water. Stay along the river for a tricky root- and rock-riddled tour.

Cross a drainage and return to the river where the bank is 8 feet above the water. Veer left here for a steep climb, crossing side drainages to gain the ridge. At the upper slope, ledge overhangs draw notice. Round to the top of the ridge, coming to a junction (1 mile): Turn right for the 0.1-mile vista spur; left continues the loop. Descending to the vantage, find an open look at the surrounding forested hills, and a pasture and pond below. Mountain laurel frames the view.

The loop traverses the ridge flat. Hemlock snags pierce the leafy woods, while ferns, grasses, Virginia creepers, and wildflowers penetrate the duff. Find a moderate descent, once again hugging the line of the slope and crossing small drainages announced by mountain laurel and skunk cabbage. Look for deer feeding on colorful fungi.

In a choked hemlock grove, take the side path heading right to a grand old oak. Resume the loop, descending among picturesque beech trees and white pines, crossing a rocky drainage at 2.2 miles. At 2.25 miles, a connector descends left across a brook to the blue-blazed Loop Trail. Keep on the orange trail, following the narrow brook downstream through mixed woods beside the laurel and azalea banks. At an unmarked junction (2.5 miles), curve left toward the covered bridge and flume. Side spurs to the right lead to views of a seasonal falls and the shore of broadened Eight Mile River. Unseen, Chapman Falls thunders upstream. Close the loop, ending at the bridge at 2.75 miles.

For the blue-blazed **Loop Trail,** cross through the bridge and turn right, following the blue and orange blazes for 0.1 mile. There turn left, touring an oak and laurel hillside, ascending to a healing fire zone, with its recovering midstory and unscathed big trees. Leave the burn, reaching the loop junction at 0.2 mile; go left, passing amid hemlock, dogwood, and maple for an easy, comfortable tour. Bypass the connector to the orange-blazed trail, top out, and then descend, again enjoying laurel. Close the loop and return to the start at 0.8 mile.

65 Hartman Recreational Park

OVERVIEW

At this 302-acre open space, find ridges trending north–south, separated by wooded valleys and wetlands. Across the property, several stone ruins and miles of stone walls recall a thriving colonial settlement. Interlocking, color-coded trails probe the park and link to the Nehantic State Forest trail system. Foot trails and cart roads from early settlement lead the way.

General description: Two main loops explore much of the park. The orange-blazed Heritage Trail strings past cultural ruins, while the red-blazed Nubble and Ridges Trail rolls from ridge to ridge, tagging interesting cliff and rock features.

General location: Northeast corner of Lyme, Connecticut.

Special attractions: Relaxing hardwood forest; interesting rock features; seventeenth-, eighteenth-, and nineteenth-century stone walls and foundations; historical cemetery; abundant mountain laurel; fall foliage; bird-watching.

Length: Heritage Trail, 3-mile loop; Nubble and Ridges Trail, 3.75-mile loop.

Elevation: Both trails show a 200-foot elevation change.

Difficulty: Both moderate.

Maps: Park map, generally available at the open-air schoolroom and picnic area.

Special concerns: No motor vehicles, fires, or collecting. In this color-coded trail system, yellow blazes indicates a connector trail, white blazes a dead end; carry a park map. Bring water, and beware of poison ivy, which is abundant throughout the park.

Season and hours: Year-round, sunrise to sunset.

For information: Lyme Parks and Recreation, Lyme Town Hall.

Key points:

Heritage Trail:
- 0.0 Trailhead.
- 0.2 Picnic area/open-air classroom.
- 0.8 Chapman Ridge
- 2.0 Jumble Ridge.
- 2.6 Cemetery.
- 2.8 Close loop at picnic area; return to trailhead.

Nubble and Ridges Trail:
- 0.0 Trailhead.
- 0.2 Picnic area/open-air classroom.
- 0.7 Hartman Field.
- 1.2 Cave Cliff.
- 2.1 Three Chimneys Ridge.
- 2.5 Park Road.
- 3.5 Close loop at picnic area; return to trailhead.

Finding the trailhead: From the Connecticut Highway 82–CT 156 junction east of Hadlyme, go south on CT 156 East for 1.7 miles and turn left (east) onto Beaver Brook Road in North Lyme. Continue east on Beaver Brook Road for 2.6 miles and turn left (north) onto Gungy/Grassy Hill Road. Find turnout parking for Hartman Park on the right-hand side of Gungy Road in 1 mile.

The hikes: For the **Heritage Trail,** cross over Park Road (a gated dirt road) to follow an orange-blazed footpath through a young forest of maple, beech, and oak. At 0.1 mile, the green-blazed Nature Loop arrives and shares the way. Find sweet pepperbush in the moister woodland reaches.

Now parallel the silver-blazed Park Road, crossing back over it at 0.2 mile. Keep to the orange blazes as the pink-blazed Beaver Pond Loop heads left.

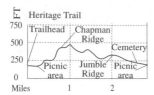

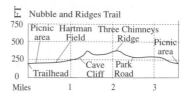

The Heritage Trail offers a glimpse at the snag–meadow marsh and beaver pond before crossing a small footbridge at the site of an old sawmill. At 0.25 mile, reach the picnic area/open-air classroom on a flat above the beaver pond and locate a mapboard and box of trail maps.

Cross Park Road and hike uphill, leaving behind the green-marked trail and crossing a yellow-blazed one. Dogwoods lend springtime bloom. At 0.5 mile, a white-blazed spur leads to the well-preserved foundation of an old barn. Shortly after, the orange-blazed trail briefly follows Park Road north. At a cellar hole and rock foundation from the Lee Farmhouse, ascend right through old fields overgrown with cedars and encroached by oaks and maples.

Where another yellow-blazed connector heads left, bear right for the "Big Scramble," a switchbacking climb through mountain laurel, topping Chapman Ridge. The trail now journeys north, skirting the various stoneworks of Chapman Farm.

At 0.95 mile, bypass the blue-blazed Chapman Path on the left to travel the shrub thicket of the power-line corridor. A spur to the right tops some rocks for a better vantage looking west out the corridor. Watch for vultures and hawks before returning to the woods at a scenic beech grove.

Descend Chapman Ridge, again finding abundant mountain laurel and passing a stone fireplace, to hike Park Road to the right. Pass beneath aspen and tulip poplar, viewing rockwork that records another old farm. Soon after, bear left from the road. A circular depression from an old charcoal kiln is at the turn.

Pass through a fern-filled glen, rounding below a huge boulder outcrop, and again ascend. At 1.7 miles, the red blazes of the Nubble and Ridges Trail briefly join the Heritage Trail on Three Chimneys Ridge. Where the two separate, a white-blazed spur leads to a compound of rockworks, including three small fireplaces. Stay on the Heritage Trail, descending past an enormous boulder against which a barn once stood.

Bear left briefly, following orange and yellow markers. Woody grapevines drape between the trees. Ahead, stay with the orange blazes for a rolling ascent of Jumble Ridge (2 miles). Along this stretch, look for a split rock measuring 6.5 feet tall. At 2.3 miles, turn left where the yellow blazes lead right. A white-blazed spur leads to the circular trench of another nineteenth-century charcoal kiln. More ruins and a second pass through the power-line corridor advance travel.

Next, pass yellow blazes to the left. To the right, white markers lead to a simple ancient cemetery atop a small knoll (2.65 miles). Low, lichen-riddled, unetched stones planted in the earth mark the burial sites. The arrangement of the stones indicates the work of humans rather than nature. Return to the orange-blazed Heritage Trail and bear right to complete the counterclockwise tour. At Park Road, go right, passing through the schoolroom/picnic site to return to the trailhead at 3 miles.

For the red-blazed **Nubble and Ridges Trail,** round the gate at the parking lot and hike north along silver-blazed Park Road. Cross a stone bridge

Hartman Recreational Park

Boulder rest stop, Hartman Recreational Park, CT.

where cardinal flowers adorn the drainage and, at 0.25 mile, pass through the picnic area/open-air schoolroom. (Pick up a trail map.)

The red blazes of the Nubble and Ridges Trail bear left, sharing the way with the pink-blazed Beaver Pond Loop. View the overgrown pond to the left, while traveling a fully shaded foot trail. At 0.4 mile, bear right, staying with the red blazes. Ferns dress the woods floor as dogwoods contribute to the overhead canopy. Before long, a white-blazed spur leads to a beaver dam.

At 0.5 mile, bypass a yellow-blazed trail on the right, coming to a T-junction with Powerline Road. Go left, passing through the shrubby corridor to follow a dirt path to the right, reentering mixed hardwood forest; watch for the turns. Rock walls again line portions of the hike.

Enter Hartman Field, overgrown with a few reclaiming red cedar, or follow the red markers along its shaded eastern edge. The paths merge where a yellow-blazed connector heads left. Resume the forest walk, finding another yellow-blazed connector to the right.

At 1.25 miles, the overhang of Cave Cliff is above the trail to the left. Other interesting rock features of quartzite, schist, and gneiss characterize the tour, including a broken overhang dubbed Snout. Find the trail rolling, fully forested, and bursting with beautiful pockets of laurel.

Next, travel atop the outcrop of Bald Nubble, a large, open rock slope that lacks views. More named, lichen-etched outcrops engage hikers before the trail descends through a forested drainage. Follow an old cart road until the trail makes a U-turn north.

At 1.9 miles, traverse the open vista-less ledge of Razorback Ridge. The trail then dips and climbs, reversing direction to top Middle Ridge and follow a rock wall along its crest. On Three Chimneys Ridge, the orange-blazed Heritage Trail shares the way; stay with the red blazes.

At 2.5 miles, turn right onto Park Road to complete the tour. Pass under power lines and through forest, returning to the picnic area/schoolroom flat at 3.5 miles, the trailhead at 3.75 miles.

66 Nayantaquit Trail

General description:	This rolling loop passes though a gentle terrain of low ridges and mixed forest, promising solitude and relaxation. A side trip to the deep, clear waters of Uncas Pond for a picnic lunch or a quick swim punctuates the tour.
General location:	5 miles southeast of Hadlyme, Connecticut.
Special attractions:	Solitude, wildlife sightings, historical stone walls and foundations, pond refreshment, fall foliage.
Length:	5 miles round trip.
Elevation:	Find a 400-foot elevation change, with the low point at Uncas Pond and the high point at Nickerson Hill.

Difficulty:	Moderate.
Maps:	Hamburg 7.5-minute USGS quad; Nayantaquit Trail map, *Connecticut Walk Book.*
Special concerns:	Swimming is at your own risk. Because periodic logging is part of forestry management, the trail may sometimes be closed for safety concerns.
Season and hours:	Year-round, depending on snow conditions. Open 8:00 A.M. to sunset.
For information:	Nehantic State Forest.

Key points:
- 0.0 Keeny Road trailhead.
- 0.2 Loop junction; go left.
- 0.9 Brown Hill.
- 1.8 Uncas Pond.
- 3.6 Nickerson Hill.
- 4.8 Complete loop; backtrack to trailhead.

Finding the trailhead: From the junction of Connecticut Highways 82 and 156 (east of Hadlyme, west of North Plain), go south on CT 156 East for 1.7 miles, reaching North Lyme. There, turn east onto Beaver Brook Road, go 1.9 miles, and turn right (south) onto Keeny Road. Reach trailhead parking on the right in 1.3 miles; the final 0.3 mile of travel is on dirt road.

The hike: Named for an Indian tribe that hunted in this part of Nehantic State Forest, this loop wins over hikers with its relaxing familiarity. From the parking area, hike in on the gated dirt road, taking an immediate left, following blue blazes. In the woods, find a trail sign and the number 1, indicating the official start. Along the loop, the numbers 1 through 10 indicate key junctions or features.

Tour a young forest of oak, maple, birch, dogwood, sassafras, shadbush, and hazelnut, with an understory of huckleberry and sarsaparilla. Cross a scenic rock wall and pass a huge boulder on the left, coming to the loop junction (site 2) at 0.2 mile. Go left for a clockwise tour, traveling a thin, mildly inclined path.

Reach a high point (site 3) near the edge of a plateau. Boulders and the occasional stump dot the forest, which, although young, provides a full leafy umbrella. Next, find a sometimes steep descent, entering a mature oak–hickory complex. As the trail weaves among the boulder outcrops and rolls, enjoy the different visuals and moods of the tour. Cross a thin (often dry) brook, pass a regal 4-foot-diameter tulip poplar, and cross a rock wall.

Next, top Brown Hill at 0.9 mile, coming to a junction in a small transition meadow. The loop continues to the left; a cutoff trail heads right for a

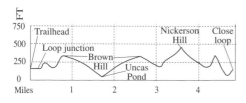

shorter hike. Along the cutoff, stone walls and foundations recall the land's domestic history as pasture and farmland. Keep left for the full loop, quickly reaching site 4, where the spur to Uncas Pond heads left; the loop turns right.

Nayantaquit Trail

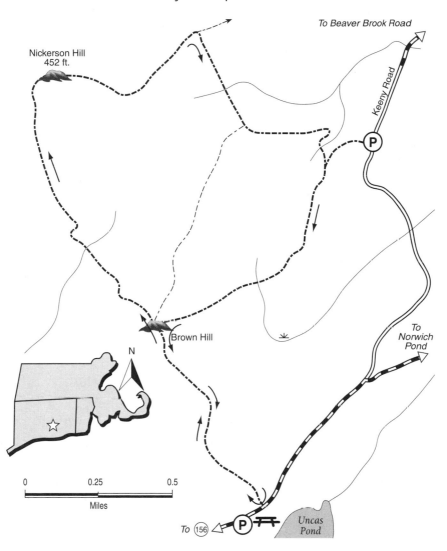

Go left for Uncas Pond, passing quietly, because wild turkey or deer may be spied. Descend from Brown Hill, passing a doghouse-size rock shelter to travel a tall mixed-deciduous woods. Roll up and over the next outcrop rise, reaching a paved road (site 10) at 1.6 miles.

Hike the road to the right and turn left, entering Uncas Pond Picnic Area, an attractive site with tables, barbecues, and pit toilets. It offers an alternative starting point for this forest trail system.

At the south end of the picnic area, reach an improved beach access (1.8 miles) where beams terrace the slope and sand greets the water. With the site's improvements, expect company in summer and a disruption from the quiet of the woods sojourn. Nevertheless, the pond's refreshment entices. Sparkling blue, the deep waters of Uncas Pond are mostly rimmed by forest with a couple of homes visible across the way. A few pond lilies decorate the edge water.

Backtrack to the loop junction (site 4) at 2.6 miles, and resume the clockwise tour (straight upon return). Follow the blazes, making a couple of quick direction changes to travel a tranquil country lane bathed in filtered lighting. Hike past a stone wall shaded by a gnarly old oak. Ahead, the lane yields to a logging road reinstated for use. Bear right, cross a drainage culvert (3 miles), and again turn right at 3.1 miles.

Just ahead, turn left off the woods road, ascending a footpath in oak, hickory, and beech to top a small hill. In 0.2 mile, cross a stone wall to travel the summit of Nickerson Hill, tagging the hike's high point (elevation 452 feet) at 3.6 miles. Here, large round boulders dot a sloping outcrop that offers limited views southeast, overlooking the tall foreground forest. Nearby stand spiny-armed snags, young deciduous trees, and cedars.

At junction 7, a spur to the left reaches a woods road that returns to parking. Bear right for the loop. In the leafy canopy, insects create the sound of high-tension wires. Next, find a series of crossings over woods roads, a brook, and a secondary trail. At 4.4 miles, reach junction 8, where the cutoff trail rejoins the hike on the right. Proceed forward.

With a steady descent, cross the width of a long meadow swath brimming with wild berry, sumac, herbs, and forbs; keep an eye out for poison ivy. Cross a plank over a small brook to tour a wetter maple woodland and pass through a goldenrod opening to close the loop at site 2. Return to the trailhead at 5 miles.

67 Bluff Point State Park and Coastal Reserve

OVERVIEW

This hike explores Connecticut's last vestige of undeveloped coast—an 800-acre wooded peninsula bounded by the Poquonock River and Mumford Cove and extending into Long Island Sound. A sandy spit offers coastal and bay discovery. Designated a coastal reserve, facilities are few and in keeping with the area's character.

General description: This easy multiple-use loop travels closed dirt roads, touring a coastal woodland, sand spit, and bluff.
General location: Eastern outskirts of Groton, Connecticut.

Special attractions: Long Island Sound and bay-shore discovery; wildlife sightings of deer, raccoon, and sea-, shore-, and woodland birds; historical 1700s homesite of Governor Winthrop.

Length: 4.8 miles round trip.

Elevation: Find a 100-foot elevation change.

Difficulty: Easy.

Maps: State park map (usually available at park).

Special concerns: Bring water; there is none at the park.

Season and hours: Year-round, 8:00 A.M. to sunset.

For information: Bluff Point State Park and Coastal Reserve.

Key points:

0.0 Picnic area trailhead.
0.1 Loop junction; go right.
1.9 Bushy Point.
2.7 Bluff Point.
3.9 Winthrop house ruins.
4.7 Close loop; end at trailhead.

Finding the trailhead: From Interstate 95, take exit 88, go 1 mile south on Connecticut Highway 117, and turn west onto U.S. Highway 1. In 0.3 mile, turn south onto Depot Road at a sign for the park. Bear right and pass under the railroad tracks to reach the gravel parking lot, picnic area, and trail in 0.4 mile.

The hike: From the center of the picnic area, hike the gated woods road paralleling the Poquonock River as it flows seaward. Swans sometimes ply the bay. Anglers line the riprap shore, while sea kayakers dig their way to Long Island Sound. Across the river sits tiny Trumbull Airport.

The hike travels at the perimeter of a mixed oak–hickory woods, with sassafras, hawthorn, cherry, and the occasional eastern red cedar. Greenbrier, wild grape, and bramble contribute to the understory tangle. At the 0.1-mile junction, go right for a counterclockwise loop. Short spurs branch to the gravelly Poquonock shore, its width dependent on tide. In spring, look for a pair of ospreys atop the offshore nesting platform.

Near an offset barricade of concrete blocks, the trail opens up, skirting a grassy tidal marsh with cattails at one end. In open areas, native beach plum, beach pea, and red and white shore roses grow. At 0.5 mile, a secondary foot trail travels closer to the bay, rejoining the road at 0.8 mile.

The main woods road passes between a bouldery, forested hill and the tight tangle of the bayward woods. A semi-overgrown colonial rock wall lines the road, adding interest and charm. At 0.7 mile, bear right; the road fork to the left offers a cutoff to shorten the hike. Where the main road and secondary bay route merge (0.8 mile), the hike offers glimpses of Long Island Sound across the tidal grass plain of the Poquonock River. This

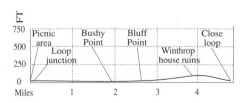

Bluff Point State Park and Coastal Reserve

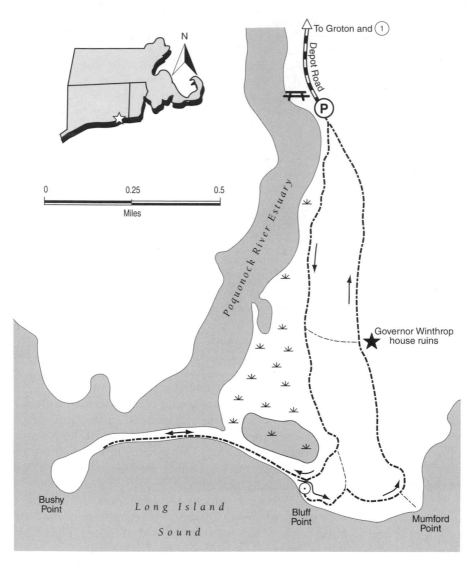

productive one hundred-acre salt marsh attracts resident and migratory birds.

At the three-pronged junction (1.1 miles), bear right for the loop. The trail passes a pair of privies set back from the trail before arriving at the beach below Bluff Point. Tidepool rocks string off the point, while pebbles, cobbles, and sun-bleached shells make up the coastal shore. Snow fences help prevent the loss of sand and vegetation.

Views sweep Long Island Sound from Groton Heights to Bluff Point and include New York's Fisher's Island and Rhode Island's Watch Hill. An attractive 200-foot-wide tombolo beach (spit) arcs west to Bushy Point. Journeying west along it, hikers can divide their time between the Sound and Poquonock bay shore; a battered boardwalk midway allows passage between the two.

Walkable at low tide, the bay shore records the tracks of wading birds and deer. On the seashore, tide-deposited strings of seaweed, sea lettuce, bladder-floated algae, skate egg cases, periwinkles, horseshoe crab shells, and flotsam and jetsam bring beachcombers to their knees. At about two-thirds of the way, stable sands replace the shifting gravels. At 1.9 miles, Bushy Point (a vegetated rock island at high tide) signals the turnaround point. Pine Island sits farther offshore, while a scenic brick lighthouse blinks to the west.

Return to the base of Bluff Point (2.7 miles). To top this 20-foot bluff, mount it from the beach or from the main dirt road rounding behind it. Views broaden, straining east; a wooden bench invites pause. Where the trail departs the east side of the bluff, a right turn leads to rocky Mumford Point. For the loop, follow the woods road bearing left. A dwarfed woods with a dense, thorny understory enfolds the tour. As the road mildly climbs, side paths branch to the rocky shore.

Beyond a study enclosure to measure the impact of deer on area vegetation, rock walls again appear. Cardinal, blue jay, hawk, and vulture may draw eyes skyward. Passing through an open area of tall grasses, keep to the main road.

At 3.9 miles, look across the rock wall to the right to discover ruins—a stone foundation, chunks of red brick, and a hard-to-see well now filled with stones. Here stood the home of Governor Fitzjohn Winthrop (grandson of the famous Massachusetts Bay governor). Circa 1700, the Winthrop house had a 300-foot tunnel connecting it to the barn, a safeguard against Indian attacks. Beware of poison ivy when exploring.

Past the Winthrop site, keep to the main woods road; a smaller track journeys right. Tall forest enfolds the trail as it completes the loop at 4.7 miles. Return to the trailhead at 4.8 miles.

Rhode Island Trails

Despite being small in geographical territory and well populated, Rhode Island remains 60 percent forested and boasts fine natural spaces. Find mildly rolling lowland forests, sandy Atlantic Ocean beaches, and rocky shores. Retired military bases now serve as vital wildlife lands, with restored cover and reclaimed runways for paths. Gulls make use of the remaining paved surfaces to break open shellfish. Elsewhere, stone walls, pens, and cellars hint at a time when the forest was tilled and partitioned for pasture. Rocky realms, meadows, ponds, and swamps complete the discovery. Enjoy bird-watching and some fine vistas.

68 George Washington Management Area

OVERVIEW

In northwest Rhode Island, this extensive management area incorporates George Washington Memorial State Forest and the adjoining Casimir Pulaski Memorial State Park. Within the management area, find a burgeoning color-coded trail system, with the Walkabout Trail and Angell Loop being prized examples of the available hikes. Tour lakeshore, woodland, and wetland, finding solitude and wildlife discovery.

General description: Designed with two cut-over trails, the Walkabout Trail allows hikers to customize both hike length and difficulty. Angell Loop offers a comfortable lakeshore–woodland circuit, passing an Indian grave site.

General location: 10 miles east of Putnam, Connecticut; 5 miles southwest of Pascoag, Rhode Island.

Special attractions: Bowdish Reservoir and Wilbur and Peck Ponds; mountain laurel; hemlock, pine, and hardwood forests; wetland habitat; wildlife sightings; fall foliage.

Length: Walkabout Trail, 2-, 6-, or 8-mile loop, with a still longer hike possible, adding the Peck Pond spur (1.2 miles round trip); Angell Loop, 1.6-mile loop.

Elevation: Walkabout Trail, 200-foot elevation change; Angell Loop, 75-foot elevation change.

Difficulty: Walkabout Trail, easy to moderately strenuous; the Angell Loop is easy.

Maps: Walkabout Trail flyer.

Special concerns: User fee area. In spring and following rains, wet conditions on the Walkabout Trail can increase its difficulty.

Season and hours: Year-round, generally spring through fall for hiking. Open sunrise to sunset.

For information: George Washington Management Area.

Key points:

Walkabout Trail:

0.0	Bowdish Reservoir trailhead.
1.0	Wilbur Pond shore.
2.9	Cross dirt road (Cold Spring Trail).
4.1	Pulaski Park; return to loop.
5.5	Cross dirt road of Inner Border Trail.
9.2	End at Bowdish Reservoir.

Angell Loop:

0.0	Boat-launch trailhead, Bowdish Reservoir.
0.8	Indian grave.
1.6	End back at reservoir.

Finding the trailhead: From the junction of Rhode Island Highways 100 and 102 and U.S. Highway 44 in Chepachet, Rhode Island, go west on US 44 for 4.2 miles and turn north for George Washington Memorial State Forest and campground. Pass the campground, finding the Walkabout Trailhead on the northeast shore of Bowdish Reservoir near the picnic area, beach, and boat launch (0.4 mile). Find the Angell Loop south of the launch.

The hikes: Built by Australian sailors awaiting the repair of their ship, the HMAS *Perth*, the **Walkabout Trail** traces its name and intent to the aborigines. Their coined name for a compelling need to wander is a *walkabout.*

Start at the marked trailhead, rounding the northeast shore of Bowdish Reservoir, touring a hemlock–hardwood forest. A tricolor blazing indicates the start. Keep to the blue blazes for a 2-mile loop, red for a 6-mile loop, and orange for the full 8-mile loop.

Canada geese sometimes ply the water or plod along the reservoir's edge. Rocks and tangled roots erupt in the trail. Find soggy drainages and fragments of boardwalk before turning away from the reservoir at 0.3 mile. A flattish granite outcrop serves up the farewell view.

The meandering woods walkabout skirts a private campground on Wilbur Pond. At 0.8 mile, the blue-blazed route breaks away, briefly on state forest road, before turning to close its loop. Continue ahead along the forest rim of Wilbur Pond for the longer hikes.

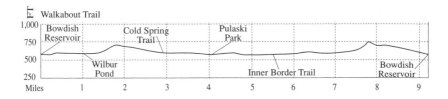

291

Wilbur Pond, George Washington Memorial State Forest, RI.

Limited openings allow only glances at this good-size pond, but its mountain laurel rim engages the eyes. At 1 mile, access a few large boulders and a 50-foot shoreline for unencumbered pond views. Ahead stretches a merry chase across the spreading inlet drainages; some require ingenuity to devise dry crossings.

While the blazes may appear excessive during the main hiking season, once the leaves drop, they are necessary. With a final look at a scenic reflecting bay-water, ascend away from Wilbur Pond (1.5 miles). Beyond the pond, encounter mostly deciduous forest with occasional pines. At 2 miles, the red-blazed trail departs to complete its loop. Follow the orange blazes for the full tour.

Because fewer obstacles riddle the trail, a relaxing woods wandering is possible. Changes in lighting, birdsongs, and a whisper of breeze contribute to the soothing message. At 2.9 miles, cross a drivable dirt road (Cold Spring Trail), then cross a grassy woods road and a second dirt road with a trailside bench at 3.2 miles. Now hike a time-healed woods road, passing through a dark hemlock grove, coming to a sign and red arrows for Pulaski Park (3.5 miles).

Detour left for Pulaski Park, Peck Pond, and the Pulaski Park trail system, ascending through rich forest and enjoying cushiony footfalls on the wood-chip-softened lane. At 4 miles, come out at an isolated pine-shaded picnic ground above Peck Pond. Pass through the park to the open beach. Multicolored pastel blazings hint at other hiking tours. Large parking areas suggest a bustling site in summer; off-season visitors share the area with wildlife. Find flush toilets and water during summer months.

Backtrack to the Walkabout Trail, retracing the red arrows to the orange-blazed trail. There, resume the clockwise tour, bearing left (4.7 miles). Pass beneath beautiful pines and cross a hemlock-lined brook, coming to a junction. The red arrows straight ahead lead back to Pulaski Park; the Walkabout Trail now heads right. By 5.1 miles, tour a skunk cabbage bog via boardwalk and, at 5.5 miles, cross the dirt road of Inner Border Trail, remaining in wetter woods.

At the Richardson Trail (a road) crossing, find a bench seat. Now round a snag-riddled wildlife pond and marsh, crossing the earthen dam. Ascend away through woods, soon to be rejoined by the red-blazed trail (6.9 miles) as snags open the forest to mountain laurel.

Next, cross Center Trail road and travel a rustic corduroy through a marshy area, before the blue-blazed trail rejoins the tour at 8.5 miles. End the hike, returning to Bowdish Reservoir along the access road to the boat launch (9.2 miles).

For the purple-blazed **Angell Loop,** round the south shore of the boat-launch cove, passing amid eastern hemlock, mountain laurel, white pine, oak, birch, and beech. The campground occupies the woods above the trail. In 300 feet, reach the loop junction and bear right, keeping to shore.

Bowdish Reservoir, large with an irregular shore-

Angell Loop

1,000 — Bowdish Reservoir
750
500 — Indian grave | Close loop
250
Miles   1   2

George Washington Management Area

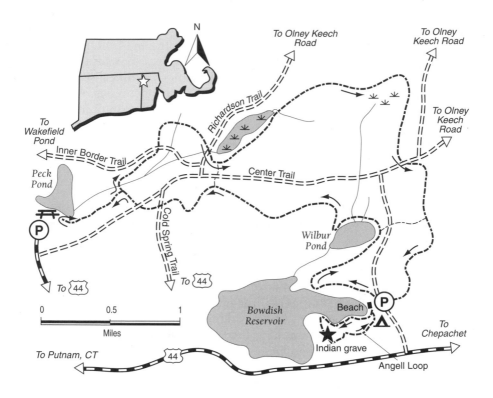

line, has a posted boat speed limit of 10 miles per hour for relative quiet. Cross a small boggy inlet, finding gaps in the tree cover to view the reservoir or cast a line. Huge rocks suggest taking a seat to admire the water and its mostly wild shore. Laurel abounds.

By 0.6 mile, gain over-the-shoulder looks at the beach area before the trail curves away left, passing some large rocks. Now travel pine–oak woods, enjoying full shade and a slow ascent. Deer, chipmunk, woodpecker, and other woodland creatures enliven a tour. At 0.85 mile, a 30-foot spur on the left leads to the Indian grave; be alert to spot it. A faded wooden sign and an arrangement of stones alone mark the site.

Find a gently rolling forested return, traveling a time-healed woods road and footpath. Forgotten natural history signs might indicate an American chestnut or a blueberry bush. Descend to close the loop and return to the trailhead at 1.6 miles.

69 George B. Parker Woodland

OVERVIEW

At this Audubon Society of Rhode Island property, visitors find rich hardwood forest, moist bottomland, peaceful brooks, and early American history. The Isaac Bowen House, a central-chimney colonial at the wildlife area headquarters, is a registered national historic place. Across the property, find foundations, stone walls, quarry sites, and inexplicable cairns that hark to the past. According to legend, Biscuit Hill traces its name to the Revolutionary War, when a food wagon of biscuits overturned en route to General Rochambeau's troops.

General description:	The Paul Cook and Milton A. Gowdey Memorial Trails, two loops joined by a connecting trail, travel the Coventry and Foster Tracts of Parker Woodland, exploring the natural and cultural wealth.
General location:	2 miles east of Vernon, Rhode Island; 4 miles northwest of Coventry Center.
Special attractions:	Solitude, bird- and wildlife-watching, historical sites, rich woods, spring and summer wildflowers, fall foliage.
Length:	7 miles round trip, traveling both loops. Hikers may explore the loops individually when the parking lot east of the headquarters is open.
Elevation:	Find about a 200-foot elevation change.
Difficulty:	Moderate.
Maps:	Wildlife area map, generally available at parking lots.
Special concerns:	Obey all posted Audubon rules, including no pets, no bicycles, no smoking, and no collecting. For this color-coded trail system, blue marks the loops; orange, the access trail; and yellow, the connecting spurs.
Season and hours:	Year-round, generally spring through fall for hiking. Open sunrise to sunset.
For information:	George B. Parker Woodland, c/o the Audubon Society of Rhode Island.

Key points:
- 0.0 Headquarters trailhead.
- 0.5 Paul Cook Memorial Trail.
- 1.0 Cross Biscuit Hill Road.
- 2.4 Milton A. Gowdey Memorial Trail.
- 3.5 Cross Pig Hill Road.
- 6.5 Complete Paul Cook loop; return to trailhead.

Finding the trailhead: From Interstate 95, take exit 5, go north on Rhode Island Highway 102 for 8.3 miles, and turn right (east) onto Maple Valley Road. Go 0.2 mile to find the headquarters parking lot for Parker Woodland on the left. Find a second parking lot east on Maple Valley Road.

The hike: From headquarters parking, follow the mowed swath along the fence to a sign. To the left is the nature center; to the right, find all trails.

Go right and, in 100 feet, follow the orange blazes to the left, passing through a beautiful mixed woods of red cedar, pine, beech, birch, maple, oak, dogwood, and hickory. The ground cover likewise displays diversity, with Canada mayflower, club moss, Virginia creeper, poison ivy, and hog peanut. At 0.25 mile, reach a T-junction; left takes you to the nature center. Continue right, gently descending to reach the loops.

Travel a moist bottomland with half a dozen fern varieties, sweet pepperbush, trillium, wood lily, false Solomon's seal, nettle, and azalea. A scenic boardwalk crosses the soggier reaches. At 0.4 mile, cross the footbridge over Turkey Meadow Brook, a slow, thin waterway adorned by drooping boughs and vegetation. A sawmill once operated alongside the brook.

At 0.5 mile, reach the Paul Cook Memorial Trail (marked in blue), and turn left for a clockwise tour of Coventry Tract. Stones stud the trail, and oak and hickory are the "big guys" of the woods. Sassafras, highbush blueberry, and huckleberry add a midstory. Rock walls grace travel.

At 1 mile, cross Biscuit Hill Road, a grassy, narrow woods road. On either side are ruins from the Vaughn farmsite: dry-laid fieldstone foundations, the cellar to a central-chimney colonial home, stairs, and a stone-lined well with its capstone ajar. The buildings dated to the mid-eighteenth century; trees now pierce the cellar floor. A sign interprets the lay of the farm.

A slow ascent follows, passing amid pine and crossing lichen-mottled outcrop. At 1.4 miles, descend and be sure to duck at the protruding rock. Cross an unnamed woods road and resume the descent, touring a mixed-hardwood forest riddled by outcrops and boulders. Expect to do some high stepping here.

The Paul Cook Memorial Trail then rolls, coming to a junction at 2 miles. The yellow-blazed trail to the left leads to the Milton A. Gowdey Memorial Trail and Foster Tract; the yellow-marked trail to the right leads to Biscuit Hill Road and parking lot 2. For the Paul Cook Memorial Trail alone, proceed forward, following blue blazes past a room-size boulder.

Opting for the full 7-mile tour, go left on rocky trail through beech–hardwood forest. Pass an even bigger boulder than the one at the 2-mile junction, and follow Pine Swamp Brook upstream, contouring the slope some 20 feet above the drainage. Mosses darken the brook's boulders.

Cross the footbridge at 2.25 miles. A root-ribbed foot trail now ascends to the blue-blazed Gowdey Trail (2.45 miles). Go left for a clockwise tour, and watch for poison ivy. The gentle incline allows for a relaxing

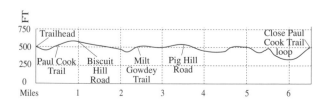

George B. Parker Woodland

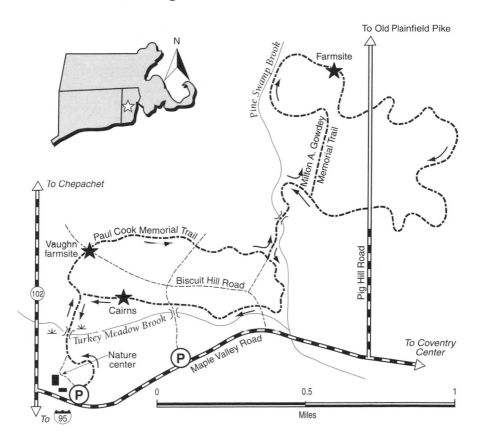

stroll. At 2.95 miles, descend back toward Pine Swamp Brook. Sweet pepperbush ushers the way, and more rocks riddle the trail.

Soon pull away from the brook, passing through another historical farmstead (3.25 miles). Rock walls, stone pens, and a 5-foot-deep foundation mark the site. Next, descend a low rise, passing among white pine and hardwoods to cross Pig Hill Road at 3.5 miles.

Pines drop from the mix on the slow descent. Where the trail passes between offset rock walls, find a boulder-dotted landscape. On the right, at 4 miles, a disturbed area with displaced rock and reclaiming vegetation signals an old quarry site.

Advance via long, sleepy trail undulations, cross Pig Hill Road a second time, and pass through a (usually gated) parking lot. Keep left when rounding the sanctuary entry post to avoid the worst of the poison ivy. At 4.95 miles, close the loop and backtrack along the yellow-blazed trail to Coventry Tract. Return to the 2-mile junction at 5.4 miles and bear left to resume hiking the blue-blazed Paul Cook Memorial Trail.

Boardwalk, George B. Parker Woodland, RI.

Descend amid outcrops, briefly passing near Pine Swamp Brook. Find showings of mountain laurel, pass another foundation on the left, and cross Biscuit Hill Road to contour above Turkey Meadow Brook at 5.9 miles. At the 6.1-mile junction, continue forward on the blue-blazed trail. The blue markers heading to the left lead to parking lot 2. The yellow ones to the right reach Biscuit Hill Road and Foster Tract.

Just ahead, discover several cairns, some 4 feet tall, others broad and squat. Their origins are unknown, but one theory attributes them to colonial field clearing, another to precolonial Celtic or Narragansett Indian sacred monuments. Pass a white-blazed trail on the right to close the loop at 6.5 miles. Retrace the 0.5-mile orange-blazed trail to the headquarters parking lot.

70 Pachaug–Tippecansett Loop

General description:	This two-state circuit beginning and ending in Rhode Island's Arcadia Management Area tags the shore of Beach Pond, travels mixed woods and rocky hilltops, passes Escoheag Fire Tower (closed to the public), and concludes with a woodland meander. Travel foot trail and woods roads; a spur to Stepstone Falls extends the tour.
General location:	On the Connecticut–Rhode Island border, 7 miles northwest of Hope Valley, Rhode Island; 16 miles northeast of Norwich, Connecticut.

Special attractions: Beach Pond views and access, mountain laurel and sweet pepperbush, intriguing rocky hilltops and slots, varied woods, wildlife, fall foliage, Stepstone Falls.

Length: 11.1-mile loop, with an optional 2.4-mile round-trip spur to Stepstone Falls.

Elevation: Find a 250-foot elevation change.

Difficulty: Strenuous.

Maps: Arcadia Management Area map; Nehantic and Pachaug Trails map, *Connecticut Walk Book.*

Special concerns: The beach parking lot on the north side of Rhode Island Highway 165 is a fee site; the fishing access on the south side is not. Expect some rough spots on this hike. Keep to the trail where it travels along and through the private South County Gun and Rod Club; pass at your own risk. October 1 through February 28, Rhode Island requires hikers as well as hunters to wear a fluorescent orange hat or vest.

Season and hours: Year-round, generally spring through fall for hiking. Open sunrise to sunset.

For information: Arcadia Management Area, Rhode Island Department of Environmental Management.

Key points:

- 0.0   Beach Pond trailhead.
- 0.5   Loop junction; go left.
- 3.5   Launch.
- 5.4   Canonicus Trail.
- 7.9   Historical cemetery/detour to Stepstone Falls.
- 9.1   Stepstone Falls; backtrack to loop.
- 13.0 End loop; backtrack to trailhead.

Finding the trailhead: From the junction of RI 3 and RI 165 (0.3 mile east of U.S. Highway 95), go west on RI 165 for 6.6 miles to reach Beach Pond Parking on either side of the road. When arriving from Voluntown, Connecticut, from the junction of Connecticut Highways 49 and 138/165, go east on CT 165/RI 165 for 4.3 miles, reaching Beach Pond. Find yellow and blue paint blazes marking the hike's start on the north side of RI 165, east of the parking lot entrance.

The hike: Follow the dual blazes of the Tippecansett Trail (yellow) and Pachaug Trail (blue), ascending stone steps and passing over a rise toward Beach Pond. Hemlocks and red oaks frame the route as it contours and curves away to the loop junction (0.5 mile). Adequate blazes guide hikers through the maze of woods roads and footpaths, leading to the junction.

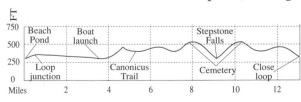

At 0.5 mile, go left onto the Pachaug Trail for a clockwise loop. The trail veers to and away from shore, dodging private landhold-

Pachaug–Tippecansett Loop

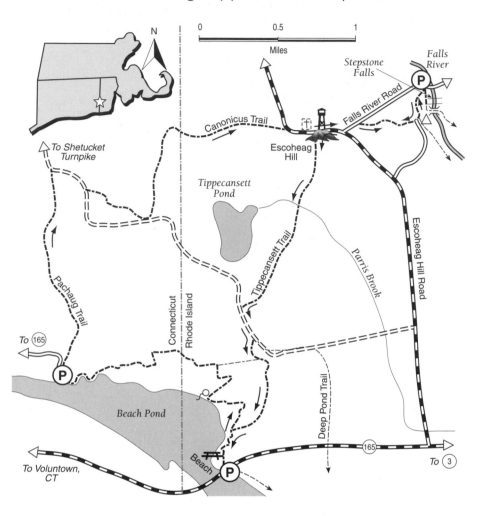

ings; keep to the blazed trail. Along shore, find lush mountain laurel, sweet pepperbush, and highbush blueberry. Rocks and wet areas mark the rolling path where it draws away from the pond. The drone of RI 165 accompanies the early distance.

By 1.25 miles, overlook a pretty, rounded cove with a gravelly bottom and dotting of reflection rocks. Across the way is a private dock; phragmites (plumed reeds) claim the cove curvature. Round above an inlet spring, find a trail register, and begin encountering stone walls. At 1.6 miles, stay left as a blue-blazed cutoff trail journeys right for a shorter loop option. Tour alternating hemlock flats and areas of oak, discovering more wet pockets. At 2.2 miles, pass a scenic boulder jumble that has deformed the trunk of a hemlock growing next to it.

At 2.25 miles, round a hillside of boulders and cliffs, cut up through a draw, circle the back of the hill, and push on to the next bouldery rise. Find overhangs, shelters, and short passageways. After resuming a mixed-woods tour, cross a dirt road at 3.2 miles.

Return to the shore of Beach Pond, now in Connecticut, reaching a boulder overlook before the launch area (3.5 miles). Shadowy perch move through the water. Keep to the right-hand side of the access road, heading uphill through the boat-launch parking area. There, resume the hike, passing north through a dark hollow in the pine border. At the parking area are chemical toilets.

Again tour woods and top outcrops, crossing a road. At 3.9 miles, descend a slot through massive boulder cliffs. The bouldery hillsides truly recommend this tour. Ascend and meander through the rocky realm, leaving the area at 4.7 miles, now in a maple–mountain laurel passage. Stone walls and stone pens hint at a former pasture. Alternately tour pine and hardwood habitats.

At a lightly used dirt road (5.4 miles), the Pachaug Trail heads left. For the loop, go right, now following the white blazes of the Canonicus Trail. Stay on the road for 0.3 mile, and then turn left onto a woods road enfolded by young pines. Wetter areas host sweet pepperbush and brier.

Upon reaching a drivable dirt road at 6.2 miles, follow it left for 200 feet. There, turn left onto a second woods road, similar to the first, although lacking the cushiony needle-strewn bed. Hardwoods replace the pines, bringing with them an understory of laurel and shrubs.

Where the route forks at 6.8 miles, continue forward on the same woods road, avoiding a side road to the left. By now, the blazes have grown scarce. Again keep right at 7 miles, passing between the South County Gun and Rod

Tippecansett Trail, Arcadia Management Area, RI.

Club and a private residence; do not stray from the woods road. At paved Escoheag Hill Road (7.75 miles), turn right, following the road.

Opposite the historical cemetery of West Greenwich at 7.9 miles, find a blazed junction. Here, end the Canonicus Trail and follow the Tippecansett Trail right for the loop. To add a visit to Stepstone Falls, follow the Tippecansett straight.

For the falls detour, follow the yellow blazes along Escoheag Hill Road for 0.1 mile, turn left onto Falls River Road for 0.3 mile, and turn right onto a foot trail entering the hardwood–pine forest. As the trail passes through woods and the Stepstone Falls Backpack Area, blue blazes merge with the yellow ones and hikers pass the Ben Utter Trail.

Reach the falls area parking turnout (1.2 miles from the cemetery); Stepstone Falls, a Northeast charmer, is just a few strides downstream along the scenic black water of the brook-size Falls River. Its four cascades spill over bedrock ledges and overhangs, with the largest cascade having a 4-foot drop. Return to the junction opposite the cemetery (10.3 miles) and follow the Tippecansett Trail left past Escoheag Fire Tower, a traditional multistory steel cage enclosed by fence.

From the tower, follow the well-blazed foot trail through oak–birch habitat, crossing outcrops and descending. At 10.9 miles, enter gun club land, heeding posted rules. Mountain laurel abounds. Cross Parris Brook and angle left across a woods road, touring a gentle landscape and relaxing woods. Stay with the blazes, leaving the gun club at 11.8 miles.

Soon after, turn left onto a rocky woods road. At 12.3 miles, turn right as the white-blazed Deep Pond Trail proceeds along the road. After skirting a gate, find the blue-blazed cutoff trail arriving on the right (12.5 miles). Continue forward on the Tippecansett Trail, meandering through pleasant mixed woods. Turn right to close the loop at 13 miles; return to the trailhead at 13.5 miles.

71 Breakheart Pond–Mount Tom Loop

General description:	In Rhode Island's Arcadia Management Area, this woodland loop unites several named trails, reaching Breakheart Pond, crossing rivers and brooks, and touring the rocky ridge of Mount Tom. Travel foot trail and woods roads.
General location:	5 miles north of Hope Valley, Rhode Island; 22 miles northeast of Norwich, Connecticut.
Special attractions:	Limited pond access; rich, varied woods; mountain laurel and sweet pepperbush; intriguing rocky hilltops; some views; wildlife; fall foliage.

Length: 13.5-mile loop.
Elevation: Find a 250-foot elevation change.
Difficulty: Moderate to strenuous.
Maps: Arcadia Management Area map; find trail maps generally stocked at the kiosk at the John B. Hudson Trailhead.
Special concerns: Permits are required for camping; contact the Rhode Island Department of Environmental Management. Expect some wet or rough spots on the hike. Keep dogs leashed from April 1 through August 15. On Mount Tom, keep to the trail to avoid straying onto private lands. October 1 through February 28, all hikers must wear a fluorescent orange hat or vest per Rhode Island regulations.
Season and hours: Year-round; spring through fall are best for hiking. Open sunrise to sunset.
For information: Arcadia Management Area, Rhode Island Department of Environmental Management.

Key points:
- 0.0 John B. Hudson Trailhead.
- 1.5 Breakheart Pond.
- 3.3 Matteson Plain Road.
- 4.1 Cross East Fork Flat River footbridge.
- 7.9 Barber Road.
- 9.1 Cross Rhode Island Highway 165.
- 11.6 RI 165 bridge.
- 13.5 End loop at John B. Hudson Trailhead.

Finding the trailhead: From the RI 3–RI 165 junction (0.3 mile east of U.S. Highway 95), go west on RI 165 for 2.5 miles and then right (north) 0.1 mile on a dirt road to reach the John B. Hudson Trail and parking for eight or nine vehicles. Look for a small sign and yellow blaze.

The hike: Follow the yellow-blazed John B. Hudson Trail north from the road closure, strolling a woods of mixed oak, maple, white pine, birch, sassafras, hickory, and beech. Fern, sweet fern, and huckleberry dress the forest floor. At 0.25 mile, proceed forward, ignoring an abandoned left spur, to encounter bigger trees and a midstory of mountain laurel exploding in June blooms. Cross a small brook and the woods road of the Tripp Trail, coming to a three-way junction. The white trail to the left leads to a backpack shelter, the center prong is the John B. Hudson Trail, and the right prong offers hikers a wet-season bypass to Breakheart Pond.

Continue forward on the John B. Hudson Trail, descending along and criss-crossing a small brook to reach fast-flowing Breakheart Brook, with its stepped cascades and green banks, at

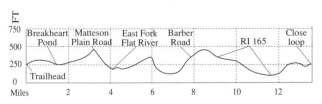

1 mile. The passage along this drainage often requires hopscotching from rock to root and may result in wet, muddy feet. Find sweet pepperbush and skunk cabbage. Where the trail travels a laurel flat, a white trail arrives from the camp shelter. Continue upstream to the dam and spillway for open views of Breakheart Pond (1.5 miles).

A thick deciduous rim and backset pines frame circular Breakheart Pond, with its lily pad mosaic, population of geese, and an eerie morning mist. Hike the dirt road to the right for 0.2 mile and turn left, staying with the yellow blazes. As the trail meanders the woodland to the pond's east, Breakheart Pond becomes but a glimmer in the distance. Mountain laurel wanes from the mix, leaving an open understory beneath the beautiful big trees.

Cross the footbridge over Breakheart Brook, passing between two beaver-dammed pools, and bear right. Multiple unmarked routes crisscross the way; keep to the blazed trail unless you carry a detailed map. A slow, steady ascent leads to Matteson Plain Road (3.3 miles); angle left across the road for a rolling descent, weaving between and rounding over rocks. Yellow pollen from the pines sometimes dusts the forest plants.

From the pine flat, cross the footbridge over East Fork Flat River, a broad dark stream (4.1 miles). Here, turn left onto a more overgrown track as indicated by the blazes. The way soon clears after the initial log step-overs, ducking, and mild bushwhacking.

Pass through pine plantation and mixed woods, coming to a rickety footbridge spanning West Fork Flat River (4.6 miles). Evaluate its safety before crossing: Wading may be necessary. Keep to the blazed route, making an occasional direction change. A corduroy aids in the crossing of a small wetland before the trail ascends to cross the shoulder of Penny Hill. At 5.75 miles, bypass the Penny Cutoff as it heads left to the Shelter Trail. A sunnier oak–huckleberry complex and open rock outcrops characterize travel on Penny Hill.

Now descend through semiopen woods, with pitch pine and a few aspen joining the oak, to cross Austin Farm Road (6.3 miles). Look for some quick direction changes before meeting Austin Farm Road a second time at 6.9 miles. Follow it left, crossing the bridge over the Falls River.

Hike past the yellow-blazed Ben Utter Trail, which hugs the upstream bank of the Falls River, and stay on the roadway another 200 feet. There take the white-blazed Escoheag Trail, heading left to continue the loop. The blue-blazed North–South Trail briefly merges with it.

As the trail enters a mature pine plantation, look for the Escoheag Trail to ascend away right, reaching a leafy woods with a sporadic appearance of mountain laurel. At Barber Road (7.9 miles), the Escoheag Trail bears right; for the loop, though, turn left, now following the Mount Tom Trail (also blazed white).

Traverse a scenic flat-ridge straightaway, exploring a forest of small-diameter trees, interrupted by arborways of laurel. At the fork (8.9 miles), bear right, descending through a fuller forest with rock ledges to cross RI 165 at a rocky road cut.

Resume slightly to the left, still following the white blazes, stone-stepping up the slope to the rockier reaches of Mount Tom Ridge. Again find low oaks

Breakheart Pond–Mount Tom Loop

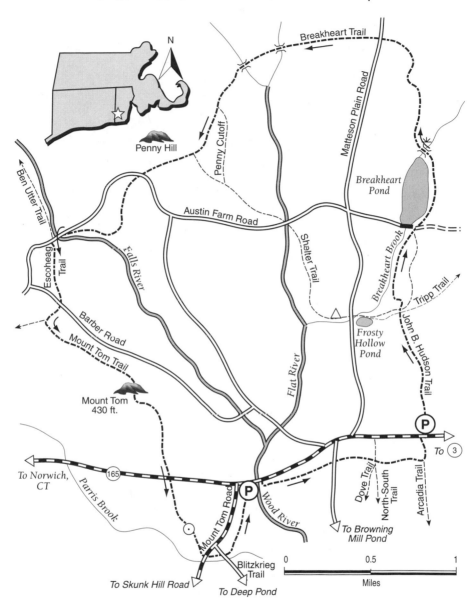

White pine, Arcadia Management Area, RI.

and sunny pockets as the trail rolls between outcrop and ledge, with filtered views seasoning the hike. After 9.8 miles, top outcrops for open southwestern views of an opposite wooded ridge and marshy woodland basin. The vista holds great autumn appeal.

Descend past balanced boulders with fern-filled seams in a pine–oak woods to reach paved Mount Tom Road (10.4 miles). Cross the road just north of Parris Brook and parallel the tannin-darkened water downstream, briefly hiking left on the Blitzkrieg Trail (a dirt road).

Just ahead, white blazes point the way through a pine plantation; be careful of the many growing ant mounds, especially if you decide to sit down. Because this piney stretch can be particularly hot and dry, carry plenty of water.

At 11.5 miles, round a gate, coming out at a Quonset hut (check station) and large parking area. Hike past the station to cross the Wood River on the RI 165 bridge. Resume on the opposite side of the river, following the blazes east into the woods, paralleling but drifting away from RI 165.

Stay mainly in pine or pine–oak woods, finding sheep laurel along a small brook before crossing it. Ascend one last ridge before dipping to cross Summit Road (12.6 miles). The rolling foot trail now parallels a scenic stone wall.

Next, bypass the North–South and Dove Trails. A wetter rock-studded woods precedes the Arcadia Trail (13.2 miles). Follow the Arcadia Trail left for a soggy passage, using stepping-stones and a rustic corduroy. Reach RI 165 at a small parking turnout and angle right across the highway to return to the John B. Hudson Trail, closing the loop at 13.5 miles.

72 Norman Bird Sanctuary

OVERVIEW

At this 450-acre privately held Aquidneck Island sanctuary, find craggy ridges trending north–south, parted by linear marshes, abandoned pasture, and rich woodland. Inland freshwater ponds expand the wildlife habitat and enrich area views, which span a dramatic rocky coastline to Rhode Island Sound. Eight miles of interlocking trails probe the property, offering a variety of tours; the selected three hikes serve as an example of the sanctuary offering.

General description:	Three hikes of varying difficulty examine woodland, field, pond, and ridge.
General location:	In Middletown, 5 miles northeast of Newport, Rhode Island.
Special attractions:	Wildlife-watching; coastal, pond, and marsh panoramas; craggy ridges and puddingstone outcrop; wildflowers; fall foliage; historical visitor center barn.
Length:	Woodland Trail, 1.1-mile loop; Hanging Rock Trail, 2 miles round trip; Gray Craig Trail, 2 miles round trip.
Elevation:	The Woodland Trail is nearly flat; the Hanging Rock and Gray Craig Trails show a maximum 70-foot elevation change.
Difficulty:	Woodland Trail, easy; the Hanging Rock and Gray Craig Trails are moderate.
Maps:	Sanctuary map.
Special concerns:	Per-person admission fee. Obey posted sanctuary rules; no pets.
Season and hours:	Year-round. Trails and center, 9:00 A.M. to 5:00 P.M. Tuesday through Sunday; open daily in summer.
For information:	Norman Bird Sanctuary.

Key points:
Woodland Trail:
- 0.0   Sanctuary trailhead.
- 0.3   Wildlife pond.
- 1.1   End at trailhead.

Hanging Rock Trail:
- 0.0   Sanctuary trailhead.
- 0.3   Wildlife pond.
- 0.7   Top Hanging Rock Ridge.
- 1.0   Hanging Rock; return to trailhead.

Gray Craig Trail:
- 0.0 Sanctuary trailhead.
- 0.3 Wildlife pond.
- 0.8 Loop junction; go left.
- 1.0 Top Gray Craig Ridge.
- 1.2 Complete loop; backtrack to trailhead.

Finding the trailhead: From the junction of Rhode Island Highway 138A (Aquidneck Avenue) and Green End Avenue in Middletown, go east on Green End Avenue for 1.5 miles and turn right onto Third Beach Road. Go 0.7 mile to enter the sanctuary on the right. Start the chosen trails, hiking southwest past the visitor center to a color-coded mapboard near the sheep pen.

The hikes: All three hikes share a common start and may be connected into a single long tour.

From the mapboard, follow the wood-chip trail straight ahead, skirting the sheep pen. At 0.1 mile, bear right for the selected hikes; the Quarry Trail journeys left through fields to an old slate quarry. A mowed track advances the hikes, passing along rock walls and through mixed woods.

At 0.2 mile, go left. (The Woodcock Trail heads right through shrubland and woods.) Deciduous trees and planted evergreens now shade the way, with sweet pepperbush, wild rose, and poison ivy in the understory. At the 0.25-mile junction, hike past the Indian Rock Trail, which heads left past a quartzite outcrop that may have been used by the early Narragansett Indians in toolmaking.

In 200 feet, again go right as a spur branches away to link up with the Quarry Trail. Pass a beautiful multitrunked maple and an outcrop sporting a memorial plaque to reach a small wildlife pond (0.3 mile). Here, find the three selected hikes. Bear left for the sanctuary ridge trails, including Hanging Rock and Gray Craig; to the right lies the Woodland Trail.

The **Woodland Trail** skirts the wildlife pond, traveling a red maple–black gum corridor, but the thick shrub understory denies pond views. Spurs to the right connect to the Woodcock Trail. Pass rock walls and some 10-foot-high humped-back outcrops of puddingstone. Boardwalk segments span the soggier reaches.

By 0.8 mile, the Woodland Trail curves back toward the visitor center, touring a tall shrub corridor. Pass an owl box and traverse a field of waist-high grasses, clover, and milkweed. Again pass the Woodcock Trail on the right, returning to the visitor center near the mapboard and animal pen at 1.1 miles.

Forgoing the Woodland Trail option at 0.3 mile, bear left for the ridge trails. A bench seat overlooks the open snag-pierced pond adorned by duckweed, cattail, and aquatic grasses. Look for ibis, heron, frog, and

Norman Bird Sanctuary

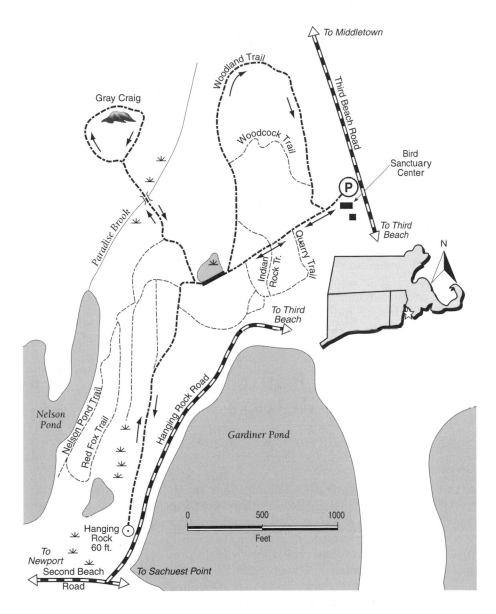

To Middletown

Woodland Trail

Gray Craig

Woodcock Trail

Third Beach Road

Bird Sanctuary Center

P

Paradise Brook

To Third Beach

Indian Rock Tr.

Quarry Trail

N

To Third Beach

Nelson Pond Trail

Hanging Rock Road

Nelson Pond

Gardiner Pond

Red Fox Trail

0   500   1000

Feet

Hanging Rock 60 ft.

To Newport

Second Beach Road

To Sachuest Point

turtle. Cross the footbridge, coming to a boardwalk junction at 0.4 mile. Here, the Hanging Rock Trail heads left, and the Gray Craig Trail heads right.

Take the popular **Hanging Rock Trail.** The Nelson Pond and Red Fox Trails quickly branch away to the right. Beyond the boardwalk, find a root-riddled woods path. At 0.5 mile, an unsigned blue dot trail heads left; keep right, passing beautiful gnarled red maple and ribbed and cobbled outcrops. The sanctuary trails narrow away from the visitor center.

Top Hanging Rock Ridge either via a spur to the right at 0.6 mile or via the main trail at 0.7 mile, and follow the crest south to the nose of the ridge. Ridge views feature Gardiner Pond, Second Beach, Sachuest Bay and Point, Rhode Island Sound, triangular Nelson Pond, and the fingery marsh isolating Hanging Rock and Red Fox Ridges. Serviceberry, dwarf juniper, oak, and wind-shaped pine vegetate the tiered and canted ledge; watch your footing. The tour halts atop Hanging Rock (1 mile). Here, find a plunging 30-foot cliff and an inspiring coastal view. Return to the visitor center for a 2-mile round trip.

If you choose the **Gray Craig Trail** at 0.4 mile, enjoy dogwood, sweet pepperbush, fern, highbush blueberry, and red maple. In 0.1 mile (0.5 mile from the visitor center), hike past a left spur to the Nelson Pond and Red Fox Trails. Where the canopy opens up, shrubs abound. Drop to the marshy flat of Paradise Brook for a boardwalk crossing. View skunk cabbage, fern, and wildflowers and afterward return to forest, where intriguing, gnarled maples still grace the hike.

Ascend to a loop junction at 0.8 mile; go left for a clockwise tour, passing through an attractive forest that alternately reveals boulders, patchy ground cover, and vine-entangled shrubs. Next, top the ridge (1 mile). Clad by red cedars and oaks, it affords only seasonal views overlooking the sanctuary toward Sachuest Point. Descend, returning to the loop junction at 1.2 miles. Retrace the first 0.8 mile to the visitor center.

73 Sachuest Point National Wildlife Refuge

OVERVIEW

At this 242-acre former naval communications station, visitors explore a jagged rocky peninsula overlooking Sachuest Bay, the broad Sakonnet River mouth, and the open waters of Rhode Island Sound. From October to mid-April, wintering harlequin ducks with their striking plumage captivate birders and casual spectators. Storms can crowd nearly a hundred of these birds onto the shoreline rocks. September flocks of tree swallows feeding on bayberry, fall migrating ospreys and hawks, snowy owls hunting the winter rodent population, and the influx of spring songbirds can suggest repeat tours. Occasionally, harbor seals haul out on the rocks.

General description: An easy perimeter loop travels the shoreline and upland habitat of Sachuest Point.

General location: 5 miles east of Newport, in Middletown, Rhode Island.

Special Attractions: Bird- and wildlife-watching, rocky shores, coastal vistas, spring-flowering shrubs, surf fishing.

Length:	2.5-mile loop.
Elevation:	The trail remains virtually flat.
Difficulty:	Easy.
Maps:	Refuge map available at the visitor center when open, or request in advance from Ninigret National Wildlife Refuge.
Special concerns:	No pets. Beware of poison ivy, and because biting insects can annoy, bring repellent.
Season and hours:	Year-round. Grounds are open from half an hour before sunrise to half an hour after sunset. Visitor center, 8:00 A.M. to 4:00 P.M. Saturday and Sunday.
For information:	Seek information in care of Ninigret National Wildlife Refuge.

Key points:

0.0   Start at southwest corner of parking.
0.6   Sachuest Point.
1.9   Flint Point.
2.5   End at parking lot.

Finding the trailhead: From the junction of Rhode Island Highway 138A (Aquidneck Avenue) and Green End Avenue in Middletown, go east on Green End Avenue for 1.5 miles. There, turn right onto Third Beach Road and stay on it for 1.8 miles, bearing right at 1.5 miles. Turn left (south) onto Sachuest Point Road to reach the visitor center and parking lot in 0.7 mile.

The hike: A perimeter loop explores the foot of this boot-shaped peninsula, visiting both Sachuest and Flint Points. For a shorter hike to a single point, take either the east or west loop from the information board near bus parking.

For a counterclockwise perimeter loop, begin at the southwest corner of the parking area and follow the paved path skirting the side of the visitor center toward Sachuest Bay. Angle left on a footpath to reach the bay-shore bluff and journey south to Sachuest Point.

Views sweep the rocky refuge shore, the cliffs and historical buildings of Middletown, and the mansions of Newport across the way. Beach plum, bayberry, poison ivy, shore rose, and tangled vines weave a dense rich border, while daisy and clover accent the tour. In early summer, enjoy a fragrant intermingling of sweet and salt air.

By 0.4 mile, the bluff flattens, allowing access to the rocky shore. In selecting a path to the rocks, beware of poison ivy. The shore consists of huge gray rockweed-clad boulders with white quartz seams. Look for mussel, crab, barnacle, and starfish within the jumble.

The trail forks at 0.5 mile; stay right at all junctions to tour the perimeter. Spurs heading left travel the upland habitat, reaching observation towers and eventually the visitor center. The untamed shrub–grassland offers chance sightings of red fox, weasel, and eastern cottontail.

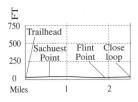

A few interpretive plaques mark the perimeter hike, the first at Sachuest Point (0.6 mile). View a lighthouse island off Sakonnet Point. On the nearby rocks, surf anglers cast for blacks, blues, and stripers (bass). An unexpected wave slapping at the point reasserts the area's wildness.

Resume the bluff stroll, heading north away from Sachuest Point. Pass at the edge of a field, snaring coastal glimpses over the top of the thick seaward shrubs. At 0.8 mile, overlook a small scenic cove with rocky tongues extending into the water. Keep to the perimeter trail; birdhouses dot the field to the left. At 1 mile, find another trail fork, a bench, and an interpretive sign—this one about ducks, which are best viewed November through March.

Coastal views now come like rapid fire, with looks at the scalloped shore, sun-bleached spits, straggled rocks, and dark waters gliding to shore. At 1.3

Sachuest Point National Wildlife Refuge

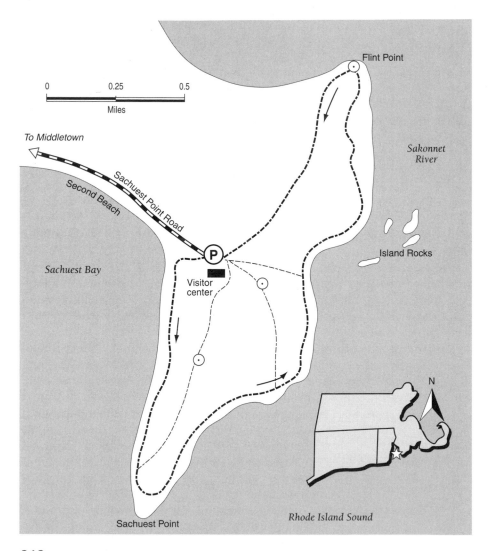

Rocky shoreline, Sachuest Point National Wildlife Refuge, RI.

miles, a mowed swath travels inland. On the perimeter hike, come upon more benches. Views now include the offshore fishing boats and Island Rocks— long, low gray outcrops piercing the water close to shore. Ahead, the shrubs grow taller and thicker, blocking views.

At 1.9 miles, on Flint Point, take the spur heading right to reach a one-story observation platform overlooking a bay cove on the Sakonnet River and Third Beach. Looks across the neck of the peninsula find Second Beach on Sachuest Bay. Capping the view, cormorants often crowd a tiny rock island between Flint Point and Third Beach.

From Flint Point, the perimeter loop swings southwest, returning to the visitor center. Pass through a shrub corridor and a shrub–field complex, where yellow warblers and swallows contribute to the finale. End at the parking lot, near the information station and bus parking (2.5 miles).

74   Vin Gormley Trail

General description: This "yellow trail" circuit travels the outlying forest, wetland, and rock habitat enfolding Watchaug Pond, with views of the pond reserved for the end of the hike. Travel public roadway, Burlingame State Park, and Kimball Wildlife Refuge, a property of the Audubon Society of Rhode Island.

General location: In southwestern Rhode Island, at the western outskirts of Charlestown.

Special attractions: A scenic boardwalk; mixed forest; azalea, sweet pepperbush, and both mountain and sheep laurel blooms; wildlife; fall foliage.

Length: 8.5-mile loop.

Elevation: Find a 150-foot elevation change.

Difficulty: Moderate.

Maps: Trail map; request a copy at the fee station or campground office (west of Prosser Trail off U.S. Highway 1).

Special concerns: Parking fee. Expect some muddy, wet stretches in spring.

Season and hours: Year-round; spring through fall are best for hiking. Open 8:00 A.M. to sunset.

For information: Burlingame State Park.

Key points:
0.0 Day-use trailhead.
0.9 Take foot trail off Kings Factory Road.
3.7 Buckeye Brook Road bridge.
5.9 Mill Brook footbridge.
7.0 Enter state park campground.
7.7 Enter Kimball Wildlife Refuge.
8.3 Watchaug Pond Fishing Access.
8.5 End at day-use trailhead.

Finding the trailhead: Access is only off US 1 South. From the junction of Rhode Island Highway 2/112 and US 1 in Charlestown, go west on US 1 South for 2.4 miles and turn right (north) onto Prosser Trail for Burlingame State Park Picnic Area and Beach. On US 1 North, go 3.4 miles east from RI 216, take the formal U-turn onto US 1 South, and turn north onto Prosser Trail in 0.4 mile. Reach day-use parking on the left in 0.7 mile.

The hike: Named for John Vincent Gormley, a dedicated trailsmith, this 8.5-mile hiker circuit offers a relaxing woodland stroll. Yellow paint and plastic blazes mark the route.

From the day-use fee station, follow the blazes east out the access road and north (left) on the Prosser Trail, a tree-lined, two-lane, lightly trafficked road. In 0.6 mile, turn left onto Kings Factory Road, hike another 0.3 mile, and turn left into woods for the natural tour. Chestnut, white, red, and black oak, birch, pine, and cherry enfold the trail; beware of poison ivy.

An enjoyable 4-foot-wide meandering trail rolls out the journey. Mayflower, starflower, club moss, wild geranium, sassafras, huckleberry, and fern variously make up the understory vegetation. Deer, toad, fox, or neighborhood dog may briefly divert attention. At 1.1 miles, angle right across a quiet paved

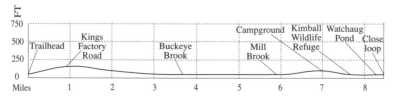

314

Colonial rockwall, Burlingame State Park, RI.

lane, entering a moist habitat with thick shrubs, including sweet pepperbush, mountain laurel, azalea, highbush blueberry, and greenbrier. Ahead, cross an inlet drainage.

The comfortable, obstacle-free trail allows eyes and thoughts to roam. At 1.6 miles, pass below a lichen-etched outcrop where mountain laurel finds a niche. From a clearing, turn right onto an attractive narrow woods road draped by hemlock–hardwood forest, with its shoulders dressed in both mountain and sheep laurel.

At 2.2 miles, bear left, heeding the blazes and arrow markers signaling direction changes. Birdsongs emanate from the leafy canopy, while Indian pipe pushes up through the forest duff. Small footbridges span a pair of slightly larger brooks. Cross a dirt road at 2.6 miles to tour a bog habitat on a rustic boardwalk of paired hewn logs. Afterward, turn left, hiking atop a flat outcrop.

Where the trail again rolls up and over rock outcrops, find 15- to 20-foot cliffs with showy fern seams. At 3.6 miles, depart the rocky area, again in low shrubs, especially pretty when the sheep laurels parade their dark pink blooms. Turn left onto Buckeye Brook Road to cross the bridge over the scenic wide slow water, accented by pond lily and arrowhead; then resume the hike on the left. Oak, tall sassafras, and pitch pine frame the narrow woods path; find stone walls and patchy shade.

At 4.4 miles, turn left, remaining in a more open woods, with poison ivy becoming common. Then, at 4.9 miles, again turn left, hiking an old woods road alongside a brook screened from view. A fuller canopy weaves above the trail. In another 0.5 mile, cross the footbridge near a scenic big maple. Afterward, encounter more of the scenic boardwalk laid by Vin Gormley.

At 5.9 miles, cross the hewn-log bridge over Mill Brook. At this spot, tranquil tannin-tinted water is accented by green grasses, ferns, and branches; dragonflies and frogs can be spied. Bog boardwalks then traverse a red

Vin Gormley Trail

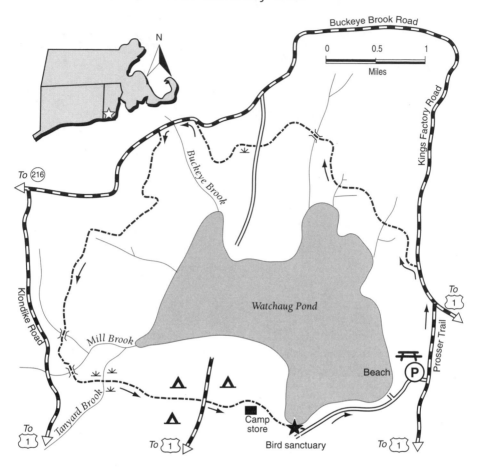

maple woodland, with skunk cabbage, azalea, and sweet pepperbush. Watch for a couple of direction changes before entering the state park campground (7 miles), with rest rooms and water available.

Hike through the open campground, following blazes, for a sunny walk. At 7.5 miles, past the playground but before the camp store, descend along the edge of a field, entering the woods at the far right corner of the field. Hardwood forest now leads to Kimball Wildlife Refuge, which next hosts travel. Obey the rules.

At the refuge, side trails branch left to Watchaug Pond, as the blazed routes from the Audubon trail system arrive and depart on the right. Keep to the yellow-blazed Vin Gormley Trail. At 7.8 miles, exit the refuge, hiking left on a dirt road past lakeshore residences; keep to the road.

At 8.3 miles, reach Watchaug Pond Fishing Access for open viewing of the huge recreational water. At 8.5 miles, complete the loop by returning to the picnic area parking at Burlingame State Park.

75 Ninigret Park, Beach Conservation Area, and National Wildlife Refuge

OVERVIEW

On the coast of Block Island Sound, this Charlestown town park, state beach conservation area, and 400-acre federal wildlife refuge offer prized recreation within a former U.S. Naval Air Station. Today's wildland features areas of upland grassland, shrubland, and woodland; marsh and pond habitats; and barrier-beach dunes, swale, and shore. The site provides a rich and varied wildlife habitat for native and migrant species and lays out some fine walks for nature lovers.

General description:	Two nature trails, a network of reclaimed runways, and a stretch of barrier beach welcome hikers.
General location:	In Charlestown, Rhode Island.
Special attractions:	Wildlife-watching, with nesting piping plover (April through August), woodcock courtship flights (dusk, mid-March through June), and wintering waterfowl; crystalline-sand beach; Rhode Island's largest coastal pond (Ninigret Pond).
Length:	Foster Cove Trail, 1-mile loop; Grassy Point Trail, 1.4 miles round trip; East Beach Hike, 7 miles round trip.
Elevation:	The terrain is gentle, virtually flat.
Difficulty:	The nature trails are easy; the beach hike is moderate.
Maps:	Refuge map.
Special concerns:	Ninigret Park, Ninigret Beach Conservation Area, and Charlestown's Blue Shutters Town Beach all charge a vehicle admission fee. Cross dunes only at designated accesses, and respect closures for nesting piping plover and habitat protection. From mid-September through March, expect to encounter beach vehicles (beach driving is by permit only). Carry insect repellent, leave pets at home, and beware of poison ivy and ticks.
	Within Ninigret National Wildlife Refuge (NWR), airstrips are being torn up, leaving interlocking hiking strips and planted native grasslands in their wake. As the trail system burgeons and matures, visitors should expect to encounter additional trail connections, leading to different avenues and loops to explore. The refuge's five-year plan calls for a resulting 3.5 miles of wheelchair-accessible trail.

Season and hours: Year-round. Ninigret Park, 7:00 A.M. to sunset;
Ninigret Beach Conservation Area, 8:00 A.M. to
sunset; Ninigret NWR, dawn to dusk; Blue Shutters
Town Beach parking area, 8:30 A.M. to 5:00 P.M.
For information: Ninigret NWR or Ninigret Conservation Area.

Key points:
Foster Cove Trail:
    0.0   NWR, western trailhead.
    0.2   Foster Cove.
    1.0   Complete loop at parking.

Grassy Point Trail:
    0.0   NWR, eastern trailhead; go left.
    0.1   Ninigret Pond.
    0.7   Grassy Point observation platform.
    1.4   Return to trailhead.

East Beach Hike:
    0.0   Blue Shutters Beach; hike east
    0.2   Ninigret Beach Conservation Area.
    2.8   Enter NWR land.
    3.5   Charlestown Breachway; backtrack to trailhead.

Finding the trailhead: Find direct access off U.S. Highway 1 North in Charlestown; U-turns are required for southbound traffic.

From the US 1–Rhode Island Highway 216 junction, go east on US 1 North, reaching the right-hand turns for East Beach Road in 0.8 mile, western Ninigret NWR (Foster Cove) in 2.6 miles, and US 1A in 2.8 miles. US 1A then leads to Ninigret Park in 0.4 mile; reach the eastern refuge and Grassy Point Trailhead at the end of the park road, past Frosty Drew Nature Center.

Southbound US 1 traffic should locate the left-lane U-turns west of RI 212. Take the U-turn in 2.8 miles for Ninigret Park and both NWR nature trails. Take the one in 4 miles for the East Beach Hike.

For the East Beach Hike, park at either Blue Shutters Town Beach or Ninigret Beach Conservation Area.

The hikes: At the west access to the NWR, the **Foster Cove Trail** leaves the southwest corner of the parking lot at the information board. Go right on the wide lane enclosed by tall shrubs, maple, oak, willow, cedar, and cherry. Poison ivy, grape, and brier entwine the sides. Springtime showers the corridor with pink and white blooms. By 0.2 mile, round Foster Cove, isolated by a thick shrub border. An occasional gap provides a view of the cove. At 0.4 mile, avoid the spur that heads right; it is overgrown with poison ivy. Animal sightings may include deer, fox, rabbit, and red squirrel, as well as a variety of songbirds.

Next, either take the hiker track heading left through a shrub corridor or proceed forward a couple of strides to a paved trail (a reclaimed runway) and turn left. Both paths allow for the loop's completion, emerging near the parking area. Head left to close the loop at 1 mile.

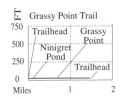

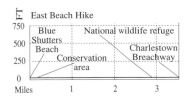

From the paved path, witness the return of the native grassland and the growth of planted shrubs. A sharp crash may explain the strange dispersal of shells. Gulls circling 20 feet above the path drop clams to break them for easy eating. Where the former runway comes within sight of the trail parking area, another paved path journeys right (east) 0.75 mile to the Grassy Point trail system.

For the NWR's **Grassy Point Trail,** start near the information board at the southeast corner of the east-access parking area. Hike left, following the hiker symbol and arrow toward Ninigret Pond, a 1,700-acre brackish coastal pond breached to the ocean.

Travel a shrub passage with wild plum, rose, poison ivy, and coastal scrub, quickly gaining access to a quiet, rocky cove and side pond rimmed by phragmites (plumed reeds). A scull may complement the image of Ninigret Pond, gulls clamor atop the rocks, and colored buoys mark crab pots. Cross-cove views include Grassy Point and the observation platform. Round the cove to the left, closing the loop back at the information board (0.25 mile).

This time, take the path to the right of the information board, again marked. Travel a shrub corridor with abundant sumac. At 0.4 mile (continuing the mileage), go left on an unmarked path for Grassy Point; a hiker symbol marks the path to the right, which completes a second loop.

En route to the point, edge a cove of Ninigret Pond, passing a bench; beach pea and poison ivy grow along the shore. Reach the one-story platform at 0.7 mile to spy a low estuarine island and brushy points, a jungle of phragmites, and egret, cormorant, osprey, and gull.

Return to the 0.4-mile junction at 1 mile and bear left, coming out at another reclaimed-runway trail at 1.1 miles. Go right to complete the second loop and backtrack to the trailhead parking area (1.4 miles). A left on the runway trail at 1.1 miles extends the hike along the upland of Ninigret Pond.

For the **East Beach Hike,** start at Blue Shutters Beach for the full 7-mile hike, or start at Ninigret Beach Conservation Area to shorten the walk. Blue Shutters has a bathhouse/rest room; find chemical toilets at the conservation area.

Bring plenty of drinking water for this sun-baked beach hike that journeys east to Charlestown Breachway, which opens Ninigret Pond to the ocean. At the west end of the tour, crowds linger close to the beach facilities. Drifting east, the strand grows more and more wild. Pass the entrance to Ninigret Beach Conservation Area at 0.25 mile. In back of the dune, primitive camping areas serve self-contained four-wheel-drive vehicles, dispersing a few more beachgoers along the barrier beach.

Ninigret Park, Beach Conservation Area, and National Wildlife Refuge

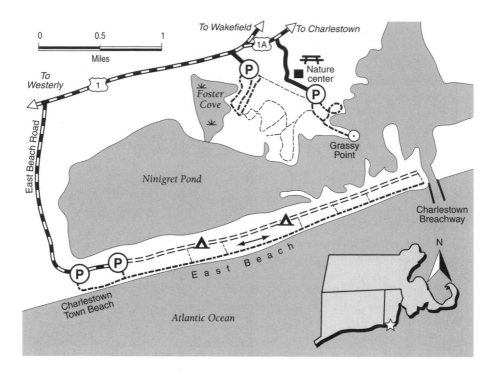

A gentle cant greets the close-breaking waves, and orange flecks contribute to the beauty of the crystalline sand. Capped by dune grass and beach pea, 4-foot-high dunes back the strand. Dips in the dunes reveal a shoreline swale and Ninigret Pond to the north. Black, purple, and green seaweed, whelk and skate egg cases, pebble patches, and a few shells complement the strand.

Offshore, view the long, flat profile of Block Island, and fishing and leisure boats. Find designated dune accesses between the camp areas and beach at 1.2, 1.5, 2.2, 2.5, 2.8, and 3.5 miles. The jetty of Charlestown Breachway gradually becomes more obvious.

At the toe of the seaward dune, piping plovers nest; grant the birds a wide safety margin. Snow fences help preserve the dune. At 2.8 miles, pass from conservation land to national wildlife refuge. East of the refuge, private parcels back the beach, so keep toward the ocean shore.

Reach the Charlestown Breachway, shaped by riprap jetties, at 3.5 miles. A glorious aqua-green water surges in and out of Ninigret Pond, while overhead an osprey commonly patrols. Views sweep Block Island Sound, the breachway, Ninigret Pond, and the far marshy shore. Seasonally, seaweed overwhelms the waves curling to shore. Turn back, enjoying a fine hike or wade.

Appendix A: Further Reading

Backpacking One Step at a Time, Fourth Edition, by Harvey Manning. Random House.

The Basic Essentials of Map and Compass by Cliff Jacobson. The Globe Pequot Press.

A Child's Introduction to the Outdoors by David Richey. Pagurian Press Limited.

The Complete Walker III by Colin Fletcher. Alfred A. Knopf.

Eastern Forests: An Audubon Society Nature Guide by Ann and Myron Sutton. Alfred A. Knopf.

A Field Guide to the Birds by Roger Tory Peterson. Houghton Mifflin Co.

Finding Your Way in the Outdoors by Robert L. Mooers, Jr. E. P. Hutton Co.

Forest Trees of Southern New England. Connecticut Forest and Park Association.

A Guide to the Properties of the Trustees of Reservations. The Trustees of Reservations.

Mountaineering First Aid, Third Edition by Martha J. Lentz, Steven C. Macdonald, and Jan D. Carline. The Mountaineers.

Mountaineering Medicine by Fred T. Darvill. Wilderness Press.

Short Nature Walks on Cape Cod and the Vineyard, Third Edition by Hugh and Heather Sadlier. The Globe Pequot Press.

The Shrub Identification Book by George W. D. Symonds. William Morrow and Co.

The Sierra Club Naturalist's Guide to Southern New England by Neil Jorgensen. Sierra Club Books.

Travel Light Handbook by Judy Keene. Contemporary Books.

Trees and Shrubs of New England by Marilyn J. Dwelley. Down East Books.

Walks and Rambles in Rhode Island by Ken Weber. Backcountry Guides.

Wild Country Companion: The Ultimate Guide to No-trace Outdoor Recreation and Wilderness Safety by Will Harmon. Falcon Press Publishing Co.

Wilderness Basics: The Complete Handbook for Hikers and Backpackers, Second Edition, by the San Diego Chapter of the Sierra Club. The Mountaineers.

Appendix B: Where to Find Maps

For trail maps produced by the managing agencies, contact the information source named in the trail summary table; turn to appendix C for the complete address and phone number.

For copies of United States Geological Survey topographic quadrangles (USGS quads), check at libraries, at most backpacking and mountaineering stores, or at specialty maps and publications stores. A state index will help you identify the name of the quad(s) that covers the area you are seeking. Or contact the United States Geological Survey Map Distribution Center, Box 25286 Federal Center, Building 41, Denver, CO 80225. Ask for the Massachusetts, Connecticut, and Rhode Island indices and a price list for the maps.

In Connecticut, USGS quads, the *Atlas of Connecticut Topographic Maps,* and other state maps and profiles may be purchased at the Department of Environmental Protection Publications Store, Store Level, 79 Elm Street, Hartford, CT 06106-5127.

The *Connecticut Walk Book: A Trail Guide to the Connecticut Outdoors,* published by the Connecticut Forest and Park Association, contains both verbal trail descriptions and simple line-drawing maps, done to scale, that locate the trail, key routes and towns, side trails, and major landmarks. Purchase current editions in area book stores and outdoor stores.

For information on ordering Trustees of Reservations maps, contact Trustees of Reservations, 572 Essex Street, Beverly, MA 01915-1530; 978–921–1944. With the purchase of a membership in this nonprofit organization, hikers not only promote the preservation of unique areas within Massachusetts, but they also receive a guidebook to the Trustees properties and free or reduced-fee admission to the sites. Send a self-addressed envelope to the above address to receive information about becoming a member.

Maps produced by the New York–New Jersey Trail Conference or Appalachian Mountain Club typically are available at backpacker and mountaineering stores or for direct order from the organizations. For an order blank and price list, contact the respective group:

New York–New Jersey Trail Conference, 232 Madison Avenue, New York, NY 10016; 212–685–9699.

Appalachian Mountain Club, 10 Water Street, Lebanon, NH, 03766; 1–800–262–4455 (for mail orders).

Appendix C: Land Management Listings

Appalachian Mountain Club
P.O. Box 582
Randolph, MA 02368
Cabin reservations for
  Ponkapoag Pond in Blue Hills
  Reservation

Appalachian Trail Conference
P.O. Box 807
799 Washington Street
Harpers Ferry, WV 25425-0807
304-535-6331

Arcadia Management Area
Rhode Island Department
  of Environmental Management
Division of Forest Environment
1037 Hartford Pike
North Scituate, RI 02857
401-647-3367

Beartown State Forest
P.O. Box 97
Blue Hill Road
Monterey, MA 01245
413-528-0904

Bigelow Hollow State Park
860-684-3430

Blackstone River and Canal Heritage
  State Park
287 Oak Street
Uxbridge, MA 01569
508-278-7604

Blue Hills Reservation Headquarters
Metropolitan District Commission
695 Hillside Street
Milton, MA 02186
617-698-1802

Blue Hills Trailside Museum
1904 Canton Avenue
Milton, MA 02186
617-333-0690

Bluff Point State Park and Coastal
  Reserve
c/o Fort Griswold Battlefield
  State Park
57 Fort Street
Groton, CT 06340
860-445-1729

Borderland State Park
257 Massapoag Avenue
North Easton, MA 02356
508-238-6566

Boxford State Forest
c/o Harold Parker State Forest
1951 Turnpike Road
North Andover, MA 01845-6326
978-686-3391

Breakheart Reservation
177 Forest Street
Saugus, MA 01906
781-233-0834

Broadmoor Wildlife Sanctuary
Massachusetts Audubon Society
280 Eliot Street
South Natick, MA 01760
508-655-2296 or 617-235-3929

Burlingame State Park
1 Burlingame Park Road
Charlestown, RI 02813
401-322-8910

Burr Pond State Park
Burr Mountain Road
Torrington, CT 06790
860-482-1817

Cape Cod National Seashore
Park Headquarters
99 Marconi Site Road
Wellfleet, MA 02667
508-349-3785
508-255-3421 (Salt Pond Visitor
Center)
508-487-1256 (Province Lands
Visitor Center)

Cockaponset State Forest
Ranger Road
Haddam, CT 06438
860-345-8521

Connecticut Department of
Environmental Protection
Bureau of Outdoor Recreation
79 Elm Street
Hartford, CT 06106-5127
860-566-2304

Conservation Commission
Berlin Town Hall
240 Kensington Road
Berlin, CT 06037
860-828-7000

D.A.R. State Forest
Route 112
Goshen, MA
413-268-7098
Mailing address: 555 East Street
Williamsburg, MA 01096

Devil's Den Preserve
The Nature Conservancy
Box 1162
Weston, CT 06883
203-226-4991

Devil's Hopyard State Park
Route 434, Hopyard Road
East Haddam, CT 06423
860-873-8566

Essex County Greenbelt Association
82 Eastern Avenue
Essex, MA 01929
978-768-7241

Gay City State Park
c/o Eastern Headquarters
209 Hebron Road
Marlborough, CT 06447
860-295-9523

George B. Parker Woodland
c/o Audubon Society of Rhode Island
12 Sanderson Road
Smithfield, RI 02917-2600
401-949-5454

George Washington Management
Area
2185 Putnam Pike
Chepachet, RI 02814
401-568-2013

Goodwin Conservation Center
23 Potter Road
North Windham, CT 06256
860-455-9534

Hancock Shaker Village
P.O. Box 927
Junction of Routes 20 and 41
Pittsfield, MA 01202
413-443-0188

Hartman Recreational Park
c/o Lyme Park and Recreation
Lyme Town Hall
Lyme, CT 06371
860-434-7733

Kettletown State Park
175 Quaker Farms Road
Southbury, CT 06488
203-264-5169

Laughing Brook Education Center
and Wildlife Sanctuary
Massachusetts Audubon Society
789 Main Street
Hampden, MA 01036
413-566-8034

Macedonia Brook State Park
159 Macedonia Brook Road
Kent, CT 06757
860-927-3238

Mashamoquet Brook State Park
RFD 2, Wolf Den Drive
Pomfret Center, CT 06259
860-928-6121

Massachusetts Audubon Society
Berkshire Sanctuaries
472 West Mountain Road
Lenox, MA 01240
413-637-0320

Massachusetts Department of
Environmental Management
Division of Forests and Parks
100 Cambridge Street, 19th Floor
Boston, MA 02202
617-727-3180
For regional headquarters:
413-442-8928 (Berkshires)
413-545-5993 (Connecticut River
Valley)
508-368-0126 (Central Region)
508-369-3350 (Northeast)
617-727-3180 (Greater Boston)
508-866-2580 (Southeast)

Metropolitan District Commission
20 Somerset Street
Boston, MA 02108
617-727-5250

Metropolitan District Commission
Quabbin Park Visitors Center,
Quabbin Administration Building
485 Ware Road
Belchertown, MA 01007
413-323-7221

Mohawk Trail State Forest
P.O. Box 7
Charlemont, MA 01339
413-339-5504

Monroe State Forest
P.O. Box 7
Charlemont, MA 01339
413-339-5504

Mount Greylock State Reservation
P.O. Box 138
Lanesborough, MA 01237
413-499-4263

Mount Tom State Reservation
P.O. Box 985
Northampton, MA 01061
413-527-4805

Mount Washington State Forest
RD 3 East Street
Mount Washington, MA 01258
413-528-0330

Nehantic State Forest
c/o Rocky Neck State Park
Box 676
Niantic, CT 06357
860-739-5471

Ninigret Conservation Area
c/o Burlingame State Park
1 Burlingame Park Road
Charlestown, RI 02813
401-322-8910 or 401-322-0450
(May to September)

Ninigret National Wildlife Refuge
Shoreline Plaza
Route 1A, P.O. Box 307
Charlestown, RI 02813
401-364-9124

Norman Bird Sanctuary
583 Third Beach Road
Middletown, RI 02842
401-846-2577

Northeast Utilities
Northfield Mountain Recreation
   and Environmental Center
99 Millers Falls Road
Northfield, MA 01360-9611
413-659-3714 or 1-800-859-2960

Norwottuck Rail Trail
136 Damon Road
Northampton, MA 01060
413-586-8706

Pachaug State Forest
P.O. Box 5
Voluntown, CT 06384
860-376-4075

Parker River National Wildlife Refuge
Northern Boulevard
Plum Island
Newburyport, MA 01950
978-465-5753

Paugussett State Forest
c/o Southford Falls State Park
175 Quaker Farms Road
Southbury, CT 06488
203-264-5169

Penwood and Talcott Mountain
   State Parks
c/o Farmington Headquarters
178 Scott Swamp Road
Farmington, CT 06032
860-242-1158

Peoples State Forest
P.O. Box 1
Pleasant Valley, CT 06063
860-379-2469

Pittsfield State Forest
Cascade Street
Pittsfield, MA 01201
413-442-8992

Purgatory Chasm State Reservation
Purgatory Road
Sutton, MA 01590
508-234-3733

Savoy Mountain State Forest
260 Central Shaft Road
Florida, MA 01247
413-663-8469

Sessions Woods Wildlife
   Management Area
P.O. Box 1550
Burlington, CT 06013-1550
860-675-8130

Sharon Audubon Center
National Audubon Society
325 Cornwall Bridge Road
Sharon, CT 06069
860-364-0520

Skinner State Park
Route 47, Box 91
Hadley, MA 01035
413-586-0350 or 413-253-2883

Sleeping Giant State Park
200 Mount Carmel Avenue
Hamden, CT 06518
203-789-7498

The Sleeping Giant Park Association
P.O. Box 14
Quinnipiac College
Hamden, CT 06518

South Cape Beach State Park
Great Neck Road
Mashpee, MA 02649
For information, phone: Waquoit Bay
    National Estuarine Research
    Reserve, 508-457-0495

Southford Falls State Park
175 Quaker Farms Road
Southbury, CT 06488
203-264-5169

The Trustees of Reservations
Central Regional Office
325 Lindell Avenue
Leominster, MA 01453
508-840-4446

The Trustees of Reservations
Northcast Regional Office
Castle Hill
P.O. Box 563
Ipswich, MA 01938
978-356-4351
978-412-2589 (beach)
978-356-4354 (recorded information)

The Trustees of Reservations
Western Regional Office
P.O. Box 792
Stockbridge, MA 01262
413-298-3239

University of Massachusetts—Amherst
Department of Forestry and Wildlife
    Management
Holdsworth Natural Resources Center
University of Massachusetts
Box 34210
Amherst, MA 01003-4210
413-545-2665

U.S. Army Corps of Engineers
Cape Cod Canal Field Office
P.O. Box J
Buzzards Bay, MA 02532
508-759-4431

Wachusett Meadow Wildlife
    Sanctuary
113 Goodnow Road
Princeton, MA 01541
978-464-2712

Wachusett Mountain State
    Reservation
Mountain Road
P.O. Box 248
Princeton, MA 01541
978-464-2987

Waquoit Bay National Estuarine
    Research Reserve
P.O. Box 3092
Waquoit, MA 02536
508-457-0495

Wellfleet Bay Wildlife Sanctuary
P.O. Box 236
291 State Highway Route 6
South Wellfleet, MA 02663
508-349-2615

West Rock Ridge State Park
c/o Sleeping Giant State Park
200 Mount Carmel Avenue
Hamden, CT 06518
203-789-7498

White Memorial Conservation
    Center
71 Whitehall Road
P.O. Box 368
Litchfield, CT 06759-0368
860-567-0857

Windsor State Forest
River Road
Windsor, MA 01270
413-684-0948

About the Authors

Over the past twenty years, the Ostertags, Rhonda (a writer) and George (a photographer), have collaborated on a dozen outdoor guidebooks and produced hundreds of articles on nature, travel, and outdoor recreation for national publication.

George was born and raised in Connecticut and brings to this book his childhood enthusiasm tempered by a reflective eye. Find the passion he holds for the region reflected in his photography.

Rhonda writes with the fresh perspective and enthusiasm of a wide-eyed westerner. Having hiked more than 2,000 miles in southern New England, the couple have become well acquainted with the trails of Massachusetts, Connecticut, and Rhode Island. This book represents firsthand information.

Other titles by the team include *Hiking New York*, Second Edition; *Hiking Pennsylvania*, Second Edition; *Scenic Driving Pennsylvania*; and *Camping Oregon* (all Falcon/Globe Pequot titles), along with *California State Parks: A Complete Recreation Guide*, Second Edition (2001) and *100 Hikes in Oregon*, Second Edition (2000), both published by The Mountaineers Books, Seattle, Washington.